Computer Science

An Overview

Second Edition

**The Benjamin / Cummings Series
in Structured Programming**

G. Booch
Software Components with Ada: Structures, Tools, and Subsystems (1987)

G. Booch
Software Engineering with Ada, Second Edition (1987)

J. Brink and R. Spillman
Computer Architecture and VAX Assembly Language Programming (1987)

F. Carrano
Assembly Language Programming for the IBM 370 (1988)

D. M. Etter
Structured FORTRAN 77 for Engineers and Scientists, Second Edition (1987)

D. M. Etter
Problem Solving with Structured FORTRAN 77 (1984)

P. Helman and R. Veroff
Intermediate Problem Solving and Data Structures: Walls and Mirrors [Pascal Edition] (1986)

P. Helman and R. Veroff
Walls and Mirrors: Intermediate Problem Solving and Data Structures—Modula II (1988)

N. Miller
File Structures Using Pascal (1987)

A. Kelley and I. Pohl
A Book on C (1984)

A. Kelley and I. Pohl
C by Dissection (1987)

A. Kelley and I. Pohl
Turbo C: The Essentials of C Programming (1988)

W. J. Savitch
Pascal: An Introduction to the Art and Science of Programming, Second Edition (1987)

W. J. Savitch
An Introduction to the Art and Science of Programming: Turbo Pascal, Second Edition (1988)

Titles of Related Interest:

M. Sobell
A Practical Guide to the UNIX System (1984)

M. Sobell
A Practical Guide to UNIX System V (1985)

Computer Science

An Overview

Second Edition

J. Glenn Brookshear

Marquette University

The Benjamin/Cummings Publishing Company, Inc.
Reading, Massachusetts • Menlo Park, California
• Don Mills, Ontario • Wokingham, U.K. • Amsterdam • Sydney •
Singapore • Tokyo • Madrid • Bogota • Santiago • San Juan

To my parents
Garland & Reba Brookshear

Sponsoring Editor: Alan Apt
Production Editor: Laura Kenney
Text Designers: Victoria Philp, Paul Quin
Cover Designer: Victoria Philp
Artists: Sally Shimizu, John Foster
Composition: Graphic Typesetting Service

Library of Congress Cataloging-in-Publication Data
Brookshear, J. Glenn
    Computer science: an overview/J. Glenn Brookshear.—
2nd ed.
    p. cm. (The Benjamin/Cummings series in structured
programming)
    Bibliography: p.
    Includes index.
    1. Electronic data processing. 2. Electronic digital
computers. I. Title. II. Series
QA76.B743   1988   87-24215
ISBN 0-8053-0903-9
BCDEFGHIJ—DO—898

The Benjamin/Cummings Publishing Company, Inc.
2727 Sand Hill Road
Menlo Park, California 94025

Preface

I wrote this book to provide a comprehensive overview of computer science, one that presents a thought-provoking introduction to the key issues and concepts throughout the field. I have done this with two primary audiences in mind.

Computer Science Majors

The first audience consists of computer science majors in the early stages of their college careers. Students at this stage tend to equate computer science with programming because that is essentially all they have seen. Yet computer science is much more than programming. In turn, beginning computer science students need to be exposed to the breadth of the subject in which they are planning to major. Providing this exposure is the purpose of this book. It gives students an overview of computer science—a foundation from which they can understand the relevance and interrelationships of future courses. Without such a perspective, students easily become immersed in the details of specialized courses and never understand the true scope and dynamics of the field. In short, this book represents the application of top-down methodologies, as taught within the curriculum, to the computer science curriculum itself.

The book is an excellent text for the second semester of a university computer science curriculum. Its content matches the four principal themes of CS2 as identified in the latest ACM model curriculum (Communications of the ACM, March 1986), and the theme throughout the text agrees with the education (as opposed to training) philosophy motivating this new curriculum. Indeed, this text presents computer science as a science, with enlightening discussions of its formal foundations, its origins in mathematics, and the role of basic principles in ongoing research.

This book is not, however, restricted to the role of a CS2 text. In fact, the first edition has served as a text for first-semester computer science courses and as a companion text in many two-semester introductory sequences. I have kept these applications in mind during the development of this new edition.

Students of Other Disciplines

I also designed this book with majors of other fields in mind. Too often, these students are channelled into courses that either concentrate on the use of today's software packages or provide an elementary introduction to programming. Unfortunately, the subject matter of these courses is often time-sensitive, limited in portability, or not developed to a depth to be useful outside the classroom. Any benefits from such courses dissipate quickly after the semester is over.

I believe that these students are seeking "computer literacy," which I loosely define as the ability to distinguish between computer science and science fiction. Providing this level of "literacy" in other fields is the purpose of such courses as general chemistry, biology, and physics. Students do not take these courses merely to develop specific skills. Rather, the major goal is to develop an understanding of the discipline—including its scope, major results and consequences, research techniques, and the current status of the field. Thus, the fact that a student might be required to develop certain skills while taking the course is merely a temporary consequence. The true benefit of the course—obtaining an overall picture of the subject—survives long after these specific items have been forgotten.

Why, then, do we insist that a computer science course for nonmajors emphasize skills? The goal should be to present an overall picture of the science, which is exactly what I have designed this book to provide. After taking a course based on this text, a student will have obtained an understanding of the science behind today's computerized society. This understanding will remain long after the details and skills "memorized" during the semester have dissipated. Indeed, the student will have been educated rather than trained.

Pedagogical Features

I developed this text over a period of years during which I was also teaching the material. As a result, the text is rich in pedagogical aids. Paramount in this regard is the abundance of problems to enhance the student's participation. Each section within a chapter closes with several Questions/Exercises to challenge students to think independently. They review the material just discussed, extend the previous discussion, or hint at related topics to be covered later. These questions are answered in Appendix F.

Each chapter concludes with a collection of Chapter Review Problems. These problems are designed to serve as "homework" problems in that they call for specific answers, can be solved in a short period of time, and are not answered in the text.

Following the Chapter Review Problems are Problems for the Programmer. These problems are designed for students who already have a programming background and serve to enhance the student's problem-solving/program-development skills as well as provide additional insights into the material in the chapter. If desired, many of these problems can be expanded into programming projects. These problems are an excellent resource when the book is used as a text for CS2 in the ACM model curriculum.

Another pedagogical aid is the use of optional sections. These sections are marked in the table of contents as well as within the chapters themselves. The fact that a section is declared optional does not mean that its material is necessarily more difficult or should be skipped. It merely means that the material in later (nonoptional) sections does not rely on these sections. The purpose of identifying these sections is to allow students to reach later portions of the text more quickly than would otherwise be possible. For example, many instructors may wish to skip or postpone much of the material on machine architecture and operating systems in order to spend more time on algorithm development and representation as discussed in chapters 4 and 5. The use of optional sections allows for this change yet leaves the material available for the more inquisitive students or courses with different goals.

The Second Edition

In addition to numerous minor changes designed to update, correct, or generally improve the text, this second edition differs from the first in the following, more significant ways.

- Chapter 4, "Algorithms," has been rewritten. The new version differs from the old in that it now introduces an informal pseudocode that is used in the remaining chapters of the book, contains an expanded discussion of algorithm development with special attention given to the role of general problem-solving theories, and introduces the topics of program verification and proof of correctness.
- Chapter 5, "Programming Languages," has been rewritten. The new version, although still emphasizing procedural languages, discusses the object-oriented and declarative paradigms as well. For example, an optional section has been added solely for the purpose of providing a more in-depth presentation of declarative programming and Prolog. (A more thorough discussion of object-oriented programming appears later in Chapter 7, "Data Structures.")
- Chapter 7, "Data Structures," has been modified to place more emphasis on abstraction and encapsulation. In keeping with this theme, the chapter now closes with an optional section on object-oriented programming.

Acknowledgments

With the development of the second edition of this text, the list of those who have contributed through their suggestions and comments has increased significantly. Today this list includes J. M. Adams, D. C. S. Allison, P. Bankston, M. Barnard, P. R. Bender, K. Bowyer, P. W. Brashear, C. M. Brown, M. Clancy, D. H. Cooley, M. J. Duncan, N. E. Gibbs, J. D. Harris, D. Hascom, P. Henderson, L. A. Jehn, K. Korb, G. Krenz, T. J. Long, C. May, S. J. Merrill, J. C. Moyer, G. Rice, N. Richert, J. B. Rogers, J. C. Simms, M. C. Slattery, D. Smith, J. Solderitsch, L. Steinberg, and M. Ziegler. To these individuals I give my sincere thanks.

As in the case of the first edition, I also thank my family, Earlene and Cheryl, for their support. They have seen how the development of a manuscript can expand to dominate an author's time. I thank them for their understanding and patience.

J.G.B.

Contents

Introduction   1

0–1	Computer Science in Perspective	1
0–2	The Role of Algorithms	4
0–3	A Short History	6
0–4	Modern Machine Architecture	11
0–5	Packaging	13
0–6	Some Computer System Examples	15

PART ONE   **Machine Architecture**   19

Part One Preview   20

Chapter 1   **Data Storage**   24

1–1	Main Memory	25
1–2	Bulk Storage	30
1–3	Coding Information for Storage	35
1–4	Dealing with Errors (optional)	39
1–5	The Binary System (optional)	43
1–6	Storing Integers (optional)	47
1–7	Storing Fractions (optional)	54
	Review Problems	57
	Problems for the Programmer	60

Chapter 2   **Data Manipulation**   61

2–1	The Central Processing Unit	62
2–2	The Stored-Program Concept	66
2–3	Program Execution	70
2–4	Other Architectures (optional)	75
2–5	Arithmetic/Logic Instructions (optional)	80
2–6	Computer/Peripheral Communication (optional)	86
	Review Problems	90
	Problems for the Programmer	93

PART TWO   **The Human/Machine Interface**   95

Part Two Preview   96

Chapter 3   **Operating Systems**   100

3–1   Functions of Operating Systems   100
3–2   Virtual Characteristics   104
3–3   The Evolution of Operating Systems   105
3–4   Operating System Architecture (optional)   111
3–5   Rudiments of Time-Sharing (optional)   115
3–6   Critical Regions and Deadlock (optional)   118
3–7   Getting It Started (optional)   123
         Review Problems   125
         Problems for the Programmer   127

Chapter 4   **Algorithms**   129

4–1   Definition   129
4–2   Algorithm Representation   131
4–3   Algorithm Discovery   141
4–4   Loop Structures   147
4–5   Recursive Structures   156
4–6   Efficiency and Correctness   172
         Review Problems   180
         Problems for the Programmer   183

Chapter 5   **Programming Languages**   184

5–1   Historical Perspective   185
5–2   Language Implementation   193
5–3   Programming Language Design   197
5–4   Third-Generation Programming Languages   202
5–5   Declarative Programming (optional)   228
         Review Problems   238
         Problems for the Programmer   240

Chapter 6	**Software Engineering**		241
	6–1	The Software Life Cycle	242
	6–2	Modular Design	246
	6–3	Coupling	251
	6–4	Cohesion	256
	6–5	Design Methodologies	259
	6–6	Documentation	263
		Review Problems	265
		Problems for the Programmer	267

PART THREE	**Data Organization**		269
	Part Three Preview		270

Chapter 7	**Data Structures**		276
	7–1	Arrays	277
	7–2	Lists	280
	7–3	Stacks	286
	7–4	Queues	291
	7–5	Trees	296
	7–6	Abstract Data Types	304
	7–7	Object-Oriented Programming (optional)	307
		Review Problems	309
		Problems for the Programmer	313

Chapter 8	**File Structures**		314
	8–1	Sequential Files	315
	8–2	Indexed Files	320
	8–3	Hashed Files	326
	8–4	The Role of the Operating System	332
		Review Problems	334
		Problems for the Programmer	335

Chapter 9   **Database Structures**   336

9–1   The Database Concept   336
9–2   Conceptual Versus Physical Organization   339
9–3   The Relational Model   343
9–4   The Network Model   350
9–5   The Hierarchical Model   360
    Review Problems   364
    Problems for the Programmer   367

PART FOUR   **The Potential of Algorithmic Machines**   369

    Part Four Preview   370

Chapter 10   **Artificial Intelligence**   374

10–1   Some Philosophical Issues   375
10–2   Image Analysis   378
10–3   Reasoning   382
10–4   Control System Activities   385
10–5   Using Heuristics   391
10–6   Applications of Artificial Intelligence   396
    Review Problems   403
    Problems for the Programmer   405

Chapter 11   **Theory of Computation**   406

11–1   A Bare Bones Programming Language   407
11–2   Turing Machines   412
11–3   Computable Functions   417
11–4   A Noncomputable Function   421
11–5   Complexity and Its Measure   426
11–6   Problem Classification   432
    Review Problems   437
    Problems for the Programmer   438

Appendix A   **Popular Codes**   440

Appendix B   **A Typical Machine Language**   441

Appendix C   **Insertion Sort in Assembly Language**   443

Appendix D   **Syntax Diagrams for Pascal**   445

Appendix E   **The Equivalence of Loop and Recursive Structures**   455

Appendix F   **Answers to Questions/Exercises**   457

Additional Reading   484

Index   487

Introduction

0–1 **Computer Science in Perspective**
0–2 **The Role of Algorithms**
0–3 **A Short History**
0–4 **Modern Machine Architecture**
0–5 **Packaging**
0–6 **Some Computer System Examples**
      A Microcomputer Application
      A Minicomputer Application
      A Mainframe Application

Computer science is the discipline that seeks a scientific foundation from which to pursue a variety of topics, including computer design, computer programming, information processing, the algorithmic solution of problems, and the algorithmic process itself. One cannot grasp the scope and dynamics of computer science by studying only one of these topics or, for that matter, by studying several of them as isolated subjects. Indeed, the science of computing involves the relationships *among* these topics as much as the individual topics themselves. The purpose of this book is to present computer science through an integrated study of the subjects it encompasses. We begin in this chapter with an informal discussion of some of the sociological, historical, and technological issues that form the background for our study.

0–1 Computer Science in Perspective

In an effort to orient our thoughts, we first consider the levels of computer involvement occurring within our society. Here we can isolate the following groups of individuals:

Group 1. Those indirectly affected by computer technology and its applications.
Group 2. Those who apply computer technology as a finished product.
Group 3. Those who apply computer technology by modifying the product to fit various applications.
Group 4. Those for whom computing is itself the major application.

It is hard to imagine anyone today not belonging to the first group. After all, computer technology is now used so extensively that its removal would undoubtedly affect even the most remote person, just as the removal of the automobile would have repercussions to those who never travel.

Although the second group does not include everyone, it is still enormous and probably contains some who are not even aware that they fall into this category. Membership in this group is obtained by using computer technology as a tool in an application often far removed from the technicalities many associate with computing. In such cases, the person using the machine merely follows directions (often supplied by the manufacturer) expressed in terms of the application rather than the internal characteristics of the underlying computer. Thus, the person using the machine thinks in terms of the application at hand without recognizing that the tool being used is a computer. Examples are microwave ovens, video games, automatic bank tellers, many office machines, and even telephones.

The third group contains individuals who have some form of programming skill. These people view a computer as a modifiable tool that can be customized to a particular application. Their knowledge includes information about both the application and the machine. One can imagine that membership in this group will grow as programming techniques are modified to require less technical knowledge. In fact, this has been the goal of many computer scientists during the past two or more decades, and with significant progress.

Most members of the fourth group are (in varying degrees) computer scientists. Indeed, the group consists of those whose interests lie in such areas as understanding cognitive processes, developing programming techniques, and advancing technology. Assisting members of groups one, two, and three is the ultimate application for members of group four. This does not mean, however, that all of computer science is geared toward immediate application. Many computer scientists are investigating questions that would probably be considered more philosophical than practical by today's society. On the other hand, the past has shown that what is philosophical today often finds practical applications tomorrow.

In summary, the required degree of computer expertise varies drastically according to an individual's goals, with the determining issue being whether the technology involved is used as an applied tool or is the subject of the application itself (Figure 0-1). In particular, someone who is satisfied with being in group one needs to know only enough to prevent any anxieties that may arise from the changing society. And, a member of group two needs only to understand how to use the particular computing tool to perform the required task.

Similar situations are common with other technologies. For instance, most members of our society relate to audio systems and automobiles at a level corresponding to group two, allowing them to take advantage of the technology without

Figure 0-1 Levels of computer involvement within our society

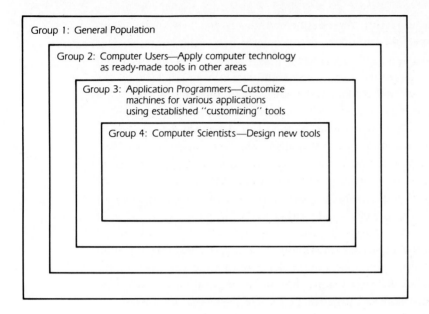

concern for its details. The only real difference between society's relationship with these devices and with computers is that individuals have learned to accept stereos and automobiles while a degree of anxiety lingers about computers. For example, the concept of a teenager building a dune buggy or wiring an apartment for quadraphonic sound now sounds old-fashioned, although a newspaper article about an 11-year-old programmer or a machine that "understands" spoken words still raises feelings of anxiety within many readers.

Whether or not it is healthy for one to accept membership in one group level without investigating the next is open to debate and probably varies with the individual and the application. Although such acceptance means that individuals can use advanced technology without developing expertise in it, it can lead to frustration and misunderstandings. Year after year, errors in data processing are traced to someone's lack of understanding in a subject that was considered irrelevant. Thus, one could argue that a wise user of a technology should obtain a higher degree of knowledge than the minimum required for the immediate application, which is why driver education courses cover such topics as changing tires and checking the oil.

We conclude that there are those in groups other than group four who would like to study the science underlying the "computer revolution." It is for these inquisitive souls that this book is written.

0–2 The Role of Algorithms

Perhaps the most significant feature of modern computers is that they are programmable. That is, a single machine can be modified to perform a variety of tasks. This versatility is achieved by designing the machine to follow step-by-step processes that can be easily altered or exchanged from outside the machine or, in fact, by the machine itself. For now, we will accept the phrase "a step-by-step process" as an informal definition of the term *algorithm*. (We will be more precise later.) The process of programming a machine involves designing an algorithm that directs the desired activities and then communicating this algorithm to the machine in a form the machine is able to understand and follow. Consequently, the design and communication of algorithms is an important subject within computer science.

It is appropriate that we take the time now to introduce the basic properties of algorithms. For this purpose, consider an algorithm that directs the construction of a kite (Figure 0-2).

In terms of this algorithm, we can highlight three major properties of algorithmic processes: the need for precision, the involvement of data, and the need for execution control. In particular, we first note that our example algorithm has been designed to be followed by humans, rather than by machines, in that it relies heavily on intuition. For example, step 1 assumes that the manner in which the sticks are to be connected will be obvious once the sticks and clip are inspected; step 2 assumes that anyone following the directions will figure out where the frame should be attached to the fabric; and so forth. The algorithm also relies on the human's knowledge, assuming, for example, that the human knows what kind of kite is being made, what form is a cross shape, and what is a kite's harness.

If this algorithm were followed by a device (such as a computer) without intuition or knowledge, such ambiguities would render the algorithm useless. Conse-

Figure 0-2 A kite construction algorithm

Step 1. Construct the kite's frame in the form of a cross by attaching the two sticks with the clip provided.

Step 2. Mount the fabric on the frame by inserting the fabric's edge string in the grooves at the ends of the sticks.

Step 3. Bow the shorter stick in the frame away from the fabric side by tying its ends together with a piece of string that is three-fourths as long as the stick itself.

Step 4. Construct the kite's harness from a piece of string slightly longer than the longer frame stick.

Step 5. If the kite is to be flown only in moderate winds, skip the next step.

Step 6. Attach the kite's tail to the bottom of the frame.

Step 7. Attach the tow line to the kite just above the middle of the harness.

Step 8. The kite is now complete.

quently, the design of algorithms for machine execution requires a higher level of precision than that to which humans are accustomed.

This gap between the precision required by machines and the lack of precision with which humans are accustomed to communicating constitutes a major obstacle in the programming process. In fact, the goal of overcoming this obstacle is ultimately the driving force behind most of the research in computer science today. Perhaps the most challenging approach to this problem is to design machines with the ability to "understand" the imprecise statements routinely offered by humans. This approach is a major topic within the subject known as artificial intelligence, which we discuss in Chapter 10.

Another approach has been to develop programming environments and methodologies that assist humans in developing the precision required by the machine. This in turn has generated interest in learning more about the design and representation of algorithms—a subject that we investigate in Chapters 4 and 5. As an example of the results in this direction, researchers have discovered general problem-solving algorithms that, once implemented, provide a problem-solving system in which the algorithms to be executed are already known to the machine. Thus, the task of a human using such a system becomes that of developing a precise description of the problem at hand rather than a precise description of a process for solving the problem—the theory being that it is easier to describe a problem than it is to find and describe a solution.

Another important property of our kite building algorithm is that it embodies an instruction selection process by which algorithm execution is passed from one instruction to the next. This process is reflected first by the fact that the steps are presented as a numbered list and second by the fact that steps 5 and 8 have as their sole purpose the control of instruction selection. Thus, the communication of an algorithm requires the ability to convey this order, and the execution of an algorithm requires the ability to select instructions (or steps) in the proper order.

Finally, we note that our example algorithm is designed to manipulate objects. The purpose of the algorithm is to accept the kite parts and produce a completed kite. Of course, the algorithm itself does not actually perform these steps but merely directs the required activities. Inherent in this observation is the fact that the overall system in which the algorithm functions must consist of three parts: the algorithm itself; a device (human or machine) that executes the algorithm; and a mechanism by which objects (in this context called data) are retrieved from the system's environment, temporarily stored for manipulation, and returned to the environment (Figure 0-3).

From our point of view, this algorithmic property has two consequences. First, in terms of algorithm communication, any system used to communicate algorithms (for instance, we used the English language to communicate our kite building algorithm) must be capable of identifying data elements and data manipulations in

Figure 0-3 Components of algorithm execution

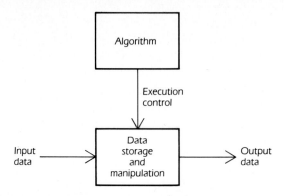

addition to reflecting the algorithm's execution order. Second, in terms of machinery, any system for executing algorithms must be able to accept data (called input) from the outside, store and manipulate the data, and pass data (called output) to its external environment.

Our informal introduction to algorithms concludes with a list of questions within computer science that we will address in this book.

- What types of instructions are necessary for expressing algorithms?
- What problems can be solved by algorithmic processes?
- How can the expression of an algorithm be made less tedious?
- How can a machine for executing algorithms be constructed?

0–3 A Short History

Our discussion of algorithms has pointed out that any machine that is to execute algorithms (which we will call an algorithmic machine) must provide certain features. In particular, it must provide a way to represent and manipulate data within the machine; the data must be accessible from the outside world in terms of both input and output; and provisions must exist for control of the steps within the algorithm. The way in which these features are implemented in modern computers is the subject of our first few chapters. For now, let us consider the history of computing in terms of how these features were incorporated in the early machines.

Although not the first computing device, the abacus might well be considered the first computing machine. Its history has been traced as far back as the ancient Greek and Roman civilizations, and it is still used today. The "machine" is quite simple, consisting of beads strung on rods that are in turn mounted in a rectangular frame. As the beads are moved back and forth on the rods, their positions represent stored values. It is in the positions of the beads that this computer represents and stores data. Data input is accomplished by a human who positions the beads; data output consists of observing the bead positions. For control of an algorithm's execution, the machine relies on the human operator. Thus, the abacus alone is merely a data storage system and must be combined with a human to create a complete algorithmic machine.

In more recent years, computing machines were designed based on the technology of gears. Among the inventors were Blaise Pascal (1623–1662) of France, Gottfried Wilhelm Leibniz (1646–1716) of Germany, and Charles Babbage (1792–1871) of England. With these machines, data was represented by the positions of gears, with data being input mechanically to establish gear positions (Figure 0-4). Output from Pascal's and Leibniz's machines was achieved by observing the final gear positions in much the same way that we read the wheels on a car's odometer. Babbage, on the other hand, envisioned a machine that would print output values on paper so that the possibility of transcribing errors would be eliminated.

As for the ability to follow an algorithm, we can see a progression of flexibility in the machines. Pascal's machine, for example, was built to follow only the addition

Figure 0-4 A prototype of Babbage's difference engine (Courtesy of International Business Machines Corporation)

algorithm. Consequently, the appropriate sequence of steps was embedded into the structure of the machine itself. In a similar manner, Leibniz's machine also had its algorithms firmly embedded in its structure. However, Leibniz's machine offered a variety of arithmetic operations from which the operator could select. Finally, Babbage's machine was designed so that the sequence of steps that the machine was to perform could be communicated to the machine in the form of holes in paper cards. Thus, this latter machine involved a more sophisticated control mechanism.

In reality, the idea of communicating an algorithm via holes in paper was not originated by Babbage. In 1801, Joseph Jacquard had applied a similar technique for controlling weaving looms in France (Figure 0-5). These looms should be considered as much the forerunners of modern computers as the machines already mentioned. The only reason they are not is that the history of computers has often been recorded as the history of numeric calculators rather than of algorithmic machines. This is a narrow and unfortunate viewpoint. The fact is that a significant number (probably the majority) of computer applications today are nonnumeric. Moreover, it was the programmable weaving loom and not the more complex gear-driven calculators that the technology of the time was able to reproduce; and it was these looms that raised the population's anxiety in ways similar to the computers of today. Indeed, many people lost their jobs to these new machines.

With this role of the Jacquard loom in mind, we should take a closer look at the loom as an algorithmic machine. The data it manipulates is the material being woven that is placed in the machine by a human in the form of thread (input) and removed in the form of cloth (output). As for instruction selection, Jacquard's looms were equipped with a control mechanism that followed the algorithm "written" on the paper cards to manipulate the data stored in the machine.

As we indicated, the technology of the time was unable to provide the precision required to popularize the complex gear-driven calculators of Pascal, Leibniz, and Babbage. It was not until electronics began to supplement mechanical devices that the technology of the day was able to support the theoretical developments taking place in the embryonic science of computing. Traditionally speaking, the door to today's electronic computers was opened in 1944 when Howard Aiken completed the electromechanical Mark I using the technology of electronically controlled mechanical relays (Figure 0-6). Of course, it is technically incorrect to give credit to one person or one machine as being the origin of today's modern electronic computers. For instance, computing devices based on relay technology had been built at Bell Laboratories, under the direction of George Stibitz, as early as 1940.

Although significantly different from Babbage's designs in terms of technology, Aiken's machine was remarkably similar to Babbage's in terms of functional design. After all, Babbage had succeeded in isolating the characteristics (data representation and storage, data manipulation, input/output, and algorithm control) required for algorithm execution. Machines today still share this functional similarity.

Figure 0-5 Jacquard's loom: (a) yesterday, (b) today. (Courtesy of (a) International Business Machines Corporation and (b) Sulzer Rutin, Inc.)

(a)

(b)

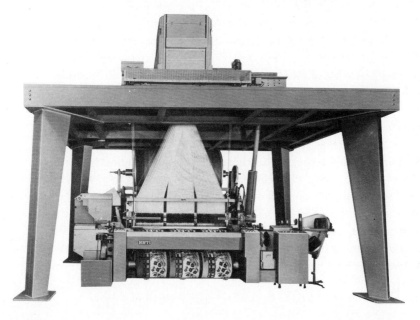

Figure 0-6 The Mark I (Courtesy of Cruft Laboratory)

From this point on, the history of computing branches in two directions: the continuing evolution of equipment (hardware) and the study and development of algorithms (software). Following the first, we witness the advancement of technology from the development of the first fully electronic computer called ENIAC (Electronic Numerical Integrator And Calculator) based on the use of vacuum tubes, through the use of transistors, and into the age of integrated circuits which today allow machines with significantly more power than the Mark I to be placed on a desk top.

The second branch involves the development of algorithms and an increased understanding of their structure. In many ways, this branch is a result of the successes of the first because such conditions as limited data storage capabilities and time-consuming programming techniques significantly restricted the complexity of the algorithms programmed into early machines. However, as limitations began to weaken, machines were applied to increasingly larger and more complex tasks. Because attempts to express the composition of these tasks in algorithmic form soon began to tax the abilities of the human mind, many research efforts turned toward the study of algorithms and the programming process. Today, computer science encompasses the study of both the technology of the machines themselves and the algorithmic processes they execute.

0–4 **Modern Machine Architecture**

As pointed out in the previous section, Charles Babbage is given credit for isolating the components necessary for an algorithmic machine. Thus, "modern" machine architecture actually dates back to the 1800s. On the other hand, one look at a piece of today's equipment quickly reveals that a lot has happened since Babbage in the way these components are implemented. In this section, we discuss the composition of today's computers in terms of their roles in algorithm execution.

We begin with data storage. Here we find that gear positions have been replaced by tiny electronic circuits, each of which is capable of storing a single digit of information called a bit (for binary digit). Large numbers of these circuits are collected into the unit of the machine called the main memory. Through coding systems in which information is represented as patterns of bit values, data is stored in the main memory along with the algorithms the machine is to execute.

To perform algorithm execution, another unit called the central processing unit (or CPU) is attached to the machine's main memory. This unit is actually responsible for two activities required for algorithm execution: the manipulation of data as requested by the algorithm and the coordination of the algorithmic steps. Thus, the CPU fetches instructions from main memory and executes them, while the execution of these instructions causes the CPU to retrieve data from main memory, manipulate the data, and possibly return results to main memory for storage.

In many respects, the CPU–main memory combination constitutes what we call "the computer." However, a computer consisting of only a CPU and main memory would prove highly restricted. In particular, without the assistance of today's peripheral devices, such as terminals, printers, disk drives, and voice synthesizers, a machine would lack the ability to communicate easily with its environment, and its ability to accept data for manipulation and return results would thus be extremely hampered. It would be more accurate to consider a complete computer as consisting of a CPU, main memory, and peripheral devices, as represented in Figure 0-7, where the close association between the CPU and main memory is shown by enclosing their respective rectangles within yet another rectangle, which is then connected to peripheral devices.

The vast collection of peripheral devices can be divided into two categories: bulk storage devices and input/output (I/O) devices. The first category is designed mainly to extend the machine's data storage capabilities beyond the capability of its main memory. A primary example consists of disk storage devices in which data is recorded magnetically on the surface of flat spinning disks. The higher capacity units use rigid disks (called hard disks) mounted one above the other on a spindle forming what is known as a disk pack. Lower capacity systems use single flexible disks, called diskettes or floppy disks, mounted in paper sleeves. Another popular

Figure 0-7 A conceptual structure of a computer system

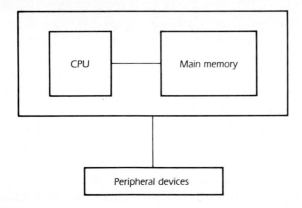

bulk storage system uses tape devices in which data is again recorded magnetically but on the surface of thin plastic tape wound on a reel.

The category of I/O devices seems to expand every day. The device most commonly known today is probably the terminal that consists of a keyboard for data input and a cathode ray tube (CRT), otherwise known as a picture tube, for output. (CRTs are also known as VDTs—short for video display tube.) Such output devices are called soft-copy devices since the output they produce does not appear in a permanent form. In contrast are the hard-copy devices such as plotters (for the production of charts, graphs, or special purpose graphics output) or printers (that range in technology from typewriterlike mechanisms operating as slow as 15 characters per second to laser printers that can print as many as 21,000 lines per minute). Other I/O devices are based on such technologies as magnetic ink character recognition (MICR), optical character recognition (OCR), and audio input and output in the form of voice recognition and voice synthesis devices. This short list, however, does not begin to exhaust the scope of I/O devices in use today. Indeed, devices exist that sense and control building temperature, monitor a patient's vital signs, and detect the speed of aircraft.

The peripheral devices we have been discussing are not normally connected directly to the CPU–main memory combination but rather are usually connected to a controller that is in turn connected to "the computer" through a connection called a port. A controller is actually a small computer and is charged with coordinating the activities of the devices attached to it as well as with dealing with each device's idiosyncrasies. Such a design relieves the central processor from the time-consuming chores of communicating with peripheral devices and allows it to concentrate on the major system activities while the potential interruptions of peripheral devices are handled by the controllers. This delegation of duties does not stop here, however. In particular, it is efficient to assign peripheral devices to controllers according to device type. One controller might handle the system's disk drives, while another might specialize in printers. Thus, a more detailed diagram than that shown in Figure 0-7 might take the form shown in Figure 0-8.

0–5 **Packaging**

The physical characteristics of computers span a spectrum from very small machines used in such home appliances as microwave ovens and vacuum cleaners where both CPU and main memory are contained on a single chip no larger than a dime to massive machines occupying large rooms and requiring special air-conditioning considerations to counteract the heat generated by their circuitry. Terminology demands that we classify these machines into three groups: microcomputers, minicomputers, and mainframe computers. Because such a classification scheme results in some rather fuzzy boundaries, it is common to find the same machine classified as a minicomputer by some and as a mainframe by others. Indeed, the minicomputer classification is being squeezed from below by microcomputers that are becoming more and more powerful as the cost/feature ratio continues to drop. At the same time, the minicomputer classification is bounded from above by the class of main-

Figure 0-8 A computer system using controllers to coordinate peripheral activity

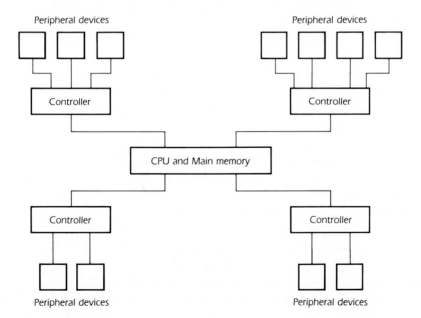

frame machines whose advancement depends on overcoming increasingly harder technology problems.

A typical microcomputer (often called a personal computer, or a PC for short) is small enough to be placed on a desk top and is used by one person at a time. Many manufacturers combine the CPU and main memory of a microcomputer in the same case along with some peripheral devices such as a keyboard, CRT, one or two floppy-disk drives, and perhaps a hard-disk system in the more expensive models. Others feel that separating certain components such as the keyboard or CRT adds to system convenience. In any case, ports are usually provided for the addition of an external printer or to allow the machine to be connected to a larger computer and thus be used as a terminal.

Because microcomputers are designed for a very cost-sensitive market, their internal architecture has changed rapidly with advances in technology and the corresponding reduction in cost/feature ratio. Early microcomputers were capable of manipulating bit patterns of 4 to 8 bits and had memories that were limited to approximately 64,000 8-bit cells. Today, many microcomputers are able to manipulate patterns of 32 bits, and although the basic models may have 128,000 to 256,000 8-bit memory cells, they are easily expanded to 640,000 or more cells.

The instruction set of a microcomputer is usually not as rich as that of a minicomputer, and thus some operations must be accomplished via short sequences of more elementary instructions. However, since microcomputers are able to execute several hundred thousand instructions per second, they are capable of processing a significant amount of data.

Minicomputers tend to have the CPU and main memory housed separately from the peripheral devices in a case placed on the floor and standing 3 to 5 feet high. The most common exception to this characteristic is the inclusion of a disk bulk storage system in the cabinet with the CPU and memory. Because minicomputers can provide simultaneous service to as many as 30 terminals, they are quite popular for small-business use. Although bulk storage for these machines may be provided by diskettes, it is more common to find larger disk packs used in situations where several terminals are being served.

The main memory of minicomputers usually consists of a few million 8-bit units, although the CPU normally fetches two or more of these units at a time and manipulates bits in units of 32. Since the instruction sets for minicomputers are richer than those found in microcomputers, steps that may require several instructions in a microcomputer can often be done with only one instruction in a minicomputer. For example, minicomputers provide instructions for supporting multiuser environments in which several requests must be serviced at the same time.

Mainframe computers are the largest machines. The CPU and main memory are housed in large cabinets surrounded by numerous large disk drives and tape units. A desk is usually nearby with a CRT terminal and perhaps hard-copy device for the use of the full-time computer operator. These systems, together with their bulk storage devices and one or more high-speed printers, normally occupy a large room with raised flooring that allows cables to be conveniently run under it for connecting the various pieces of equipment. Moreover, the heat generated by the equipment requires air-conditioning to keep the room at a comfortable temperature.

At such installations, computer users seldom come in direct contact with the machine but use one of a hundred or more remote terminals either permanently connected to the machine or temporarily connected by telephone lines or other long-distance communication methods.

Mainframe machines have extensive instruction repertoires that allow the manipulation of bit strings of 32 or more bits with execution speeds on the order of a million or more instructions per second.

0–6 Some Computer System Examples

This chapter closes with a look at some examples of typical computer installations.

A Microcomputer Application

Our first example is a small business that designs, makes, and sells sails for a variety of sailboats. To support its everyday business needs, this company owns seven medium-size microcomputers that are used for maintaining mailing lists, producing form letters, and performing general functions for which typewriters were used in the past. (The company has essentially adopted the policy of buying microcomputers rather than typewriters—the argument being that for a little more money, the company obtains a much more flexible piece of equipment.) In addition, the company owns a large microcomputer (containing a hard-disk storage system with a capacity of 25 million characters) that is used for maintaining business records such as accounts receivable, accounts payable, etc.

A more novel computer application is found in the activities particular to the company's product. Although the business manufactures a few styles and sizes of sails on a routine basis, at least 90% of its production consists of custom-made sails. Thus, the sail designers are constantly considering variations of numerous sails to maximize performance on different boats under different conditions. To support this design process, each designer is provided with a medium-size microcomputer.

With these machines, a designer first selects the basic type of sail (genoa, spinnaker, etc.) to be designed and describes the particular refinements desired by typing appropriate parameters at the keyboard. The business has designed programs capable of converting this information into a description of the various pieces of cloth from which the desired sail should be constructed together with a report on additional characteristics that the finished sail will have. This information is stored on a floppy disk or, at the designer's option, can be printed at the printer for future reference or current discussion.

Once a suitable design is refined, the description of the sail on the floppy disk is taken to the cutting room where a second microcomputer system, similar to the first, is attached to a plotter 70 by 5 feet. With this system, the pieces of cloth are both cut and marked directly from the information on the disk.

As we observe in the case of sail design, data is currently transferred from one of the company's machines to another by recording the data on a floppy disk that is then carried to the other machine where the data is needed. However, as more and more of the company's activities are becoming "computerized," the company has observed such data transfers taking place on a large scale throughout the organization. Thus, management is currently considering a system by which all the company's machines would be connected electronically so that data transfer from one machine to another could be performed more efficiently.

A Minicomputer Application

Our second example focuses on a small business that buys oil in large quantities and prepares special blends for its customers who consist mainly of bulk industrial users. The company also produces motor oil in quart containers for local sale under a regional brand name.

The computer system owned by the business is centered around a minicomputer described by the block diagram in Figure 0-9. The machine occupies a corner of a large room on the first floor of the company's two-story building. The same room is occupied by both the receptionist and the office manager. The CPU, main memory, and all disk units (diskette and disk packs) are contained in the same cabinet. The diskette unit is used mainly for recording data to be used for backup purposes. Data accessed on a routine basis is kept on the two permanently mounted disk packs, which together are capable of holding more than 50 million characters.

Next to the computer cabinet is the high-speed printer used for producing such items as invoices, sales reports, and other reports required by management. A slower letter-quality printer is located closer to the two employees who use it for printing the final copy of letters and other documents after first entering and correcting the text through CRT terminals at their desks. Although not the latest technology, the business has found it cost-effective to enter all data through the terminals. Thus, a major role of the office manager and receptionist is to update the stored records as the information is collected.

A third CRT terminal is located next to the computer for use by management personnel who occasionally stop in to obtain information not provided by one of the routine reports produced by the machine on a daily, weekly, monthly, or yearly basis. A fourth CRT terminal is located in the laboratory upstairs, where it provides

Figure 0-9 A block diagram of a typical minicomputer installation

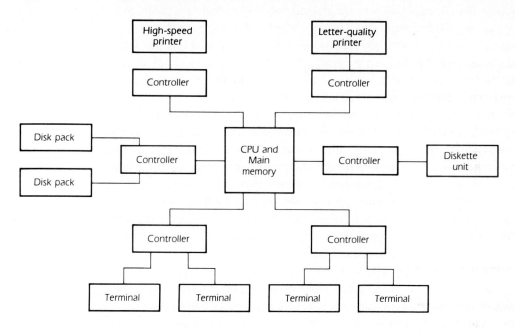

access to the machine for the more mathematical or scientific applications associated with new product development.

The system is used for maintaining the normal business records (inventory, accounts receivable, accounts payable, payroll, etc.) and correspondence in addition to research and development. The one exception is the executive payroll, which is handled by the company's bank.

A Mainframe Application

Our last example is a large bank located in a metropolitan area with 12 branch offices. The bank owns two mainframe machines that occupy most of a floor in the bank's central office building along with numerous disk drives, tape units, printers, and special purpose devices such as an optical scanner and five magnetic ink character recognizers that routinely process over a million checks a day. The mainframe machines are configured to share the workload or provide backup for one another in case of maintenance problems. These machines are mainly used to provide a central storage and retrieval system for records pertaining to the complete range of banking and business activities. Customer records such as checking, savings, and loan accounts are maintained in the computers in addition to the business records of both the bank itself and individual businesses that contract with the bank for such services.

Another significant use of the machines includes research and development on a variety of levels. For example, some personnel use the machines as tools for economic forecasting, while others use them for program development in an effort to keep up with changes in laws and regulations and to offer competitive services to the bank's customers. Because of this program development, another floor of the bank's central building is used to house computer support personnel whose jobs are solely to maintain the computing facilities.

Access to the bank's machines can be obtained in one of two ways. One is to carry data stored on media such as magnetic tapes or disks to the computer installation where it can be read into the machine and processed. This technique is typical when dealing with medium to large amounts of data on a routine basis. For instance, the bank processes the payroll for other businesses that regularly deliver preprocessed time sheets in such a recorded form. (On the other hand, more and more businesses are finding it convenient to record information on time sheets in a form that can be read by the bank's optical scanning equipment as this removes the need for preprocessing the data before presenting it to the bank.)

The second and more popular method of access to the machines is via remote devices. For example, within the central building are numerous terminals used by tellers, administrators, and programming personnel. However, these terminals represent only a small part of the total remote use. Each branch office houses terminals to support many of the same activities supported at the central office. Moreover, each of the 200 automatic tellers positioned in convenient locations such as shopping centers around the area is connected to the machines as a restricted-use terminal. And, many businesses that contract with the bank for accounting and other business services transfer data to and from the machines over their own terminal devices.

We see, then, that the two machines in the bank's central office serve a variety of purposes, are connected to a host of peripheral devices, and are highly likely (in fact almost always) required to serve numerous requests at the same time. How these requests are coordinated and honored in a timely fashion is yet another subject of computer science.

1

Machine Architecture

Chapter 1   Data Storage

Chapter 2   Data Manipulation

Part One Preview
Machine Architecture

A modern computer consists of three components: a main memory where data is stored, a central processing unit (CPU) where algorithm execution and data manipulation take place, and peripheral devices that either provide a means of communication between the machine and its environment (input/output devices) or extend the machine's information storage capabilities (bulk storage devices). The design of this equipment, along with the theoretical basis on which the design is constructed, is a major part of computer science. Since these design principles are often reflected in the external properties of the machines, it is reasonable to start out with a brief coverage of today's architecture and its ramifications.

Chapter 1 begins by considering the structure of a machine's main memory, which is essentially nothing more than a collection of small electronic circuits capable of storing either one of two "symbols." These symbols are called bits and are often represented as 1 and 0 (also on and off, or set and clear). Most computer memories can store millions of these bits collected into groups (or, more precisely, into short strings) known as memory cells. A typical memory cell size is 8 bits, a size that is often referred to as a byte. The cells in a computer's memory are thought of as being in a row with the location of a cell in this row being the cell's address.

To extend a machine's memory capabilities and to allow for the external storage of data, today's machines can be accompanied by numerous bulk storage devices. The two leading storage device technologies are tape storage and disk storage. Tape storage is based on the magnetic recording of bit patterns on long strips of plastic tape that can be wound on a reel for storage. The major drawback to this system is that all reading and writing of information must be done sequentially. That is, to retrieve information from the middle of a tape, we must scan the information recorded earlier to reach the desired data. Consequently, a significant amount of winding and rewinding would be required if we needed the information in any order other than that in which it was recorded. On the other hand, reels of tape are easily removed from tape read/write units (placed off-line), stored externally for later use, and reinserted in tape read/write units (placed on-line) when needed. Tape storage systems therefore remain popular for long-term storage of data for backup purposes.

Disk storage systems are designed to overcome the drawback of inherently sequential tape technology. With these systems, information is recorded (again magnetically) on the surface of flat plastic disks that rotate within the disk access device. Reading or writing information on the disk is accomplished by read/write heads that remain stationary as the disk rotates so that the heads traverse closed circles, called tracks, on the disk's surface. Segments of the recorded data can be retrieved merely by selecting the correct track instead of being forced to traverse all the previously recorded data. Today, flexible disks called floppy disks or diskettes that are easily inserted into and removed from disk read/write units have become quite popular as a replacement for tape systems for long-term storage.

In addition to discussing the structure of data storage devices, Chapter 1 deals with the techniques and consequences of coding information for storage. Because of the bit system used by today's computers, all information in these machines must be coded in terms of 1s and 0s. To see how this is done, we first note that since a memory cell contains a collection of bits, a variety of different bit patterns can be stored in each cell. If we agreed to represent the letter A by one of these patterns, B by another, etc., we could store information in a machine's main memory by placing the appropriate character codes in a row of memory cells. One popular code for this purpose is the American Standard Code for Information Interchange (ASCII, pronounced as'—kee), described in Appendix A.

More compact storage techniques that take advantage of the base two representation system are available if the information being stored is numeric. You can count in base two by imagining a car's odometer that has been modified to contain only the digits 0 and 1. Thus, each time a 1 rolls out of sight, it leaves a 0 behind, and the digit to its left is also changed (just as in the case of the 9 on a normal odometer). The sequence of readings thus appears as follows:

$$
\begin{array}{c}
0000 \\
0001 \\
0010 \\
0011 \\
0100 \\
0101 \\
0110 \\
\cdot \\
\cdot \\
\cdot
\end{array}
$$

which is the base two version of the more common sequence:

$$
\begin{array}{c}
0 \\
1 \\
2 \\
3 \\
4 \\
5 \\
6 \\
\cdot \\
\cdot \\
\cdot
\end{array}
$$

In reality, a computer usually uses a modified version of the base two system, depending on the properties of the values being stored. One such variation is known as two's complement notation, which is popular when storing integer values. Another variation, called floating-point notation, allows the storage of values with fractional parts.

It is important to recognize that because each computer is physically limited in the number of bits it can maintain, the size and accuracy with which numbers can be stored are limited. Such restrictions can lead to inaccurate results because of either overflow errors (the result of attempting to store a value that is too large to be represented in the coding system being used) or found-off errors (the result of attempting to store a value whose fractional part requires more precision than is available in the coding system being used). The development of techniques to avoid such problems is an important part of the branch of mathematics known as numerical analysis.

Chapter 2 focuses on the CPU, where bit patterns are manipulated and the machine's activities are coordinated. Within this unit is a relatively small collection of storage cells (normally no more than 32) called registers. It is in these registers that the CPU stores bit patterns that are about to be or have just been manipulated. Thus, manipulating data stored in memory consists of moving the data from memory into a register in the CPU, performing the desired operations within the CPU, and then moving the result from a register into memory. Operations performed by a typical CPU include the usual arithmetic operations; rotating bit patterns within a register; and the logic operations known as AND, OR, and EXCLUSIVE OR, which get their names from their relationships to the truth tables associated with these terms. Our point here is that all the more complex activities that machines are doing every day are constructed from these very elementary capabilities.

For a machine to perform a task, it must be told what to do by means of a programming process. For this reason, each machine is designed to respond to a variety of instructions expressed in bit patterns and known as the machine language. Through this language, a sequence of instructions describing the task to be performed can be stored within the machine's memory in the same manner that data is stored.

Once a program is stored in a machine's memory, the CPU can execute it by repeatedly performing its machine cycle consisting of three steps: fetch, decode, and execute. During the fetch step, the CPU fetches an instruction from memory; in the decode step, the CPU decodes the instruction just fetched; and in the execute step, the CPU actually performs the requested action. To aid in the fetching of instructions, the CPU contains a register, known as the program counter, in which it keeps track of its location in the memory being executed. Normally, the instructions are fetched in the order stored in memory. However, to alter this sequence, machine languages provide instructions that cause the program counter to be modified (called branch or jump instructions). In this way, a program or program segment stored in one area of memory can initiate the execution of a program in another area.

Because accepting information from the outside world and returning processed information to the machine's environment is an important component of a computer's overall task, Chapter 2 includes an introduction to some of the issues associated with such communication. In particular, it provides a discussion of the role of controllers as well as such issues as memory mapped input/output and serial versus parallel interfaces.

As mentioned in the Introduction, a major goal in computer science is to design systems that allow computing machinery to be used by those who are not aware of the internal characteristics outlined here. Thus, many topics in computer science have their roots in the technicalities of today's, as well as yesterday's, equipment. The purpose of Part One is to provide us with enough background in machine architecture to allow us to approach the other topics in our study with a level of understanding that might otherwise be replaced with an aura of mystery.

1 Data Storage

1–1 **Main Memory**
    Storage of Bits
    Main Memory Organization
    Organization Within a Cell
    Hexadecimal Notation

1–2 **Bulk Storage**
    Tape Storage
    Disk Storage
    Logical Versus Physical Records

1–3 **Coding Information for Storage**
    Symbol Representation
    Representing Numeric Values

1–4 **Dealing with Errors** (optional)
    Parity Bits
    Error Correcting Codes
    Issues of Application

1–5 **The Binary System** (optional)
    Binary Addition
    Fractions in Binary

1–6 **Storing Integers** (optional)
    Sign-Magnitude Notation
    Excess Notation
    Two's Complement Notation

1–7 **Storing Fractions** (optional)
    Floating-Point Notation
    Round-Off Errors

As already noted, a machine for executing algorithms must be able to store data internally. Over the years, many technologies have been used to accomplish this (for example, beads on rods, gear positions, and electromagnetic relays). Theoretically, the technology used for data storage has no effect on the computing power of the machine. Indeed, Chapter 11 demonstrates that a very simple machine has the same "power" as any of today's multimillion-dollar computers. In reality, however, the technology applied and the techniques used in its implementation have an enormous impact on the issues of practicality and are repeatedly reflected in the external characteristics of the system. Thus, just as a knowledge of anatomy is essential in the practice of medicine, a familiarity with a machine's internal storage techniques pays regular dividends throughout the study of computer science. Consequently, we begin our study by acquiring this beneficial background.

1–1 **Main Memory**

Fundamental to the storage of data within today's algorithmic machines is the concept of a *bit* (short for *binary digit*), which can be represented by a device that can exist in one of two states, such as on or off (a switch), open or closed (a relay), or even raised or lowered (a flag on a flagpole), although such a device would not be conducive for use in an electronic circuit. Of course, the actual technology used for bit storage in machines varies as new and more cost-effective techniques are devised. Because it might be helpful to have a particular device in mind as you read the following sections, we will take a brief look at a popular technology for bit representation in computers today: the capacitor.

Storage of Bits

Suppose two metal plates are placed parallel to one another with a short distance separating them, as shown in Figure 1-1. If we were to connect these plates to opposite terminals of a battery, we would find that the positive and negative charges from the battery would distribute themselves over the plates to which each terminal was connected. If we then were to disconnect the battery, the plates would be left holding these charges. In this charged condition, the plate combination would behave as a power source similar to the battery. In particular, if the plates were connected either directly or indirectly through an electronic circuit, an electric current would flow through the connection until the charges on the plates were neutralized. A capacitor is nothing more than such a system of plates and can be made so small that several thousand capacitors made up of these plates can be assembled on a single wafer (called a *chip*) no larger than a dime.

As we stated, the significance of a capacitor from our point of view is that it is an electronic device that can be placed in one of two states (in this case charged or discharged) and will remain in that state until later tested. In reality, we seldom use the terms *charged* and *discharged* when referring to the status of a bit in a machine since not all bits are represented with capacitor technology. Instead, it is more common to use the terms *one* and *zero*. (Other popular terms frequently used in place of one are *true, set, on,* and *high*. Moreover, each of these has its corresponding substitute for zero, which is *false, reset* (or *clear*), *off,* and *low,* respectively.)

Figure 1-1 The charging and discharging of a capacitor

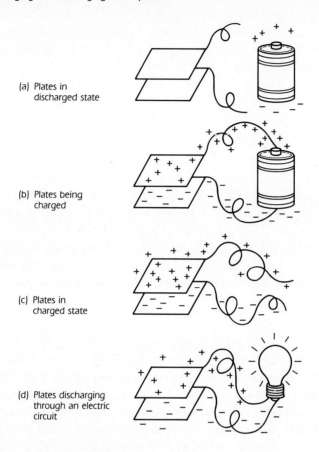

(a) Plates in
    discharged state

(b) Plates being
    charged

(c) Plates in
    charged state

(d) Plates discharging
    through an electric
    circuit

Main Memory Organization

It is clear that little information can be stored in a circuit that can represent only one bit. Thus, information is represented by means of a coding system in which different bit patterns are used to represent different symbols such as the letters of the alphabet, digits, or punctuation. For this reason, we find that a computers **main memory** (in contrast to the machine's bulk storage or secondary memory discussed in the next section) consists of a large collection of circuits capable of storing numerous bits. For reasons of practicality, this bit reservoir is divided into manageable units called **cells** (or words), with a typical cell size being 8 bits (Figure 1-2). In fact, bit collections of size eight are often used to represent individual symbols in the machine's coding system and have become so popular that the term **byte** is now widely used in reference to bit collections of that size. We adopt this terminology here, even though there are still those in the field who use the term *byte* for bit collections of sizes other than eight.

Figure 1-2 An 8-bit memory cell containing the pattern 10100100

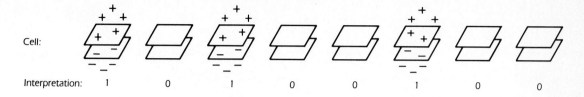

A tremendous variation exists in the number of cells appearing in the memories of different machines. For instance, the small computers used in such household devices as microwave ovens may have memory sizes measured in hundreds of cells or fewer, whereas large computers used to store and manipulate extensive amounts of data can have billions of cells in their main memories. It is customary to state the size of a machine's main memory in terms of 1024-cell units. (The value 1024, being a power of two, is more natural as a unit of measure within a computer than an even 1000.) The letter K (short for kilo, as in kilobyte) is used to indicate this unit of measure. Therefore, a memory of size 16K contains 16,384 (16 × 1024) cells.

To identify individual cells in a machine's main memory, each cell is assigned a unique name, called its ***address.*** The system is analogous to, and uses the same terminology as, the technique of identifying houses in a city by addresses. In the case of memory cells, however, the addresses used are completely numeric since there are no street names involved. To be more precise, one envisions all the cells being placed in a single row and then being numbered in this order starting with the value zero. Thus, the cells in a machine with a 64K memory would be addressed as 0, 1, 2, . . . , 65535. Note that such an addressing system not only gives us a way of uniquely identifying each cell but also associates an order to the cells (Figure 1-3). Thus, phrases such as "the next cell" or "the previous cell" make sense.

To complete the main memory of a machine, the circuitry that actually holds the bits is combined with the circuitry required to allow other circuits to store and retrieve data from the memory cells. Thus, other circuits can get data from the memory by electronically asking for the contents of a certain address (called a read operation) or record information in the memory by requesting that a certain bit pattern be placed in the cell at a particular address (called a write operation).

A common analogy to a main memory's organization is the collection of mailboxes at a post office, where you find numerous boxes (cells) consecutively numbered on the outside (addresses). This analogy breaks down, however, when we consider the insertion and removal of data. First, we note that a mailbox does not have a well-established capacity. (It seems that one more envelope can always be squeezed into it.) On the other hand, a memory cell can only retain so many bits. If more bits are stored, the old ones are lost. Second, when "data" is extracted from a mailbox,

Figure 1-3 Memory cells arranged by address

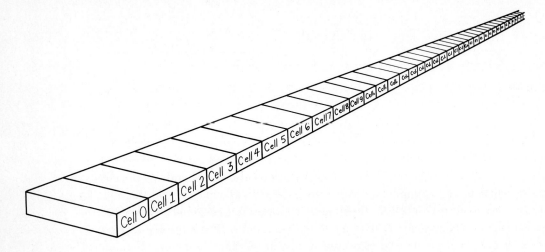

the box becomes empty. In contrast, when data is retrieved from a memory cell, a copy of that data remains behind. Thus, the same data can be extracted over and over.

Organization Within a Cell

Returning now to the memory cells themselves, we should note that the bits found there are not merely "thrown in a pile" but are arranged in a sequential order similar to the arrangement of the cells. Thus, a memory cell is conceptually like an egg carton except that instead of containing two rows of eggs, a cell contains a single row of bits. We call one end of this row the **high order** end and the other the **low order** end. Although there is no left and right within a machine, as humans we imagine the bits arranged in a row from left to right with the high order end on the left. The bit at this end is often called either the high order bit or the **most significant bit**; similarly, the bit at the other end is referred to as the low order bit or the **least significant bit.** Thus, we may represent the contents of a byte-size cell, as shown in Figure 1-4.

An important consequence of the ordering of both the cells and the bits within each cell is that the entire collection of bits within a machine's main memory is

Figure 1-4 The organization of a byte-size memory cell

essentially ordered in one long row. Thus, pieces of this long row can be used to store bit patterns that may be longer than the length of a single cell. In particular, if the memory is divided into byte-size cells, one can still store strings of length 16 by merely using two consecutive memory cells.

Hexadecimal Notation

At this point, it would probably not be difficult to convince you that anyone dealing with the internal characteristics of a computer might well spend a lot of time looking at strings of bits and that such a job can be extremely tedious and error prone. It is not surprising that shorthand notations have been developed for expressing strings of bits. The most popular of these, and the one we use in this book, is known as *hexadecimal notation.* The technique is to group the string that is to be represented into a sequence of short 4-bit blocks and then represent each of these blocks with a single symbol. Note that a block might contain only one of 16 different patterns. These patterns, along with the symbol we use to represent them, are shown in Figure 1-5.

Using this system, we see that the 8-bit pattern 01011010 would be represented by the condensed pattern 5A and that the 32-bit pattern 10100100011000001110101100010011 reduces to the more palatable form of A460EB13.

Questions/Exercises

1. If the memory cell whose address is 5 contains the value 8, what is the difference between writing the value 5 into cell number 6 and moving the contents of cell number 5 into cell number 6?

Figure 1-5 A hexadecimal table

Bit pattern	Hexadecimal representation
0000	0
0001	1
0010	2
0011	3
0100	4
0101	5
0110	6
0111	7
1000	8
1001	9
1010	A
1011	B
1100	C
1101	D
1110	E
1111	F

2. Suppose you wanted to interchange the values stored in memory cells 2 and 3. What would be wrong with the following sequence of steps:

   Step 1. Move the contents of cell number 2 to cell number 3.
   Step 2. Move the contents of cell number 3 to cell number 2.

   Design a sequence of steps that correctly interchanges the contents of these cells.

3. How many bits would be in the memory of a computer with 4K memory cells if each cell had a capacity of one byte?

4. Using a square to represent the pattern 00, a triangle to represent 01, a circle for 10, and a diamond for 11, represent the bit pattern 01001011111001.

5. Use hexadecimal notation to represent the following bit patterns:
   a. 0110101011110010   b. 11101000010101010000010111   c. 01001000

6. What bit patterns are represented by the following hexadecimal patterns:
   a. 5FD97   b. 610A   c. ABCD   d. 0100

7. What would be the hexadecimal representation of the largest memory address in a memory with 4K cells?

1–2 Bulk Storage

Regardless of the size of a machine's main memory, it seems that applications always require still more data storage area. Thus, most machines are provided with a **bulk storage** system (also called **secondary memory**) in addition to their main memory. As we will see, these bulk storage systems have both advantages and disadvantages. Paramount among the disadvantages is that secondary storage systems require mechanical motion; therefore, the process of either storing or retrieving data with such systems is relatively slow compared with the machine's main memory. Among the advantages is that in most cases, the medium on which the data is recorded in bulk storage can be removed from the machinery and stored elsewhere for backup purposes or shipped to another location where it may be needed.

You will hear the terms **on-line** and **off-line** in relation to devices that can be either attached to or detached from a machine. On-line means that the device or information is connected and readily available to the machine without human intervention. In contrast, off-line means that human intervention is required before the device or information can be accessed by the machine. This may be because the device must be turned on or the medium holding the information must be inserted into some mechanism.

Tape Storage

A traditional bulk storage technology is centered around the use of magnetic tape (Figure 1-6). Here, data is recorded on a magnetic coating of a thin plastic tape that

Figure 1-6 A tape storage mechanism

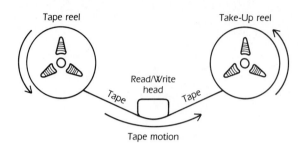

Tape reel

Take-Up reel

Read/Write
head

Tape

Tape

Tape motion

is in turn wound on a reel for storage. To access the data, this tape is mounted in a device called a tape drive that can typically read, write, and rewind the tape under control of the computer.

An important consequence of tape storage is that data so stored has a sequential order associated with it because of its physical organization on the tape. In contrast to the order of main memory cells, this sequential order is not accompanied by an address system by which individual parts can be referenced independently. Thus, when processing data on a tape, the information at the beginning of a tape must be scanned to retrieve data from the middle. Moreover, adding information to the middle of the tape means that the data physically following it must be moved further down. This situation usually means that updating information stored on a tape requires moving the entire collection of data to a second tape.

Tape storage devices range in size from small cassette units that were used in conjunction with early home computers to large reel-to-reel units standing approximately 5 feet high. The typical tape used on these larger units is one-half inch wide and 2400 feet long. Although the capacity of such a tape depends on how the data is stored, it is safe to say that in a typical situation, a 2400-foot tape can hold several million characters. (A million characters is roughly equivalent to a 300-page novel.) This information is divided into manageable units that are recorded as individual blocks on the tape one after the other.

Writing one of these blocks of information on a tape involves starting the tape moving, waiting for it to reach the proper speed, transferring the data to the tape, and stopping the tape. (These steps are normally accomplished by the machine without human intervention. That is, the machine normally communicates directly with the tape unit via electronic signals.) The important thing to note is that the start and stop process results in blank sections of tape, called *inter-record gaps*, between the blocks (Figure 1-7). These gaps consist of the length of tape that passes by the read/write head while the tape is starting and stopping between consecutive write commands. Such gaps are on the order of one-half inch to an inch in length, and their existence can result in very inefficient use of tape. For example, if separate

Figure 1-7 Data recorded in blocks on tape

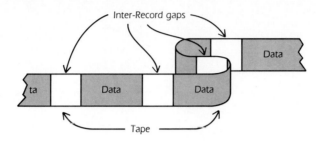

blocks no larger than 800 characters each (a significant amount of data) are written on a tape that holds 1600 characters per inch (a typical value for the larger tape units), then two-thirds of the tape may remain blank and is thus wasted since each one-half-inch block of data would be followed by a one-inch inter-record gap.

A major advantage of tape technology is that in addition to providing on-line storage, it provides an excellent off-line storage medium. This is because a reel of tape is a compact, rugged package with a large storage capacity that is easily mounted or dismounted on a tape drive. In fact, one of the major uses of tape storage today is for long-term (such as a month, year, or longer) storage of data for backup purposes.

Disk Storage

To overcome the drawbacks associated with sequential systems, storage devices using direct access techniques have been developed that allow one to skip directly to the data desired. Paramount among these devices are the disk units in which a thin continuously spinning disk with a magnetic coating, rather than a long strip of tape, is used to hold the data. Read/write heads are placed above and/or below the disk so that as the disk spins, the heads traverse a circle, called a *track*, around its upper and/or lower surface. Each track is divided into arcs called *sectors* on each of which data is recorded as a continuous string of bits (Figure 1-8).

A sector is therefore similar to a short piece of tape in that the data stored on it is sequential. However, by moving a read/write head closer to the center of the disk or farther out to the edge, we can quickly change to sectors on other tracks. The entire disk can therefore be thought of as a collection of short tapes that can be quickly and individually selected. Thus, the information on a sector can be updated without disturbing the data on the other sectors. Moreover, to obtain data stored in the middle of the disk, much of the unwanted data can be bypassed by moving the read/write head directly to the correct track. Thus, the difference between data retrieval from a disk rather than from a magnetic tape is analogous to the difference between playing a particular portion of a phonograph record where the

Figure 1-8 A disk storage system

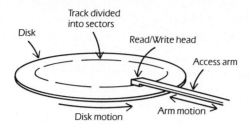

tone arm can easily be positioned in the correct groove rather than searching for the desired passage on a stereo tape player.

Traditionally, disk systems have been developed using several disks, called a pack, mounted on a spindle one on top of the other with enough space for read/ write heads to slip between the platters. Such an arrangement might consist of 10 disks providing a total of 20 surfaces for data storage. Some disk packs are constructed to be easily removed from the disk units, while others are permanently mounted in the disk device. This permanent mounting reduces flexibility but greatly increases the mechanical precision of the device. Consequently, the permanently mounted systems are normally able to hold more data and provide for more rapid data transfer than are corresponding removable systems. For example, a large, permanently mounted disk pack might have a maximum capacity on the order of a billion characters and be able to transfer the characters at the rate of a million per second, whereas such figures for a similar removable pack would typically be reduced by a factor of at least five.

In recent years, another form of disk storage has become very popular, especially on small computer systems. This technique uses a single plastic disk known as a diskette or, since the disk is quite flexible, by the less prestigious title of floppy disk. (In contrast, the rigid disks previously discussed are often called hard disks.) These diskettes are available in a variety of sizes, with diameters of 8, 5¼, and 3½ inches being the most common. (The 3½-inch varieties, being housed in rigid plastic cases, do not constitute as flexible a package as their larger cousins that are housed in paper sleeves.) Diskettes are easily inserted and removed from their corresponding read/write units and are easily mailable. As a consequence, diskettes now rival tape systems for long-term data storage and transportation.

Logical Versus Physical Records

As mentioned earlier, bulk storage techniques require mechanical motion whose duration is usually measured in milliseconds (thousandths of a second). Although this seems fast, it is actually quite slow when compared to the speed at which activities take place within the computer itself. (Activities within a machine are accomplished electronically and are measured in time increments of microseconds or nanoseconds, that is, millionths or billionths of a second.) As a result, the moving of data to and from bulk storage devices often proves to be the bottleneck in computer systems.

It is not surprising that an attempt is made to minimize the number of times such a device is accessed. One technique for this is to transfer large conglomerates of data, called *physical records*, between bulk storage and the machine at one time. The strategy here is twofold. First, once a tape is moving, we keep it moving, or once we have found the beginning of a sector on a disk, we use the entire sector. Second, alterations of individual data items within the conglomerate can be performed in the context of main memory. That is, to modify information stored in bulk storage, we first transfer an entire physical record to main memory, update it in this more efficient environment, and return the updated block to bulk storage.

The actual size of a physical record is largely determined by the desire to make efficient use of bulk storage media. That is, it is necessary to design the physical records to "fit" the bulk storage device being used. In the case of disk storage, this means making sure that the size of the physical records allows the records to fit conveniently on the tracks; for tape storage, the concern is that inter-record gaps do not dominate the tape. Thus, physical considerations play a major role in determining the size of physical records.

In contrast to the division of data into physical records whose size is determined by machine characteristics, we find that the data being stored usually has natural divisions. For example, a company's employee data is conveniently divided into a block of information for each employee. Such blocks of data are called *logical* (or *conceptual*) *records.* The logical record size rarely constitutes a good choice for the physical record size. In fact, the desired physical record size is often considerably larger than the logical record size. In such cases, several logical records are blocked together and stored as one physical record (Figure 1-9). The number of logical records making up one physical record is called the *blocking factor.*

Questions/Exercises

1. Suppose you were going to store a mailing list on a magnetic tape with a density of 1600 characters per inch and inter-record gaps of one inch. If each entry (consisting of a name, address, city, state, and zip code) totals 100 characters, what blocking factor should you use to waste only half of the tape to inter-record gaps? What if you were willing to waste only one-third of the tape?
2. Why should the data in a reservation system that is constantly being updated be stored on a disk pack instead of on tape?
3. What sequence of events might transpire when a program requires data from a tape that is currently on-line? What if the tape is off-line?

Figure 1-9 Blocking logical records on a disk and tape

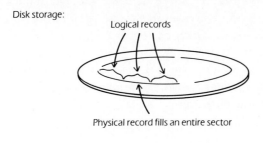

Disk storage:

Logical records

Physical record fills an entire sector

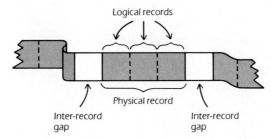

Tape storage:

Logical records

Physical record

Inter-record
gap

Inter-record
gap

4. When only one side of a disk is used for storing data, it is called single-sided. When both surfaces are used, we say it is double-sided. Drives for double-sided disks are provided with two read/write heads (one for each side) that are mechanically linked so that they move as a single unit and always traverse tracks directly opposite each other on the two surfaces. When recording data on a double-sided disk, should we fill a complete side before starting the other or alternate between the surfaces by filling each opposing track pair before moving to the next pair?

1–3 **Coding Information for Storage**

It is time now to take a closer look at the techniques used for representing information in terms of bit patterns.

Symbol Representation

As alluded to earlier, one popular procedure for representing symbols within a machine is to design a code in which different symbols (such as the letters of the alphabet or punctuation marks) are assigned unique bit patterns and to store the information as sentences in main memory or on bulk storage media. Unfortunately, over the years, many such codes have been designed and used in connection with

different pieces of equipment, producing a corresponding proliferation of communication problems. To alleviate this situation, the American National Standards
Institute has adopted what is known as the *American Standard Code for Information
Interchange* (*ASCII*, pronounced as'–kee), which has become extremely popular.
This code, which partially appears in Appendix A, uses 7 bits to represent each
symbol and is therefore referred to as a 7-bit code. You should note that the code
includes upper- and lower-case letters, digits, punctuation marks, and a space. As
an example, Figure 1-10 shows that the bit pattern:

1001000110100101000001010011111010111001010101110

represents the sentence "Hi Sue."

Although ASCII is probably the most common code in use today, others continue to be used, and you should be aware of their existence. One such code is Binary
Coded Decimal (BCD). In the past BCD referred to the 6-bit code shown in Appendix
A that has the disadvantage of not providing for lower-case characters. Today the
term *BCD* is more often used in reference to a 4-bit code representing only the digits
0 through 9. This 4-bit code consists of the least significant 4 bits of the 6-bit BCD.
Thus, the 4-bit BCD representing 5 would be 0101 whereas the code for 9 would
be 1001. Another popular code is Extended Binary Coded Decimal Interchange Code
(EBCDIC). This is an 8-bit code and, as with ASCII, it includes both upper-case and
lower-case characters. Finally, we should mention that there is also an 8-bit version
of ASCII, called ASCII–8.

Representing Numeric Values

Although the method of storing information as coded characters is quite popular,
it is extremely inefficient when the data being recorded is purely numeric. To see
why, suppose we wish to store the number 25. If we insist on storing it as coded
symbols in ASCII, we would need a total of 14 bits (7 to represent the symbol 2 and
7 more for the symbol 5). Moreover, the largest number we could store using 14
bits would be 99. Although many machines do provide for numeric data to be stored
and manipulated in such a form (except that the 4-bit BCD is usually used rather
than ASCII since it is more compact), it is rather wasteful and inefficient to do so.
A more efficient technique is to store the value in its base two, or binary, representation. To see why, let us first investigate the base two concept.

Figure 1-10 The message "Hi Sue." in ASCII

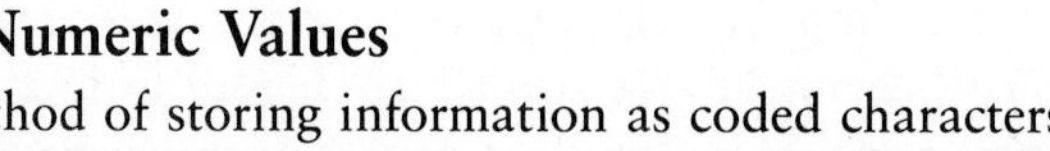

Consider a car's odometer. When the car is new the odometer appears:

0 0 0 0 0 0 0 0

Each 0 is actually painted on a wheel, and on each wheel are also painted the digits 1, 2, 3, 4, 5, 6, 7, 8, and 9. As the car is driven, the right-most wheel (the low order wheel) begins to turn, causing the digits painted on it to appear in the correct sequence until the odometer has the following appearance:

0 0 0 0 0 0 0 9

At this point, as the right-most wheel continues to turn, it hooks the wheel next to it and pulls it over one notch. The result is that as the right-most wheel cycles back to its original 0 position, the wheel next to it is rotated one notch to expose the 1 painted on it. The odometer now appears as follows:

0 0 0 0 0 0 1 0

As the car continues to be driven, the right-most wheel continues to rotate alone until its 9 is again showing. At this point, the adjacent wheel once more rotates as the right-most wheel returns to its 0 position. Thus, the odometer changes from:

0 0 0 0 0 0 1 9

to

0 0 0 0 0 0 2 0

Counting in base two is the same process, except that each wheel has only two digits, 0 and 1, painted on it, and the adjacent wheel rotates every time the 1 rotates over to expose the 0 instead of the 9 rotating to expose the 0. If cars had base two odometers, the sequence of odometer readings would appear, as in Figure 1-11, as a new car was driven for its first few miles.

Thus, Figure 1-11 represents the symbols obtained when counting from 0 to 6 in base two. If moving from 00000011 to 00000100 bothers you, think again about what the car odometer does when it moves from 00000099 to 00000100 and remember that changing a digit from 9 to 0 on the odometer coincides with changing a digit from 1 to 0 when counting in base two.

Figure 1-11 Binary odometer readings starting from zero

00000000
00000001
00000010
00000011
00000100
00000101
00000110

This counting technique not only provides a down-to-earth introduction to binary notation but also constitutes a brute force system for converting back and forth between the binary and decimal notations. In the case of large values in which counting becomes impractical, a more efficient technique exists that we discuss in Section 1-5. In reality, however, learning the binary system is much like learning a foreign language or foreign currency system. Once you use it for a while, you over-come the need to translate back into your original notation.

Recall now our original problem of storing numeric data. Using binary nota-tion, we see that in 1 byte we can store any integer between 0 and 255 (00000000 to 11111111), and given 14 bits we can store the integers from 0 to 16383. This is a drastic improvement over the ability to store only the integers from 0 to 99 when coding characters using ASCII.

For this and other reasons, it is far more common to store numeric information in a form of binary notation rather than in coded symbols. We say "a form of binary notation," because in reality, the straightforward binary system just described is only the basis for several numeric storage techniques used within machines. Some of these variations of the binary system are discussed later in this chapter. For now, we will merely note that a system called **two's complement notation** is common for storing whole numbers since it provides a convenient method for representing negative numbers as well as positive. For representing numbers with fractional parts such as 4½ or ¾, still another technique, called **floating-point notation**, is used. Thus, a particular value (such as 25) may be represented by several different bit patterns (coded characters, two's complement notation, or in floating-point notation as 25 0/2); conversely, a particular bit pattern may be given several interpretations.

At this point, we should mention a significant problem with numeric storage systems that we deal with in more depth later. Regardless of the pattern size that a machine might allocate for the storage of numeric values, there will still be values too large or fractions too small to be stored in the space allotted. The result is the constant potential for errors such as **overflow** (values too large) and **round-off** (frac-tions too small) that must be dealt with, or an unsuspecting computer user can soon be faced with a multitude of erroneous data.

Questions/Exercises

1. Here is a message coded in ASCII. What does it say?

           1000011 1101111 1101101 1110000 1110101 1110100
           1100101 1110010 0100000 1010011 1100011 1101001
           1100101 1101110 1100011 1100101

2. In the ASCII code, what is the relationship between the codes for an upper-case letter and the same letter in lower case?

3. Code these sentences in ASCII:
   a. I like milk.
   b. Where are you?
   c. "How?" Cheryl asked.
   d. 2 + 3 = 5.
4. Describe a device from everyday life that can be in either of two states (other than our earlier example of a flag on a flagpole). Assign the symbol 1 to one of the states, 0 to the other, and show how the ASCII representation for the letter b would appear when stored with such bits.
5. Convert each of the following binary representations to its equivalent decimal form:
   a. 0101   b. 1001   c. 1011   d. 0110   e. 10000   f. 10010
6. Convert each of the following decimal representations to its equivalent binary form:
   a. 6   b. 13   c. 11   d. 18   e. 27   f. 4
7. What is the largest numerical value that could be represented with 21 bits if each digit were coded using ASCII? What if binary notation were used?

1–4 **Dealing with Errors** (optional)

When data is transferred back and forth among the various parts of a computer, transmitted from the earth to the moon and back, or for that matter, merely left in storage, a chance exists that the bit pattern finally retrieved may not be identical to the original one. For instance, particles of dirt or grease on a magnetic recording surface or a malfunctioning circuit may cause data to be incorrectly recorded or read. Moreover, in the case of some technologies, background radiation can alter patterns stored in a machine's main memory.

Of course, today's technology allows us to build extremely reliable devices. A disk drive, for example, may have an error rate of no more than one error per million bits. However, when considered in an application, this error rate translates into one possible error for every 30 pages of a novel. Thus, if the material were transferred often, the error rate could easily become intolerable.

To resolve this problem, a variety of coding techniques have been developed to allow the detection and even the correction of errors. Today, because these techniques are largely built directly into the components of a computer system, they are not apparent to the personnel using the machine, just as a machine's internal use of ASCII is not readily apparent to a computer user. Nonetheless, their presence is extremely important and represents a significant contribution to scientific research.

In fact, many of these techniques are prime examples of the contributions made by theoretical mathematics, often scorned as too abstract to be applicable. It is fitting for us to briefly investigate some of these techniques that lie behind the reliability of today's equipment.

Parity Bits

A popular and extremely simple method of detecting errors is based on the principle that if each of the bit patterns being manipulated has an odd number of 1s and a pattern is found with an even number of 1s, an error must have occurred.

To use this principle, we need a system in which each pattern contains an odd number of 1s. This is easily obtained by first adding an additional bit, called the *parity bit*, to each pattern in a system already available (usually at the high order end). (Thus, the 7-bit ASCII code will become an 8-bit code or a 16-bit pattern representing a value in two's complement notation will become a 17-bit pattern.) In each case, we assign the value 1 or 0 to this new bit so that the resulting pattern will have an odd number of 1s. Thus, as Figure 1-12 shows, the ASCII code for A would become 11000001 (parity bit 1), and the ASCII for I would become 01001001 (parity bit 0). Although the 7-bit pattern for A had an even number of 1s in it and the 7-bit pattern for I had an odd number of 1s, both the 8-bit patterns have an odd number of 1s. Once our coding system has been modified in this way, a pattern with an even number of 1s will indicate that an error has occurred and that the data being manipulated is incorrect.

The particular parity system just described is called *odd parity*, because we designed our system so that each pattern would contain an odd number of 1s. Another technique is to use *even parity*. In such a system, each pattern is designed to have an even number of 1s in it, and thus an error is signaled by the occurrence of a pattern with an odd number of 1s.

Figure 1-12 The ASCII codes for A and I adjusted for odd parity

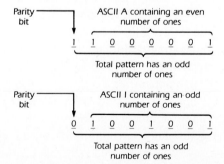

Today, it is not unusual to find parity bits being used in a microcomputer's main memory. Thus, whereas we envision these machines having memory cells of 8 bits, in reality they may have 9-bit cells, 1 bit of which is used as a parity bit.

Error Correcting Codes

Although the use of a parity bit is designed to allow the detection of an error, it does not provide the information needed to correct the error. Many people are surprised that codes, known as *error correcting codes*, can be designed so that errors not only can be detected but also can be corrected. After all, intuition says that one cannot correct errors in a received message unless one already knows the information in the message. However, a simple code with such a corrective property is presented in Figure 1-13.

To understand how this code works, we first define the *Hamming distance* (named after R. W. Hamming, who pioneered the search for error correcting codes after becoming frustrated with the lack of reliability of the early relay machines of the 1940s) between two patterns to be the number of bits in which the two differ. Thus, the Hamming distance between A and B in the code in Figure 1-13 is 4, and the Hamming distance between B and C is 3. The important feature of the code is that any two patterns are separated by a Hamming distance of at least three. If a single bit is modified by a malfunctioning device, the error can be detected since the result will not be a legal pattern. (We must change at least 3 bits in any pattern before it will look like another legal pattern.) If a single error has occurred in a pattern, we can also figure out what the original pattern was, because the modified pattern will be a Hamming distance of only one from its original form but at least two from any of the other legal patterns. To decode a message, we simply compare each received pattern with the patterns in the code until we find one that is within a distance of one of the received pattern. This we consider to be the correct symbol for decoding. For example, suppose we received the bit pattern 010100. If we compared this pattern to the patterns in the code, we would obtain the table in

Figure 1-13 An error correcting code

Symbol	Code
A	000000
B	001111
C	010011
D	011100
E	100110
F	101001
G	110101
H	111010

Figure 1-14 Decoding the pattern 010100 using the code in Figure 1-13

Character	Distance between the received pattern and the character being considered
A	2
B	4
C	3
D	1 (Smallest distance)
E	3
F	5
G	2
H	4

Figure 1-14 and thus conclude that the character transmitted must have been a D since this is the closest match.

You will observe that using this technique with the code in Figure 1-13 actually allows us to detect up to two errors per pattern and to correct one error. If we designed the code so that each pattern was a Hamming distance of at least five from each of the others, we would be able to detect up to four errors per pattern and correct up to two. Of course, the design of efficient codes associated with large Hamming distances is not a straightforward task and constitutes a part of the branch of mathematics called algebraic coding theory.

Issues of Application

As mentioned earlier, the use of parity bits or error correcting codes today is almost always a concern handled within the equipment itself and is rarely visible to the person using the machine. The average computer user may be concerned with these concepts only when it is necessary to connect two pieces of equipment such as a printer and a computer. In such cases, most devices have switches whose settings determine the communication technique to be used. Under these circumstances, it is the user's responsibility to adjust the switches so that both pieces of equipment are set for the same technique. For instance, you could imagine that little would be accomplished if a computer sent characters with an odd parity to a printer that was expecting an even parity.

The decision as to whether to use parity checks or an error correcting code depends on the application at hand and to what extent one is willing to go for the added reliability. Observe that neither technique is foolproof when detecting errors. If too many errors occur in the code for a single character when using an error correcting code, the result can look like another legal pattern. On the other hand, the parity technique will not detect the occurrence of an even number of errors in a single pattern since the result will have the same parity as the original.

Based on the correcting ability alone, one is tempted to conclude that the use of an error correcting code is superior to the use of parity bits. However, the use of an error correcting code requires longer patterns to represent the same number of symbols than the use of a parity bit. Consequently, you will find that both techniques are quite popular, with error correcting codes being used in cases where the need for accuracy or the likelihood of errors overrides the cost of a more lengthy code. For example, most popular among tape devices is the use of parity bits, with odd parity being more common than even parity. This preference of odd parity exists because a blank tape is usually interpreted as all 0s. Consequently, an accidentally erased portion of a tape would have even parity (no 1s) and thus would be detected as an error only if odd parity were being used.

The use of error correcting codes is becoming more and more popular in conjunction with bulk storage devices. It is not uncommon to find such a technique being used by high-speed, large-capacity disk units. In such devices, the need for accuracy far outweighs the overhead expenses introduced by correcting methods.

Questions/Exercises

1. The following bytes were originally coded using odd parity. In which of them do you know that an error has occurred?
   a. 10101101 b. 10000001 c. 00000000 d. 11100000 e. 11111111
2. Could errors have occurred in a byte from question 1 without your knowing it? Explain your answer.
3. How would your answers to questions 1 and 2 change if you were told that even parity had been used instead of odd?
4. Code these sentences in ASCII using odd parity by adding a parity bit at the high order end of each character code:
   a. I like milk.
   b. Where are you?
   c. "How?" Cheryl asked.
   d. 2 + 3 = 5.
5. Using the same error correcting code presented in the text, decode the following messages:
   a. 001111 100100 001100
   b. 010001 000000 001011
   c. 011010 110110 100000 011100
6. Construct a code for the characters A, B, C, and D using bit patterns of length five so that the Hamming distance between any two patterns is at least three.

1–5 **The Binary System** (optional)

The remaining sections of this chapter take a closer look at numeric storage techniques with the goal of better understanding the role of each and the problems of overflow and round-off mentioned earlier. We begin this pursuit with a more thorough treatment of the base two representation system.

In a base two representation of a number, each bit position is assigned a quantity (often called a weight) according to its position within the pattern. These quantities are specified from right to left as one, two, four, eight, etc. The rule is that the quantity assigned each position is twice that of the position to its right. Thus, the 1 in the binary representation 10000 is in the position assigned the quantity 16.

To decode a binary representation, you merely multiply each position's quantity by the value of the bit at that position and then add these results. For example, the binary number 101101 is found to be equivalent to 45 in our usual base ten notation (Figure 1-15). (The technique of multiplying each bit value by the corresponding position quantity is based on a general procedure for converting representations from other bases as well. For those who wish the utmost in simplicity, the effect of this process in the binary case is merely to add the quantities of those positions occupied by 1s.)

Binary Addition

You will note that the assignment of quantities to the digit position is common to other base systems as well. In particular, our more common base ten system uses the same concept, except that the quantity assigned to each position is ten times that to its right instead of two times. This common approach allows us to use the same addition process in base two as that used in the base ten system to which we are accustomed. Thus, to add two values represented in binary notation we begin, just as we did with base ten in elementary school, by memorizing the addition facts (Figure 1-16).

The binary facts are used to add two strings of bits in the same way the decimal facts are used to add two strings of decimal digits. That is, add the digits in the right-hand column, write the least significant digit of this sum under the column, carry the more significant digit of the sum (if there is one) to the next column to the left, and proceed by adding that column. Thus, to solve the following problem we proceed as follows:

$$\begin{array}{r} 00111010 \\ +00011011 \\ \hline \end{array}$$

Figure 1-15 Decoding the binary representation 101101

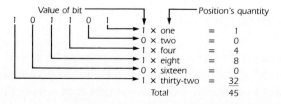

Figure 1-16 The binary addition facts

```
  0      1      0      1
+ 0    + 0    + 1    + 1
───    ───    ───    ────
  0      1      1     10
```

Add the right-most 0 and 1, obtaining 1, which we write below the column. Now add the 1 and 1 from the next column, obtaining 10. Write the 0 from this 10 under the column and carry the 1 to the top of the next column. At this point, our solution looks like this:

```
         1
    00111010
  + 00011011
  ──────────
          01
```

Add the 1, 0, and 0 in the next column, obtaining 1, which we write under this column. The 1 and 1 from the next column total 10; we write the 0 under the column and carry the 1 to the next column. Now our solution looks like this:

```
         1
    00111010
  + 00011011
  ──────────
        0101
```

The 1, 1, and 1 in the next column total 11; we write the low order 1 under the column and carry the other 1 to the top of the next column. Here it is added to the 1 and 0 in that column to obtain 10. Again, the low order 0 is recorded and the 1 is carried to the next column. We now have this:

```
         1
    00111010
  + 00011011
  ──────────
      010101
```

Now add the 1, 0, and 0 from the next to the last column, obtaining 1, which we record below the column with nothing to carry. Finally, we add the last column, which yields 0, and record this under the column. Our final solution is this:

```
    00111010
  + 00011011
  ──────────
    01010101
```

Fractions in Binary

To extend binary notation to accommodate fractional values, we use a *radix point* in the same role as the decimal point in decimal notation. That is, the digits to its left represent the integer part of the value and are interpreted as in the binary system discussed previously. The digits to its right represent the fractional part of the value and are interpreted in a manner similar to the other bits, except their positions are assigned fractional quantities. That is, the first position to the right of the radix is assigned the quantity one-half, the next position the quantity one-fourth, the next one-eighth, etc. Note that this is merely a continuation of the rule stated previously that each position is assigned a quantity twice the size of the one to its right. With these quantities assigned to the bit positions, decoding a binary representation containing a radix point requires the same procedure as used without a radix point. In particular, we multiply each bit value by the quantity assigned to that bit's position in the representation. Thus, the binary representation 101.101 decodes to 5⅝, as shown in Figure 1-17.

Again, when it comes to addition, the techniques applied in the base ten system are also applicable in binary. That is, to add two binary representations having radix points, we merely align the radix points and apply the same addition process as before. Thus, 10.011 added to 100.11 produces 111.001, as shown below:

$$\begin{array}{r} 10.011 \\ +\ 100.11\ \\ \hline 111.001 \end{array}$$

Questions/Exercises

1. Convert each of the following binary representations to its equivalent decimal form:

    a. 101010   b. 100001   c. 10111   d. 0110   e. 11111

2. Convert each of the following decimal representations to its equivalent binary form:

    a. 32   b. 64   c. 96   d. 15   e. 27

3. Convert each of the following binary representations to its equivalent base ten form:

    a. 11.01   b. 101.111   c. 10.1   d. 110.011   e. 0.101

4. Express the following values in binary notation:

    a. 4½   b. 2¾   c. 1⅛   d. 5/16   e. 5⅝

Figure 1-17 Decoding the binary representation 101.101

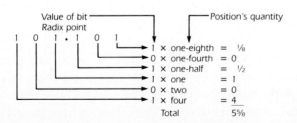

5. Perform the following additions in binary notation:

a.	11011	b.	1010.001	c.	11111	d.	111.11
	+ 1100		+ 1.101		+ 1		+ .01

1–6 **Storing Integers** (optional)

When searching for an efficient technique for representing whole numbers as bit patterns, we might try the binary notation presented in Section 1-5, except that there is often a need to store negative values as well as positive ones. Thus, we need a notational system that encompasses both positive and negative integers. Mathematicians have long been interested in numerical notational systems, and many of their ideas have turned out to be very compatible with the design of electronic circuitry and thus are used extensively in computing equipment. In this section we consider some of these notational systems (sign-magnitude, excess, and two's complement notation). Then, we consider a major limitation of these systems as it is reflected in the problem of overflow.

Sign-Magnitude Notation

One method of representing both positive and negative integers, called *sign-magnitude notation,* is to reserve the high order bit in the bit string to indicate the sign of the value being stored. When so used, this high order bit is known as the *sign bit.* It is common to use a sign bit value of 0 to represent a nonnegative value and a 1 to represent a negative value. Thus, if we were using one byte to store a value in sign-magnitude notation, the bit at the high order end would be the sign bit, and the other 7 bits of the byte would be used to store the magnitude of the number. For example, Figure 1-18 shows that 9 would be stored as 00001001 and −9 would be 10001001.

Excess Notation

Although sign-magnitude notation seems like a natural method, other techniques are more easily manipulated by electronic circuitry. One such technique is *excess notation.* Here, we first decide what length of bit patterns our system will use and then we write down all the different bit patterns of that length in the order they would appear if we were counting in binary. Next, we observe that the first pattern with a 1 as its most significant bit appears approximately halfway through the list. We pick this pattern to represent zero; the patterns following this are used to represent 1, 2, 3, . . . ; and the patterns preceding it are used for −1, −2, −3, ... The resulting code, when using patterns of length four, is shown in Figure 1-19. Note that contrary to the sign-magnitude notation, nonnegative values are recognized by the fact that their high order bit is 1.

Figure 1-18 A sign-magnitude representation of 9 and − 9

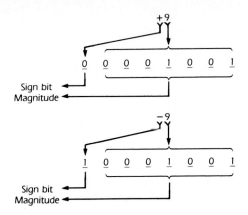

We should say a few words about why the code in Figure 1-19 is called excess eight. The insight regarding the code will also provide a means of coding or decoding individual values without constructing the entire table. The secret is to interpret the patterns using the traditional binary system and compare the results to the values represented in the excess code. In the table of Figure 1-19, you will find that each of the traditional binary values exceeds the value being represented in the code by eight. For example, the pattern 1100 represents 12 in the traditional binary system, but in our excess system it represents 4; 0000 normally represents 0, but in the excess system it represents − 8; etc. In a similar manner, an excess system based on patterns of length five would be called excess 16 notation since the pattern 10000, for instance,

Figure 1-19 An excess eight conversion table

Bit pattern	Value represented
1111	7
1110	6
1101	5
1100	4
1011	3
1010	2
1001	1
1000	0
0111	− 1
0110	− 2
0101	− 3
0100	− 4
0011	− 5
0010	− 6
0001	− 7
0000	− 8

Figure 1-20 A two's complement notation using bit patterns of length four

Bit pattern	Value represented
0111	7
0110	6
0101	5
0100	4
0011	3
0010	2
0001	1
0000	0
1111	−1
1110	−2
1101	−3
1100	−4
1011	−5
1010	−6
1001	−7
1000	−8

would be used to represent 0 rather than its usual value of 16. Likewise, you may wish to confirm (by making a table) that the 3-bit excess system would be known as excess four notation.

Two's Complement Notation

We have introduced excess notation for two reasons. First, it is a popular way of representing the exponent field in floating-point notation, as we will learn in Section 1-7. Second, it is similar to the more popular notation called **two's complement notation.** In fact, we can obtain a table for two's complement notation simply by changing the highest order bit of each pattern in the table for the excess method. That is, instead of using the pattern 1011 to represent the value three as in our excess eight table, two's complement notation would use 0011. The complete two's complement notation system using bit patterns of length four is described in Figure 1-20.

We will see that the use of two's complement notation allows the operations of addition, subtraction, multiplication, and division to be performed using only two electronic circuits. Such economy is the main reason for the system's popularity. For now, we demonstrate how values can be coded and decoded when using the two's complement system without building a complete table.

The cornerstone of this process is the important, yet simple, operation of forming the **complement** of a bit pattern, which is merely the process of changing the 0s in the pattern to 1s and the 1s to 0s. (The complement of the pattern 1101 is 0010.) Starting with any value (except −8) in the system of Figure 1-20, we can find the pattern representing its negation by first forming the complement of the value's representation and then adding one, using the binary addition process. For example, starting with the value 5, we can obtain the pattern for −5 by complementing 0101 (the representation for 5) to get 1010 and adding one to obtain 1011. Similarly, if we started with −5, we could get the pattern for 5 by complementing 1011 (the pattern for −5) to obtain 0100 and adding one to obtain 0101.

The coding of a value using the two's complement system is really quite simple. Nonnegative values are represented by the bit pattern that corresponds to their base two representations. Thus, coding these values is nothing more than writing them in binary notation. Coding negative values is just about as easy. Following the negation process already described, the coding of a negative value consists of first coding the corresponding positive value, then negating it by forming its complement, and then adding one (Figure 1-21). Thus, to code −4, we would write down the pattern 0100, which is the binary representation for 4, complement it to obtain 1011, and add one to get 1100.

Decoding two's complement representations is a similar process. Again our procedure depends on whether or not the value in question is negative. The first step in decoding a value is to look at its high order bit. If this bit is 0, the value is nonnegative and is obtained by reading the bit pattern as if it were a binary number. If, however, this bit is 1, we negate the pattern by means of the complement and increment process (to obtain the bit pattern representing the corresponding positive value), decode this positive value, and place a negative sign in front of the result. As an example, consider the problem of decoding the bit pattern 1010. In this case, because the high order bit is 1, the value represented is negative. Thus, we negate the pattern by complementing it to get 0101 and then increment it to get 0110. This result is the binary representation of 6; we conclude that the original two's complement pattern 1010 represents the value −6.

Addition in Two's Complement Notation

The source of popularity for two's complement notation lies in the simplicity and scope of the addition process used in conjunction with it. To understand this, we first note that adding values represented in two's complement notation is the same process as the binary addition previously described, except that all bit patterns,

Figure 1-21 Coding −5 in two's complement notation using eight bits

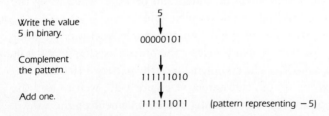

including the answer, are the same length. This means that when adding in a two's complement system, any extra bit generated on the left of the answer by a final carry must be truncated. Thus, "adding" 0101 and 0010 would produce 0111, and "adding" 0111 and 1011 would result in 0010 (0111 + 1011 = 10010, which would be truncated to 0010).

With this understanding, consider the three addition problems in Figure 1-22. In each case, we have translated the problem into two's complement notation (using four bits), performed the addition process previously described, and decoded the result back into our usual decimal notation.

Observe that when using the traditional techniques taught in elementary school, the third problem would require an entirely different process (subtraction) than the previous problems. On the other hand, by translating the problems into two's complement notation, we are able to compute the correct answer in all cases by applying the same computational process. This, then, is the advantage of two's complement notation. Indeed, addition of any combination of signed numbers can be accomplished using the same process.

In contrast to elementary schoolchildren who are first taught to add and later to subtract, a machine using two's complement notation needs only to know how to add. For example, the subtraction problem $7 - 5$ is the same as the addition problem $7 + (-5)$. Consequently, if a machine were asked to subtract 5 (stored as 0101) from 7 (stored as 0111), it would first change the 5 to -5 (represented as 1011) and then perform the addition process of 0111 + 1011 to obtain 0010, which represents 2 as represented below:

$$\begin{array}{ccccc} 7 & & 0111 & & 0111 \\ -5 & \longrightarrow & -0101 & \longrightarrow & +1011 \\ \hline & & & & 0010 \longrightarrow 2 \end{array}$$

Consequently, if we build a circuit to negate values (which with two's complement is little more than a complementing circuit) and another to perform the above addition process, these two circuits provide the ability to solve both addition and subtraction problems. The benefits do not stop there, however. Multiplication is

Figure 1-22 Addition problems converted to two's complement notation

$$\begin{array}{ccccc} 3 & & 0011 \\ +2 & \longrightarrow & +0010 \\ \hline & & 0101 \longrightarrow 5 \end{array}$$

$$\begin{array}{ccccc} (-3) & & 1101 \\ +(-2) & \longrightarrow & +1110 \\ \hline & & 1011 \longrightarrow -5 \end{array}$$

$$\begin{array}{ccccc} 7 & & 0111 \\ +(-5) & \longrightarrow & +1011 \\ \hline & & 0010 \longrightarrow 2 \end{array}$$

merely repeated addition, and division is repeated subtraction (6/2 is the number of times 2 can be subtracted from 6 without getting a negative result). Thus, we can ultimately get all four of the standard arithmetic operations of addition, subtraction, multiplication, and division from these two circuits.

The Problem of Overflow

One problem we have avoided in the preceding examples is inherent in the addition process of two's complement notation: in any two's complement system there is a limit to the size of the values that can be represented. For example, when using patterns of four bits, the value 9 has no pattern associated with it. Thus, we could not hope to obtain the correct answer to the problem 5 + 4. In fact, the result would appear as −7. Such an error is called *overflow.* When using two's complement notation, this might occur when adding two positive values or when adding two negative values. In either case, the condition can be detected by checking the sign bit of the answer. That is, an overflow is indicated if the addition of two positive values results in the pattern for a negative value or if the sum of two negative values appears to be positive.

The point is that contrary to public belief, computers can make mistakes. So, the person using the machine must be aware of the dangers involved. Of course, because most machines manipulate longer bit patterns than we have used here, larger values can be computed without causing an overflow. For example, many large machines use patterns of 32 bits for storing two's complement notation, allowing for positive values as large as 2,147,483,647 to accumulate before overflow occurs. If still larger values are needed, the technique called *double precision* is often used. This means that the length of the patterns used is doubled from that which the machine normally uses. Another approach to the problem is to change the units of measure. For instance, finding a solution in terms of miles instead of inches will result in smaller numbers being used and may still provide the accuracy required.

Questions/Exercises

1. Convert each of the following sign-magnitude representations to its equivalent decimal form:
   a. 0111   b. 1001   c. 0000   d. 00101   e. 10110   f. 1111
2. Convert each of the following decimal representations to its equivalent sign-magnitude form using patterns of 8 bits:
   a. 5   b. −5   c. 17   d. −20   e. 9   f. −13
3. When using sign-magnitude notation, what is similar about the values represented by 0000 and 1000?
4. Convert each of the following excess eight representations to its equivalent decimal form without referring to the table in the text:
   a. 1110   b. 0111   c. 1000   d. 0010   e. 0000   f. 1001

5. Convert each of the following decimal representations to its equivalent excess eight form without referring to the table in the text:
   a. 5   b. −5   c. 3   d. 0   e. 7   f. −8

6. Can the value 9 be represented in excess eight notation? What about representing 6 in excess four notation? Explain your answer.

7. Convert each of the following two's complement representations to its equivalent decimal form:
   a. 00011   b. 01111   c. 11100   d. 11010   e. 00000   f. 10000

8. Convert each of the following decimal representations to its equivalent two's complement form using patterns of 8 bits:
   a. 6   b. −6   c. −17   d. 13   e. −1   f. 0

9. Suppose the following bit patterns represent values stored in two's complement notation. Find the two's complement representation of the negative of each value:
   a. 00000001   b. 01010101   c. 11111100
   d. 11111110   e. 00000000   f. 01111111

10. Suppose a machine stores numbers in two's complement notation. What are the largest and smallest numbers that could be stored if the machine uses bit patterns of the following lengths?
    a. 4   b. 6   c. 8

11. In the following problems, each bit pattern represents a value stored in two's complement notation. Find the answer to each problem in two's complement notation by performing the addition process described in the text. Then check your work by translating the problem and your answer into decimal notation.

a.	b.	c.	d.	e.
0101	0011	0101	1110	1010
+0010	+0001	+1010	+0011	+1110

12. Solve each of the following problems in two's complement notation, but this time watch for overflow and indicate which answers are incorrect because of this phenomenon.

a.	b.	c.	d.	e.
0100	0101	1010	1010	0111
+0011	+0110	+1010	+0111	+0001

13. Translate each of the following problems from decimal notation into two's complement notation using bit patterns of length four, then convert each problem to an equivalent addition problem (as a machine might do), and finally perform the addition. Check your answers by converting them back to decimal notation.

a.	b.	c.	d,	e.
6	3	4	2	1
+1	−2	−6	+4	−5

14. Can an overflow ever occur when adding values in two's complement notation when one value is positive and the other is negative? Explain your answer.

1−7 **Storing Fractions** (optional)

In contrast to the storage of integers, the storage of a value with a fractional part requires that we store not only the pattern of 0s and 1s representing its binary representation but also the position of the radix point. A popular way of doing this is called *floating-point notation.* We explain this technique with an example using only one byte of storage. Our example is representative of actual systems used and therefore serves to demonstrate the important concepts of such storage techniques.

Floating-Point Notation

We first designate the high order bit of the byte as the sign bit. Once again, a 0 in the sign bit will mean that the value stored is nonnegative and a 1 will mean that the value is negative. We divide the remaining 7 bits of the byte into two groups, or fields, called the *exponent field* and the *mantissa field.* Let us designate the next three bits as the exponent field and the remaining four bits as the mantissa field. The byte is therefore divided as shown in Figure 1-23.

We explain the meaning of the fields by considering the following example. Suppose a byte contained the bit pattern 01101011. Analyzing this pattern with the preceding format, we see that the sign bit is 0, the exponent is 110, and the mantissa is 1011. To decode the byte, we first extract the mantissa and place a radix point on its left side obtaining:

.1011

Next, we extract the contents of the exponent field (110) and interpret it as an integer stored using the 3-bit excess method. Thus, the pattern in the exponent field in our example represents a positive 2. This tells us to move the radix in our solution to the right 2 bits. (A negative exponent would mean to move the radix to the left.) Consequently, we obtain:

10.11

which represents 2¾. Next, we note that the sign bit in our example is 0; the value represented is thus nonnegative. We can conclude that the byte 01101011 represents 2¾.

As another example, consider the byte 10111100. We extract the mantissa to obtain:

.1100

Figure 1-23 Floating-point notation components

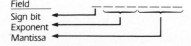

and move the radix one bit to the left since the exponent field (011) represents a negative 1. We therefore have:

$$.01100$$

which represents ⅜. Since the sign bit in the original pattern is 1, the value stored is negative. We conclude that the pattern 10111100 represents −⅜.

To store a value using floating-point notation, we reverse the above process. For example, to code 1⅛, first we express it in binary notation and obtain 1.001. Next, we copy the bit pattern into the mantissa field from left to right, starting with the first nonzero bit in the binary representation. At this point, the byte looks like:

$$1\ 0\ 0\ 1$$

We must now fill in the exponent field. To this end, we imagine the contents of the mantissa field with a radix point at its left and determine the number of bits and the direction the radix must be moved to obtain the original binary number. In our example, we see that the radix in .1001 must be moved one bit to the right to obtain 1.001. Because the exponent should therefore be a positive 1, we place 101 (which is positive 1 in excess four notation) in the exponent field. Finally, we fill the sign bit with 0 since the value being stored is nonnegative. The finished byte looks like this:

$$0\ 1\ 0\ 1\ 1\ 0\ 0\ 1$$

Round-Off Errors

Let us consider the annoying problem that occurs if we try to store 2⅝ with our floating-point system. We first write 2⅝ in binary, which gives us 10.101. But now when we copy this into the mantissa field, we run out of room, and the last 1 (which represents the last ⅛) is lost (Figure 1-24). If we ignore this problem for now and continue by filling in the exponent field and the sign bit, we will end up with the bit pattern 01101010, which represents 2½ instead of 2⅝. What has occurred is

Figure 1-24 Coding the value 2⅝

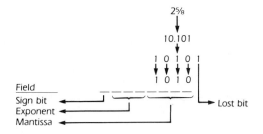

called a **_round-off error_**, and in this case it was caused by the fact that our mantissa field contains only 4 bits, whereas 5 were required for accuracy. This suggests the solution of lengthening this field, which is exactly what is done on real machines. As with integer storage, it is common to use something like 32 bits for storing floating-point notation instead of the 8 we have used here. This approach also allows for a longer exponent field at the same time. Even with these longer formats, however, there are still times when more accuracy is required. Again we find the concept of **_double precision_** being applied when extreme precision is required.

Another source of round-off errors is a phenomenon that you are already accustomed to in decimal notation. This is the problem of nonterminating expansions such as those found when trying to express ⅓ in decimal form. Some values cannot be accurately expressed regardless of how many digits we use.

The difference between our normal decimal notation and binary notation is that more values have nonterminating representations in binary than in decimal notation. For example, the value one-tenth is nonterminating in binary. (Imagine the problems this might cause the unwary person using floating-point notation to store and manipulate dollars and cents. In particular, if the dollar is used as the unit of measure, the value of a dime could not be stored accurately. A solution in this case is to manipulate the data in units of pennies so that all values will be integers that can be accurately stored using a method such as two's complement.)

Round-off errors and their related problems are an everyday concern for people working in the area of numerical analysis. This branch of mathematics deals with the problems involved when doing actual computations that are often massive and require significant accuracy.

We close this section with an example of a general rule that would warm the heart of any numerical analyst. Suppose we are asked to add the following three values using our one-byte floating-point notation defined previously:

$$2\tfrac{1}{2} + \tfrac{1}{8} + \tfrac{1}{8}$$

If we add the values in the order listed, we first add 2½ to ⅛ and obtain 2⅝, which in binary is 10.101. Unfortunately, because this value cannot be stored accurately (as seen previously), the result of our first step ends up being stored as 2½ (which is the same as one of the values we were adding). The next step is to add this result to the last ⅛. Here again a round-off error occurs, and our final result turns out to be the incorrect answer 2½.

Now let us add the values in the opposite order. We first add ⅛ to ⅛ to obtain ¼. In binary this is .01; so the result of our first step is stored in a byte as 00111000, which is accurate. We now add this ¼ to the next value in the list, 2½, and obtain 2¾, which we can accurately store in a byte as 01101011. The result this time is the correct answer.

In summary, when adding values in floating-point notation, the order in which they are added can be extremely important. The general rule is to always add the smaller values together first; however, even this does not guarantee accuracy.

Questions/Exercises

1. Decode the following bit patterns using the floating-point format discussed in the text:

   a. 01001010   b. 01101101   c. 00111001   d. 11011100   e. 10101011

2. Code the following values into the floating-point format discussed in the text. Indicate the occurrence of round-off errors.

   a. $2\frac{3}{4}$ b. $5\frac{1}{4}$ c. $\frac{3}{4}$ d. $-3\frac{1}{2}$ e. $-4\frac{3}{8}$

3. In terms of the floating-point format discussed in the text, which of the patterns 01001001 and 00111101 represents the larger value? Describe a simple procedure for determining which of two patterns represents the larger value.

4. When using the floating-point format discussed in the text, what is the largest value that can be represented? What is the smallest positive value that can be represented?

Chapter 1 Review Problems

(Asterisked problems are associated with optional sections.)

1. The following table represents (using hexadecimal notation) the addresses and contents of some cells in a machine's main memory. Starting with this memory arrangement, follow the sequence of instructions below and record the final contents of each of these memory cells:

Address	Contents
00	AB
01	53
02	D6
03	02

   Step 1. Move the contents of the cell whose address is 03 to the cell at address 00.
   Step 2. Move the value 01 into the cell at address 02.
   Step 3. Move the value stored at address 01 into the cell at address 03.

2. What bit patterns are represented by the following hexadecimal notations:

   a. BC   b. 67   c. 9A   d. 10   e. 3F

3. What is the value of the most significant bit in the bit patterns represented by the following hexadecimal notations:

   a. FF   b. 7F   c. 8F   d. 1F

4. Express the following bit patterns in hexadecimal notation:

   a. 101010101010   b. 110010110111
   c. 000011101011

5. Suppose the screen of a microcomputer (with a 64K memory) displayed 24 rows containing 80 text characters each. If the image on the screen were stored in memory by representing each character by its ASCII code (one character per byte), what portion of the machine's memory would be required to represent the entire screen image?

6. How many characters could be stored on a 2400-foot tape if they are stored in blocks of 3200 characters at a density of 1600 characters per inch with half-inch inter-record gaps? What if the blocks consisted of only 1600 characters each?

7. What portion of the tape in the preceding problem would be wasted because of inter-record gaps with a block size of 3200 characters? What about 1600 characters?

8. Suppose you needed to store logical records, each consisting of 300 characters, on the tape described in problem 6. What blocking factor should you

use to reduce the space allotted to inter-record gaps to no more than one-third of the tape? Using this blocking factor, how many logical records could you store on the tape?

9. Suppose 1000 employee records, each consisting of 2000 characters, are to be stored on a 2400-foot tape using a blocking factor of 2. If the recording density is 1600 characters per inch and inter-record gaps are one-half inch long, what fraction of the tape will be required for storage of the records (including inter-record gaps)? How much of the 2400 feet of tape will actually have data recorded on it?

10. Suppose a 5¼-inch floppy disk contained 40 tracks, each of which is divided into sectors capable of holding 256 characters. How many characters would the disk hold if each track were divided into 10 sectors? What if each track contained 16 sectors? How do these capacities compare to the size of a 400-page novel in which each page contains 3500 characters?

11. If the 16-sectored floppy disk in problem 10 were spinning at the rate of 300 revolutions per minute (rpm), at approximately what rate, measured in characters per second, would the data pass by the read/write head?

12. If the microcomputer using the floppy disk in problem 11 executed one instruction every 2 microseconds (millionths of a second), how many instructions could it execute in the time between consecutive characters passing the read/write head?

13. Observe that once it is determined that a certain block of data is desired from a disk, the machine will have to wait for that data to rotate around to the read/write head. This means that on the average, the time required for the disk to make half a rotation (called the latency time) will be wasted each time data is extracted. If the disk is rotating at 300 revolutions per minute and the machine can execute an instruction in 2 microseconds (millionths of a second), how many instructions could the machine perform during this average wait?

14. Compare the latency time of the typical floppy disk in problem 13 with that of a typical full-size disk drive spinning at 60 revolutions per second.

15. Approximately how many 350-page novels with approximately 3300 characters per page could be recorded on a typical full-size disk pack with a total of 16,650 tracks, each having a capacity of 20,000 characters?

16. Here is a message in ASCII. What does it say?

    1010111 1101000 1100001 1110100 0100000
    1100100 1101111 1100101 1110011 0100000
    1101001 1110100 0100000 1110011 1100001
    1111001 0111111

17. List the binary representations of the integers from 6 to 16.

18. a. Write the number 13 by representing the 1 and 3 in ASCII.
    b. Write the number 13 in binary representation.

*19. Code the following sentences in ASCII using a parity bit and odd parity:
    a. 100/5 = 20
    b. To be or not to be?
    c. The total cost is $7.25.

*20. The following message was originally transmitted with odd parity in each short bit string. In which strings have errors definitely occurred?

    11011 01011 10110 00000 11111 10101 10001
    00100 01110

*21. Suppose a 21-bit code were generated by representing each symbol by three consecutive copies of its ASCII representation (for example, the symbol A would be represented by the bit string 100000110000011000001). What error correcting properties would this new code have?

*22. Using the error correcting code described in Figure 1-13, decode the following words:
    a. 111010 110110
    b. 101000 100110 001100
    c. 011101 000110 000000 010100
    d. 010010 001000 001110 101111
       000000 110111 100110
    e. 010011 000000 101001 100110

*23. Convert each of the following binary representations to its equivalent decimal form:
    a. 111   b. 0001   c. 11101
    d. 10001   e. 10111   f. 000000
    g. 100   h. 1000   i. 10000
    j. 11001   k. 11010   l. 11011

*24. Convert each of the following decimal representations to its equivalent binary form:
    a. 7   b. 12   c. 16   d. 15   e. 33

*25. Convert each of the following sign-magnitude representations to its equivalent decimal form:
a. 0011 b. 1011 c. 11110
d. 01000 e. 111

*26. Convert each of the following decimal representations to its equivalent sign-magnitude form using patterns of 6 bits:
a. 7 b. −7 c. 31 d. −16 e. −12

*27. Convert each of the following excess 16 representations to its equivalent decimal form:
a. 100007 b. 10011 c. 01101
d. 01111 e. 10111

*28. Convert each of the following decimal representations to its equivalent excess four form:
a. 0 b. 3 c. −3 d. −1 e. 1

*29. Convert each of the following two's complement representations to its equivalent decimal form:
a. 10000 b. 10011 c. 01101
d. 01111 e. 10111

*30. Convert each of the following decimal representations to its equivalent two's complement form using patterns of 7 bits:
a. 12 b. −12 c. −1 d. 0 e. 8

*31. Perform each of the following additions assuming the bit strings represent values in two's complement notation. Identify each case in which the answer is incorrect because of overflow.

a.	00101	b.	01111	c.	11111
	+01000		+00001		+00001

d.	10111	e.	00111	f.	00111
	+11010		+00111		+01100

g.	11111	h.	01010	i.	01000
	+11111		+10101		+01000

j. 01010
  +00011

*32. Solve each of the following problems by translating the values into two's complement notation (using patterns of 5 bits), converting any subtraction problem to an equivalent addition problem, and performing that addition. Check your work by converting your answer to decimal notation. (Watch out for overflow.)

a.	7	b.	7	c.	12
	+ 1		− 1		− 4

d.	8	e.	12	f.	4
	− 7		+ 4		−11

*33. Convert each of the following binary representations into its equivalent base ten form:
a. 11.001 b. 100.1101 c. .0101
d. 1.0 e. 10.01

*34. Express each of the following values in binary notation:
a. 5¾ b. 1/16 c. 7⅞
d. 1¼ e. 6⅝

*35. Decode the following bit patterns using the floating-point format discussed in this chapter:
a. 01011100 b. 11001000
c. 00101010 d. 10111001

*36. Code the following values using the floating-point format discussed in this chapter. Indicate each case in which a round-off error occurs.
a. ½ b. 7½ c. −3¾
d. ³⁄₃₂ e. ³¹⁄₃₂

*37. What is the best approximation to the square root of 2 that can be expressed in the floating-point format of Section 1-7? What value would actually be obtained if this approximation were squared by a machine using this floating-point format?

*38. In each of the following addition problems, interpret the bit patterns using the floating-point format discussed in Section 1-7, add the values represented, and code the answer in the same floating-point format. Indicate those cases in which round-off errors occur.

a.	01011100	b.	01101010
	+ 01101000		+ 00111000

c.	01111000	d.	01011000
	+ 00011000		+ 01011000

*39. In each of the following cases the different bit strings represent the same value but in different numeric coding systems that we have discussed. Identify each value and the coding systems used to represent it.
a. 1101 0011 1011
b. 11111101 10000011 11101100
c. 1010 0010 01101000

*40. If you doubled the length of the bit strings being used to represent integers in binary from 4 bits to 8 bits, what change would be made in the value of the largest integer you could represent? What if you were using two's complement notation?

*41. What would be the hexadecimal representation of the largest memory address in a memory consisting of 16K cells?

Problems for the Programmer

1. What is the largest integer your language/machine combination can conveniently handle? As an experiment, write a loop that initializes an integer at 1 and repeatedly multiplies by 2 seventy times while printing the result at each step. Explain the results.

2. What statements does your language provide for identifying how the various data items in your programs are to be coded by the machine?

3. Does your language provide a convenient technique for handling overflow?

4. Write a program that requests two integers from the terminal, adds them, and displays the result. What happens if the values typed are very large? Can you modify your program so that it prints the message "overflow occurred" when such is the case?

5. What statements in your programming language allow access to data
   a. in main memory?
   b. in bulk storage?

6. Write a loop that initializes a real variable at 0.01 and repeatedly increments it by 0.01 up to the value 1, printing its value at each step. Does it print the correct values? Why would you suspect that it may not? Experiment with different initial values and step sizes.

7. Does your language allow you to mix data types in the same instruction? For example, can you add an integer value to a floating-point value and place the result in a floating-point field? How about placing the result in an integer field? What activities must be done by the language/machine system to accomplish such a procedure?

8. Write a program to convert binary numerals into Roman numerals. (Recall that 1 = I, 5 = V, 10 = X, 50 = L, 100 = C, 500 = D, and 1000 = M.)

2   Data Manipulation

2–1 **The Central Processing Unit**
Registers
CPU/Memory Interface
Machine Instructions

2–2 **The Stored-Program Concept**
Instruction Components
A Typical Machine Language

2–3 **Program Execution**
An Example of Program Execution
Special Program Counter Applications

2–4 **Other Architectures** (optional)
Microprogrammed Machines
Pipelining
Multiprocessor Machines
Data-Driven Machines
Demand-Driven Machines

2–5 **Arithmetic/Logic Instructions** (optional)
Logical Operations
Rotation and Shift Operations
Arithmetic Operations

2–6 **Computer/Peripheral Communication** (optional)
Communication Through Ports
Controllers
Parallel and Serial Communication

In Chapter 1, we studied the concepts relating to the storage of data and a computer's memory. In addition to being able to store data, an algorithmic machine must be able to manipulate the data as directed by the algorithm. Thus, the machine must have the mechanism for performing operations on data and coordinating the sequence of these operations. In today's machines, this mechanism is called the central processing unit. This unit is conceptually divided into two smaller units: one that coordinates the machine's activities and one that performs the requested operations. It is the study of these units and related topics on which this chapter concentrates.

2–1 **The Central Processing Unit**

The circuitry in today's computers that performs the operations (such as addition and subtraction) on data is not directly connected to the storage cells in the machine's main memory. Instead, this circuitry is isolated in an area of the computer called the **central processing unit,** or **CPU.** This unit is actually charged with two conceptually different tasks since as we observed in the introduction, the execution of an algorithm requires not only that operations be performed on data but also that the sequential order of these operations be coordinated. Consequently, the CPU actually consists of two parts: the **arithmetic/logic unit** containing the circuitry that performs data manipulation and the **control unit** that contains the circuitry for coordinating the machine's activities.

Registers

Since the CPU is a separate device from the machine's memory, it contains special memory cells, called **registers**, that are used as temporary holding places for data being manipulated. In particular, these registers, which are connected to the arithmetic/logic unit's circuitry, hold the inputs to this circuitry and provide a storage place for the result. When an operation is to be performed on data, it is the control unit's responsibility to see that the data is placed in the registers, to inform the arithmetic/logic unit as to which registers hold the data, and to activate the appropriate operation circuitry in the arithmetic/logic unit.

Many machines assign special roles to certain registers. For example, it is not uncommon to find the same register connected to the output of all the operation circuits in the arithmetic/logic unit. Thus, regardless of the operation performed, the result will always be left in this register. Such a register is referred to as the **accumulator,** or A register, since it is in this register that the result accumulates.

It is instructive to consider registers in the context of a machine's overall memory facilities. Registers are used to hold the data immediately applicable to the operation at hand; main memory is used to hold the data that will be needed in the near future; and bulk storage is used to hold data that will likely not be needed in the near future.

CPU/Memory Interface

To perform an operation on information stored in memory, the data must first be copied from memory into the registers in the CPU. Having completed the operation, it is highly likely that we will want the result placed somewhere in memory. For this purpose the CPU is connected to main memory by a collection of wires called a **bus** (Figure 2-1). Through this bus, the CPU is able to extract, or read, data from main memory by supplying the address of the pertinent memory cell along with a read

Figure 2-1 A CPU/main memory architecture

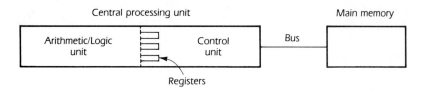

signal. In a similar manner, the CPU can place, or write, data in memory by providing the address of the destination cell and the data to be stored together with a write signal.

With this mechanism in mind, we see that performing an operation such as addition on data stored in main memory involves more than the mere execution of the operation itself. The process involves the combined efforts of both the control unit, which coordinates the transfer of information between the registers and main memory, and the arithmetic/logic unit, which performs the operation of addition when instructed to do so by the control unit. The complete process of adding two values stored in memory might be broken down into the steps listed in Figure 2-2.

Machine Instructions

Note that each step in Figure 2-2 is written in the form of an instruction as though we were speaking to the control unit. Such a sequence of instructions is called a program, and the process of developing programs and communicating them to the computer is called programming the machine.

Programming a machine requires an understanding of which instructions the control unit is able to execute since telling the unit to do anything else would be unproductive. Thus, a brief look at the types of instructions that a typical machine might be able to execute should be helpful at this point (a more in-depth discussion appears later in the chapter). You may be surprised to learn that the list is really quite short. One of the fascinating aspects of computer science is that once a machine can perform certain elementary but well-chosen tasks, adding more features does

Figure 2-2 Adding values stored in memory

Step 1. Get one of the values to be added from memory and place it in a register.

Step 2. Get the other value to be added from memory and place it in another register.

Step 3. Activate the addition circuitry with the registers used in steps 1 and 2 as inputs with another register designated to hold the result.

Step 4. Store the result in memory.

Step 5. Stop.

not increase the machine's theoretical capabilities. In other words, beyond a certain point, additional features only increase such things as convenience and speed but add nothing to the machine's basic abilities. We discuss these ideas further in Chapter 11.

When discussing the instructions in a machine's repertoire, it is helpful to recognize that they can be classified into three categories: the data transfer group (sometimes called the data movement group), the arithmetic/logic group, and the control group.

Data Transfer

The first group of instructions consists of instructions that request the movement of data from one location to another. Steps 1, 2, and 4 in Figure 2-2 fall into this category. As in the case of main memory, it is unusual for the data being transferred from any location in a machine to be erased from its original location. The process involved in a transfer instruction is more like copying the data into another location rather than moving it. In this sense, the popular *transfer* or *move* terminology is actually a misnomer, with a more descriptive term being *copy*. While on the subject of terminology, we should mention that special terms are used when referring to the transfer of data between the CPU and main memory. A request to fill a register with the contents of a memory cell is commonly referred to as a LOAD instruction; conversely, a request to transfer the contents of a register to a memory cell is called a STORE instruction. Thus, steps 1 and 2 in Figure 2-2 are LOAD instructions, while step 4 is a STORE instruction.

An extremely important group of instructions within the data transfer category consists of the commands for communicating with devices outside the CPU–main memory context. Since these instructions handle the input/output (I/O) activities of the machine, they are classified as the I/O instructions and are sometimes considered as a category in their own right. On the other hand, we will see in Section 2-6 that these I/O activities are often handled by the same instructions that request data transfers between the CPU and main memory, and placing them in a separate category would therefore be somewhat misleading.

Arithmetic/Logic

The arithmetic/logic group consists of the instructions that tell the control unit to request an activity within the arithmetic/logic unit. Step 3 in Figure 2-2 falls into this group. As its name suggests, the arithmetic/logic unit is capable of performing operations other than the basic arithmetic operations. For instance, the common logic operations are AND, OR, and EXCLUSIVE OR, which we discuss later. For now, we merely mention that these operations are often used for manipulating individual bits within a register without disturbing the rest of the register. Another collection of operations available within most arithmetic/logic units allows the con-

Figure 2-3 Dividing values stored in memory

Step 1. LOAD a register with a value from memory.

Step 2. LOAD another register with another value from memory.

Step 3. If this second value is zero, jump to step 6.

Step 4. Divide the contents of the first register by the second register and leave the result in the accumulator.

Step 5. STORE the contents of the accumulator in memory.

Step 6. Stop.

tents of registers to be moved to the right or the left within the register. These operations are known as either SHIFT or ROTATE operations, depending on whether the bits that "fall off the end" of the register when its contents are moved are merely discarded (SHIFT) or are used to fill the holes left at the other end (ROTATE).

Control

The control group consists of those instructions that direct the execution of the program rather than the manipulation of data. Step 5 in Figure 2-2 falls into this category, although it is an extremely elementary example. This group contains many of the more interesting instructions in a machine's repertoire such as the family of JUMP (or BRANCH) instructions used to direct the control unit to execute an instruction other than the next one in the list. These JUMP instructions appear in two varieties: unconditional jumps and conditional jumps. An example of the former would be the instruction to "skip to step number 5"; an example of the latter would be "if the value obtained is 0 then skip to step number 5." Thus, the distinction is that a conditional jump will result in a "change of venue" only if a certain condition is satisfied. As an example, Figure 2-3 displays a sequence of instructions for dividing two values where step 3 is a conditional jump that protects against the possibility of division by zero.

Questions/Exercises

1. Draw an analogy between a CPU extracting information from memory and a shoe store customer requesting to try on some shoes for purchase consideration.
   a. What corresponds to memory?
   b. What corresponds to registers?
   c. What corresponds to an address?
   d. What corresponds to the contents of a memory cell?
   e. What are some differences between the two systems?
2. What sequence of events do you think would be required in a machine to move the contents of one memory cell to another?

3. What information must the CPU supply to the main memory circuitry to write a value into a memory cell?

4. Why might the term *move* be considered an incorrect name for the operation of moving data from one location in a machine to another?

5. What is the difference between the terms *write* and *store*? How about *read* as opposed to *load*?

6. In the text, jump instructions were expressed by identifying the destination explicitly by stating the name (or step number) of the destination within the jump instruction (e.g., "jump to step 6"). This technique's drawback is that if an instruction name (number) is later changed, we must be sure to find all jumps to that instruction and change that name also. Describe another way of expressing a jump instruction so that the name of the destination is not explicitly stated.

7. Is the instruction "If 0 equals 0, jump to step 7" a conditional or unconditional jump?

2–2 The Stored-Program Concept

Early computing devices were not known for their flexibility, as the program that each device executed tended to be built into the control unit as a part of the machine. Such a system is analogous to a music box that always plays the same tune when what is needed is the flexibility of a record player. One approach used to gain this flexibility in early electronic computers was to design the control units so they could be conveniently rewired. This flexibility was accomplished by means of a pegboard arrangement similar to old telephone switchboards in which the the ends of jumper wires were plugged into holes.

A breakthrough (credited, perhaps incorrectly, to John von Neumann) came with the realization that a program, just like data, can be coded and stored in main memory. If the control unit is designed to extract the program from memory, decode the instructions, and execute them, a computer's program could be changed merely by changing the contents of the computer's memory instead of rewiring the control unit. (This technique even allows the machine to change its own program.) This stored-program concept has become the standard approach used today. To apply it, a machine is designed to recognize certain bit patterns as representing certain instructions. This collection of instructions along with the coding system is called the **machine language** because it defines the means by which we can communicate with the machine.

The discovery of the stored-program concept is an example of a common phenomenon. The concept of storing a program in memory is not difficult at all. What made it difficult to think of originally was that everyone thought of programs and data as different entities: data was stored in memory; programs were part of the control unit. The result was a prime example of not being able to see the forest for the trees. It is easy to be caught in such ruts, and the development of computer science might well remain in many of them today without our knowing it. Indeed, part of the excitement of the science is that new insights are constantly opening doors to new theories and applications.

Instruction Components

To code a machine's instructions for storage in memory, it is customary to assign a unique bit pattern to each of the elementary operations such as STORE, SHIFT, EXCLUSIVE OR, and JUMP. Such a bit pattern is called an *operation code*, or *op-code* for short, since it is the code describing the basic operation. Following the op-code, we attach an additional bit pattern that more fully describes the instruction being coded. For example, in the case of a STORE operation, we must identify which register is to have its contents stored and which memory cell is to receive the data. Such a bit pattern constitutes the *operand field* of the instruction since it is here that the operands of the operations such as ADD, SHIFT, and OR are identified.

A Typical Machine Language

With these ideas in mind, let us see how the instructions of a typical machine might be coded. The machine that we will use for our discussion is described in Appendix B and summarized in Figure 2-4. It has 16 registers, named R0 through R15 (R0

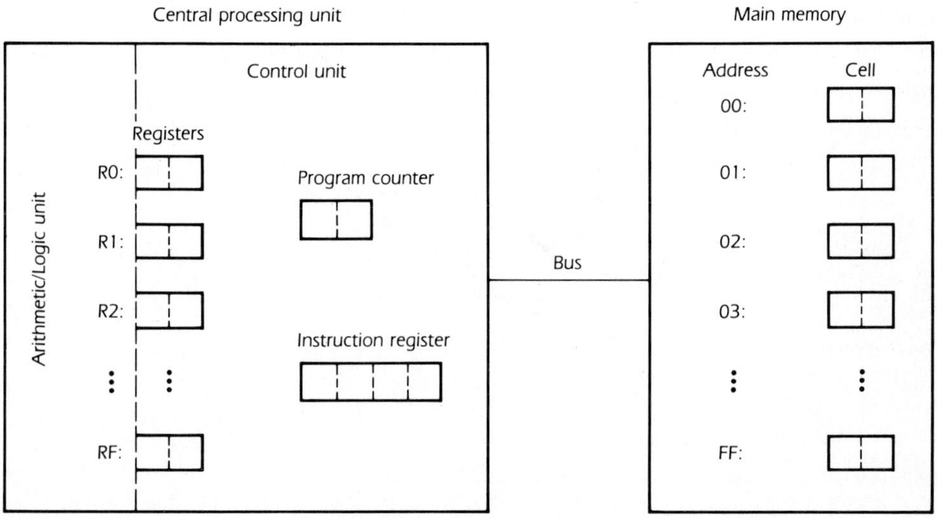

Figure 2-4 The architecture of the machine of Appendix B

through RF in hexadecimal). Moreover, the machine has 256 cells in its main memory. Consequently, each memory cell is uniquely addressed, or identified, by an integer in the range from 0 to 255. As we mentioned earlier, memory cells containing 8 bits are quite popular, so let us pretend that the memory cells in our machine are also one byte. Since the registers are used to hold data from memory cells on a temporary basis, it makes sense to have each register also consist of 8 bits.

Op-Codes

Referring to the machine language listing in Appendix B, you will find that each instruction is coded with a total of 16 bits, represented in the listing by four hexadecimal digits (Figure 2-5). The op-code for each instruction consists of the first 4 bits, or equivalently, the first hexadecimal digit. The entire instruction list consists of only 12 basic instructions whose op-codes are represented by the hexadecimal digits 1 through C. Thus, any instruction code starting with the bit pattern 0011 (hexadecimal 3) refers to a STORE instruction, and any instruction code starting with 1010 (hexadecimal A) refers to a ROTATE instruction.

The machine has two ADD instructions. One is a binary ADD and the other is a floating-point ADD. This distinction results from the fact that different operations are required to add two bit patterns, depending on how the patterns are to be interpreted. That is, adding bit patterns that represent values coded in binary notation requires different activities within the arithmetic/logic unit than when adding floating-point notation.

Operands

Now we take a look at the operand field. It consists of 12 bits, or three hexadecimal digits, and in each case (except for the HALT instruction, which needs no further refinement) clarifies the general instruction given by the op-code. For example, if the first 4 bits of an instruction were 0001 (the op-code for loading from

Figure 2-5 The format of a machine instruction

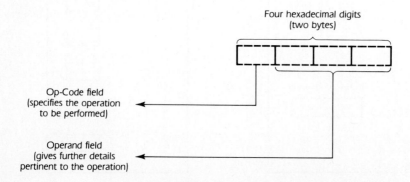

Four hexadecimal digits
(two bytes)

Op-Code field
(specifies the operation
to be performed)

Operand field
(gives further details
pertinent to the operation)

memory), the next 4 bits of the instruction would indicate which register is to be loaded, and the last 8 bits would indicate which memory cell is to provide the data. Thus, the instruction 1347 translates to the statement "load register R3 with the contents of the memory cell at address 47." In the case of the op-code hexadecimal 7, which requests that the contents of two registers be ORed, the next 4 bits indicate where the result should be placed, while the last 8 bits of the operand field are used to indicate which two registers are to be ORed. Thus, the instruction 70C5 translates to the statement "OR the contents of R12 (C in hexadecimal is 12 in decimal) with the contents of R5 and leave the result in register R0."

A subtle distinction exists between our machine's two LOAD instructions. Here we see that the op-code 0001 (hexadecimal 1) refers to the instruction that loads a register with the contents of a memory cell, whereas the op-code 0010 (hexadecimal 2) refers to the instruction that loads a register with a particular value. The difference is that the operand field in an instruction of the first type contains an address, whereas in the second type, it contains the data that is to be loaded.

An interesting situation occurs in the case of the JUMP instruction (op-code hexadecimal B). The first 4 bits of the operand field indicate which register is to be compared with register R0. If this register contains the same pattern as R0, the machine jumps to the instruction at the address indicated by the last 8 bits of the operand. Otherwise, the execution of the program continues as usual. In general, this provides a conditional jump. However, if the first 4 bits of the operand field are 0000 (hexadecimal 0), the instruction would request that R0 be compared with R0. Since a register will always be equal to itself, the comparison will always be equal, and thus the jump will always be taken. Consequently, any instruction whose code starts with the hexadecimal digits B0 will translate to an unconditional jump.

A Program Example

We close this section with the following coded version of the memory in Figure 2-2. We have assumed that the values to be added are stored in binary notation at memory addresses 6C and 6D and the sum is to be placed in memory at address 6E.

Step 1.	156C
Step 2.	166D
Step 3.	5056
Step 4.	306E
Step 5.	C000

Questions/Exercises

1. The following are instructions written in the machine language described in Appendix B. Rewrite them in English.

   a. 368A   b. BADE   c. 803C   d. 40F4

2. What is the difference between the instructions 15AB and 25AB in the machine language of Appendix B?

3. Here are some instructions in English. Translate each of them into the machine language of Appendix B.
   a. LOAD register number 3 with the hexadecimal value 56.
   b. ROTATE register number 5 three bits to the right.
   c. JUMP to the instruction at location F3 if the contents of register number 7 is equal to the contents of R0.
   d. AND the contents of register number 10 (hexadecimal A) with the contents of register number 5 and leave the result in register number 0.

2–3 Program Execution

A computer follows a program stored in its memory by moving the instructions from memory to the control unit as needed. Once in the control unit, each instruction is decoded and obeyed. The order in which the instructions are fetched from memory corresponds to the instructions' address order unless otherwise specified by a jump instruction. To understand how the overall execution process takes place, it is necessary to take a closer look at the control unit inside the CPU. Within this unit are two special purpose registers called the **program counter** and the **instruction register.** The program counter contains the address of the next instruction to be executed, thereby serving as the machine's way of keeping track of where it is in the program. The instruction register is used to hold the instruction being executed.

The control unit performs its job by continually repeating what is called the **machine cycle,** which consists of three steps: fetch, decode, and execute (Figure 2-6). During the fetch step, the control unit requests that main memory provide it with the next instruction to be executed. The unit knows where the next instruction is in memory because its address is kept in the program counter. The control unit

Figure 2-6 The machine cycle

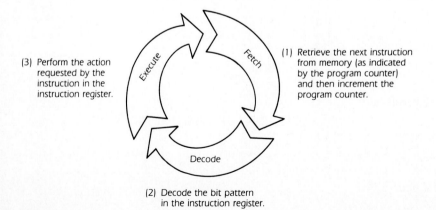

(3) Perform the action requested by the instruction in the instruction register.

Execute

Fetch

(1) Retrieve the next instruction from memory (as indicated by the program counter) and then increment the program counter.

Decode

(2) Decode the bit pattern in the instruction register.

places the instruction received from memory in its instruction register and then increments the program counter so that the counter contains the address of the next instruction.

With the instruction now in the instruction register, the control unit begins the decode phase of the machine cycle. At this time, it analyzes the op-code and operand fields to determine what action the instruction is requesting.

Having decoded the instruction, the control unit enters the execute phase during which it activates the correct circuitry to perform the requested task. For example, if the instruction were a load from memory, the control unit would cause the load to occur; if the instruction were for an ADD operation, the control unit would activate the appropriate ADD circuitry in the arithmetic/logic unit with the correct registers as inputs.

When the instruction has been executed, the control unit again begins the machine cycle with the fetch phase. Observe that since the program counter was incremented at the end of the previous fetch phase, it again provides the control unit with the correct instruction address.

An Example of Program Execution

Let us follow this process through the program we coded at the end of Section 2-2. We first need to put the coded program somewhere in memory. For our example suppose the program is stored in consecutive addresses, starting at address A0 hexadecimal. A table representing the contents of this area of memory would thus appear as shown in Figure 2-7. With the program stored in this manner, we can cause the machine to execute it by placing the address (A0) of the first instruction in the program counter and starting the machine.

The control unit begins its fetch phase by extracting the instruction at location A0 and placing this instruction (156C) in its instruction register. Notice that, in our machine, instructions take up two cells of memory. The control unit is designed to take this into account so that it knows to retrieve the contents of both cells. It then adds two to the program counter so that this register contains the address of the

Figure 2-7 Our "add" program stored in memory starting at address A0

Address	Contents
A0	15
A1	6C
A2	16
A3	6D
A4	50
A5	56
A6	30
A7	6E
A8	C0
A9	00

next instruction. Thus, at the end of the fetch phase of the first machine cycle, the program counter and instruction register contain the following data:

Program Counter: A2
Instruction Register: 156C

Next, the control unit analyzes the instruction in its instruction register and concludes that it is to load register R5 with the contents of the memory cell at address 6C. This load activity is performed during the execution phase, and the control unit then returns to the fetch phase of the machine cycle.

During this fetch phase, the control unit obtains the instruction 166D from the two memory cells starting at address A2, places this instruction in its instruction register, and increments the program counter to A4. The values in the program counter and instruction register therefore become the following:

Program Counter: A4
Instruction Register: 166D

Now the control unit decodes the instruction 166D and determines that it is to load register R6 with the contents of memory address 6D. It then enters the execute phase during which register R6 is actually loaded.

Since the program counter now contains A4, the control unit extracts the next instruction starting at this address. The result is that 5056 is placed in the instruction register, and the program counter is incremented to A6. The control unit now decodes the contents of its instruction register and enters the execution phase by activating the binary addition circuitry with the inputs R5 and R6.

During this execution phase, the arithmetic/logic unit performs the requested addition, leaves the result in R0 (as requested by the control unit), and reports to the control unit that it has finished. The control unit then begins another fetch phase of the machine cycle. Once again, with the aid of the program counter, it fetches the next instruction (306E) from the two memory cells starting at memory location A6 and increments the program counter to A8. This instruction is decoded during the next decode phase and executed during the next execute phase. At this point the sum is placed at memory location 6E.

The next instruction is fetched starting from memory location A8, and the program counter is incremented to AA. The contents of the instruction register (C000) are now decoded as the halt instruction. Consequently, the machine stops during the next execute phase of the machine cycle, and the program has been completed.

In summary, we see that the execution of a program stored in memory involves nothing mysterious. In fact, the process is similar to the process you and I might use if we needed to follow a detailed list of instructions. Whereas we might keep our place by checking the instructions off as we do them, the computer keeps its place by using the program counter. After determining which instruction to execute next, we would read the instruction and extract its meaning just as the machine decodes its instructions. Finally, we would perform the task requested and return to the list for the next instruction in the same manner that the machine executes its instructions during the execute phase and then continues with another fetch.

The significant differences between humans and machines when following such a list of instructions are accuracy and speed. Machines do not tire of doing the same task over and over as do humans. The control unit faithfully repeats the machine cycle again and again without any tendency or desire to cut corners and, thus, without errors. Humans, on the other hand, quickly become bored, think they see what is to be done, and hurry to do it without giving each instruction its fair attention. The result is that the bolts we have left to attach the swing to the chain are the ones that were supposed to connect the ladder to the swingset.

As for speed, technology continues to amaze us with faster and faster equipment. Today it is not unusual to find machines that execute a million or more instructions in a single second. There are signs, however, that there will be a limit to the speed with which machines can execute instructions, and technology is already turning toward alternatives. This is the subject of Section 2-4.

Special Program Counter Applications

Before leaving this section, we should note the ease with which the machine can execute a jump instruction. All that needs to be done during the execute phase is to change the contents of the program counter to the address to which the jump is directed. The next machine cycle will then start by extracting the correct instruction from memory since it blindly uses the program counter as the address.

Such an example brings us to an important property of modern machines. In particular, many programs can be stored simultaneously in a computer's main memory so long as they occupy different locations. Which program will be run when the machine is started can then be determined merely by setting the program counter appropriately.

One must keep in mind, however, that data is also contained in memory, and since it is also coded in terms of 0s and 1s, the machine alone has no way of knowing what is data and what is program. A common error is to accidentally set the program counter to the address of data instead of to the address of the desired program. The result is that the computer, not knowing any better, extracts the data bit patterns as though they were instructions and executes them. What happens depends on what the data was.

Care must be taken at this point not to assume that this feature is all bad. Once again, the concept of programs and data being completely different entities can be severely limiting. In reality, providing programs and data with a common appearance in a machine's memory has proven a useful attribute since it allows one program to manipulate other programs (or even itself) as it would data. Indeed, we will see that what may be data to one program often turns out to be another program.

Questions/Exercises

1. Suppose the memory cells from addresses 00 to 05 in the machine described in Appendix B contained the (hexadecimal) values given in the following table:

Address	Contents
00	14
01	02
02	34
03	17
04	C0
05	00

If we started the machine with its program counter containing 00, what would be the contents of the memory cell whose address is hexadecimal 17 when the machine halts?

2. Suppose the memory cells at addresses B0 to B8 in the machine described in Appendix B contained the (hexadecimal) values given in the following table:

Address	Contents
B0	13
B1	B8
B2	A3
B3	02
B4	33
B5	B8
B6	C0
B7	00
B8	0F

a. If the program counter starts at B0, what will be the contents of register number 3 after the first instruction has been executed?

b. What will be the contents of memory cell B8 when the halt instruction is executed?

3. Suppose the memory cells at addresses A4 to B1 in the machine described in Appendix B contained the (hexadecimal) values given in the following table:

Address	Contents
A4	20
A5	00
A6	21
A7	03
A8	22
A9	01
AA	B1
AB	B0
AC	50
AD	02
AE	B0
AF	AA
B0	C0
B1	00

Answer the following questions assuming that the machine is started with its program counter containing A4:

a. What will be in register 0 the first time the instruction at address AA is executed?

b. What will be in register 0 the second time the instruction at address AA is executed?

c. How many times will the instruction and address AA be executed before the machine halts?

4. Suppose the memory cells at addresses F0 to F9 in the machine described in Appendix B contained the (hexadecimal) values described in the following table:

Address	Contents
F0	20
F1	C0
F2	30
F3	F8
F4	20
F5	00
F6	30
F7	F9
F8	FF
F9	FF

If we start the machine with its program counter containing F0, what will the machine do when it reaches the instruction at address F8?

2–4 **Other Architectures** (optional)

To broaden our perspective, let us consider some alternatives to the machine architecture we have discussed so far.

Microprogrammed Machines

We begin by considering the conflict between cost (in terms of size, power consumption, design complexity, etc.) and performance. At issue is the decision regarding how a machine's fetch-decode-execute cycle should be implemented. One option is to build a machine that is able to decode and execute a wide variety of instructions. Such a machine would be easier to program than a machine with a smaller instruction set, because a single instruction could be used to accomplish some tasks that would require multi-instruction sequences on another, less endowed machine. However, implementing these more elaborate instructions would require a more complex CPU than would otherwise be necessary. Thus, on the one hand we are encouraged to build a CPU with an extensive instruction set while on the other we desire a machine with a limited instruction repertoire.

One method of dealing with these contradictory desires is to build a machine with a limited instruction set and then program it to handle more elaborate instructions. This approach follows the observation that programming a machine to execute a complex instruction is easier than building the circuitry to execute the instruction directly. Following this approach, many manufacturers build machines with an additional, high-speed memory called micromemory from which the circuitry in the CPU is designed to fetch, decode, and execute a limited collection of instructions called microinstructions. Then, in terms of these microinstructions, a program called a *microprogram* is written that directs the CPU to fetch, decode, and execute instructions from main memory according to the machine cycle discussed in the previous sections. The end result is a machine with the enriched instruction set that was desired all along but with less circuitry than would have been required to implement these instructions directly.

We have introduced this layered approach to machine architecture for two reasons. First, it is an example of the trade-offs typically found in any design process. On one hand one desires a powerful, flexible machine, and on the other hand one seeks economy and efficiency. The microprogram approach provides a compromise since very complex machine language instructions can be implemented merely by describing them in the microprogram yet the actual circuitry in the CPU needs to execute just the limited set of microinstructions.

The second reason for introducing the concept of a microprogrammed machine is that it represents the foundation of a much more extensive layered system that typifies the structure of modern computing systems. Indeed, in the coming chapters we will learn that today's typical computer system is the result of numerous layers, each level dealing with certain details so that the next higher level will be more compatible with the machine's external environment.

Pipelining

In Section 2-3, we indicated that a barrier exists to the development of faster machines. This occurs because data and control signals are transferred electronically within a computer and electric pulses travel through a wire no faster than the speed of light. Since light travels approximately one foot in a nanosecond (one billionth of a second), it will require at least two nanoseconds for the control unit in the CPU to fetch an instruction from a memory cell that is one foot away. (The read request must be sent to memory, requiring at least one nanosecond, and the instruction must be sent back to the control unit, requiring at least another nanosecond.) Consequently, to fetch, decode, and execute an instruction in such a machine would require several nanoseconds. Thus, increasing the execution speed of a machine ultimately becomes a miniaturization problem, and although fantastic advances have been made in this area, there would appear to be a limit.

In an effort to solve this dilemma, computer scientists have turned to the concept of *throughput* rather than execution speed. Throughput refers to the total amount of work the machine can do, that is, how much processing the machine can accomplish in a given amount of time rather than how long it takes to do one task. One example of how a machine's throughput can be increased without requiring an increase in execution speed is the technique called *pipelining.* This term comes from the analogy of pushing objects—in our case instructions—into a pipe at one end and having them emerge from the other. At any given time, there are several instructions in the pipe, each at a different stage of being executed. In particular, while one instruction is being executed, another instruction is being decoded, while still another is being fetched.

With such a system, although each instruction requires the same amount of time to be fetched, decoded, and executed, the total throughput of the machine is increased by a factor of three since three instructions are processed at once. (In reality, an increase of a factor of three is seldom achieved because of the occurrence of jump instructions. For example, if an instruction is a jump, the pipe must be emptied since the instructions in it are not the ones needed after all. Thus, any gain that would have been obtained by prefetching will not be realized.)

Multiprocessor Machines

Pipelining can be viewed as a special case of the more general concept called *parallel,* or *concurrent, processing*, which refers to the process of performing several activities simultaneously. Many futurists believe that parallel processing represents the trend of tomorrow. One argument supporting this claim looks to the human mind as a model. Today's technology is rapidly approaching the ability to construct electronic circuitry with roughly as many switching circuits as there are neurons in the human brain (neurons are believed to be nature's switching circuits), yet the capabilities of today's machines still fall far short of those of the human mind. This, so it is claimed, is because of the inefficient use of the machine's components as dictated by the machine's architecture. After all, if a machine is constructed with a lot of memory circuits but only a single CPU, then most of its circuitry is destined to be idle most of the time. In contrast, much of the human mind can be active at any given moment. Thus, the proponents of parallel processing argue in favor of a machine with many processing units, each having access to a small amount of memory. This, they argue, results in a configuration with the potential of a much higher utilization factor.

The major obstacle remaining before the full potential of these multiprocessor machines can be realized is to develop the ability to organize tasks in a manner that takes advantage of the parallel architecture. We must learn how to divide tasks into subtasks that can be executed at the same time. On the other hand, others argue that presenting this obstacle as merely a slight problem to be resolved may prove to be overly simplistic. We are reminded of the promises of nuclear power in the 1950s when "all that remained" was to solve the problems of radiation from plant malfunctions and nuclear waste.

Data-Driven Machines

Still other alternative architectures are based on removing the reliance on a program counter for processor control. This is because the use of a program counter requires that programs be developed as a sequence of instructions in which the order can be extremely important. For example, if our program needs to calculate the total cost of an item by adding the sales tax to the base price, we must be certain that these two items have been calculated before we attempt to add them together. Thus, developing a program for such a system requires two steps: deciding which operations should be performed and arranging these operations in the correct order.

When developing large programs, the second step can become surprisingly complex. This problem can be recognized as originating from the rigid process that is used to determine which instruction is to be executed next. Here we use the term *rigid* to refer to the fact that the control process performs its task without any knowledge of the purpose, action, or requirements of the instructions being executed. The execution of the program is determined entirely by the control procedure. Such machines (which include today's computers) are consequently called ***control-driven machines.***

In contrast to control-driven machines, consider a computer whose program takes the form of a variety of instructions waiting to be performed with no explicit order associated with them. Each instruction consists of a statement as to the operation requested together with a definition of the data required for its proper execution. In such a machine, the execution of a program proceeds simply by executing those instructions whose input data is available.

As instructions are executed, their results satisfy the input requirements for other instructions, which consequently become eligible for execution. In our cost calculation example, the addition of sales tax and base cost would be triggered by the availability of the sales tax and base cost values rather than by the occurrence of its turn in some previously defined order. The fact that execution of an instruction is triggered by the presence of its input data results in such machines being referred to as ***data-driven machines.*** Note that in a data-driven machine, the data for many instructions may well be available at the same time. Consequently, computers designed on this principle would be much more conducive to parallel processing than would control-driven machines. Moreover, the data-driven design removes one of the steps from the programming process because program development is reduced to a thorough definition of each operation to be performed with no concern for the relative times at which the actions should take place.

Demand-Driven Machines

Returning again to our cost-computing example, we see that in a data-driven machine the addition of sales tax and base price will occur when the necessary inputs become available whether or not the resulting total is really required elsewhere. It could well be that this instruction is needed only under certain conditions, that the total cost is not required elsewhere in the program, and that its calculation would therefore be a waste of time.

The concept of a **demand-driven machine** removes the possibility of such wasted efforts. In these machines, programs are conceptually the same as in data-driven machines. The difference is that in a demand-driven machine, an instruction is not executed until its output is needed. Consequently, the addition of sales tax and base price would not be triggered until the total cost was required. The machine would then recognize the need for the values of sales tax and base price, and the instructions that provide those values would in turn be activated. This process would continue until all the required instructions were initiated and completed.

Data-driven and demand-driven machines are at the stage that control-driven machines were during the 1940s. Although some experimental results are available, such machines are far from being put to popular use. Whether or not they will be the computers of the future is yet to be seen. The important point for now is that we should not close our minds to innovative ideas.

Questions/Exercises

1. Why does the CPU in a microprogrammed machine require two program counters and two instruction registers?
2. Referring back to question 3 of Section 2-3, if the machine used the pipeline technique discussed in the text, what will be in "the pipe" when the instruction at address AA is executed? Under what conditions would the pipelining technique not be beneficial at this point in the program?
3. What conflicts must be resolved when running the program in question 4 of Section 2-3 on a pipeline machine?
4. Suppose there were two "central" processing units attached to the same memory and executing different programs. Furthermore, suppose that one of these processors needs to add one to the contents of a memory cell at roughly the same time that the other needs to subtract one from the same cell. (Thus, the net effect should be that the cell ends up with the same value with which it started.)
   a. Describe a sequence in which these activities could occur that would result in the cell's ending up with a value one less than its starting value.
   b. Describe a sequence in which these activities could occur that would result in the cell's ending up with a value one greater than its starting value.

5. Below is a list of instructions stored in a data-driven machine. If we start the machine with the available inputs being price-one and price-two and the required output being total-cost, in what order will the instructions be executed?
   a. Multiply subtotal by .05 giving total-tax.
   b. Add price-one and price-two giving subtotal.
   c. Multiply price-two by .05 giving tax-two.
   d. Add subtotal and total-tax giving total-cost.
   e. Multiply price-one by .05 giving tax-one.

6. How would your answer to question 5 change if the machine were a demand-driven machine?

2–5 **Arithmetic/Logic Instructions** (optional)

As previewed earlier in the chapter, the class of arithmetic/logic instructions consists of instructions requesting arithmetic, logical, or shift operations. We have already discussed the arithmetic operations in the context of their relationship with information coding techniques. In many ways, their early introduction is unfortunate since it tends to give the operations an air of priority over the other operations in this class of instructions. The fact is the majority of computer applications today are not in the numeric area but are centered around the manipulation of strings of characters such as names and addresses. For this reason, we now emphasize the nonnumeric operations by beginning our more detailed discussion of the arithmetic/logic instructions with them.

Logical Operations

Three popular operations within the group of logical operations are AND, OR, and EXCLUSIVE OR. They are similar to addition and subtraction in that each accepts two operands (or inputs) and produces a single result. (In contrast, consider an operation that finds the values that, when squared, produce a given positive number. It accepts one operand and produces two results; for example, given the operand 4, it will produce the outputs 2 and −2.) We will, therefore, introduce these operations, as we did binary addition, by first looking at the results they produce when both operands are single bits and then extending them to more complex operands.

The AND Operation

Figure 2-8 shows a table indicating the results of the AND operation when applied to single-bit operands. Note that the only way the result can be 1 is for both operands to be 1. That is, both the first *and* the second operands must be 1 for the result to be 1.

Figure 2-8 The AND operation

```
        1          1          0          0
    AND 1      AND 0      AND 1      AND 0
    ─────      ─────      ─────      ─────
        1          0          0          0
```

In contrast to the addition operation for which operands of single bits can produce a multiple-bit output, all such results from the AND operation are single bits. Consequently, extending the table in Figure 2-8 to include cases where the operands are strings of bits involves nothing more than applying the basic rules to each individual column without any interplay between columns as with the carry process in addition. For example, ANDing the bytes 10011010 and 11001001 results in:

$$
\begin{array}{r}
10011010 \\
\text{AND } 11001001 \\
\hline
10001000
\end{array}
$$

One of the major uses of the AND operation is for placing zeros in one part of a bit pattern while not disturbing the other part. Consider, for example, what would happen if the byte 00001111 were the first operand of an AND operation. Without knowing the contents of the second operand, we could still conclude that the 4 most significant bits of the result would be 0s. Moreover, the 4 least significant bits of the result would be a copy of that part of the second operand as shown in the following example:

$$
\begin{array}{r}
00001111 \\
\text{AND } 10101010 \\
\hline
00001010
\end{array}
$$

This use of the AND operation is an example of the process called **masking.** Here one operand, called the **mask**, is used to determine which part of the other operand will affect the result. In the case of the AND operation, masking is used to produce a result that is a partial replica of one of the operands with 0s occupying the nonduplicated positions. A need for such an operation might arise when attaching parity bits to character codes. In particular, suppose the lower order 7 bits of a byte contains the ASCII code for the character C (1000011) and we wish to transmit this character using odd parity. The byte transmitted must, therefore, have a parity bit equal to 0. By ANDing the byte we already have with the byte 01111111, we will obtain the byte 01000011 regardless of the value of the parity bit in the original byte.

The OR Operation

Now let us take a look at the OR operation. Its basic rules are shown in Figure 2-9. Note in this case that the only way the result can be 0 is for both operands to be 0. That is, if either the first operand *or* the second operand is 1, the result will be 1.

Figure 2-9 The OR operation

```
     1           1           0           0
  OR 1        OR 0        OR 1        OR 0
     1           1           1           0
```

Again, the basic rules can be expanded to strings of bits by applying the operation to the individual columns as shown by the following:

```
   10011010
OR 11001001
   11011011
```

Where the AND operation could be used to duplicate a part of a string while placing 0s in the nonduplicated part, the OR operation can be used to duplicate a part of a bit string while putting 1s in the nonduplicated part. For this we again use a mask, but this time we indicate the bit positions to be duplicated with 0s and use 1s to indicate the nonduplicated positions. For example, ORing any byte with 11110000 will produce a result with 1s in its most significant 4 bits and a copy of the other operand in the least significant 4 bits, as demonstrated by the following example:

```
   11110000
OR 10101010
   11111010
```

Consequently, just as the AND operation and the mask 01111111 can be used to produce bytes with parity bits equal to 0, the OR operation along with the mask 10000000 can be used to produce bytes with parity bits equal to 1.

The EXCLUSIVE OR Operation

The basic rules for the EXCLUSIVE OR (XOR) operation are shown in Figure 2-10. In this case, to obtain a 1 for the result, exactly one of the operands must be 1. That is, one operand *or* the other must be 1, *exclusive* of the other. As before, the result of EXCLUSIVE ORing two strings together can be calculated by applying these rules to each column as seen by the following example:

```
    10011010
XOR 11001001
    01010011
```

Figure 2-10 The EXCLUSIVE OR operation

```
      1           1           0           0
  XOR 1       XOR 0       XOR 1       XOR 0
      0           1           1           0
```

A major use of this operation is in forming the complement of a bit string. For example, note the relationship between the second operand and the result in the following example:

$$
\begin{array}{r}
11111111 \\
\text{XOR } \underline{10101010} \\
01010101
\end{array}
$$

EXCLUSIVE ORing any byte with a byte of 1s will produce the complement of the first byte.

Rotation and Shift Operations

The operations in this class provide a means for the movement of bits within a register and are often used in solving alignment problems such as preparing a byte for future use in masking operations or for manipulating the mantissa of floating-point representations. These operations are classified as to the direction of motion (right or left) and as to whether or not the process is circular. Within these classification guidelines are numerous variations with mixed terminology. Let us take a quick look at the ideas involved.

If we consider starting with a byte of bits and shifting its contents one bit to the right or the left, we might imagine the bit on one end falling off the edge and a hole appearing at the other end. What happens with this extra bit and the hole is the distinguishing feature among the various shift operations. One technique is to place the extra bit in the hole at the other end. The result is a circular shift, or a rotation. Thus, if we perform a right circular shift on a byte eight times, we will obtain the same bit pattern we started with, and seven right circular shifts will be equivalent to a single left circular shift.

Another technique is to discard the bit that falls off the edge and always fill the hole with a 0. The term *logical shift* is often used to refer to these operations. Such shifts to the left can be used for multiplying two's complement representations by two. After all, shifting binary digits to the left corresponds to multiplication by two, just as a similar shift of decimal digits corresponds to multiplication by 10. Moreover, division by two can be accomplished by shifting the binary string to the right. In either shift, care must be taken to preserve the sign bit when using certain notational systems. Thus, we often find right shifts that always fill the hole (which occurs at the sign bit position) with its original value. Shifts that leave the sign bit unchanged are sometimes called *arithmetic shifts.*

Arithmetic Operations

Although we have already mentioned the arithmetic operations of add, subtract, multiply, and divide, a few loose ends must still be connected. First, as we have mentioned, this collection of operations can often be generated from the single add operation and a negation process. For this reason, many of the small computers are designed with only the add or perhaps only the add and subtract instructions.

We should also mention that for each arithmetic operation, numerous variations exist. We have already alluded to this in relation to the add operations available on our machine in Appendix B. In the case of addition, for example, if the values to be added are stored in two's complement notation, the addition process should be performed as a straightforward binary add. However, if the operands are stored as floating-point values, the addition process must extract the mantissa of each, shift them right or left according to the exponent fields, check the sign bits, perform the addition, and translate the result into floating-point notation. We see, then, that although both operations are considered addition, the action of the machine is not the same. As far as the machine is concerned, the two operations may have no relationship at all. Consequently, it is common to find machines with a variety of add instructions.

We should also mention an operation conceptually similar to the process of subtraction: comparing the relative size of two values. In many machines, such as the one in Appendix B, this process appears only under the disguise of the conditional jump instruction. In other machines, however, it appears as an isolated instruction where it is used to establish a context in which future instructions are interpreted. Thus, an instruction sequence might take the form of "Compare cost to cash. If equal jump to . . ." rather than "If cost equal cash jump to . . . ." In either case, two values could be compared within a machine by subtracting them and testing to see if the result is positive, zero, or negative. On the other hand, implementing the test in this fashion is often quite costly in terms of time. (Performing subtraction with two floating-point values would require the same time-consuming decoding process that addition does.) Thus, shortcuts are often sought for this comparison process.

An example of such a shortcut involves the use of excess notation for the exponent field in floating-point notation. This notation essentially reduces the process of comparing the relative size of two values to scanning them from left to right, looking for the first bit in which the two patterns differ. For example, if both sign bits are 0, the larger of the two values being compared is the one containing a 1 in the first bit position from the left in which the two patterns differ.

The comparison process can be extended to nonnumeric cases as well. For example, when characters are stored using ASCII, the binary values associated with the character codes increase in size according to alphabetical order. Thus, the ability to compare the relative sizes of the binary values gives us the ability to alphabetize the character data represented by the patterns.

Questions/Exercises

1. Perform the indicated operations.

   a.   01001011
      AND 10101011

   b.   10000011
      AND 11101100

   c.   11111111
      AND 00101101

d.	01001011	e.	10000011	f.	11111111
	OR 10101011		OR 11101100		OR 00101101

g.	01001011	h.	10000011	i.	11111111
	XOR 10101011		XOR 11101100		XOR 00101101

2. Suppose you wanted to isolate the middle 3 bits of a 7-bit string by placing 0s in the other 4 bits without disturbing the middle 3 bits. What mask would you use together with what operation?

3. Suppose you wanted to complement the 3 middle bits of a 7-bit string while leaving the other 4 bits undisturbed. What mask would you use together with what operation?

4. a. Suppose we EXCLUSIVE ORed the first 2 bits of a string of bits and then continued down the string by successively EXCLUSIVE ORing each result with the next bit in the string. How would our result be related to the number of 1s appearing in the string? For example, if there were an odd number of 1s in the string, would our final result be 1 or 0?

   b. How does this problem relate to determining what the appropriate parity bit should be when coding a message?

5. It is often convenient to use a logical operation in place of a numeric one. For example, the logical operation AND combines two bits in the same manner as multiplication. Which logical operation is almost the same as adding two bits, and what goes wrong in this case?

6. What logical operation together with what mask could you use to change ASCII codes of lower-case letters to upper-case? What about upper-case to lower-case?

7. What is the result of performing a 3-bit right circular shift on the following bit strings:

   a. 01101010   b. 00001111   c. 01111111

8. What is the result of performing a one-bit left circular shift on the following bytes represented in hexadecimal notation? Give your answer in hexadecimal form.

   a. AB   b. 5C   c. B7   d. 35

9. A right circular shift of 3 bits on a string of 8 bits is equivalent to a left circular shift of how many bits?

10. What bit pattern represents the sum of 01101010 and 11001100 if the patterns represent values stored in two's complement notation? What if the patterns represent values stored in the floating-point format discussed in Chapter 1?

11. When coding characters in ASCII, would the upper-case A precede or follow the lower-case a "alphabetically"?

12. Using the machine language of Appendix B, write a program that will place a 1 in the most significant bit of the memory cell whose address is A7 without modifying the remaining bits in the cell.

13. Using the machine language of Appendix B, write a program that will copy the middle 4 bits from memory cell E0 into the least significant 4 bits of memory cell E1, while placing 0s in the most significant 4 bits of that same cell.

2–6 **Computer/Peripheral Communication** (optional)

In this section we discuss the communication between a machine's CPU and its peripheral devices. This communication is carried out through a variety of plugs normally found on the back of the machine. Although there are numerous technical issues associated with these connections, our purposes allow us to consider them as merely locations through which data can enter and/or leave the machine. In fact, this perspective is the reason these connections are called *ports.*

Communication Through Ports

With respect to the control unit within the CPU, the ports are identified by port numbers, just as memory cells are identified by addresses. In many machines, ports are actually disguised as memory cells occupying certain addresses in memory. In other words, the port replaces the memory cell in such a way that when the CPU writes something to that location in memory (as in a STORE instruction), the data is really transferred to the port. In a similar fashion, if the CPU tries to read data from that location in memory (as in a LOAD instruction), what it really gets is the data that has arrived at the port from a peripheral device. Such a system is called *memory mapped I/O* and is represented conceptually by Figure 2-11. It has the advantage of not requiring special machine language instructions for I/O purposes since the regular LOAD and STORE instructions fill the bill. On the other hand, it has the disadvantage of cluttering the machine's memory with fake memory cells.

To transfer data in and out of ports in machines not using memory mapped I/O, extra instructions, called I/O instructions, are provided in the machine's language. These instructions are classified in the data transfer group. In such cases, we might find an instruction that transfers the contents of a register to a port, with the port number indicated in the instruction's operand field. Likewise, there might be an instruction to load a register with the data from a port, again with the port identified in the operand field.

We should point out here that more information than merely the data being transferred is passed through a port. This is because of the communication required between the peripheral device and the machine. For example, in most cases, the machine can produce characters to be printed much faster than a printing device can print them because of the difference between the electronic properties of the machine and the mechanical properties of the printing device. Consequently, with-

Figure 2-11 A conceptual representation of memory mapped I/O

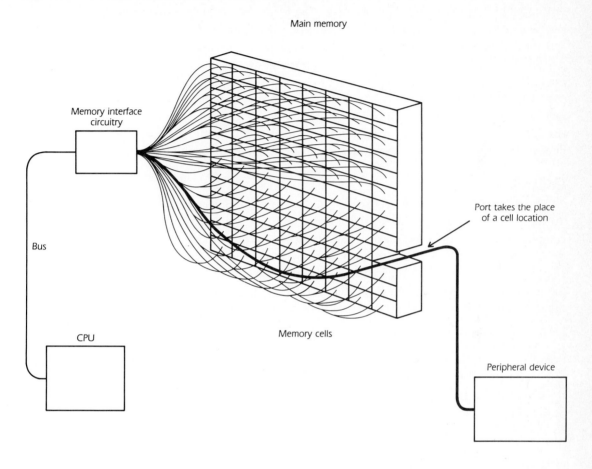

Main memory

Memory interface
circuitry

Port takes the place
of a cell location

Bus

CPU

Memory cells

Peripheral device

out additional communication between the machine and the printer, the printer would quickly fall behind.

To rectify such problems, most systems allow a two-way communication, called **handshaking,** to take place between the peripheral device and the machine in addition to allowing the passing of data. Thus, in our printing example, the printer not only would have the circuitry and mechanisms to receive and print characters but also would have the circuitry required to transmit the printer's status in a coded form back to the computer. The program being executed by the computer can then be written so that the machine waits for the appropriate status information from the printer before a character is transmitted through the port.

We thus see that two-way communication is often taking place even though it may appear to the casual observer that information is flowing in only one direction.

Most communication lines between computers and peripheral devices employ two-way (*duplex*) systems rather than one-way (*simplex*) systems. There are, however, two ways of implementing duplex systems: one called **half duplex** and the other called **full duplex.** Half-duplex systems allow for two-way communication but allow only one direction at a time. Full-duplex systems allow communication in both directions at the same time. Telephone systems are based on full-duplex communication (except in the case of some very long distance calls that are actually half duplex although the system is implemented so subtly that the callers seldom notice the difference). In contrast, the communication between a CPU and memory is half duplex since data can be transferred in either direction, but not simultaneously.

Controllers

At times it is necessary to connect several devices to a computer at the same port. You can imagine that such an arrangement would increase the communication's complexity since it would become necessary to coordinate the activities of the various devices competing for the use of the port. In such cases, we normally find additional circuitry, called a **controller** (or by the less generic term of **channel**), positioned at the junction of the device cables and the port. This circuitry is obligated to coordinate the devices attached to it and often takes the form of a small computer in itself.

The use of controllers can result in a much more efficient system since it provides a form of parallel processing as mentioned in Section 2-4. For example, it is common to connect the controller to main memory in the same fashion as the CPU. That is, the controller takes the form of another CPU connected to the same main memory as the original CPU. In this case, the controller is said to have **direct memory access (DMA).**

In DMA systems, the CPU can prepare a complete line of text in memory and direct the controller to send the line to a particular printer. Thus, the controller handles the character-by-character communication with the printer as it extracts the character codes from memory, and the CPU is free to begin preparing the next line in another area of memory. The controller plays a similar role in the case of data entering the system from a peripheral device. In particular, the controller takes care of the communication with the device until the data has been received and placed in main memory. Then it informs the CPU that data has been read and is ready for processing.

Such delegation of device communication to controllers have proven to be so effective that many computer systems use the technique even though only one device may be connected to a port. One common use of this delegation occurs in the case of communication with bulk storage devices where the controller is assigned the duty of moving the physical records back and forth between main memory and the secondary memory device. All the CPU must do is send the directions to the controller (through the port), telling it what physical record is to be read and where in memory the record is to be placed. In the case of sending a memory to bulk storage, the CPU merely places the data in a block of main memory cells and requests the controller to copy that block into bulk storage.

The area of memory used for the transfer of data between the CPU and the controller as just described is called a *buffer.* In a more general sense, a buffer is any location where one system can leave data to be picked up later by another system. Thus, the registers in a CPU serve as buffers between the control unit and the arithmetic/logic unit or between the CPU as a whole and the main memory. The process of moving data from one system to another through a buffer is called *buffering*.

Parallel and Serial Communication

Before leaving this section on computer/peripheral communication, we should say a few words about parallel versus serial communication. These terms refer to the manner in which the bit patterns are transferred with respect to time. With *parallel communication*, all the bits in a character's code are transferred at the same time, each on a separate line. Such a technique is capable of transferring data rapidly but requires a relatively complex communication path, which results in the use of large multiwire cables. On the other hand, *serial communication* tends to be slower but requires a simpler data path since the bits of a character's code are transferred over the same line as a sequence of bits.

The simpler data path required for serial communication allows computer data transfers to take place over existing communication systems that were originally developed for other purposes. One common example of this is the use of telephone lines where the digital data is converted into audio signals by a *modem* (short for modulator-demodulator), serially transferred via the existing telephone system, and converted back into digital form when it is received. Such communication would not be feasible using parallel techniques because of the inherent properties of the existing telephone system.

The speed of serial communication is measured in bits per second (*bps*) with common speeds ranging from 110 bps to 9600 bps. Another common but often misused measure is *baud rate*, which refers to the rate at which the communication line transfers states. Let us clarify this with an example. If we apply a tone at one end of a telephone connection, the tone can be detected at the other end. Consequently, we could send messages over the phone system by agreeing that a certain note would be used to represent a 0 and another note would represent a 1. In such a system, the communication line could be in one of two states: carrying one of the notes or carrying the other. Since each state represents a single bit, the rate in which states are communicated is the same as the rate in which bits are communicated; thus, the baud rate would be the same as the bps. However, if we change our protocol to include four possible states (notes), each state could represent 2 bits. For example, we might agree to use a low pitch to represent the bits 00, a higher pitch to represent the bits 01, a still higher pitch to represent the bits 10, and the highest pitch to represent the bits 11. In this system, the rate at which bits are transferred will be twice the rate that states (or notes) are transferred since each state represents 2 bits. Thus, the bps would be twice the baud rate.

Questions/Exercises

1. Suppose a serial communication system is capable of transmitting and receiving eight different states. If bit patterns are assigned to each of the eight states so that each state represents a total of 3 bits, how would the baud rate of the system compare to the measure of bps?
2. Give examples of simplex, half-duplex, and full-duplex communication occurring in situations outside the computer field.
3. Suppose the computer described in Appendix B uses memory mapped I/O without the added advantage of a controller and a printer is connected to the port represented by memory location FA (hexadecimal).
   a. Assuming that the ASCII code for a character is currently in register number 5, what machine language instruction would cause this character to be printed at the printer?
   b. If the machine executes 200,000 instructions per second, how many times could this character be sent to the printer in one second?
   c. Could the printer keep up with the characters being sent to it in part b?
4. What are some status messages that a printer might send to the computer?
5. Why are input terminals normally connected to the computer by full-duplex lines rather than merely by simplex lines?

Chapter 2 Review Problems

(Asterisked problems are associated with optional sections.)

1. Suppose three values (x, y, and z) were stored in a machine's memory. Describe the sequence of events (loading registers from memory, saving values in memory, etc.) that would lead to the computation of $x + y - z$. How about $(2x) + y$?

2. The following are instructions written in the machine language described in Appendix B. Translate them into English.
   a. 407E   b. 9028   c. A302
   d. B3AD   e. 2835

3. Suppose a machine language is designed with an op-code field of 4 bits. How many different instruction types could the language contain? What if the op-code field were increased to 8 bits?

4. Translate the following instructions from English into the machine language described in Appendix B.
   a. Load register R8 with the contents of memory cell 55.
   b. Load register R8 with the hexadecimal value 55.
   c. Rotate register R4 3 bits to the right.

d. AND the contents of registers RF and R2 leaving the result in register R0.

e. Jump to the instruction at memory location 31 if the contents of register R0 equals the value in register RB.

5. Classify each of the following instructions (in the machine language of Appendix B) in terms of whether its execution changes the contents of the memory cell at location 3B, retrieves the contents of the memory cell at location 3B, or is independent of the contents of the memory cell at location 3B.

a. 153B   b. 253B   c. 353B

d. 3B3B   e. 403B

6. Suppose the memory cells at addresses 00 through 03 in the machine described in Appendix B contain the following hexadecimal values:

Address	Contents
00	23
01	02
02	C0
03	00

a. Translate the first instruction into English.

b. If the machine is started with its program counter containing 00, what value will be in register R3 when the machine halts?

7. Suppose the memory cells at addresses 00 through 05 in the machine described in Appendix B contain the following (hexadecimal) values:

Address	Contents
00	10
01	04
02	30
03	45
04	C0
05	00

Answer the following questions assuming that the machine starts with its program counter equal to 00:

a. Translate the instructions that would be executed into English.

b. What value will be in the memory cell at address 45 when the machine stops?

c. What value will be in the program counter when the machine stops?

8. Suppose the memory cells at addresses F0 through FD in the machine described in Appendix B contain the following (hexadecimal) values:

Address	Contents
F0	20
F1	00
F2	21
F3	01
F4	23
F5	05
F6	B3
F7	FC
F8	50
F9	01
FA	B0
FB	F6
FC	C0
FD	00

If we started the machine with its program counter equal to F0, what would be the value in register R0 when the machine finally executes the halt instruction at location FC?

9. If the machine in Appendix B executes an instruction every microsecond (a millionth of a second), how long will it take to complete the program in problem 8?

10. Suppose the memory cells at addresses 00 through 05 in the machine described in Appendix B contained the following (hexadecimal) values:

Address	Contents
00	25
01	B0
02	35
03	04
04	C0
05	00

If we started the machine with its program counter equal to 00, when would the machine halt?

11. In each of the following cases, write a short program in the machine language described in Appendix B to perform the requested activities. Assume that each of your programs will be placed in memory starting at address 00.

a. Move the value at memory location 8D to memory location B3.

b. Interchange the values stored at memory locations 8D and B3.

c. If the value stored in memory location 45 is 00, then place the value CC in memory location 88; otherwise, put the value DD in memory location 88.

12. A popular game among computer hobbyists is core wars—a variation of battleship. (The term *core* originates from an early memory technology in which 0s and 1s were represented as mag-

netic fields in little rings of magnetic material.) The game is played between two opposing programs, each stored in different locations of the same computer's memory. The computer is assumed to alternate between the two programs, executing an instruction from one followed by an instruction from the other. The goal of each program is to destroy the other by writing extraneous data on top of it; however, neither program knows the location of the other.

a. Write a program in the language of Appendix B that approaches the game in a defensive manner by being as small as possible.

b. Write a program in the language of Appendix B that tries to avoid any attacks from the opposing program by moving to different locations. More precisely, write your program to start at location 00, copy itself to location 70, and then jump to this new copy.

c. Extend the program in part b to continue relocating to new memory locations. In particular, make your program move to location 70, then to E0 (70 + 70), then to 60 (70 + 70 + 70), etc.

*13. Suppose the following instructions and input values for truck weight, total weight, shipping cost, and shipping charge were given to a data-driven machine. Identify those instructions that will be executed and the order of this execution if the desired output is profit per pound. What is the desired output were total profit?

a. Divide shipping charge by load weight giving charge per pound.

b. divide load weight by shipping cost giving cost per pound.

c. Subtract shipping cost from shipping charge giving total profit.

d. Subtract truck weight from total weight giving load weight.

e. Subtract cost per pound from charge per pound giving profit per pound.

*14. Reanswer problem 13 assuming that the machine is a demand-driven one rather than a data-driven one.

*15. Suppose the registers R4 and R5 in the machine described in Appendix B contain the hexadecimal values 3C and C8, respectively. What would be left in register R0 after executing each of the following instructions:

a. 5045   b. 6045   c. 7045
d. 8045   e. 9045

*16. Using the machine language described in Appendix B, write programs to perform each of the following tasks:

a. Copy the value stored in memory location 66 into memory location BB.

b. Change the least significant 4 bits in the memory cell at location 34 to 0s while leaving the other bits undisturbed.

c. Copy the least significant 4 bits from memory location A5 into the least significant 4 bits of location A6 while leaving the other bits at location A6 undisturbed.

d. Copy the least significant 4 bits from memory location A5 into the most significant 4 bits of A5. (Thus, the first 4 bits in A5 will be the same as the last 4 bits.)

*17. Perform the indicated operations:

a.	111000 AND 101001		b.	000100 AND 101010
c.	000100 AND 010101		d.	111011 AND 110101
e.	111000 OR 101001		f.	000100 OR 101010
g.	000100 OR 010101		h.	111011 OR 110101
i.	111000 XOR 101001		j.	000100 XOR 101010
k.	000100 XOR 010101		l.	111011 XOR 110101

*18. Identify both the mask and the logical operation needed to accomplish each of the following objectives:

a. Put 0s in the middle 4 bits of an 8-bit pattern without disturbing the other bits.

b. Complement a pattern of 8 bits.

c. Complement the most significant bit of an 8-bit pattern without changing the other bits.

d. Put a 1 in the most significant bit of an 8-bit pattern without disturbing the other bits.

e. Put 1s in all but the most significant bit of an 8-bit pattern without disturbing the most significant bit.

*19. Identify a logical operation (along with a corresponding mask) that, when applied to an input string of 8 bits will produce an output string of all 0s if and only if the input string is 10000001.

*20. Describe a sequence of logical operations (along with their corresponding masks) that, when applied to an input string of 8 bits, will produce an output byte of all 0s if the input string both begins and ends with 1s. Otherwise, the output should contain at least one 1.

*21. What would be the result of performing a 4-bit left circular shift on the following bit patterns:
a. 10101   b. 11110000   c. 001
d. 101000   e. 00001

*22. What would be the result of performing a one-bit right circular shift on the following bytes represented in hexadecimal notation (give your answers in hexadecimal notation):
a. 3F   b. 0D   c. FF   d. 77

*23. List the symbols +, (, [, m, 5, $, and G in the "alphabetical" order they inherit by means of being coded in ASCII.

*24. Could a printer, printing 40 characters per second, keep up with a string of ASCII characters (each with a parity bit) arriving serially at the rate of 300 bps? What about 1200 bps?

*25. Suppose a person is typing 30 words per minute at a terminal keyboard. (A word is considered to be five characters.) If a machine executes one instruction every 3 microseconds (millionths of a second), how many instructions would the machine execute during the time between the typing of two consecutive characters?

*26. How many bits per second must a terminal transmit to keep up with a typist typing 30 words per minute? (Assume each character is coded in ASCII along with a parity bit and each word consists of five characters.)

*27. A communication system capable of transmitting any sequence of eight different states at the rate of at most 300 states per second could be used to transfer information at what rate in bps?

*28. Suppose the machine described in Appendix B communicates with a printer using the technique of memory mapped I/O. Suppose also that address FF is used to send characters to the printer and address FE is used to receive information about the printer's status. In particular, suppose the least significant bit at the address FE indicates whether or not the printer is ready to receive another character (with a 0 indicating "not ready" and a 1 indicating "ready"). Starting at address 00, write a machine language routine that will wait until the printer is ready for another character and then send the character represented by the bit pattern in register R5 to the printer.

Problems for the Programmer

1. Even though the programming language you may know may not be a machine-level language, does it still use a structure similar to the op-code/operand system found in machine languages? That is, does it use a few basic statement forms, identified perhaps by a key word, that have numerous variations depending on the specifics of the rest of the statement?

2. Which statements in your language are straightforward applications of the traditional machine language operations discussed in this chapter? Which are not?

3. Pick a simple statement in a programming language you know and translated it into the machine language of this chapter.

4. What notation does your programming language use to indicate arithmetic addition? What determines whether this addition will ultimately be performed by the machine's floating-point instruction or by its integer instruction?

5. Write a program to simulate the machine in Appendix B.

2 Part Two

The Human/Machine Interface

Chapter 3   Operating Systems

Chapter 4   Algorithms

Chapter 5   Programming Languages

Chapter 6   Software Engineering

Part Two Preview
The Human/Machine Interface

In Part One we discussed the major components from which a computer is constructed. These components, which are tangible, are classified as hardware. In contrast, the programs that the hardware executes are intangible and are classified as software. In Part Two we turn our attention to the topics associated with software. The issues discussed here are perhaps the most fundamental topics within a computer science curriculum. After all, it is through software that machines are told what to do. And consequently, the issues of development, communication, and understanding of software are the cornerstones of the human/machine interface.

In Chapter 3 we begin our study of software and the role the software plays in human/machine communication by investigating the activities of a machine's operating system, which is the program that begins executing when the machine is first turned on (through a process known as bootstrapping) and establishes the context through which the machine communicates with the outside world. In particular, the operating system continually monitors the various peripheral devices attached to the machine and responds to any input from these devices according to its programmed logic. In this way, the operating system embellishes the machine with the ability to interact with its environment.

In addition to providing a communication interface between the machine and its environment, most operating systems encompass a number of prewritten routines, some of which are structured as independent programs while others are program segments that can be incorporated into programs being written by the machine's users. By means of these routines, a user of a machine can store information in bulk storage, print data at a printer, or cause words to be spoken by a voice synthesizer without acquiring the technical skills that might otherwise be required. Another important task of an operating system is to coordinate all requests for the machine's resources. (Imagine, for example, the appearance of the printed output that would result from two users engaging a printer at the same time.) The techniques for handling this coordinating responsibility constitute a major subject in the study of operating systems and are introduced in the latter part of Chapter 3.

A very important concept introduced in Chapter 3 is that of a virtual feature, which is nothing more than an illusory feature created by software rather than a feature directly implemented in the hardware. For example, an operating system can create the illusion of a machine that can understand commands in English while in reality the machine only "understands" its machine language. Another prominent example is the result of time-sharing (rapidly shifting a single machine's attention from one program to another), a technique by which an operating system creates the illusion of several machines, each running a separate program. Thus, we speak of the operating system creating several virtual machines from a single real machine.

In Chapter 4 we study the concept of an algorithm (which is essentially a step-by-step process), with our emphasis being on the techniques of algorithm development and the role of methodologies. We distinguish between the process of discovering an algorithm and expressing it once discovered. This distinction is important when considering the role of design methodologies. In particular, the expression of an algorithm once formulated in one's mind is more conducive to the application of rules than is the more creative process of discovering the algorithm in the first place. This is not to·say that the discovery phase cannot be assisted through the use of design methodologies but rather that a significant amount of research remains to be done on the subject.

Another important topic discussed in Chapter 4 is the control of repetitive processes within an algorithm. One such process is represented by a loop structure in which the steps involved are executed in a circular fashion until a certain condition is met (as in "continue to make tuition payments until your account is zero"). In contrast are recursive structures in which the process being repeated is effectively contained within itself in a manner reminiscent of the way an image of yourself looking at yourself can be produced by two opposite mirrors. In either case, dealing with the subtleties of controlling the repetition can easily become more complex than the design of the process being repeated.

In Chapter 5 we consider the problem of programming a machine. We learn that there are several approaches to this problem. One is based on the traditional procedural paradigm in which the programmer develops a sequence of instructions that tells the machine what to do. Another approach is the declarative paradigm in which the machine is given a general-purpose problem-solving algorithm in advance, and hence the task of applying the machine to a particular problem is that of describing the problem to the machine. Still another approach is the object-oriented paradigm in which the programmer's task is that of identifying and simulating those components pertinent to the problem's solution.

These various approaches to the programming process make it difficult to classify all programming languages on the traditional linear scale of first-generation languages, second-generation languages, etc. Our approach, then, is to investigate the historical development of programming languages. From this perspective, we see the development of procedural languages as the central theme with the other paradigms branching off as they are discovered and pursued.

As just indicated, the dominant paradigm in the development of programming languages is the procedural one, and thus we take the time in Chapter 5 to investigate the features found in most of the traditional third-generation procedural languages. In most of these cases, programs tend to consist of two parts: the declaration part, where the data manipulated by the algorithm is described, and the procedural part, where the algorithmic process is described.

Within the declaration part, descriptive names are usually associated with the data units together with the definition of the type and structure of the data. The type of a data unit refers to the manner in which the bit pattern representing the data in the machine should be interpreted. For example, a pattern might be interpreted as a numeric value stored in an integer or floating-point format (integer or real type), a string of characters stored in ASCII (character type), or as the numeric address of another location in memory (pointer type). The structure of a unit of data refers to the data's organization. That is, it may consist of a single element, a list of elements, or an array consisting of rows and columns.

The description of an algorithmic process within the procedural part requires the use of control statements in addition to statements that directly apply to the task at hand. Indeed, a major part of Chapter 5 is devoted to the features in high-level procedural languages for expressing algorithm control structures. Control statements are divided into two classes: the statement-level control statements that implement their control in terms of statements or short sequences of statements and the unit-level control statements used to control the execution of entire program units known as subprograms.

Subprograms consist of isolated program segments that can be effectively inserted in other programs or program segments when needed. We say "effectively inserted" because a subprogram is not physically placed in the location where it is needed but rather is executed as though it were. That is, if an activity performed by a subprogram is required in a program, the programmer merely inserts a single control statement that requests the execution of the subprogram at that point. When the program is ultimately run, this statement will cause the control of execution to be transferred to the subprogram and then returned to continue with the original program when the subprogram has completed.

The importance of subprograms is emphasized in Chapter 6 in the discussion of software engineering. The point is that the use of subprograms allows the more detailed or technical parts of an algorithm to be isolated from the main flow of the program. A major advantage of this approach is that the program can be expressed in a modular fashion (that is, in individual units, each of which performs a distinct part of the overall task).

The importance of expressing a program, or even a complete software system, in a modular fashion is best appreciated by considering the software life cycle (also presented in Chapter 6), which points out that once a program is developed, it enters a pattern of being repeatedly used and modified. It is in this modification process that the benefits of a modular design become increasingly pronounced. Indeed, to modify a program, it is first necessary to understand the program's relevant activities. Isolating the various activities into modules according to function allows one's attention to be more easily focused on the portion of the program pertinent to the modification than would be possible without the modular approach.

In summary, Part Two deals with the topics of algorithm design and programming. These subjects have attracted computer scientists for some time, with the goal being the development of a human/machine interface that not only accommodates but also assists humans in the art of problem solving.

3 Operating Systems

3–1 **Functions of Operating Systems**
3–2 **Virtual Characteristics**
3–3 **The Evolution of Operating Systems**
      Batch Processing
      Interactive Processing
      Multiuser Systems
3–4 **Operating System Architecture** (optional)
      Major Operating System Components
      Utility Software
3–5 **Rudiments of Time-Sharing** (optional)
      Interrupt Handling
      Time-Sharing
3–6 **Critical Regions and Deadlock** (optional)
      Coordinating the Use of Resources
      Critical Regions
      Deadlock
3–7 **Getting It Started** (optional)
      Memory Technology
      The Bootstrap Process

The previous chapters have largely been devoted to the equipment making up a computer system. The collection of all such tangible equipment, including the computer itself, printer paper, printers, magnetic tape, disk packs, etc., is classified as *hardware.* Hardware alone is of little use to anyone since without programs to control it, the equipment does little more than occupy space. Consequently, the intangible programs called *software* are just as important to a computer installation as is the hardware.

This chapter discusses a major software unit called the operating system, including its role in a variety of computer systems, some of the problems involved, and a look at how some of these problems might be resolved.

3–1 Functions of Operating Systems

Let us first say a few words about the terminology that we will be using in relation to software. A program is the intangible logic, normally expressed as a sequence of instructions, that a machine follows to perform a task. Although we recognize that it is the hardware that actually performs the task, it is common to give credit to the controlling software in our terminology. For example, we may say that a program sorts a list of names, whereas in reality it is the machine that actually sorts the list by executing the program.

With this understanding in mind, we turn our attention to operating systems and what they do. Suppose that you are sitting at a terminal connected to a computer. How do you get the computer to do something for you? The answer is that a program (or, more accurately, one of a collection of programs) called the *operating system* is already being executed by the computer. This program accepts input from the terminal and compares the character pattern received with the patterns constituting the commands that it was designed to obey. Such a command might be to read a program from disk to memory and execute it or perhaps to copy some information in memory to a disk so that it can be saved for future use. If the operating system finds that the characters received constitute a legal command, it performs the requested action. Otherwise, it sends an appropriate message such as "ILLEGAL COMMAND" to the CRT screen at the terminal and continues to watch the keyboard for other commands.

An operating system therefore contains the logical procedures that define how the computer is to interact with the outside world. In most cases this interaction takes place with a person called the user, although it may be with other controlling intelligence such as another computer. How elaborate the interaction is depends on the requirements of the computer system, but the following features are common to many operating systems:

1. **Control Access to the Machine.** If numerous terminals are connected to the machine or if devices can be connected via the telephone, somehow use of the machine must be reserved for approved personnel and denied to others. A typical solution is to provide the operating system with access codes, or passwords, known only by the approved personnel and to design the operating system to request and verify these codes before performing any tasks for the would-be user.

2. **Maintain Accounting Data.** It is often necessary to have a record of the machine's use over a period of time for billing purposes or for evaluating the machine's performance. Such records might include who used the machine and for how long and what features of the machine were used. Such records are commonly maintained by the operating system and made available to management personnel on a regular basis or on special request.

3. **Control Data and Its Access.** Here we consider data in its broad sense, including both what would normally be considered data and programs. (Remember that what is considered data at one stage may be a program at another.) Each such

item resides in the computer system as a collection of records called a file and is normally held in bulk storage from which it can be copied into main memory and used. The operating system is responsible for taking care of this manipulation of files. All access to data or execution of programs is handled by the operating system following the appropriate request from the user. To do this the operating system keeps a record of what files are stored, where in bulk storage they are stored, and (in systems used by several people) who should be allowed access to which files.

4.   **Provide for Efficient Device Access.** A great variety of peripheral devices can be attached to a computer, and you can imagine that developing programs to communicate with many of them would require a major programming effort. Most operating systems include those routines needed to conveniently use the peripheral devices attached to the machine. Thus, if within our own program we need to communicate with a peripheral device, we can use the prewritten operating system routines for this rather than develop our own. As an example, let us see how this technique simplifies the use of bulk storage devices. We learned in Chapter 2 that although our data may conveniently be divided into units called logical records, it is best to store it in blocks called physical records whose size is determined by the properties of the bulk storage device. If we write our own routines to store and retrieve data, we must therefore concern ourselves with blocking and unblocking data. On the other hand, if we use the prewritten operating system routines, these details will be handled for us so we can develop our own program entirely in terms of logical records. This is because as our program asks the operating system to store logical records on the device, the records are actually held until an appropriate physical record size is obtained and then written as a single block on the device. Conversely, if our program requests the retrieval of a logical record, the operating system routines—knowing how the records were blocked originally—are able to retrieve the correct physical record, unblock it, and return the desired logical record. By using these prewritten routines, we need never be concerned with the details of the physical records being used.

5.   **Manage Resources.** The resources of a computer system include such things as memory area, peripheral devices, and programs. Section 3-2 explains how some operating systems allow several people to use the same machine at the same time. When this is being done, it is important to keep track of which devices, areas of memory, and programs are being used and by whom. For example, if two users were allowed to use the same printer at the same time, their outputs would be intertwined and worthless to both. Even when only one person is using a machine, such conflicts are possible since because of parallel processing techniques, more than a single action may be taking place at a given time. Most

operating systems are given the responsibility of resource management so that such conflicts will not occur.

Our discussion of operating system functions thus far has concentrated on a system's role in relation to the coordination of machine activities. Another function of operating systems is found on a completely different level in the form of the systems' significant contribution toward the standardization of the human/machine interface across the entire computer industry. For example, even though two machines might be significantly different in terms of their internal design and construction, their operating systems can be constructed so that their dialogues with a user are essentially the same. Thus, if a person is trained to communicate with one piece of equipment through the use of a universal operating system, that training can be applied to other equipment as well. Such standardization is common in other industries. For example, the accelerator and the brake on most cars are operated with the right foot, and the clutch (if there is one) is operated with the left foot.

The first real application of this standardizing effect was implemented by IBM with the System/360 series of machines introduced in the 1960s. This series consisted of a variety of machines ranging from designs for small-business applications to large machines for businesses with significant needs. These machines were all supplied with operating systems that made them communicate with their environments in essentially the same manner. Thus, as a business grew, it could change to a larger machine in the 360 series without major reprogramming and retraining efforts.

Today such uniformity bridges the boundaries between the equipment of different manufacturers. The operating system UNIX (developed at Bell Laboratories) is now available on numerous machines including both minicomputers and microcomputers. Even among the avalanche of microcomputers on the market today, one finds the human/machine interface often standardized through the use of similar operating systems. One example is MS-DOS (developed by Microsoft Corporation), which has gained popularity because of its adoption by IBM for use in its line of personal computers. Another example, both in the past as well as today, is the CP/M system (from Digital Research), which over the years has supplied a uniform interface to more than 3000 different hardware configurations.

Questions/Exercises

1. Describe an analogy to the distinction between hardware and software in the following settings:
   a. record players   b. television   c. novels
2. Which of the five features of an operating system presented in the text would be least prominent in a microcomputer system?
3. How would you expect an operating system to respond if you typed "PLEASE DELETE THE FILE I ENTERED YESTERDAY" at a terminal?

3–2 **Virtual Characteristics**

The common thread running throughout Section 3-1 is that the role of the operating system is to make the machine more compatible with its environment. Although the actual hardware responds only to its machine language instructions and "thinks" in terms of bits, with the addition of an operating system the machine is able to respond intelligently to our requests such as to retrieve and execute programs stored in bulk storage, to make copies of files, or to list the names of the files currently in bulk storage.

Thus, the operating system significantly alters the machine's characteristics so that when using such a system, one gets the illusion of dealing with a different and usually more application-oriented piece of equipment than is actually present. In particular, through the operating system the machine is given the ability to understand commands stated in a human-compatible form, whereas the hardware alone only "understands" the machine language. By restricting unauthorized access to data in bulk storage, the operating system creates the illusion of containing only a single user's data, whereas in reality the machine's bulk storage might contain data belonging to a multitude of users. Through its I/O routines, the operating system creates the illusion of data being stored in units of logical records, whereas the data is actually stored in physical blocks compatible with the particular storage device being used.

We use the term *virtual* to refer to a characteristic whose existence is simulated with software rather than actually existing within hardware (Figure 3-1). Thus, the illusionary, more application-oriented machine created by an operating system is called a virtual machine. In general, a machine with the same characteristics could be constructed entirely by hardware, although the result would be a more rigid, more expensive, and less practical device than its virtual counterpart.

Figure 3-1 Virtual versus real characteristics

Virtual Characteristics	Real Characteristics
Data stored in logical blocks	Data stored in physical blocks
Presence of only data pertinent to a single user	Presence of data belonging to all users
Ability to "understand" commands in human-compatible language	Ability to "understand" only machine language
Same internal characteristics as other machines	Significantly different internal characteristics from other machines

The term *virtual* is important enough for us to consider the following analogy. Consider a family-owned-and-operated mail-order business that operates out of a converted garage where two family members fill each day's orders. The business obtains orders by running large, impressive magazine advertisements. It is incorporated, has its own letterhead, and handles all its sales through the mail. With this arrangement, a customer's image of the business is likely to be quite different from reality. The advertisements, letterheads, etc., are designed to create an image (a virtual business) for the customer consisting of a large warehouse, various departments, and numerous employees. The fact that this virtual business is not the same as the actual one is not important so long as the system continues to function like the virtual business from the customer's point of view. If, however, a customer is trying to resolve a problem of an incorrectly filled order, it might well be advantageous to know more about the actual business structure involved.

Such is the case with computer systems. The operating system creates the illusion of a machine (a virtual machine) that communicates more conveniently with its environment than does the actual hardware and relieves the user from the burden of understanding the technical details of the hardware activities. The fact that this illusion does not accurately reflect the true internal characteristics of the machine is an asset so long as the virtual machine is faithfully simulated. With the correct operating system, a person can use a computer without any knowledge of the internal functions. On the other hand, just as when dealing with the above business, an understanding of the activities behind the scene can often increase one's ability to use the system efficiently or to resolve problems that might occur.

Questions/Exercises

1. Describe an analogy (other than the mail-order business in the text) of a virtual entity.
2. In what ways is the distinction between virtual and real characteristics important to the computer user?
3. Construct a table contrasting the virtual and real characteristics of the mail-order business described in this chapter.

3–3 The Evolution of Operating Systems

The algorithmic machines of the 1940s and 1950s were not extremely flexible or efficient. The execution of a program required significant preparation of the equipment in terms of mounting tapes, placing punched cards in the card reader, setting switches, etc. Thus, each program (also called a job) was handled as an isolated entity. In situations where several programmers were required to share the same machine, sign-up sheets on which the various users could reserve the machine for particular blocks of time were common. During the time period allocated to a programmer, the machine was totally under that programmer's control. The session usually began with program setup, followed by short periods of program execution, and was often completed in a hurried effort to do just one more thing ("It will take only a minute") while the next programmer was impatiently starting to set up.

Batch Processing

Operating systems were spawned as systems for simplifying program setup and for streamlining the overall process of transition between programs. One early development in this direction was the separation of programmers and equipment to eliminate the physical transition of people in and out of the computer room. For this purpose a computer operator was hired to perform the actual operation of the machine. Anyone wanting a program run was required to submit it (along with any required data and special directions about the program's requirements) to the operator and return later for the results. The operator in turn would load these materials into the machine's bulk storage where the operating system could access it for execution. This was the beginning of **batch processing**, which refers to the execution of jobs by first collecting them and their associated data in a single batch in bulk storage and then executing them independent of the user's control.

To further streamline the operation, operating systems were designed to allow the operator to insert jobs into bulk storage as they were submitted. Thus, several jobs could be waiting in bulk storage at any one time. Each time the job being executed terminated, the operating system merely selected another job from bulk storage according to some selection process and started it. Such a process resulted in a job storage system called a **job queue** in which jobs waited before being executed (Figure 3-2).

A queue is a collection of objects (in our case jobs) ordered in a **first-in-first-out (FIFO)** fashion. That is, the objects are removed from the queue in the order in

Figure 3-2 Batch processing

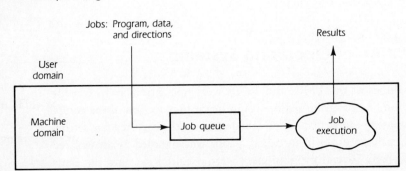

which they arrived. (The word *queue* is used in some parts of the world in place of the word *line,* which is common in America. In England, for example, people queue up at a bus stop and form a queue to buy theater tickets.) Most job queues do not rigorously follow the FIFO structure (and thus the term *queue* is a misnomer in the literal sense) since most operating systems provide for consideration of job priorities. As a result, it is possible for a job waiting in the job queue to be bumped by a higher priority job.

In early batch processing systems, any instructions pertaining to the requirements of a program being submitted for execution had to be communicated to the operator since the person making the request would not be present when the program ran. However, with a job queue, the time at which the program would actually be run was determined by the operating system; this, in turn, complicated the operator's task of associating instructions with jobs. Thus, a coding system, called a ***job control language (JCL)***, was designed by which these special instructions could be stored with the job in the queue. When the job was finally selected for execution, the operating system would print these instructions at a printer where they could be read and followed by the operator.

The development of job control languages meant that a person-to-person meeting between the operator and user was no longer necessary. Soon the users were provided with input devices such as card readers by which they could submit their jobs and instructions directly into the job queue rather than indirectly through the operator. As the sophistication of operating systems developed, more and more of these instructions could be obeyed by the operating system without the aid of the operator. Today job control languages are used more for sending instructions to the operating system than to the computer operator.

Interactive Processing

The major drawback to a batch processing system is that the program and its data cannot be altered once they are in the job queue. This system is acceptable for such applications as processing payroll or performing scientific calculations since in these cases, all the data and decisions about how it is to be manipulated are made before the execution of the program. On the other hand, applications exist in which the data that the program is to manipulate is not available until the program is running and thus cannot be submitted with the program into the job queue. A major example consists of data retrieval and update applications such as a reservation system where the program must interact with a person by means of a terminal to report vacancies or record reservations as they occur. Another example is the process of program development where it is convenient to stop, modify, and restart new programs to correct errors. In such cases it is inherent in the application that the computer user be allowed to interact with the machine during program execution.

Figure 3-3 Interactive processing

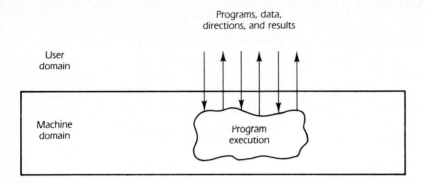

To accommodate these needs, new operating systems were developed to provide *interactive processing* rather than batch processing (Figure 3-3). These systems were designed to carry on a dialogue with the user as described at the beginning of Section 3-2 and to allow user access to the machine (through terminals) during program execution. Instead of requests to the system being placed in a queue for later attention, they were acted on immediately, and the result or an appropriate error message was returned to the requester in a conversational fashion.

Interactive processing is closely associated with another concept called *real-time processing*, which refers to the requirement that the software coordinate its activities with those of its environment. Such requirements do not surface in relation to batch processing since the only constraint is that the job be completed without an unreasonable delay. In contrast, when controlling the flight of an aircraft, it is not sufficient merely to raise and lower the landing gear; major consideration must be given to the actual (or real) time frame in which this action is performed. Likewise, a reservation system must respond to the agent requesting service in a reasonable amount of time or the system becomes ineffective. Today, interactive real-time systems dominate the scene, with batch processing mainly relegated for processing large managerial record-keeping projects.

Multiuser Systems

Recall that one of the major issues in the origins of batch processing systems was the need to coordinate the requirements of several users competing for the same machine. If an interactive system is to be used in a similar environment, it too must be able to coordinate the needs of several users. Batch processing achieved this coordination by essentially postponing requested activities (by placing them in the job queue) until time was available. In an interactive environment, requests from the various users must be acted upon at the time of the request. One solution would be to allow only one user to make requests at a time, although this is reminiscent of the old sign-up sheets that proved awkward years ago.

Instead, the development of interactive operating systems for large multiuser machines was accomplished by the development of *time-sharing*, which we discuss later in more detail. For now we simply note that time-sharing is a technique by which the attention of the machine alternates among the various tasks being performed in such a way that the machine appears to be performing the tasks at the same time. In particular, the time available is divided into short periods called time slices that are awarded to the various tasks in an alternating fashion. Thus, using time-sharing techniques, interactive operating systems appear to serve users at different terminals at the same time.

The reason time-sharing was not a viable solution to the competition among users of the early machines is largely that the machines of that period were not capable of the execution speeds and storage capacities required for multiuser applications. The irony is that now that technology has provided equipment capable of efficient multiuser applications, it has also removed much of the need for such systems. The price and size of equipment have decreased to the point that competition among users can often be resolved by merely supplying each user with a different machine running its own single-user interactive operating system.

In a sense, the irony is twofold. As more and more users acquire their own machines there seems to be more and more desire to link the machines for the exchange of information. Thus, coupled computer systems called *networks* are becoming extremely popular. Along with this popularity is the growing need for operating systems to coordinate the activities of networks, and this has generated new research directions in the field of operating systems.

Today, the state of the art is essentially what might be called a network of operating systems rather than an operating system for the network. That is, networks are generally constructed of machines, each of which operates under its own operating system that has been patched to accommodate the network communication protocol. The goal, on the other hand, is a truly distributed operating system—a single operating system that resides networkwide.

Numerous network configurations are in use today, and the actual arrangement used can affect the problems in the design of an operating system. One configuration is the ring structure (Figure 3-4). Another is a system in which each computer has a direct path to each of the others, and still another uses one machine as the hub through which all other machines in the network must communicate. Which structure is applicable in a given situation depends largely on logistics and cost considerations.

We have chosen to represent the closed ring since it readily suggests some problems that must be considered in developing an operating system for use within the network. These problems center around the transferring of messages among the

Figure 3-4 A computer network

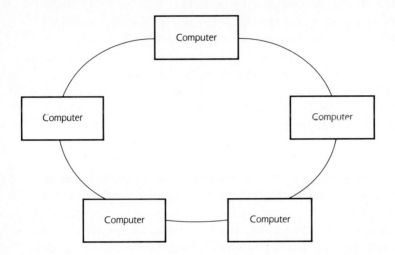

machines in the network. For example, if a message is to be sent to another machine in the system, in which direction should it be directed? How active should the operating system at one machine become in transferring a message that is "just passing through" on its way to another machine? How can an operating system handle messages coming from both directions at once, or must the software be designed to avoid this situation altogether? How can a message be protected against eavesdropping of machines at locations other than its destination? Such concerns constitute a major extension of operating system functions and are the subject of much experimentation and debate.

It is important to note that a system representing the latest advances in the evolution of operating systems need not be the best in any given case. Batch processing, for example, remains an efficient way of updating records on a periodic basis from data collected between updates such as in the processing of payroll. Moreover, the use of a network introduces operating system complexities not present when the single-machine concept is used. For example, in the case of a reservation system, the use of a single machine provides a natural place for the storage of reservation data where it can be accessed by all the agents. However, when this same application is implemented in a network, the major problem of assuring that each agent has an up-to-date version of the reservation status to prevent overbookings suddenly appears.

Questions/Exercises

1. What are some examples of queues in everyday life? In each example, indicate any situations in which the strict queue structure (FIFO) is violated.
2. Which of the following activities would require real-time processing:
   a. Displaying the letters typed at the keyboard on the CRT screen.

b. Printing a sequence of mailing labels.

c. Maintaining the checking and savings account balances of a bank's customers.

3. Which of the following activities could be handled conveniently in a batch processing environment:

a. Printing mailing labels.

b. Executing a program that predicts the state of next year's economy.

c. Executing a video game.

4. In the circular network presented in the text, what are some disadvantages of restricting the transfer of messages to a single direction?

5. In the closing paragraph of this section, we alluded to the problem of maintaining a reservation system within a computer network. In particular, what problems must be overcome if a separate copy of the database is kept in each machine in the system?

3–4 **Operating System Architecture** (optional)

A productive approach to understanding and constructing any complicated system is to analyze the system in terms of its parts. This was our approach to the study of computer hardware, where we saw that a machine consists of units such as main memory, bulk storage systems, a central processing unit, and peripheral devices. Such a decomposition is viable in the case of software systems as well and is the major theme of Chapter 6. In this section we apply such a modular analysis to our study of operating systems with the goal of acquiring a better understanding of the activities of an entire system.

Our approach is to assume that a user sitting at a terminal has just requested that a program (which is stored in bulk storage) be executed. With this as our starting point, we will follow the activities of a simplified yet representative operating system as it obeys the request. We further assume that the system is an interactive time-sharing one.

Major Operating System Components

The first unit we should introduce is the ***command processor*** since this part of the operating system handles the dialogue with the user. The command processor "watches" the terminals attached to the machine and interprets the commands typed as mentioned earlier in this chapter. Thus, this unit gives the system much of its personality by establishing the communication format to which any user of the system must conform.

Once the command processor has determined that the command typed at the terminal is valid and discovered that it is a request for the execution of a program, it resorts to the assistance of the ***scheduler.*** As the name suggests, the scheduler arranges for the execution of the program. In a batch processing environment, this would involve placing the program in the job queue according to its priority. In an interactive time-sharing environment, the scheduler's job is to place the requested program within the collection of other activities currently sharing time.

Before this is done, the scheduler must seek the services of two other units within the operating system. One is the *file manager*, the unit that maintains the records pertaining to the information stored in bulk storage. This unit is required by the scheduler for accessing the requested program.

The file manager is also in charge of protecting files in bulk storage against unauthorized access. In particular, if the file manager discovers that the user should not be allowed to execute the requested program, it reports to the scheduler, which in turn reports the problem back to the command processor instead of scheduling the program for execution. (In this case the command processor would properly chastise the user for making an unauthorized request.)

Assuming all goes well with the file manager, the scheduler must also be assisted by the *resource allocator*, which coordinates the assignment of resources within the computer system. If the activity being scheduled requires a resource not currently available, the resource allocator reports the situation to the scheduler. Otherwise, the required resources are allocated to the new activity and the activity, which in our case is the running of a program, is scheduled for execution. (We have stretched the facts here to the point that a word of caution is in order. Resource allocation might be required at numerous times during the process of program scheduling and execution. For example, the file manager might need to acquire additional disk storage space, or a program already in the scheduled pool might return to the resource allocator with requests for the use of additional peripheral devices.)

The final step of executing the program is handled by the operating system unit called the *dispatcher.* This unit, in a time-sharing system, coordinates the switching of the machine's attention among the various activities scheduled for execution. We discuss the function of the dispatcher in more detail in the next section. For now we merely note that the dispatcher oversees the actual execution of the requested program (along with the others scheduled for execution) and reports back to the scheduler when the program is completed. The scheduler is then able to inform the resource allocator that the resources used by the program are no longer needed and to report the completion of the program to the command processor, which in turn can notify the user.

Our choice of approaching the structure of an operating system from the viewpoint of a machine user was not completely arbitrary. Such a point of view is also used to produce the popular onion-skin diagram of an operating system's architecture, as shown in Figure 3-5. The purpose behind the diagram is to reflect the levels of activities taking place within the system. We envision the computer users on the outside (of the onion). From there, all that is visible is the outer layer consisting of

Figure 3-5 An onion-skin diagram of an operating system

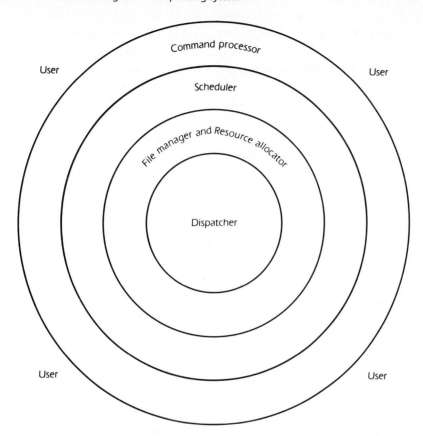

the command processor. The command processor in turn communicates with the scheduler, represented by the next inner layer of the onion. Within this layer are the file manager and resource allocator. Finally, deep inside the system is the dispatcher quietly overseeing the execution of the requested activities and reporting the results back to the layers surrounding it.

Utility Software

Earlier we suggested that an operating system consisted of more than one program. To a large extent this was meant to reflect the fact that the various layers just presented are essentially different programs combined into a coordinated system. On the other hand, today's operating systems do contain (or are accompanied by) a variety of other programs and partial programs called *utility software* (or application software). This utility software is provided to reduce the user's programming burden by supplying prewritten routines for performing often-required chores.

An example of utility software normally associated with an operating system consists of a collection of programs for manipulating files. Within this collection one commonly finds programs for copying, deleting, merging, and sorting files, which in an interactive system can be scheduled for execution by typing the appropriate command along with the name of the file or files on which to operate.

Paramount among the file maintenance programs is the *editor*, which provides an interactive way of creating and modifying files by means of a terminal. Historically, editors were initially designed as a programming tool and provided a convenient means by which programs, in an appropriately coded form, could be typed at the keyboard of a terminal, saved by the operating system for execution, and later retrieved at the terminal for modification.

Because of their classification as merely programming tools, early editors were developed with only rudimentary editing features such as the ability to delete unwanted lines or to insert new lines. Perhaps the most powerful feature of these early editors was their ability to search a document for the occurrence of a designated character pattern and possibly change those occurrences to another pattern.

The state of the art now encompasses the design of elaborate editors, known as word processors, that provide powerful features including automatic page formatting, the ability to exchange large blocks of text within a document, and the insertion of one document within another. The power of these processors centers around the flexibility of the soft-copy CRT for modifying the document before producing the final paper copy. After all, replacing characters or reformatting a paragraph because a phrase was removed is much more efficient on a CRT screen than it is on a hard-copy device. Today it is not uncommon to find interactive operating systems that provide a variety of editors to fit various needs.

In many applications easy access to utility software is the most important feature of and operating system, and many interactive systems are designed with this in mind. One result of this emphasis is the concept of viewing utility programs as building blocks from which larger programs (or more accurately program sequences) can be constructed. For example, in addition to providing separate utility programs to perform such tasks as searching documents for certain syntactic forms (such as underscored or boldfaced words), sorting lists, and printing files, an operating system might well provide a means by which utilities can be strung together to produce the appearance of one large program that will print an index for a document by locating the underscored words, sorting these words, and then printing them along with their corresponding page numbers. The process of stringing together utility programs is often called piping, which should not be confused with the term *pipelining* in Chapter 2 in reference to the technique of fetching instructions in advance.

The utility routines just discussed are stand-alone programs in the sense that they are ready to execute with no additional programming required by the user. Another class of utility software consists of partial routines for inclusion in user-written programs. An example of such software is the collection of routines for controlling peripheral devices. In addition, many installations provide specialized routines for frequently needed calculations, including routines for statistical analysis, graphics applications, and economic forecasting. Such routines are commonly provided in a file called a *library* and are inserted into (or more accurately linked to) the user program by another stand-alone utility program called the linker. We discuss this process in more detail in the following chapters.

Questions/Exercises

1. List the components of an interactive time-sharing operating system. Summarize the role of each component with a short phrase.
2. Draw an onion-skin diagram of the mail-order business described in Section 3-2.
3. From an editor's point of view, why is it convenient to have the computer's program divided into cells of byte sizes?
4. To keep up with user files and utility software the operating system must keep records in files of its own. Why should these files be stored on disk instead of on tape?
5. What is the difference between user-written programs and utility programs provided by the operating system?

3–5 Rudiments of Time-Sharing (optional)

In Section 3-4 we indicated that the illusion of several activities occurring at the same time within a single machine is created by the dispatcher through the technique of time-sharing, but we avoided a discussion of how such a process was actually accomplished. In this section we investigate the rudiments of this technique. First, however, we need to understand the hardware *interrupt* feature.

Interrupt Handling

If you are interrupted while performing a task, you normally stop what you were doing, record in some manner where you were, take care of the interrupting entity, and later return to the original task. Interrupts in computers provide for a similar process to occur in relation to the execution of a program. When an interrupt signal occurs within the computer system, it causes the CPU to stop executing the current program, save its position in the program, and then start executing another program located elsewhere in memory. Let us take a closer look at the last two steps in this process.

First note that when you are interrupted while reading a book, your place in the book consists not only of the current page number but also of the information (some of which may be incomplete) that you have gained to that point. Your ability to continue reading at a later time depends on your ability to remember both the page number at which to start and the accumulated information. Similarly, the CPU's position in a program consists not only of the value in the program counter but also of the information in the other registers and memory cells being used by the program. This collection of information, including the value in the program counter, is called the ***program's state*** (or its context).

To save the CPU's position in the current program therefore involves saving the program's entire state. This is typically done by copying the contents of the registers into a collection of cells in memory. Having done this, the complete state will be preserved in main memory so that the CPU can be used to process other programs and later return to the previous program where it left off by reloading the state from memory.

The last step in the interrupt process—to start executing another program—is implemented by changing the contents of the program counter to contain the location of the desired program and starting the fetch phase of the machine's cycle. The location of this other program is predetermined and is called the interrupt entry point since it is the point at which the CPU enters the software system after an interrupt has occurred. The program stored at this location is called the ***interrupt routine*** since it is the routine executed by the CPU immediately after being interrupted.

To review the interrupt process we see that upon an interrupt signal being generated, the register contents are saved in memory and the CPU starts executing the program located at the interrupt entry point.

Time-Sharing

Now that we have discussed the interrupt process, let us see how the dispatcher in an operating system can execute several programs at the same time. Suppose two programs are scheduled for execution and stored in different locations in main memory. To start one of the programs, the dispatcher merely executes a jump to that program's location in memory. However, before doing this, it starts a timer circuit that will generate an interrupt signal after a certain time has lapsed.

The first program will therefore be interrupted after a period of time, called a ***time slice***, and the interrupt routine will be started. Here the interrupt routine—a part of the dispatcher—again sets the timer and jumps to the beginning of the second program. Upon the completion of the next time slice, the second program is interrupted and control is again given to the interrupt routine within the dispatcher. Now the dispatcher, knowing where the first program's state was stored in memory, is able to reload the registers as they were when the first program was interrupted and continue that program's execution. Thus, aided by interrupt circuitry, the dispatcher can coordinate the alternating execution of several programs (Figure 3-6).

Figure 3-6 Time-sharing between program A and program B

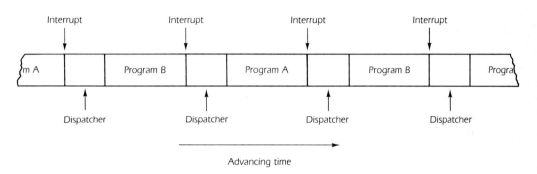

Activity of CPU:

Advancing time

The process of alternating the CPU's attention between different programs is called time-sharing. On large machines it is not uncommon to find 50 or more activities sharing the time of a single CPU. Since the length of a time slice is in the range of 10 milliseconds to 100 milliseconds, the appearance of all these programs running at the same time is produced even though only one program is actually executing at any instant. For example, if interactive programs are communicating with people through terminals, then each person has the illusion of having his or her own machine. Thus, we again find the virtual machine concept since the operating system has created numerous virtual machines (one for each terminal), while in reality only one machine exists.

It is reasonable that each virtual machine created by a time-sharing system is slower than the real machine, and when many routines are sharing time this slowness can become quite noticeable. Several techniques are available for controlling this machine sluggishness. One approach is to assign priorities to the activities in the sharing pool so that important jobs execute quickly at the expense of less important activities. This might be done by either giving the high-priority jobs longer time slices or giving them preferred treatment when selecting the activity to receive the next time slice.

Another approach to improving the performance of a sluggish time-sharing system is to remove as much of the machine's load as possible. Following this line of thought, many computer installations with a large number of interactive users have substituted microcomputers in place of terminals. Used in this way, a microcomputer constitutes what is called an intelligent terminal since a significant amount of processing can be done within itself. Competition with other users for a time slice thus occurs only when features available solely on the large machine are needed.

It is important to recognize that interactive and batch processing are contrasting ways of handling the machine/user interface. Time-sharing, on the other hand, is a technique for executing programs where several are available. Thus, time-sharing can be applied within batch processing systems as well as within interactive ones.

The technique of time-sharing often improves the total throughput of a batch processing system since the operating system can remove several jobs from the job queue and allow them to share time in hopes of obtaining a mix of jobs that will make judicious use of the machine's resources. For example, if one job requires significant use of a tape drive and another job consists mainly of manipulating data in main memory, the second job can be running during those time intervals in which the first job is waiting for data to arrive from the tape. In such cases the two jobs together will be completed in much less time than if they had been executed separately because, through time-sharing, one program is allowed to use the time that would otherwise have been wasted by the other.

Questions/Exercises

1. We mentioned in the text that each program in a time-sharing system would run slower than it would in a nonsharing environment. What about several programs as a group? More precisely, would it take less total time to run two programs by allowing them to share time or by executing the first completely and then running the second?
2. In a time-sharing system, how could high-priority programs be allowed to run faster than others?
3. Summarize the activities of a machine when handling an interruption.
4. What are the major activities involved in restarting a program for the next time slice?
5. If time slices in a time-sharing system are 50 milliseconds, how many programs can share one second?

3–6 **Critical Regions and Deadlock** (optional)

Saying that the development of a major operating system is a significant undertaking is like telling a child that the stars are big and far away. Although true, the statement oversimplifies the real complexities involved. An excellent example occurs within the design of the resource allocator, which in a time-sharing environment is charged with the job of coordinating the use of the machine's resources among the various user programs (as well as among the units of the operating system itself). It is the subtleties involved in this task that we will investigate in this section.

Coordinating the Use of Resources

We begin by noting that the resources of a machine can be placed in one of two categories: those that are shareable and those that are not. Disk units go into the first category since data for different programs can be stored on different tracks of the same disk without interference. Tape units are in the second category since, because of their sequential nature, two programs trying to use the same tape independently for data storage would greatly interfere with one another. Printers also fall into the second category since the sharing of a printer would result in rather confusing output.

The major role of the resource allocator is the prevention of such clashes over nonshareable resources. The first step in this direction is to establish the resource allocator as the central clearinghouse for all requests for resources under its control. (In reality, some resources are controlled by other units in the system. For example, the dispatcher allocates time slices.) Closely associated with this step is the need to design the system in a way that enforces the policies of the allocator. After all, little is gained if, once in execution, a program is allowed to do as it pleases. To accomplish these goals, user programs in time-sharing environments are not allowed to communicate directly with the peripheral devices of the machine. Rather, all such communication is done through the operating system at the request of the user programs. This places the operating system in a position whereby it can assure that once a program has been allocated a nonshareable resource, other programs are denied its use until the first program has finished.

The next step in the control of resources is to establish a reliable allocation procedure for the resource allocator. As a solution to this problem one might first suggest a technique based on the concept of a flag. (A flag refers to a bit in memory that can be in one of two states: set or clear.) Our proposed solution is to establish a flag for each of the nonshareable resources. When we begin, all flags will be clear. If a program requests the use of a nonshareable resource, the resource allocator will check the corresponding flag. If the flag is still clear, no other program is using the resource and the resource allocator will grant the request and also change the flag to its set state. If another program later requests the use of the same resource, the flag will be found in its set state (indicating the resource is already in use) and the resource allocator will deny the request of the second program. Finally, when a program finishes with a nonshareable resource, the resource allocator will clear the corresponding flag, indicating the resource's availability.

Although this solution looks good at first glance and the flag concept is very useful in many cases, a major flaw exists in this application. The problem is that when a program requests the use of a nonshareable resource, the process of testing and possibly setting the corresponding flag requires several machine steps. It is therefore possible for the process to be interrupted after a clear flag has been retrieved but before the flag has been set. Let us take a look at a sequence of events that exemplifies this situation.

Suppose a printer is currently available and a program requests use of it. The corresponding flag is checked and found to be clear, indicating that the printer is available. However, at this point the process is interrupted and another program begins to execute. It too requests the user of the printer. Thus, the flag is checked and found still clear since the previous process was interrupted before it had time to set it. Consequently, the resource allocator allows this second program to begin using the printer. Later the original program resumes execution where it left off. Since in the environment of this program the flag was already tested and found to be clear, the resource allocator honors the original program's request even though the flag is actually set. Thus, the two programs share the nonshareable printer.

Critical Regions

The problem in our proposed solution can be corrected by recognizing that the process of testing and possibly setting the flag is an example of a *critical region.* That is, it is a sequence of steps that once started must be completed without competition. Critical regions have attracted the attention of computer scientists for some time now, and many techniques have been developed for implementing them. A technique that works in our case is to use the interrupt disable and interrupt enable instructions provided in most machine languages to take advantage of the role interrupts play in coordinating the execution of the programs. When executed, the interrupt disable instruction causes the CPU to delay recognition of any interrupt signals until an interrupt enable instruction is executed. Any interrupt signals generated in the interim must wait. Therefore, if we were to start our test flag routine with an interrupt disable instruction and end with an interrupt enable instruction, once the routine had started because of a request from one program, no other entries to the routine could be made until the first request had been processed.

We should point out that this solution using the control of interrupts does not work in a true parallel processing environment. Recall from Chapter 2 that there are cases where, to improve throughput, more than one CPU is integrated into the same computer system. The result is much like having several separate computers except that when I/O is required, the separate machines compete with one another for the available resources. In this setting the two programs in our example would literally be running at the same time using different CPUs instead of sharing time under the control of operating systems. Consequently, the disabling of interrupts would not prevent the two programs from concurrently entering the critical test-and-set process since neither program would interrupt the other anyway. In such cases more subtle coordination techniques are required.

Deadlock

Assuming that our critical region problem has been solved, let us look at another problem that might arise. Suppose two programs are sharing time. One requests the use of the printer and receives it while the other requests the use of the tape drive and receives it. Later, the first program needs the tape drive in addition to the printer but is denied its use since the other program is using it. The first program must therefore wait for the second one to finish with the tape drive. However, while it is waiting the second program reaches a point where it needs the use of the printer. The operating system also denies this request since the printer is assigned to the first program; thus each program ends up waiting for the other to finish. Such a condition is called *deadlock* and, just as in other settings (Figure 3-7), can severely degrade a system's performance if not properly handled.

Analysis of the deadlock problem has revealed that it cannot occur unless all three of the following conditions are satisfied:

1. There is competition for nonshareable resources.
2. The resources are requested on a partial basis; that is, having received some resources, a program will return later to request more.
3. Once a resource has been delegated, it cannot forcibly be retrieved.

The point of isolating these conditions is that deadlock in a system can be prevented by removing any one of them, and in fact techniques attacking each are used in systems today. For example, requiring each user program to request all its required resources at one time removes the second condition, or allowing the operating system to take back resources removes the third condition. Perhaps the more

Figure 3-7 A deadlock resulting from competition for nonshareable railroad intersections

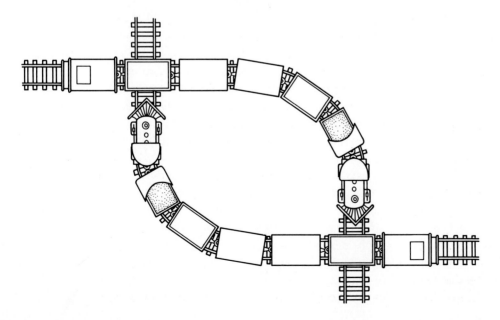

elaborate techniques involve the removal of the first condition. Let us take a look at how this might be done.

The trick is not to remove the competition directly by controlling the requests but to remove it indirectly by converting nonshareable resources into shareable ones. For example, suppose the nonshareable resource in question is a printer and a variety of user programs are doing statistical analysis, the results of which are to be printed. Each time a program requests the use of a printer, the operating system grants the request. However, instead of sending the data to an actual printer, the operating system sets aside storage area on a disk pack to hold the data until a printer becomes available. Thus, each program, thinking it has the use of a printer, executes in its normal way. In this manner the operating system has made the nonshareable resource appear shareable by creating the illusion of many virtual printers that can be used simultaneously. This technique of holding data for output at a later but more convenient time is called *spooling* and is quite popular on systems of all sizes.

Questions/Exercises

1. Suppose program one and program two are sharing time on the same machine and each needs the same nonshareable resource for short periods of time. (For example, each program may be printing a series of independent, short reports.) Thus, each program may repeatedly acquire the resource, release it, and later request it again. What would be a drawback to controlling access to the resource in the following manner:

    > Begin by assigning a flag the value zero. If program one requests the resource and the flag is zero, grant the request. Otherwise, make program one wait. If program two requests the resource and the flag is one, grant the request. Otherwise, make program two wait. Each time program one finishes with the resource, change the flag to one. Each time program two finishes with the resource, change the flag to zero.

2. Suppose a two-lane road converges to one lane to go through a tunnel. To coordinate the use of the tunnel, the following signal system has been installed: A car entering either end of the tunnel causes red lights above the tunnel entrances to be turned on. As the car exits the tunnel, the lights are turned off. If an approaching car finds a red light on, it waits until the light is turned off before entering the tunnel. What is the flaw in this system?

3. Suppose the following solutions have been proposed for removing the deadlock that occurs on a single-lane bridge when two cars meet. Identify which condition for deadlock given in the text is removed by each solution.
    a. Do not let a car onto the bridge until the bridge is empty.
    b. If cars meet, make one of them back up.
    c. Add a second lane to the bridge.

4. Suppose we represent each program in a time-sharing system with a dot and draw an arrow from one dot to another if the program represented by the first

dot is waiting for a resource being used by the second. Mathematicians call the resulting picture a directed graph. What property of the directed graph is equivalent to deadlock in the system?

3–7 **Getting It Started** (optional)

We began this chapter by asking how we get the machine to do something for us and answered by saying that the operating system, which is already running, is designed to respond to our requests. That leaves the question open as to how the operating system gets started. To understand this process we first take a closer look at main memory technology.

Memory Technology

Memory techniques used in computers can be divided into two broad categories: volatile and nonvolatile. Volatile means that the memory circuit does not retain the stored information when it is turned off. Any data in it is lost each time power is disconnected, and when power is restored the memory either is blank (often all zeros) or contains miscellaneous garbage. An example of such memory is the capacitor technology discussed in Chapter 1 since the tiny capacitors used for computer memory lose their charge in a manner of a few milliseconds if not recharged by what is known as the memory refresh circuit.

Nonvolatile techniques retain the stored information after power loss. An example of this technology is found in the use of magnetic media, which are popular in bulk storage systems. For use in main memory systems, magnetic material can be formed into tiny donut-shaped rings called *cores*, each capable of representing one bit. Such technology was quite popular in the past, but its size, cost, and energy requirements have caused it to lose favor in recent years.

In an effort to construct memories that do not change when their power source is removed, some technologies are used that might be considered extreme in the sense that the memory contents cannot be changed even by the computer itself. Since the machine cannot write information into it, such memory is often referred to as *read only memory (ROM)*. Once information is placed in ROM by a special process during the machine's construction, it will remain there whether the machine is on or off.

In contrast to ROM, memory that the machine can both write to and read from is called *random access memory (RAM)*. Although popular, the use of such terminology conveys the incorrect notion that ROMs do not provide for random access. Information stored in ROMs can be extracted in just as random a fashion as can that in RAMs, and when installed in a machine, both appear as a collection of cells uniquely identified by addresses.

The Bootstrap Process

With these concepts in mind, let us see what happens when a computer is first turned on. A CPU is constructed so that each time it is turned on it initializes its program counter to a predetermined address before starting its first machine cycle, therefore it will interpret the contents of the memory cells beginning at this predetermined location as the program that is to be executed. Thus, it is necessary to construct this area of memory using a nonvolatile technology such as ROM and see that the correct program is stored there. In home appliance applications such as microwave ovens, this ROM constitutes a majority of the machine's memory. The elementary operating system that monitors the keyboard on the front of the oven and correspondingly controls the (rather specialized) peripheral devices is stored here. Each time the oven is plugged into a power socket, the controlling computer automatically begins performing its supervisory tasks.

Figure 3-8 The bootstrap process

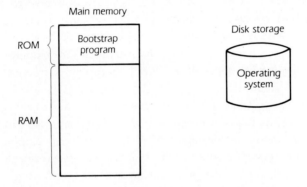

(Step 1) Machine starts by executing the bootstrap program already in memory. Operating system is stored in bulk storage.

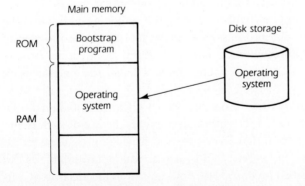

(Step 2) Bootstrap program directs the transfer of the operating system into main memory and then transfers control to it.

This technique is convenient for specialized applications where no modifications to the software will ever be made. When greater flexibility is required, however, it is not practical to reserve a major block of main memory in the form of ROM. We thus find that in general purpose machines the ROM used is quite small and contains a very short program called the ***bootstrap.*** (Its role in loading the operating system is analogous to that of the small tab on a boot that is necessary when putting on a boot but is of little use afterward.) This program is not the operating system but rather is a program that reads a predetermined area of bulk storage (normally on disk) into an area of memory constructed from RAM, assumes the data read is the beginning of the operating system, and executes a jump to the beginning of this memory area. In this manner, when the machine is turned on, the operating system, which is permanently held in bulk storage, is automatically loaded into memory and then executed (Figure 3-8). In keeping with the bootstrap terminology, this process is known as ***bootstrapping*** or sometimes simply booting.

In some cases, the program loaded from bulk storage is not a general purpose operating system but rather a more specialized program such as a word processor. Hence, this specialized program automatically starts executing when the machine is turned on. Such arrangements, called ***turnkey systems*** (in reference to the fact that the machine is started with the ease of turning a key to start a car), are popular in office environments where the personnel operating the equipment have little understanding of the equipment's interior functions.

Questions/Exercises

1. Turnkey systems are provided as a means of simplifying a machine's operation procedure. What is a disadvantage of this technique?
2. What analogy can be drawn between the bootstrap routine in a computer and the starter in a car?
3. Summarize the bootstrapping process found in a general purpose computer. How does this process differ from that found in a turnkey system?

Chapter 3 Review Problems

(Asterisked problems are associated with optional sections.)

1. In each of the following cases identify which item is hardware and which is software:
   a. newspapers, news
   b. music, player pianos
   c. recipe, cake
2. Explain the distinction between real and virtual characteristics.
3. Explain how operating systems can be used to make different machines appear to be the same.

4. List five activities of a typical operating system.
5. Summarize the distinction between batch processing and interactive processing.
6. What is the difference in the meaning of the terms *interactive processing* and *real-time processing*?
* 7. Draw an onion-skin diagram of a restaurant.
* 8. Suppose a time-sharing operating system is allotting time slices of 50 milliseconds. If it normally takes 8 milliseconds to position a disk's read/write head over the desired track and another 17 milliseconds for the desired data to rotate around

to the read/write head, how much of a program's time slice could be spent waiting for a read operation from a disk to take place? If the machine is capable of executing one instruction each microsecond, how many instructions could be executed during this waiting period? (This is why a time-sharing system will normally allow another program to run while the first program is waiting for the services of a peripheral device.)

* 9. What activities must the operating system perform when a program requests a logical record from a physical record that:
   a. has not yet been read from tape?
   b. is already held in main memory because of a previous read request?

   In which of these cases will the program's time slice (in a time-sharing system) most likely be terminated? Why?

*10. A program is said to be I/O-bound if it requires a lot of I/O operations, whereas a program that consists of mostly computations within the CPU/memory system is said to be compute-bound. If both a compute-bound routine and an I/O-bound routine are waiting for a time slice, which should be given priority? Why?

*11. Would greater throughput be achieved by a system running two programs in a time-sharing environment if both programs were I/O-bound (refer to problem 10) or if one was I/O-bound and the other was compute-bound? Why?

*12. In addition to the machine's location within a program, what must be saved when a program is interrupted so that it can later be restarted?

*13. List in chronological order the major events that take place when a program is interrupted.

*14. A banker with only $100,000 loans $50,000 to each of two customers. Later both customers return with the story that before they can repay their loans they must each borrow another $10,000 to complete the business deal in which their previous loans are involved. The banker resolves this deadlock by borrowing the additional funds from another source and passing this loan (with an increase in the interest rate) on to the two customers. Which of the three conditions for deadlock has the banker removed?

*15. In the text we briefly indicated that in reality resource allocation is performed by units within the operating system other than the resource allocator. In each of the following cases identify a resource that would be allocated by the particular operating system unit:
   a. command processor
   b. file manager
   c. dispatcher

*16. Students who wish to enroll in Model Railroading II at the local university are required to obtain permission from the instructor and pay a laboratory fee. The two requirements are fulfilled independently in either order and at different locations on campus. Enrollment is limited to 20 students; this limit is maintained by both the instructor, who will grant permission to only 20 students, and the financial office, which will allow only 20 students to pay the laboratory fee. Suppose that this registration system has resulted in 19 students having successfully registered for the course, but with the final space being claimed by two students—one who has only obtained permission from the instructor and another who has only paid the fee. Which requirement for deadlock is removed by each of the following solutions to the problem:
   a. Both students are allowed in the course.
   b. The class size is reduced to 19, and thus neither of the two students is allowed to register for the course.
   c. The competing students are both denied entry to the class and a third student is given the 20th space.
   d. It is decided that the only requirement for entry into the course is the payment of the fee. Thus, the student who has paid the fee gets into the course and entry to the other student is denied.

*17. Identify the critical region in each of the following processes:
   a. An airplane taking off.
   b. A stunt car performing a long jump from a ramp.
   c. Placing a cash order with a questionable mail-order business.
   d. The exchange of captured spies between two countries.

*18. Programs in a time-sharing system are normally considered as being in one of three states: executing (the routine enjoying the current time slice), ready (the routines waiting for a time slice), and not ready (the routines that couldn't make use of a time slice since they are waiting for the

assignment of some required resource, input from a terminal, or perhaps data to arrive from a bulk storage device). In each of the following cases, identify the classification to which the described program will be moved:
   a. The executing program at the normal end of a time slice.
   b. The program at the head of the ready queue at the end of a time slice.
   c. The executing program that has just requested data from bulk storage.
   d. A program in the not ready state that has just been allotted the resource for which it has been waiting.

*19. Each of two robot arms is programmed to lift assemblies from a conveyor belt, test them for tolerances, and place them in one of two bins depending on the results of the test. The assemblies arrive one at a time with a sufficient interval between them. To keep both arms from trying to grab the same assembly, the computers controlling the arms share a common memory cell. If an arm is available as an assembly approaches, its controlling computer reads the value of the common cell. If the value is nonzero, the arm lets the assembly pass. Otherwise, the controlling computer places a nonzero value in the memory cell, directs the arm to pick up the assembly, and places the value zero back into the memory cell.
   a. What sequence of events in this control system constitutes a critical region?
   b. Without protection for this critical region, what sequence of events could lead to a tug-of-war between the two arms?

*20. Suppose each computer in a ring network is programmed to transmit simultaneously in both directions those messages that originate at that station and are addressed to all the other stations belonging to the network. Moreover, suppose this is done by first acquiring access to the communication path to the machine's left, retaining this access until access to the path to the right is acquired, and then transmitting the message.

Identify the deadlock that would occur if all the machines in the network tried to originate such a message at the same time.

*21. Identify the use of a queue in the process of spooling output to a printer.

*22. The pavement in the middle of an intersection can be considered as a nonshareable resource for which cars approaching the intersection compete. A traffic light rather than an operating system is used to control the allocation of the resource. If the light is able to sense the amount of traffic arriving form each direction and is programmed to give the green light to the heavier traffic, the lighter traffic might suffer from what is called starvation. What is meant by starvation? What could happen in a multiuser computer system where routines are assigned priorities and competition for resources was always resolved strictly by priority?

*23. What subtle problem could occur in a time-sharing system if the dispatcher always assigned time slices according to a nondynamic priority system? (Hint: What would be the priority of the routine that just completed its time slice in comparison to the routines that had been waiting, and consequently which routine would get the next time slice?)

*24. What is the similarity between deadlock and starvation? (Refer to problem 22.) What is the difference between deadlock and starvation?

*25. What problem arises as the length of the time slices in a time-sharing system are made smaller and smaller? What about as they become longer and longer?

*26. List five resource whose use a time-sharing operating system might have to coordinate.

*27. In what way is deadlock avoided in the simple operating system described in Section 3-4?

*28. List the major steps in a general bootstrap process in chronological order.

Problems for the Programmer

1. What utility routines do you use to prepare and execute a program in your language?

2. What utility routines can you request from within a program in your language?

3. If you are using an interactive time-sharing system, how can you find out how many users are using the system with you? Does system response become sluggish as this number increases? Why might you expect it to?

4. Write a program that passes an imaginary token back and forth among four potential owners named A, B, C, and D under the restriction that the token can have only one owner at any given time. In particular, a request to give the token to a letter is implemented by typing that letter at the keyboard. If the token is available, your program should respond with the message "Token is now assigned to X" where X is the letter that was typed. On the other hand, your program should respond with the message "Token is not available" if the token is not available (if it is currently owned by another letter). Typing the letter currently owning the token should cause the token to be released and the program to respond with the message "Token is now available". What similarities and dissimilarities does your program have with a resource allocator controlling access to a non-shareable resource?

5. Expand your program in programming problem 4 to control two tokens called X and Y that might be requested by any of the potential owners. Design your program to avoid deadlock.

6. Write an elementary operating system simulator consisting of a command processor, a file manager, and a scheduler. That is, write a program that accepts commands of the form:

EXECUTE name
DELETE name
CREATE name
LIST

(where "name" implies a character string identifying a fictitious file to be maintained by the system) from the keyboard and responds correctly. More precisely, the command LIST should cause the command processor to ask the file manager to list the names of the files currently being held in the simulated system, and the commands CREATE and DELETE should result in the file manager being requested to insert or remove (respectively) the indicated file. The EXECUTE command should cause the command processor to request the scheduler to schedule the identified program for execution. In this case, of course, the scheduler should check with the file manager to see that the requested program is in fact available. As a way of simulating the scheduling of a program for execution, design the scheduler so that it prints a message such as "PROGRAM X SCHEDULED FOR EXECUTION" at your terminal.

4 Algorithms

4–1 **Definition**

4–2 **Algorithm Representation**
    Syntax and Semantics
    Primitives
    Pseudocode
    Modular Design

4–3 **Algorithm Discovery**
    The Theory of Problem Solving
    Getting a Foot in the Door

4–4 **Loop Structures**
    The Sequential Search Algorithm
    Loop Control
    The Insertion Sort Algorithm

4–5 **Recursive Structures**
    The Binary Search Algorithm
    Recursive Control
    The Quick Sort Algorithm

4–6 **Efficiency and Correctness**
    Algorithm Efficiency
    Software Verification

We have seen that before a computer can perform a task it must be given a list of instructions (an algorithm) telling it precisely what to do. Consequently, the study of such instruction sequences is the cornerstone of much of computer science. In this chapter we introduce many of the concepts relating to this study. In particular, we investigate the issues of algorithm discovery and representation as well as the major control concepts of loop and recursive structures. In so doing we also present a few well-known algorithms for searching and sorting.

4–1 Definition

In the introductory chapter, we referred to an algorithm informally as a step-by-step process. We should now look more closely at the meaning of this term. Our situation is analogous to the need for more precise definitions of terminology in other fields such as the terms *work* in physics and *real property* in law.

Technically speaking, computer science defines the term **algorithm** as a finite sequence of unambiguous, executable steps that will ultimately terminate if followed. You may think that the latter part of this definition (requiring a finite sequence of steps to terminate) is redundant. However, the fact that a list of directions contains only a finite number of steps does not necessarily mean that the described task will ever be completed if followed. For example, the single instruction that reads "Do this step again" will result in an endless process, whereas "If you have done this step four times then stop, otherwise do it again" will terminate. In summary, the latter part of the definition of an algorithm means that an algorithm must be both definable in a finite number of steps and executable in a finite amount of time.

The use of the term *unambiguous* in the definition of an algorithm means that at each step the action to be performed next must be uniquely determined by the instruction and the data available at that time. Observe that this does not mean that the instruction alone must be enough to determine the desired action. Merely knowing that a person is about to execute the "if" instruction from the previous paragraph is not enough information to determine what that person's action is going to be. We must also know how many times the person has already executed the instruction.

The requirement that each step in an algorithm be executable rules out the possibility of an algorithm containing steps whose execution is impossible. For instance, the sequence of steps:

Step 1. Make a list of all the positive integers.
Step 2. Arrange this list in descending order (from largest to smallest).
Step 3. Extract the left-most integer in the resulting list.
Step 4. Stop.

is not an algorithm since the execution of some of its steps is impossible. One cannot make a list of all the positive integers as requested by step 1, and the positive integers cannot be arranged in descending order as requested by step 2. Computer scientists use the term *effective* to capture this concept of executable. That is, they speak of an algorithm being effective, whereas we might say that an algorithm must be doable.

The technical definition of an algorithm given above originated in the study of computability, a subject we will consider in Chapter 11. The underlying goal of this subject is to determine what problems have solutions that can be obtained by a computational process and thus can be solved by computational machines. Inherent in the concept of computing the solution of a problem is the ability to recognize when the solution has been obtained and thus terminate the computational process. In this sense, then, one is interested in only those computational processes that ultimately stop. This is the source of the termination requirement in our formal definition of an algorithm.

On the other hand, there are numerous applications in data processing that require a nonterminating computational process. One such case involves the monitoring of a patient's vital signs. Indeed, the process used in this setting should continue performing its task indefinitely. Another example is that of a computer operating system that continues serving the needs of the machine's users in a cyclical fashion. Applications such as these and the lack of a definitive source of terminology within the computing community have resulted in the informal, and technically incorrect, use of the term *algorithm* in reference to processes that may not terminate. Thus, one must be aware of these variations and not jump to the assumption of termination without first considering the context of the discussion. In this text, however, those processes referred to as algorithms terminate.

Questions/Exercises
1. Give some examples of algorithms with which you are familiar. Are they really algorithms in the precise sense?
2. Why would a natural language such as English not be suited for the communication of algorithms?
3. Why is the following instruction sequence not an algorithm in the precise sense? Modify it so that it is an algorithm.

   Step 1. Take a coin out of your pocket and put it on the table.
   Step 2. Return to step 1.

4–2 Algorithm Representation

We begin by noting that an algorithm, being a sequence of steps, is purely conceptual and abstract. Thus, to communicate an algorithm (perhaps to another person or to a computer), we must find a way to represent the algorithm. The issues involved in algorithm representation constitute the subject of this section.

Syntax and Semantics

Paramount to the subject of algorithm representation is the distinction between syntax and semantics. The term *syntax* refers to the representation, whereas *semantics* refers to the object or concept represented. Thus, the syntactic structure *air* is merely a collection of three letters, but the object represented (the semantics) is a gaseous substance surrounding the entire world.

A major goal in algorithm representation is to ensure that the syntax accurately reflects the intended semantics. Examples abound in language in which such associations are not well defined. For instance, does the statement, "Visiting grandchildren can be nerve-racking" mean that the grandchildren can be nerve-racking when they visit or that going to see them can be nerve-racking?

Another concern is that the syntax should reflect the underlying semantics in an accessible manner. Let us explain by an example. First, consider the algorithm for folding a bird from a square piece of paper as represented in Figure 4-1. Our first observation is that the representation of an algorithm can take on a variety of syntactic forms—even a sequence of pictures. Moreover, the form chosen can significantly affect the accessibility of the algorithm being represented. For instance, although you may argue that the representation in Figure 4-1 is not ideal, most would agree that the pictorial form is much more accessible than any representation we might develop if we chose to express the algorithm in a narrative form using ordinary English sentences and paragraphs.

The search for syntactic structures for representing algorithms in an unambiguous, accessible manner is a continuing effort in computer science.

Primitives

Let us reconsider Figure 4-1, which although superior to a narrative representation still has some communication deficiencies. One results from the fact that two-dimensional line drawings often fail to capture the reality of three-dimensional space, and thus the drawings are at times ambiguous. Another is that in some cases the difference between two consecutive drawings is too great to communicate the steps involved in bridging the gap.

These problems are actually special cases of general algorithm representation issues, one being the need for an unambiguous syntax, the other being the need for a well-established level of detail at which the algorithm should be expressed. Computer science attacks both of these issues through the use of primitives. A *primitive* consists of a well-defined semantic structure together with an unambiguous syntax for representing it. Using this approach, the aforementioned problems in algorithm representation are overcome by first establishing a rich enough collection of primitives so that any algorithm can be expressed as a combination of them and then expressing all algorithms in these terms. Such a collection of primitives along with the rules by which they can be combined to represent more complex structures is called a programming language.

As an example, we could go a long way toward producing a better representation of the bird-folding algorithm by first establishing the general origami primitives shown in Figure 4-2. Then, we could describe the algorithm for folding the bird using these primitives as building blocks. A portion of the result is shown in Figure 4-3, where we have concentrated on the process of forming the bird's head.

To obtain a collection of primitives to use in representing algorithms for computer execution, we could turn to the individual instructions that the machine is designed to execute. After all, if an algorithm is expressed at this level of detail, we

Figure 4-1 Folding a bird from a square piece of paper

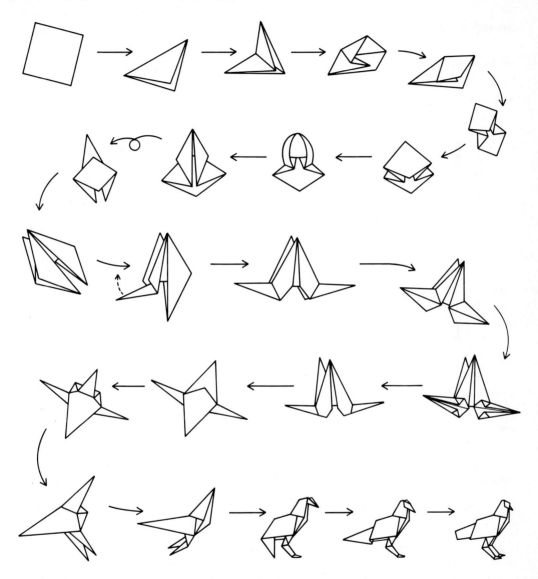

will certainly have a program suitable for machine execution. However, expressing algorithms at this level is extremely tedious, and hence, one normally uses a collection of "higher-level" primitives, each of which can be constructed by combining the primitives provided in the machine's language. The result is a programming language in which algorithms can be expressed in a conceptually higher form than in the actual machine language. Such languages are called high-level programming languages and are discussed in the next chapter.

Figure 4-2 Origami primitives

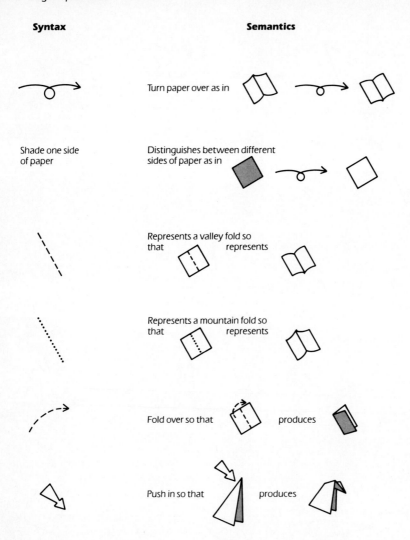

Pseudocode

For now, we forego the introduction of a formal high-level programming language in favor of a less formal, more intuitive notational system known as **_pseudocode._** Our goal is to establish a notational system somewhere between the unrestricted use of the entire English language and that of the strict use of only formal primitives. After all, even when the ultimate intention is to represent an algorithm in a formal language, one rarely insists on the strict adherence to the rules of that language in

Figure 4-3 Forming the bird's head

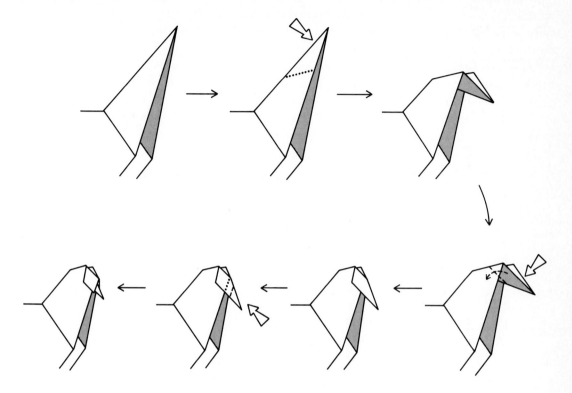

the early stages of writing. Instead, one tends to sketch informally until ideas materialize and the need to adhere to formal rules becomes important. (When representing the bird-folding algorithm, one is likely to draw numerous sketches before becoming involved with the details of dotted versus dashed lines or which sections of a drawing should be shaded and which should not. When writing a term paper, one often sketches an outline before filling in the details using complete, grammatically correct sentences.)

One method of obtaining a pseudocode is simply to loosen the rules of the formal language in which the final product is to be expressed. This is a common approach in computer programming in those settings in which the target programming language is known in advance. There the pseudocode used during the early stages of program development consists of syntax-semantic structures similar to, but less formal than, those used in the target programming language.

Our goal, however, is to consider the issues of algorithm development and representation without confining our discussion to a particular programming language. Thus, our pseudocode will be developed by an alternate approach. We begin with the observation that when representing an algorithm, one's goal is not to achieve a creative literary style but rather to convey the algorithm in a straightforward, unambiguous manner. Moreover, since our pseudocode will be used for jotting down ideas, we would like its syntax to be terse, yet expressive enough to reflect its associated meaning. Our approach to pseudocode, then, is to develop a consistent, concise notation for representing recurring ideas. In turn, these structures will become the primitives in which we attempt to express future ideas.

For example, the need to select one of two possible activities depending on the truth or falsity of some condition is a common algorithmic structure. Examples include:

> If you have a younger sister, give her your outgrown clothes; otherwise give them to charity.

> Should your older sister have bad taste in clothing, encourage her to give her outgrown clothes to charity; otherwise encourage her to give them to you.

and

> In those cases in which you know the clothes being purchased will ultimately be given to you, take an active role in their selection; otherwise pay no attention.

Each of these statements could be rewritten to conform to the structure

$$\text{if } (condition) \text{ then } (activity)$$
$$\text{else } (activity)$$

where we have used the key words if, then, and else to announce the different substructures within the main structure and parentheses to delimit the boundaries of these substructures. By adopting this syntactic structure for our pseudocode, we acquire a uniform and readily accessible way in which to express this common semantic structure. This, then, is exactly what we do. In fact, we also adopt the shorter syntax

$$\text{if } (condition) \text{ then } (activity)$$

for those cases not involving an else activity. Thus, whereas the statement

> Depending on whether or not tomorrow is a workday, either set the alarm or merely wind the clock.

may possess a more creative literary style, we will consistently opt for the straightforward

$$\text{if (tomorrow is workday)}$$
$$\text{then (wind clock and set alarm)}$$
$$\text{else (wind clock)}$$

and

> Should it be the case that all seats are taken, wait for the next performance.

will be reduced to

> if (all seats are taken) then (wait for next performance)

Another common algorithmic structure involves the need to continue executing a statement or sequence of statements as long as some condition remains true. Informal examples include

> As long as there are tickets to sell, continue selling tickets.

and

> While there are tickets to sell, keep selling tickets.

For all such cases, we adopt the uniform pattern

> while *(condition)* do *(activity)*

for our pseudocode. In short, such a statement means to check the *condition* and if it is true perform the *activity* and return to check the *condition* again. If the *condition* is ever found to be false, move on to the next instruction following the while structure. Thus, both of the preceding statements would reduce to

> while (tickets remain to be sold) do (sell a ticket)

A third recurring activity is the association of a value with a name. After all, the request to divide SalesQuota by SizeOfSalesForce is more descriptive than the command divide 120 by 30. Of course, to use the more descriptive form we must have a way of establishing the association between the name SalesQuota and the value 120. This we will do with an assign statement of the form

> assign *name* the value *value*

meaning that *name* is to be associated with the value *value*. In particular, to associate SalesQuota with the value 120, we would write

> assign SalesQuota the value 120

Keep in mind that the value being assigned may not be numeric. For example, the statement

> assign LastName the value "Smith"

would associate the name LastName with the string of letters S, m, i, t, and h.

Modular Design

Up to this point we have been discussing the role of syntax-semantic relationships in reference to the goal of producing unambiguous programs. However, the removal of ambiguity is not the only concern in algorithm representation. Equally important is that the final program be easy to understand and modify. This, in fact, is the reason we will use indentation in our pseudocode. The statement

```
if (item is taxable)
    then (if (price > limit)
             then (pay x)
             else (pay y))
    else (pay z)
```

is easier to comprehend than the otherwise equivalent

```
if (item is taxable) then (if (price > limit) then (pay x)
else (pay y)) else (pay z)
```

We see, then, that the organization of an algorithm's representation is as important to clarity as the design and selection of primitives. One technique for obtaining a well-organized representation is to construct it in a modular fashion. That is, we divide the task performed by the algorithm into small units (or modules) and represent each of these modules separately. Then, these modules can be used to construct other modules that tackle larger portions of the overall task. The result is a representation that is organized in varying levels of detail. At the highest level, we find the steps of the algorithm stated in terms of large units whose functions are closely related to the overall task at hand. As we shift our attention to lower levels in the hierarchy, we find each individual task defined in more detail and in terminology more closely associated with the primitives in which all tasks are ultimately defined. Thus, anyone approaching such a representation is able to grasp its composition with relative ease and to evaluate it (or part of it) at the degree of detail desired.

Because of these advantages, modular design is used as an organizational methodology in a variety of applications throughout our society. For example, businesses normally delegate responsibilities to their employees in such a manner. The president of a company is concerned with the overall functioning of the business, the vice-presidents are concerned with significant yet particular parts of the business (such as finance, personnel, or marketing), and ultimately an employee on the assembly line is concerned with bolting assembly A to assembly B. Another example is the technique (sometimes called parts explosion) of describing the structure of complex machinery. An entire machine (such as a car) might be represented as being composed of several subassemblies (body, drive assembly, electrical system, steering system, etc.) that are in turn represented in terms of smaller assemblies (the drive assembly consists of the motor, transmission, differential, etc.).

With these examples and benefits in mind, we might consider applying the concept of modular design to our presentation of the bird-folding algorithm. The result might appear as in Figure 4-4, where we have described the algorithm in terms of major subtasks such as folding the base, forming the leg structure, and shaping the body. Each of these activities can then be presented in more detail in another

Figure 4-4 Folding a bird using modules

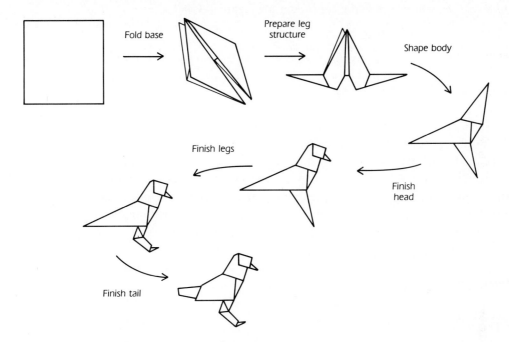

Fold base

Prepare leg structure

Shape body

Finish head

Finish legs

Finish tail

drawing where the additional precision will not contribute to the clutter of detail from the other steps. In particular, the process of forming the head could be described as already shown in Figure 4-3.

In light of our discussion, we should extend our pseudocode to allow for the modular representation of algorithms. For this we first allow a module to be given a name by beginning that module with a statement of the form

procedure *name*

where *name* is the name to be given the module consisting of the instructions that follow this statement. Then, we allow that module to be used elsewhere merely by inserting the module's name at the location at which its services are required. As an example, if two modules were given the names ProcessLoan and RejectApplication, then they could be used to simplify an otherwise complex if-then-else structure by writing

if (. . .) then (ProcessLoan)
else (RejectApplication)

which would result in the execution of the procedure ProcessLoan if the tested condition were true or in the execution of RejectApplication if the condition were false. As another example, if the steps requested in Figure 4-4 (FoldBase,

PrepareLegStructure, etc.) were written in our pseudocode as modules with the corresponding names, we could express the equivalent for Figure 4-4 as

> FoldBase
> PrepareLegStructure
> ShapeBody
> FinishHead
> FinishLegs
> FinishTail

At times the module being requested may be designed to perform some activity on an object (or objects) that must be specified when the module is requested. For instance, if the module named Sort is designed to sort a list into alphabetical order, then we may need to specify the target list when we request the services of Sort. We allow for this in our pseudocode by means of a parenthetical statement following the module's name at the point of the request. Thus, we might write something such as:

> Sort (stamp club membership list)

or

> Sort (wedding guest list)

depending on our needs.

Keep in mind that the purpose of our pseudocode is to provide a means of jotting down rough outlines of algorithms—not the writing of complete, formal programs. Thus, we will feel free to insert informal phrases that request activities whose details are not rigorously specified. (How these details are resolved is not so much a feature of the algorithm being expressed as it is a property of the language in which the formal program is ultimately written.) If, however, we find a particular idea recurring in our outlines, we will adopt a consistent syntax for representing it and thus extend our pseudocode.

Questions/Exercises

1. A primitive in one context may turn out to be a composite of primitives in another. For instance, our *while* statement is a primitive in our pseudocode, yet it is implemented as a composite of machine language instructions. Give two other examples of this phenomenon in a noncomputer setting.
2. In what sense is the construction of modules the construction of primitives?
3. The Euclidean algorithm finds the greatest common divisor of two positive integers X and Y by the following process:

   As long as the value of neither X nor Y is zero, continue dividing the larger of the values by the smaller and assigning X and Y the values of the divisor and remainder, respectively. (The final value of X is the greatest common divisor.)

   Express this algorithm in our pseudocode.

4. Describe a collection of primitives that are used in a subject other than computer programming.

4–3 Algorithm Discovery

The development of a program consists of two activities—discovering the underlying algorithm and representing that algorithm as a program. Up to this point we have been concerned with the issues of algorithm representation without considering the question of how algorithms are found in the first place. Yet algorithm discovery is usually the more challenging step in the software development process. After all, to discover an algorithm is to find a method of solving that problem whose solution the algorithm is to compute. Thus, to understand how algorithms are discovered is to understand the problem-solving process.

The Theory of Problem Solving

The techniques of problem solving and the need to learn more about them are not unique to computer science, but rather they are topics pertinent to almost any field. On the other hand, the close association between the process of algorithm discovery and that of general problem solving has caused computer scientists to join with those of other disciplines in the search for better problem-solving techniques. Ultimately, one would like to reduce the process of problem solving to an algorithm in itself, but this has been shown to be impossible. (This is a result of the material in Chapter 11, where we show that there are problems that do not have algorithmic solutions.) Thus, the ability to solve problems remains more of an artistic skill to be developed than a precise science to be learned.

As evidence of the illusive, artistic nature of problem solving, the loosely defined problem-solving phases presented by the mathematician G. Polya in the late 1940s remain the major principles on which attempts to teach problem-solving skills are based today. (Actually, Polya's work was preceded by the research of H. von Helmholtz [late 1800s], J. Dewey [1930s], and others who studied the problem-solving process in general settings. Polya is usually quoted by computer scientists because his work dealt with problem solving in the context of mathematics—a close cousin of computer science.) Polya's problem-solving phases are:

Phase 1. Understand the problem.
Phase 2. Devise a plan for solving the problem.
Phase 3. Carry out the plan.
Phase 4. Evaluate the solution for accuracy and for its potential as a tool for solving other problems.

Translated into the context of program development, these phases become:

Phase 1. Understand the problem.

Phase 2. Get an idea as to how an algorithmic procedure might solve the problem.

Phase 3. Formulate the algorithm and represent it as a program.

Phase 4. Evaluate the program for accuracy and for its potential as a tool for solving other problems.

Having presented Polya's list, we should emphasize that these phases are not steps to be followed when trying to solve a problem but rather phases that will be completed sometime during the solution process. The key word here is *followed*. One does not solve problems by following. Rather, to solve a problem, one must take the initiative and lead. If you were to approach the task of solving a problem in the frame of mind depicted by "Now I've finished phase 1, it's time to move on to phase 2," you would most likely not be successful. However, if you became involved with the problem and ultimately solved it, you would most likely be able to look back at what you had done and realize that Polya's four phases had been completed.

Another important observation is that Polya's four phases are not necessarily completed in sequence. Contrary to the claim made by many authors, successful problem solvers often start formulating strategies for solving a problem (phase 2) before the problem itself is entirely understood (phase 1). Then, if these strategies fail (during phases 3 or 4), the potential problem solver gains a deeper understanding of the intricacies of the problem and, based on this deeper understanding, can return to form other and hopefully more successful strategies.

Keep in mind that we are discussing how problems are solved—not how they should be solved. Ideally, we would like to eliminate the waste inherent in the trial-and-error process just described. In the case of developing large software systems, discovering a misunderstanding as late as phase 4 represents a tremendous, and usually devastating, loss in resources. Avoiding such catastrophes is a major goal of software engineers (Chapter 6), with the principal technique being to insist on a thorough understanding of a problem before proceeding with a solution. On the other hand, one could argue that a true understanding of a problem is not obtained until a solution has been found. The mere fact that a problem is unsolved implies a lack of understanding. Thus, to insist on a complete understanding of the problem before proposing any solutions is somewhat idealistic.

As an example, consider the following problem:

Person A is charged with the task of determining the ages of person B's three children. B tells A that the product of the children's ages is 36. After considering this clue, A replies that another clue is required, so B tells A the sum of the children's ages. Again, A replies that another clue is needed, so B tells A that the oldest child plays the piano. After hearing this clue, A tells B the ages of the three children. How old are the three children?

At first glance the last clue seems to be totally unrelated to the problem. However, it is this clue that allows A to finally determine the ages of the children. How can this be? Let us proceed by formulating a plan of attack and following this plan, even though we still have many questions about the problem. Our plan will be to trace the steps described by the problem statement while keeping track of the information available to person A as the story progresses.

The first clue given A is that the product of the children's ages must be 36. This means that the triple representing the three ages must be one of those listed in Figure 4-5(a). The next clue is the sum of the desired triple. We are not told what this sum is, but we are told that this information is not enough for A to isolate the correct triple; therefore, the desired triple must be one whose sum appears at least twice in the table of Figure 4-5(b). But the only triples appearing in Figure 4-5(b) with identical sums are (1,6,6) and (2,2,9), both of which produce the sum 13. This is the information available to A at the time the last clue is given. It is at this point that we finally understand the significance of the last clue. It has nothing to do with playing the piano; rather it is the fact that there is an oldest child. This rules out the triple (1,6,6) and thus allows us to conclude that the children's ages are 2, 2, and 9.

In this case, then, it is not until we attempt to implement our plan for solving the problem (phase 3) that we gain a complete understanding of the problem (phase 1). Had we insisted on completing phase 1 before proceeding, we would probably never have found the children's ages. Such irregularities in the problem-solving process are fundamental to the difficulties in developing systematic approaches to problem solving.

Another irregularity is the mysterious inspiration that may come to a potential problem solver who, having worked on a problem without apparent success, may at a later time suddenly see the solution while doing another task. This phenomenon was identified by Helmholtz as early as 1896 and was discussed by the mathema-

Figure 4-5

(1,1,36)	(1,6,6)
(1,2,18)	(2,2,9)
(1,3,12)	(2,3,6)
(1,4,9)	(3,3,4)

(a) Triples whose product is 36

1 + 1 + 36 = 38	1 + 6 + 6 = 13
1 + 2 + 18 = 21	2 + 2 + 9 = 13
1 + 3 + 12 = 16	2 + 3 + 6 = 11
1 + 4 + 9 = 14	3 + 3 + 4 = 10

(b) Sums of triples from part **a**

tician Henri Poincaré in a lecture before the Psychological Society in Paris. There Poincaré described his experiences of realizing the solution to a problem he had worked on after he had set it aside and begun other projects. The phenomenon is as though a subconscious part of the mind continues working and, if successful, immediately forces the solution into the conscious mind. Today, the period between consciously working on a problem and the sudden inspiration is known as an incubation period, and its understanding remains a goal of current research.

Getting a Foot in the Door

We have been discussing problem solving from a somewhat philosophical point of view while avoiding a direct confrontation with the question of how one should go about trying to solve a problem. There are, of course, numerous problem-solving approaches, each of which can be successful in certain but not all settings. We will identify some of these shortly. For now we note that there seems to be a common thread running through these techniques, which simply stated is "get your foot in the door." As an example, let us consider the following simple problem.

> Before A, B, C, and D ran a race they made the following predictions:
>
> > A predicted that B would win.
> > B predicted that D would be last.
> > C predicted that A would be third.
> > D predicted that A's prediction would be correct.
>
> Only one of these predictions was true, and this was the prediction made by the winner. In what order did A, B, C, and D finish the race?

After reading the problem and analyzing the data, it should not take long to realize that since the predictions of A and D are equivalent and only one prediction was true, the predictions of both A and D must be false. Thus, neither A nor D were winners. At this point we have our foot in the door, and obtaining the complete solution to our problem is merely a matter of extending our knowledge from here. If A's prediction was false, then B did not win either. The only remaining choice for the winner is C. Thus, C won the race and C's prediction was true. Consequently, we know that A came in third. That means that the finishing order was either CBAD or CDAB. But, the former is ruled out since B's prediction must be false. Therefore, the finishing order was CDAB.

Of course, being told to get our foot in the door is not the same as being told how to do it. Obtaining this toehold, as well as realizing how to expand this initial thrust into a complete solution to the problem, requires creative input from the would-be problem solver. There are, however, several general approaches that have been proposed by Polya and others for how one might go about getting a foot in the door. One of these is to try working the problem backward. For instance, if the problem is to find a way of producing a particular output from a given input, one might start with that output and attempt to back up to the given input. This approach is typical of someone trying to discover the bird-folding algorithm in the previous section. They tend to unfold a completed bird in an attempt to see how it is constructed.

Another general problem-solving approach is to look for a related problem that is either easier to solve or has been solved before and then try to apply its solution to the current problem. This technique is of particular value in the context of program development. Often the major difficulty in program development is not that of solving a particular instance of a problem but rather of finding a general algorithm that can be used to solve all instances of the problem. More precisely, if we were faced with the task of developing a program for sorting lists of names, our task would not be to sort a particular list but to find a general algorithm that could be used to sort any list of names. Thus, although the instructions

> Move the name Bob to the first of the list.
> Place the name Carol after Bob.
> Place the name David after Carol.

correctly sort the list Carol, Bob, David, they do not constitute the general purpose algorithm we desire. What we need is an algorithm that will sort Carol, Bob, David as well as other lists we may encounter. This is not to say that our solution for sorting a particular list is totally worthless in our search for a general purpose algorithm. We might, for instance, get our foot in the door by considering such special cases in an attempt to find general principles that could in turn be used to develop the desired general purpose algorithm. In this case, then, our solution will have been obtained by the technique of solving a collection of related problems.

Still another approach to getting a foot in the door is to apply *stepwise refinement,* which is essentially the technique of not trying to conquer an entire task (in all its gory detail) at once. Rather, stepwise refinement proposes that one first view the problem at hand in terms of several subproblems. The idea is that by breaking the original problem into subproblems, one is able to approach the overall solution in terms of steps, each of which is easier to solve than the entire original problem. In turn, stepwise refinement proposes that these steps be decomposed into smaller steps and these smaller steps be broken into still smaller ones until the entire problem has been reduced to a collection of easily solved subproblems.

In this light, stepwise refinement is a top-down methodology in that it progresses from the general to the specific. In contrast are bottom-up methodologies that progress from the specific to the general. Although contrasting in theory, the two approaches actually complement each other in practice. For instance, the decomposition of a problem proposed by the top-down methodology of stepwise refinement is often guided by the problem solver's intuition, which is working in a bottom-up mode.

Note that solutions produced by stepwise refinement possess a natural modular structure, and herein lies a major reason for the popularity of stepwise refinement in algorithm design. Indeed, if an algorithm has a natural modular structure, then it is easily adapted to a modular representation, which we have seen is conducive to the development of a manageable program. Furthermore, the subproblems produced by stepwise refinement are compatible with the concept of team programming, in which several people are assigned the task of developing a software project as a team. After all, once the task of the software has been broken into subproblems (or potential modules), the personnel on the team can work independently on these subtasks without getting in each other's way.

These advantages of stepwise refinement in the context of software development have produced many followers of the technique. However, with all its good points, stepwise refinement is not the final word in algorithm discovery. Rather, it is essentially an organizational tool, whose problem-solving attributes are consequences of this organization. Stepwise refinement is a natural methodology to use when writing a term paper, developing a marketing strategy, or planning a sales convention. Similarly, most software development projects in the data processing community have a large organizational component. The task is not so much that of discovering a startling new algorithm as it is a problem of organizing the tasks to be performed into a coherent package. Thus, stepwise refinement has correctly become a major design methodology in data processing and is a technique in which potential programmers and systems analysts should be trained. But, stepwise refinement remains only one of many design methodologies of interest to computer scientists, and thus one should not be misled into believing that all algorithm discoveries can be achieved by means of stepwise refinement.

In the last analysis, then, algorithm discovery remains a challenging art that must be developed over a period of time rather than taught as an isolated subject consisting of well-defined methodologies. Indeed, to train a potential problem solver to follow certain methodologies is to squash those creative skills that should instead be nurtured.

Questions/Exercises

1. a. Among all the lists of positive integers whose sum is 2001, find the list whose product is the largest.
    b. Use the insight gained from solving part a to obtain an algorithm for solving the same problem for values other than 2001.
2. a. Suppose we were given a checkerboard consisting of 2^n rows and 2^n columns of squares, for some positive integer n, and a box of L-shape tiles, each of which can cover exactly three squares on the board. If any single square is cut out of the board, could we cover the remaining board with tiles such that tiles do not overlap or hang off the edge of the board?
    b. Explain how your solution to part a could be used to show that $2^{2n} - 1$ is divisible by 3 for all positive integers n.
    c. How are parts a and b related to Polya's phases of problem solving?

3.   Decode the following message. Then, explain how you got your foot in the door.

> Pdeo eo pda ydnnayp wjosan.

4–4 **Loop Structures**

Our goal now is to study some of the repetitive structures used in describing algorithmic processes. In this section we discuss the loop structure, exemplified by the while statement in our pseudocode, and in the next section we introduce the technique of recursion. Moreover, as examples, we introduce some popular algorithms for searching and sorting—the sequential and binary searches and the insertion and quick sorts—since they involve excellent applications of the repetitive structures being considered. We begin, then, by introducing the sequential search algorithm.

The Sequential Search Algorithm

Consider the problem of searching a list for the occurrence of a particular target value. We wish to develop an algorithm that determines whether or not that value is in the list. If the value is in the list, we will consider the search a success; otherwise we will consider it a failure. We assume that the list is sorted according to some rule for ordering its entries. For example, if the list is a list of names, we assume the names appear in alphabetical order, or if the list is a list of numbers, we assume its entries appear in order of increasing magnitude.

To get our foot in the door, we imagine how we might search a guest list of perhaps 20 entries for a particular name. In this setting, it is possible that we would scan the list from its beginning, comparing each entry with the target name. If we should find the target name, the search would terminate as a success. However, if we should reach the end of the list or reach a name greater than (alphabetically) the target name, our search would terminate as a failure. (Remember, the list is arranged in alphabetical order, so reaching a name greater than the target name indicates that the target does not appear in the list.) In summary, our rough idea is to continue searching down the list as long as there are more names to be investigated and the target name is less than the name currently being considered.

In our pseudocode, this process could be represented as

> Establish the current entry as the first entry in the list.
> while (target value > current entry and
>   there remain entries to be considered)
>   do (set the current entry to the next entry in the list)

Upon terminating the while structure, either the current entry is no less than the target name or else it is the last name in the list. In either case, we can detect a successful search by comparing the current entry to the target value. If these are equal, the search has been successful. Thus, we add the statement

> if (target value = current entry)
>   then (declare the search a success)
>   else (declare the search a failure)

to the end of the pseudocode routine presented above.

Finally, we observe that the first statement in our search routine is based on the assumption that the list in question contains at least one entry. We might reason that this is a safe guess, but just to be sure we could position our routine as the else option of the statement

> if (list empty)
>   then (declare the search a failure)
>   else (...)

which produces the pseudocode program shown in Figure 4-6. (Precautions such as protecting against the occurrence of an empty list make our final program more robust, a quality that should always be in the back of our minds when developing software. Indeed, options that may seem ridiculous when an algorithm is being developed have a tendency to seem quite logical after the algorithm has been implemented.)

In summary, the algorithm represented by Figure 4-6 directs a sequential search, considering the entries in the order in which they occur in the list. For this reason the algorithm is called the *sequential search algorithm.* Because of its simplicity, it is often used for short lists or in cases where other concerns dictate its use. However, in the case of long lists, sequential searches are not as efficient as other techniques (as we shall soon see).

Figure 4-6 The sequential search represented in pseudocode

```
if (list empty)
    then
        (declare search a failure)
    else
        (establish the current entry as the first entry in list,
        while (target value > current entry and
                there remain entries to be considered)
            do (set current entry to next entry in list),
        if (target value = current entry)
            then (declare search a success)
            else (declare search a failure))
```

Loop Control

The repetitive use of an instruction sequence is an extremely important algorithmic concept. One method if implementing such repetition is the **loop structure** (also known as the *iterative structure*), in which a collection of instructions, called the body of the loop, is executed in a repetitive fashion under the direction of some control process. A typical example is found in the sequential search algorithm represented in Figure 4-6. Here we have used a while statement to control the repetition of the single statement "set current entry to next entry in list." Indeed, the while statement

while (condition) do (body)

exemplifies the concept of a loop structure in that its execution traces the cyclic pattern

check the condition
execute the body
check the condition
execute the body
.
.
.

until the condition fails.

As a general rule the use of a loop structure produces a higher degree of flexibility than would be obtained merely by writing the body several times. For example, although the loop structure

Execute the following statement three times:
Pick up a marble and put it in the basket.

is equivalent to the sequence

Pick up a marble and put it in the basket.
Pick up a marble and put it in the basket.
Pick up a marble and put it in the basket.

we cannot produce a similar sequence that is equivalent to the loop described by

while (there are marbles on the floor) do
(pick up a marble and put it in the basket)

since we do not know in advance the number of marbles that will be involved.

With these examples in mind, let us take a closer look at the composition of loop control. You may be tempted to view this part of a loop structure as having minor importance. After all, it is typically the body of the loop that directly takes on the responsibility of accomplishing the task at hand (e.g., picking up the marbles)—the control activities appear merely as the overhead involved because we chose to execute the body in a repetitive fashion. However, experience has shown

Figure 4-7 Components of repetitive control

Initialize:	Establish an initial state that will be modified toward the termination condition
Modify:	Change the state in such a way that it moves toward the termination condition
Test:	Compare the current state to the termination condition and terminate the repetition if equal

that the control of a loop is the more error-prone part of the structure and therefore deserves our attention.

The control of a loop actually consists of the three activities initialize, modify, and test (Figure 4-7), with the presence of each being required for successful loop control. The test activity has the obligation of causing the termination of the looping process by watching for a condition that indicates termination should take place. It is for the purpose of this test activity that we provide a condition within each while statement of our pseudocode. This is the condition under which the body of the loop should be executed. That is, the repetitive execution of the body will continue as long as this condition is true. Thus, the termination condition is the negation of the condition stated in the while structure.

The other two activities in the loop control are meant to assure the termination condition will ultimately occur. The initialization step establishes a starting condition, and the modification step moves this condition toward the termination condition. For instance, in Figure 4-6 initialization takes place in the establish statement preceding the while statement. Here the current entry is established as the first list entry. The modification step in this case is actually accomplished within the loop body, where our position of interest is moved toward the end of the list. Thus, having executed the initialization step, repeated application of the modification step will result in the termination condition being reached. (If we never find the target value, we will ultimately reach the end of the list.)

We should emphasize that the initialization and modification steps must lead to the appropriate termination condition. This characteristic is critical for proper loop control, and thus one should always double-check for its presence when designing a loop structure. Failure to make such an evaluation can lead to errors even in the simplest cases. A typical example is the use of a termination condition such as testing a location for the value 6, initializing the location at 1, and then using the addition of 2 as the modification step. In this case, as the loop cycles, the location

Figure 4-8 The **while** loop structure

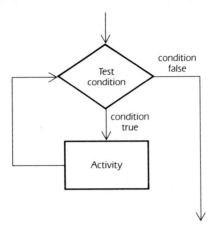

in question will contain the values 1, 3, 5, 7, 9, etc., but never the value 6. Thus, the loop will never terminate.

Finally, we note that the relative position of the various components of a loop structure can have a profound effect on the overall operation of the loop. For instance, having initialized the loop control, we may choose to execute the loop body and then test for termination or we could test for termination and then execute the loop body. More precisely, the structure of our pseudocode while statement

while *(condition)* do *(activity)*

is represented by the flow diagram in Figure 4-8. In contrast is the structure represented in Figure 4-9, in which the repetitive process begins by performing the loop's body rather than testing the condition. Thus, in this alternate structure the loop's body will always be executed at least once, whereas in the while structure the body will never be executed if the termination condition is satisfied the first time it is tested.

To provide a convenient notation for representing this alternate loop structure, we extend our pseudocode to include the statement form

repeat *(activity)* until *(condition)*

whose semantics is shown in Figure 4-9. Thus, the statement:

repeat (take a coin from your pocket)
until (there are no coins in your pocket)

assumes there is a coin in your pocket at the beginning, but:

while (there is a coin in your pocket)
do (take a coin from your pocket)

does not.

Figure 4-9 The **repeat** loop structure

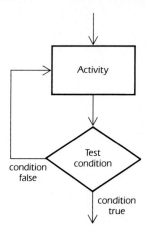

The Insertion Sort Algorithm

As an additional example of the use of loop structures, let us consider the problem of sorting a list of names into alphabetical order. But, before proceeding we should identify the constraints under which we will work. Simply stated, our goal is to sort the list "within itself." In other words, we want to sort the list by shuffling its entries as opposed to moving the list to another location. This rules out, for example, the technique of reconstructing the list in another location in such a way that the new version is sorted.

Our situation is analogous to the problem of sorting a list whose entries are recorded on separate cards spread out on a crowded desk top. We have cleared off enough space for the cards but are not allowed to push additional materials back to make more room. This restriction is typical in computer applications, not because the work space within the machine is necessarily crowded like our desk top, but simply because we want to use the storage space available in an efficient manner.

Let us get a foot in the door by considering how we might sort the names on the desk top. To be more precise, consider the list of names

Fred
Alice
David
Bill
Carol

One approach to sorting this list is to note that the list consisting of only the top name, Fred, is sorted but a list consisting of the top two names, Fred and Alice, is not. Thus, we might pick up the card containing the name Alice, slide the name Fred down into the space where Alice was, and then place the name Alice in the

hole at the top of the list, as represented by the first row in Figure 4-10. At this
point our list would be:

Alice
Fred
David
Bill
Carol

Figure 4-10 Sorting the list Fred, Alice, David, Bill, and Carol

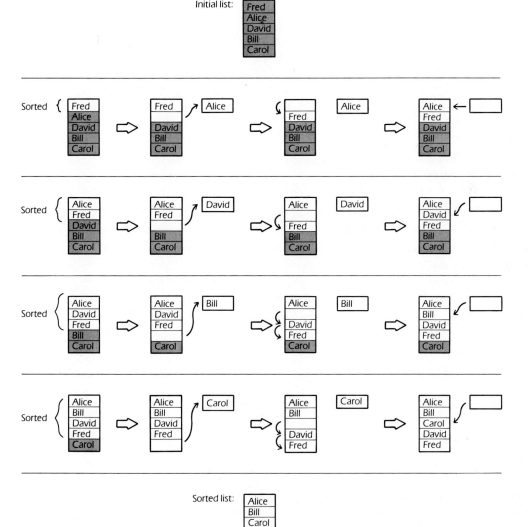

Now we note that the top two names form a sorted list but the top three do not. Thus, we might pick up the third name, David, slide the name Fred down into the hole where David was, and then insert David in the hole left by Fred, as summarized in the second row of Figure 4-10. The top three entries in the list would now be sorted. Continuing in this fashion, we could obtain a list in which the top four entries are sorted by picking up the fourth name, Bill, sliding the names Fred and David down, and then inserting Bill in the hole (see the third row of Figure 4-10). Finally, we can complete the sorting process by picking up Carol, sliding Fred and David down, and then inserting Carol in the remaining hole (see the fourth row of Figure 4-10).

Having analyzed the process of sorting a particular list, our task now is to generalize this process to obtain an algorithm for sorting general lists. To this end we observe that each row of Figure 4-10 represents the same general process—pick up the first name in the unsorted portion of the list, slide the names greater than the extracted name down, and insert the extracted name back in the list where the hole appears. If we identify the extracted name as the pivot entry, this process can be expressed in our pseudocode as

```
move the pivot entry to a temporary location leaving a hole in the list
while (there is a name above the hole and that name is greater than the pivot) do
    (move the name above the hole down into the hole leaving a hole above the name)
move the pivot entry into the hole in the list
```

Next, we observe that this process should be executed repeatedly, starting with the pivot being the second list entry and then advancing the pivot assignment one entry down the list before each additional execution until the last list entry has been positioned. This advancement of the pivot assignment is indicated in Figure 4-10 by means of shading. At any point in the figure, the portion of the list below the last pivot assignment is shaded. Each row in the figure begins by picking the top entry from the shaded portion to be the pivot and removing the shading from this position in the list. Thus, we can control the repetition of the preceding pseudocode routine with the statements

```
shade the portion of the list from the second entry through the last entry
repeat
    (remove the shading from the first name in the shaded portion of the list and
        establish this name as the pivot entry

            .
            .
            .    )
until (the entire list is unshaded)
```

where the dots indicate the location where the previous routine should be placed.

Of course, our routine so far assumes that there are at least two entries in the list to be sorted, an assumption that should not be made in general. On the other hand, if the list in question has fewer than two entries, it must be sorted already. Thus, we can extend our routine to handle such cases merely by starting with the statement

> if (there are two or more entries in the list)
>   then (. . .)

Our complete pseudocode program is shown in Figure 4-11. In short the program sorts a list by repeatedly removing an entry and inserting it into its proper place. It is because of this repeated insertion process that the underlying algorithm is called the *insertion sort.*

Note that the structure of Figure 4-11 is that of a loop within a loop, the outer loop being expressed by the repeat statement and the inner loop represented by the while statement. Each execution of the body of the outer loop results in the inner loop being initialized and executed until its termination condition is obtained. Thus, a single execution of the outer loop's body will result in several executions of the inner loop's body.

The initialization component of the outer loop's control consists of shading the portion of the list from the first entry to the last. The modification component is handled by the statement

> remove the shading from the first name in the shaded
>   portion of the list and establish this name as the
>   pivot entry

Figure 4-11 *The insertion sort expressed in pseudocode*

```
if (there are two or more entries in the list) then
    (shade the portion of the list from the second entry
            through the last entry
    repeat
        (remove the shading from the first name in the shaded
                portion of the list and establish this name as the
                pivot entry
        move the pivot entry to a temporary location leaving
            a hole in the list
        while (there is a name above the hole and that name
                    is greater than the pivot) do
            (move the name above the hole down into the hole
                    leaving a hole above the name)
        move the pivot entry into the hole in the list)
    until (the entire list is unshaded))
```

The termination condition occurs when the shaded portion of the list becomes empty, as indicated by the until clause.

The inner loop's control is initialized by removing the pivot entry from the list that creates a hole. The loop's modification step is accomplished by moving entries above the hole down, thus moving the hole up. The termination condition consists of the hole being immediately below a name that is not greater than the pivot or of the hole reaching the top of the list.

Questions/Exercises

1. Modify the sequential search program in Figure 4-6 to allow for lists that are not sorted.

2. Convert the pseudocode routine:

> assign Z the value 0
> assign X the value 1
> while (X < 6) do
>   (assign Z the value Z + X
>   assign X the value X + 1)

to an equivalent routine using a repeat statement.

3. Suppose the insertion sort as presented in Figure 4-11 was applied to the list George, Cheryl, Alice, and Bob. Describe the organization of the list at the end of each execution of the body of the repeat structure.

4. Why would we not want to change the phrase "greater than" in the while statement in Figure 4-11 to "greater than or equal to"?

4–5 Recursive Structures

Recursive structures provide an alternative to the loop paradigm for repetitive structures. As an introduction to the technique, we consider the binary search algorithm.

The Binary Search Algorithm

Let us again tackle the problem of searching a sorted list to see if it contains a particular entry, but this time we imagine that the list is a long tray of cards such as those found in the reference section of a library. In this case it is highly likely that we would not approach the problem by interrogating the first card, then the second card, etc. Rather, when faced with a search problem in this environment, we tend to begin by looking at a card in the area in which we believe the target entry will be found, or if we have no inclination as to where the target may be, we might pick an entry from the middle of the tray. If we are lucky, we will pick the card we are looking for on our first try, in which case our search succeeds. If we are not so lucky, we will have to continue searching. But, knowing the value on the selected

Figure 4-12 The core of the binary search

Specify the "middle" entry in the list as the current entry.
Perform one of the following instructions depending on which
    case is satisfied:

(target value = current entry):
    declare search a success.

(target value < current entry):
    search (the portion of the list preceding the current entry),
    if (that search is successful)
        then (declare search a success)
        else (declare search a failure).

(target value > current entry):
    search (the portion of the list following the current entry),
    if (that search is successful)
        then (declare search a success)
        else (declare search a failure).

card and the order of the list, we will be able to narrow the remaining search to a restricted portion of the list. In particular, if the target entry belongs in front of the chosen card, we would narrow our search to the earlier portion of the list; otherwise, we would search the latter portion.

In our pseudocode this process could be represented as shown in Figure 4-12. Note that we have placed the word *middle* in quotation marks to indicate the possibility that a list with an even number of entries has no middle entry. In this case the middle entry will refer to the first entry in the second half of the list.

Our problem now is how to perform the search required if the entry chosen first is not the target one. The routine in Figure 4-12 requires a program segment named search for performing this task. Thus, to complete our program we must provide a module named search that describes how this secondary search is to be performed. Note that this module must be robust enough to handle a request to search an empty list. For instance, if the routine in Figure 4-12 is given a list containing only one entry that does not agree with the target value, then the module will be requested to search either the sublist above or below the single entry, both of which are empty.

We could use the sequential search developed in the previous section as the required module, but this is not the technique we would probably use when searching the card tray in a library. Rather, we would probably repeat the same process on the restricted portion of the tray that we used for the whole tray. That is, we would select an entry toward the middle of that portion of the tray and use it to narrow our search further.

We can implement this in our pseudocode by first modifying the routine in Figure 4-12 to handle the case of an empty list and then giving the resulting program segment the name search to obtain the pseudocode program shown in Figure 4-13. Thus, if we were following the routine and came to the instruction "search (the portion of the list . . .)," we would apply the same search technique to the smaller list that we were applying to the original one. If that search succeeded, we would return to declare our original search successful; if this secondary search failed, we would declare our original search a failure.

Figure 4-13 The binary search in pseudocode

```
procedure search

if (list empty)
    then
        (declare search a failure)
    else
        (specify the "middle" entry in the list as the current entry,
        and perform one of the following instructions depending on
        which case is satisfied:

        (target value = current entry):
            declare search a success.

        (target value < current entry):
            search (the portion of the list preceding the
                current entry),
            if (that search is successful)
                then (declare search a success)
                else (declare search a failure).

        (target value > current entry):
            search (the portion of the list following the
                current entry),
            if (that search is successful)
                then (declare search a success)
                else (declare search a failure))
```

To clarify this process, let us apply the algorithm represented in Figure 4-13 to the list Alice, Bill, Carol, David, Evelyn, Fred, and George with the target name being Bill. Our search begins by selecting David (the middle entry) as the current entry under consideration. Since the target value (Bill) must precede this current entry, we are instructed to apply the module named search to the list of entries preceding David—that is, the list Alice, Bill, and Carol. Thus, we create a second copy of the search module and assign it to this secondary task.

For a while we will have two copies of our search module being executed, as summarized in Figure 4-14. Progress in the original copy is temporarily suspended

Figure 4-14

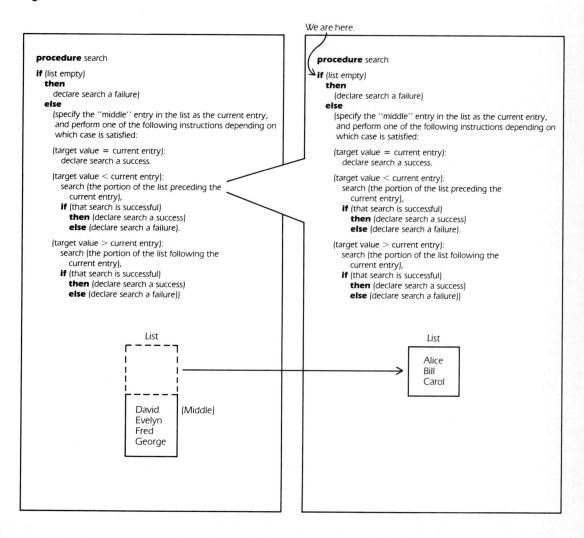

at the instruction

search (the portion of the list preceding the current entry)

while we apply the second copy to the task of searching the list Alice, Bill, and Carol. Once we complete this secondary search, we will discard the second copy of the module, report its findings to the original copy, and continue progress in the original. Thus, the second copy of the module executes as a subordinate to the original, performing the task requested by the original module and then disappearing.

The secondary search selects Bill as its current entry since that is the middle entry in the list Alice, Bill, and Carol. Consequently, its current entry is the same as the target value, so it declares its search to be a success and terminates.

At this point we have completed the secondary search as requested by the original copy of the module, and therefore we are able to continue the execution of that module. Here we are told that if the secondary search was successful, we should declare the original search a success. Thus, our process correctly determines that Bill is a member of the list Alice, Bill, Carol, David, Evelyn, Fred, and George.

Let us now consider what would happen if we asked our routine to search the list Alice, Carol, Evelyn, Fred, and George for the entry David. This time the original copy of the module would select Evelyn as its current entry and conclude that the target value must reside in the preceding portion of the list. It will therefore request another copy of the module to search the list of entries appearing in front of Evelyn— that is, the two-entry list consisting of Alice and Carol. At this stage our situation is as represented in Figure 4-15.

The second copy of the module will select Carol as its current entry and conclude that the target value must lie in the latter portion of its list. Thus, it will request a third copy of the module to search the list of names following Carol in the list Alice and Carol, which is empty. Thus, the third copy of the module has the task of searching the empty list for the target value David. Our situation at this point is represented by Figure 4-16. The original copy of the module has the task of searching the list Alice, Carol, Evelyn, Fred, and George with the current entry being Evelyn; the second copy is searching the list Alice and Carol with its current being Carol; and the third copy is about to begin searching the empty list.

Of course, the third copy of the module quickly declares its search to be a failure and terminates. The completion of the third copy's task allows the second copy to continue its task. It notes that the search it requested was unsuccessful, declares its own task to be a failure, and terminates. This report is what the original copy of the module has been waiting for, so it can now proceed. Since the search it requested failed, it declares its own search to have failed and terminates. Thus, our routine has correctly concluded that David is not contained in the list Alice, Carol, Evelyn, Fred, and George.

In summary, if we were to look back at the previous examples, we could see that the process employed by the algorithm represented into Figure 4-13 is to repeat-

Figure 4-15

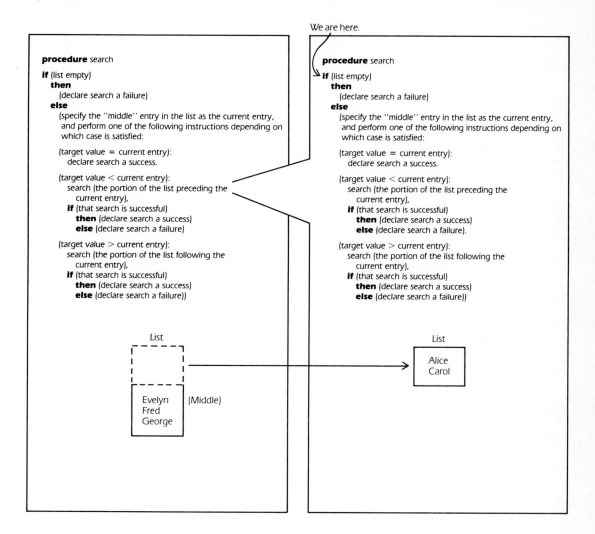

edly divide the list in question into two smaller pieces in such a way that the remaining search can be restricted to only one of these pieces. This divide-by-two approach is the reason why the algorithm is known as the ***binary search.***

Recursive Control

The binary search algorithm is similar to the sequential search in that each algorithm requests the execution of a repetitive process. However, the implementation of this repetition is significantly different. Whereas the sequential search involves a circular form of repetition, the technique employed by the binary search is to have each stage

Figure 4-16

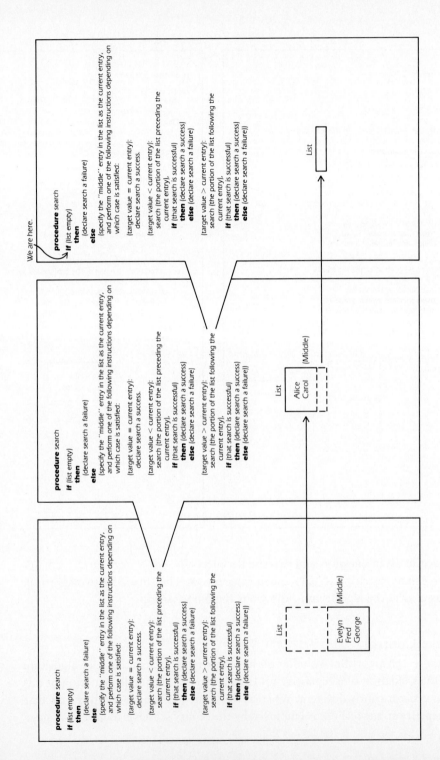

of the repetition executed as a subtask of the previous stage. This technique is known as *recursion.*

As we have seen, the illusion created by the execution of a recursive algorithm is the existence of multiple copies of itself, called activations, that appear and disappear as the algorithm advances. Of those activations existing at any given time, only one is actively progressing. The others are effectively in limbo, with each waiting for another activation to terminate before it can continue.

Being a repetitive process, recursive systems are just as dependent on proper control as are loop structures. For example, just as in loop control, recursive systems are dependent on testing for a termination condition and on a design that assures this condition will be reached. In fact, proper recursive control involves the same three ingredients—initialization, modification, and test for termination—that are required in loop control.

In general, a recursive routine is designed to test for the termination condition (often called the base case) before requesting further activations. If this condition is not met, the routine assigns an activation to the task of solving a revised problem that is closer to the termination condition than that assigned to the current activation. However, if the termination condition is met, a path is taken that avoids further recursive action. Thus, the current activation will terminate without creating additional activations. This means that one of the activations in limbo will be allowed to continue execution, complete its task, and in turn allow yet another activation to continue. In this fashion all the activations that are generated ultimately terminate, leaving the original task completed.

Let us see how the initialization and modification phases of repetitive control are implemented in our recursive binary search routine of Figure 4-13. In this case the creation of additional activations is terminated once the target value is found or the task is reduced to that of searching an empty list. The process is initialized implicitly by being given an initial list and a target value. From this initial configuration, the routine modifies the task it is assigned to that of searching a smaller list. Since the original list is of finite length and each modification step reduces the length of the list in question, we are assured that the target value will ultimately be found or the task will be reduced to that of searching the empty list. Thus, we conclude that the repetitive process is guaranteed to cease.

Having seen both the iterative and recursive control structures, you may wonder if the two are equivalent in power. That is, if an algorithm were designed using a loop structure, could another algorithm using only recursive techniques be designed that would solve the same problem and vice versa? Such questions are important in computer science since their answers tell us what features should be provided in a programming language in order to obtain the most powerful programming system possible. We return to these ideas in Chapter 11, where we consider some of the more theoretical aspects of computer science and its mathematical foundations. With this background, we will then be able to prove the equivalence of iterative and recursive structures in Appendix E.

The Quick Sort Algorithm

For another application of recursion, we reconsider the problem of sorting a list of names. Once again, we work within the constraints of sorting the list within itself, as dictated by the crowded desk top analogy described in our introduction to the insertion sort in Section 4-4.

The *quick sort* approaches its task by selecting one name, which we will call the pivot entry, finding this name's correct position, and placing the name in that position. To find the correct position for the pivot, the algorithm essentially divides the list into two smaller lists: the first consists of the names that should precede the pivot in the final order; the second consists of the names that should follow the pivot. Consequently, the correct location for the pivot entry will be between these two sublists.

To start the quick sort we must select a list entry as the pivot. Not knowing anything about the list, we might as well pick the name currently at the top. Next, we must divide the list into the two sublists just described. For this purpose we place an arrow, which we call a pointer, at the first name in the list (which is the pivot entry) and another pointer at the last name. Our algorithm will direct the movement of these pointers toward each other in such a way that the following assertion is always satisfied:

> **Assertion 1:**
> The names above the top pointer are less than (alphabetically) or equal to the pivot entry, while those below the bottom pointer are greater than the pivot.

This assertion states that the pointers identify two groups within the list. One group contains only entries that should precede the pivot entry (the names above the top pointer) in the final sorted list, while the other group contains only entries that should follow the pivot (the names below the bottom pointer).

To describe how the pointers are moved, we consider the problem of sorting the list:

> Jane
> Bob
> Alice
> Tom
> Carol
> Bill
> George
> Cheryl
> Sue
> John

We begin with the configuration:

$\rightarrow$ Jane   (Pivot entry)
Bob
Alice
Tom
Carol
Bill
George
Cheryl
Sue
$\rightarrow$ John

Next, we move the bottom pointer up the list comparing the name pointed to with the pivot entry at each step. As long as this name is greater than the pivot entry, we keep moving the pointer. Ultimately we will have to reach a name less than or equal to the pivot entry since the top name certainly fits this criterion. Once such a name has been reached, we stop moving the pointer. In our example, because this happens when the pointer reaches Cheryl, we stop moving the pointer at that position, producing the following configuration:

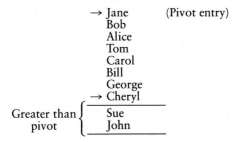

Now we begin moving the top pointer down the list comparing the names pointed to with the pivot entry. This time, however, we keep moving the pointer as long as the name in the list is less than or equal to the pivot entry or until the two pointers coincide. As we will see, this latter condition indicates that the correct location for the pivot has been found. On the other hand, the former condition would present us with a dilemma since any further movement of either pointer would destroy the validity of assertion 1. This is demonstrated in our example, which at this stage appears as follows:

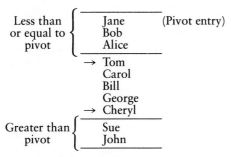

Observe that this deadlock can always be broken by interchanging the names designated by the pointers, after which we can again move the bottom pointer up (and then the top pointer down) without violating assertion 1. This, then, is what we do. Immediately after the interchange, our example has the following configuration:

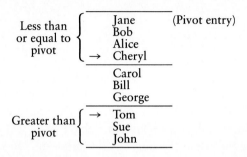

By continuing the process of moving the pointers and then interchanging names to break the deadlock, the two pointers must at some point coincide. In our example, this meeting occurs after the bottom pointer has stopped at George and the top pointer has moved down to it, producing the situation that appears as follows:

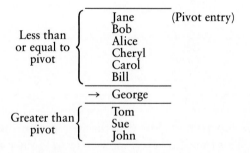

Once the pointers coincide, how does the identified entry compare to the pivot? To answer this question we first justify the following assertion:

Assertion 2:
At the beginning of the sort process and after each interchange for breaking a deadlock, the top pointer points to a name less than or equal to the pivot.

This assertion is certainly true at the beginning of the sort since at this time the top pointer points to the pivot entry itself. Furthermore, since each time a deadlock occurs the bottom pointer must point to a name less than or equal to the pivot entry, the interchange performed to break the deadlock will result in the top pointer pointing to an entry that is less than or equal to the pivot. We conclude that assertion 2 holds.

Based on assertion 2, we claim:

Assertion 3:
If the pointers coincide, the entry they identify is less than or equal to the pivot.

To justify this claim, we consider the two processes that could lead to the coincidence of the pointers. First, the bottom pointer could move up to the top pointer. In this case, assertion 2 confirms that the top pointer must point to an entry less than or equal to the pivot before the bottom pointer began to move. Thus, if the bottom pointer should reach the top one, assertion 3 will be satisfied. The other process that could lead to common pointer positions is for the top pointer to move down to the bottom one. But, in this case the bottom pointer would have previously stopped at an entry that is less than or equal to the pivot, so again assertion 3 will be satisfied.

Combining assertion 1 and assertion 3, we conclude that once the pointers coincide, the entries in the list below the pointers are all greater than the pivot and those entries at or above the common pointers are all less than or equal to the pivot. Indeed, in our example we find the following configuration:

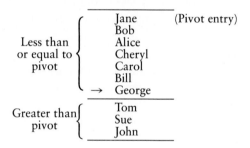

We are now ready to position the pivot entry; it belongs between the two sublists we have formed. To place it there we could remove the pivot from the list, repeatedly move names up one notch in the list until a hole is generated at the position of the common pointers, and then insert the pivot in this hole. This action would generate a tremendous amount of motion on our desk top as we pushed cards up to make room for the pivot, so, we prefer to simply interchange the pivot with the entry identified by the common pointers. After all, this entry belongs in front of the pivot (by assertion 3), and this interchange involves the movement of only two names instead of many. After this interchange our example takes on the following appearance:

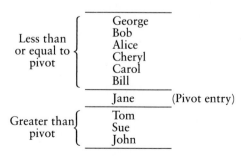

What we have accomplished at this stage is the correct positioning of one name. Admittedly, this does not sound like much, but the fact is that we are almost done from the algorithm point of view. If the portions of the list above and below the name just positioned had been sorted, the entire list would now be sorted. Thus, the problem is reduced to sorting these two portions as though they were two separate lists.

Note that having started with the problem of sorting one list, we have arrived at the problem of sorting two lists. At first glance you might conclude that we are getting farther from the solution rather than closer. However, such a conclusion overlooks the fact that the two lists that must now be sorted are each shorter than the original one. This observation leads to the conclusion that by applying this same algorithmic process to these shorter lists, we would obtain even more, but still shorter lists to sort. Successive applications of the process would ultimately reduce the initial sort problem to the problem of sorting numerous lists, each of which contained no more than one name. (We use the phrase "no more than one" to allow for the occurrence of a list with no names in it. Such a case would arise, for instance, if the pivot entry turned out to belong at the first of the list, resulting in the list of names above it being empty.) Since such lists are already sorted by default, we see that repeated applications of the process would at some stage no longer be required; at this point, the original list would be sorted.

With these ideas in mind, we are in position to present the complete quick sort algorithm, as shown in Figure 4-17.

In summary, let us apply the quick sort algorithm to the list:

> Bob
> Elaine
> David
> Alice
> Cheryl

We check the length of the list, establish Bob as the pivot entry, position pointers at the top and bottom of the list, move the bottom pointer up to the name Alice, move the top pointer down to the name Elaine, and interchange Elaine and Alice. Our situation now is as follows:

> Bob   (Pivot entry)
> → Alice
> David
> → Elaine
> Cheryl

Now we move the bottom pointer up to Alice but are unable to move the top pointer down since the pointers already coincide. Thus, we interchange the names Bob and Alice. At this point our list appears as follows:

Alice
Bob   (Pivot entry)
David
Elaine
Cheryl

We are now requested to sort the portion of the list above the pivot, which is the list containing the single name Alice. It is important to keep in mind that for a while we will have two activations of our algorithm. One is temporarily suspended at the instruction

sort (the portion of the list above the pivot)

while the second is charged with the task of sorting the list Alice. Our situation is analogous to that represented in Figure 4-18.

Actually, the second activation of the algorithm does not last long. It recognizes that the list it is charged with sorting has fewer than two entries and declares its task complete. Thus, we discard the second activation and return to continue in the first, where we find the instruction:

sort (the portion of the list below the pivot)

Figure 4-17 The quick sort in pseudocode

```
procedure sort
if (the list contains fewer than two entries)
    then
        (declare the list sorted)
    else
        (select the first entry in the list as the pivot,
        place pointers at the first and last entries of the list,
        while (the pointers do not coincide) do
            (move the bottom pointer up to the nearest entry less than
                or equal to the pivot but not beyond the top pointer,
            move the top pointer down to the nearest entry greater
                than the pivot but not beyond the bottom pointer,
            if (the pointers do not coincide)
                then (interchange the names indicated by the pointers))
        interchange the pivot entry with the entry indicated by
            the common pointers,
        sort (the portion of the list above the pivot),
        sort (the portion of the list below the pivot))
```

Figure 4-18

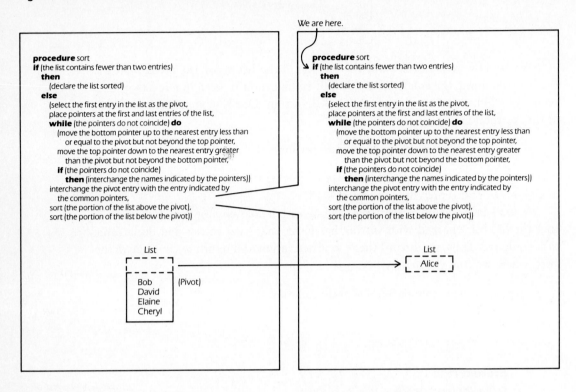

This requests that we establish another activation of the sort algorithm and assign it the task of sorting the list David, Elaine, and Cheryl. This activation establishes David as its pivot entry, interchanges Elaine and Cheryl, and then interchanges David (the pivot) and Cheryl (the name identified by the common pointers). Thus, the list under consideration by this activation of the algorithm has the structure

Cheryl
David   (Pivot entry)
Elaine

At this point the current activation reaches the instruction:

sort (the portion of the list above the pivot)

so it requests yet another activation to sort the list Cheryl. This results in a total of three activations currently underway. As the third of these activations begins, our situation is that of Figure 4-19. The original activation is waiting for the lower portion of its list to be sorted by the second activation. The second activation is waiting for the upper portion of its list to be sorted by the third activation. The third activation is about to begin its task.

Figure 4-19

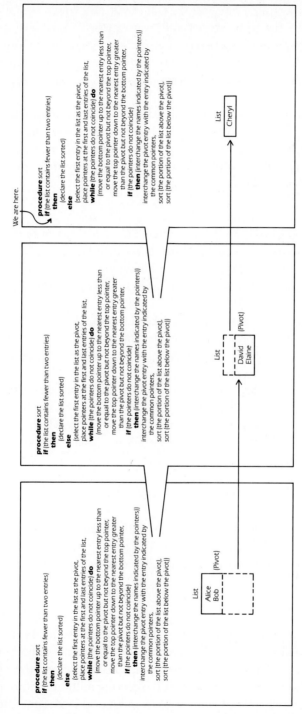

Here again the task of sorting a one-entry list does not take long. The third activation simply declares its list to be sorted and terminates. Thus, the second activation is able to proceed by requesting that the lower portion of its list be sorted. This, of course, creates another third activation charged with the task of sorting the list Elaine. This third activation does its job, terminates, and allows the second activation to continue once more.

At this stage the second activation has completed its task. Thus, it terminates and allows the original activation to continue. The original activation has been suspended at its last instruction, which requested the lower portion of its list to be sorted. Since that request has now been fulfilled, the original activation is finished and terminates. Indeed, the entire list has now been sorted.

Questions/Exercises

1. What names will be interrogated by the binary search (Figure 4-13) when searching for the name Joe in the list Alice, Bob, Carol, David, Evelyn, Fred, George, Henry, Irene, Joe, Karl, Larry, Mary, Nancy, and Oliver?
2. What is the maximum number of entries that must be interrogated when applying the binary search to a list of 200 entries?
3. If we applied the quick sort (Figure 4-17) to the list Carol, Alice, Bob, Larry, and John, what would be the order of the names immediately after the first interchange of names? What about after executing the next-to-the-last instruction in the first activation of the program?
4. What would happen if the quick sort were applied to a list that was already sorted? What if the list were in exactly reverse order?
5. What would happen if the quick sort were applied to a list in which all the names were the same?

4–6 Efficiency and Correctness

Of the remaining topics that could be discussed as a part of our formal introduction to algorithms, this section discusses two that should linger in your mind as you pursue the task of developing programs on your own. The first of these is efficiency, and the second is correctness.

Algorithm Efficiency

We discuss the issues of algorithm efficiency more thoroughly in Chapter 11 in the context of algorithm complexity. For now, however, we emphasize the importance of this topic by taking a few paragraphs to introduce the idea of comparative efficiency. Even though today's machines are capable of executing millions of instructions each second, efficiency remains a major concern in algorithm design. Often the choice between efficient and inefficient algorithms can make the difference between a practical solution to a problem and an impractical one.

Let us consider the problem of a university registrar who is faced with the task of retrieving and updating student records. Although the university has an enrollment of approximately 10,000 students, it actually maintains a current record of more than 30,000 students since it maintains each student's record for several years after graduation. For our purposes we can envision these records as being stored in the registrar's computer as a list ordered by student identification numbers. Thus, to find a student's record, the registrar essentially searches a sorted list for a particular identification number.

We have presented two algorithms for searching such a list: the sequential search and the binary search. Our question now is whether the choice between these two algorithms would make any difference in the case of the registrar. We consider the sequential search first.

Given a student identification number, the sequential search algorithm starts at the beginning of the list and compares the entries it finds to the number desired. Not knowing anything about the source of the target value, we cannot conclude how far into the list this search must go. We can say, though, that after many searches we would expect the average depth of the searches to be half way through the list; some will be shorter, but others will be longer. We conclude that over a period of time, the sequential search will have investigated roughly 15,000 records per search. Thus, if retrieving and checking a record for its identification number requires a millisecond (one thousandth of a second), each search will require an average of 15 seconds. Since an eight-hour workday contains 28,800 seconds, this means that the sequential search would allow the registrar to perform an average of no more than 2000 searches during a day. Thus, to retrieve each of the 10,000 active student records would represent more than a week's work. Moreover, this does not allow time for using or updating the information retrieved.

In contrast, the binary search proceeds by comparing the target value to the middle entry in the list. If this is not the desired entry, then at least the remaining search is restricted to only half of the original list. Thus, after interrogating the middle entry in the list of 30,000 student records, the binary search will have at most 15,000 records still to consider. After the second enquiry, at most 7500 will remain, and after the third retrieval, the list in question will have been reduced to no more than 3750 entries. Continuing in this fashion we find that if the target record is in the list, it will be found after retrieving at most 15 entries from the list of 30,000 records. Thus, if each of these retrievals could be performed in one millisecond, the process of searching for a particular record would require only 0.015 second. This means that the process of searching for each of the 10,000 active student records one at a time would consume at most 2.5 minutes—a substantial improvement over the sequential search algorithm.

Thus, one would certainly prefer the binary search over the sequential one in our example. But, before we blindly accept this as a correct conclusion, we must admit that our example is somewhat simplistic. To use the binary search requires that the student records be stored in a manner that allows the middle entries of successively smaller sublists to be retrieved without undue hardship. In short, the ultimate efficiency of the algorithm is closely associated with the details of its implementation. Our example here is rather typical in that a major concern regarding the algorithm's implementation is data organization. Indeed, the relationship between algorithms and data organization is the underlying theme of Part Three of this text.

We conclude that the issue of efficiency is quite important. In fact, the search for efficient solutions to problems and for techniques of measuring efficiency is a major topic in the area of complexity theory, which we discuss in Chapter 11.

Software Verification

Recall that the fourth phase in Polya's analysis of problem solving (Section 4-3) is to evaluate the solution for accuracy and for its potential as a tool for solving other problems. The significance of the first part of this phrase is exemplified by the following example:

> A traveler with a gold chain of seven links must stay in an isolated hotel for seven nights. The rent each night consists of one link from the chain. The hotel requires that each night's lodging be paid the following morning, and the traveler is not willing to pay in advance. What is the fewest number of links that must be cut so that the traveler can pay the hotel one link of the chain each morning without paying for lodging in advance?

We first realize that not every link in the chain must be cut. For instance, if we cut the second link, we could free both the first and second links from the other five. Following this insight we are led to the solution of cutting only the second, fourth, and sixth links in the chain, a process that releases each link while cutting only three (Figure 4-20). Furthermore, any fewer cuts will leave two links connected, and thus we conclude that the correct answer to our problem is three.

However, upon reconsidering the problem, we might make the observation that if only the third link in the chain is cut, we would obtain three pieces of chain of lengths one, two, and four (Figure 4-21). With these pieces we could proceed as follows:

> On the first morning, give the hotel the single link.
> On the second morning, retrieve the single link and give the hotel the two-link piece.
> On the third morning, give the hotel the single link.
> On the fourth morning, retrieve the three links held by the hotel and give the hotel the four-link piece.
> On the fifth morning, give the hotel the single link.
> On the sixth morning, retrieve the single link and give the hotel the double-link piece.
> On the seventh morning, give the hotel the single link.

Consequently, our first answer, which we were sure was correct, is incorrect. How, then, can we be sure that our new solution is correct? We might argue as follows:

Figure 4-20 Separating the chain using only three cuts

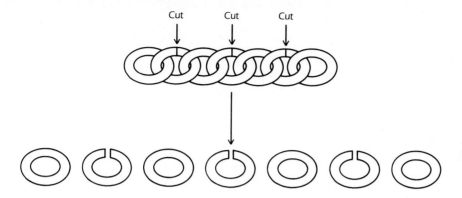

Since a single link must be given to the hotel on the first morning, at least one link of the chain must be cut, and since our new solution requires only one cut, it must be optimal.

Translated into the programming environment, this example emphasizes the distinction between a program that is believed to be correct and a program that is correct. Indeed, the two are not necessarily the same. The data processing community is rich in horror stories involving software that although "known" to be correct still failed at a critical moment because of some unforeseen situation. Thus, verification of software is an important undertaking, and the search for efficient verification techniques constitutes an active field of research in computer science.

One current line of research in this area attempts to apply the techniques of formal logic to prove the correctness of a program. The underlying thesis is that by reducing the verification process to a formal procedure, one is protected from the

Figure 4-21 Solving the problem with only one cut

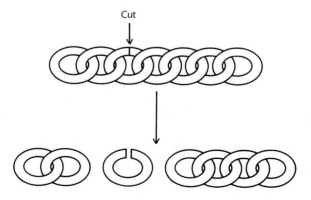

inaccurate conclusions that may be associated with intuitive arguments, as was the case in the gold chain problem. Let us consider this approach to program verification in more detail.

Just as a formal mathematical proof is based on axioms (geometric proofs are often founded on the axioms of Euclidean geometry while other proofs may be based on the axioms of set theory), a formal proof of a program's correctness is based on the specifications under which the program was designed. Thus, to prove that a program correctly sorts lists of names, we are allowed to begin with the assumption that the program's input is a list of names, or if the program is designed to compute the average of one or more positive numbers, we can assume that the input does, in fact, consist of one or more positive numbers. In short, a proof of correctness begins with the assumption that certain conditions, called preconditions, are satisfied at the beginning of program execution.

The next step in a proof of correctness is to consider how the consequences of these preconditions promulgate through the program. For this purpose, researchers have analyzed various program structures to determine how a statement, known to be true before the structure is executed, is affected by executing the structure. As a simple example, if a certain statement about the value assigned to Y is known to hold prior to executing the instruction

assign X the value of Y

then that same statement can be made about X after the instruction has been executed.

A slightly more involved example occurs in the case of an if-then-else structure such as:

if *(condition)* then *(instruction* 1)
else *(instruction* 2)

Here, if some statement is known to hold before execution of the structure, then upon executing *instruction* 1 we know that both that statement and the condition tested are true, whereas if *instruction* 2 is executed we know the statement and the negation of the condition must hold.

Following rules such as these, a proof of correctness proceeds by identifying statements, called assertions, that can be established at various points in the program. The result is a collection of assertions, each being a consequence of the program's preconditions and the sequence of instructions that lead to that point in the program at which the assertion is established. If the assertion so established at the end of the program corresponds to the desired output specifications, we can conclude that the program is correct.

To be more specific, let us consider a program consisting of the typical repeat loop structure represented in Figure 4-22. Suppose as a consequence of the precon-

Figure 4-22 The assertions associated with a typical **repeat** structure

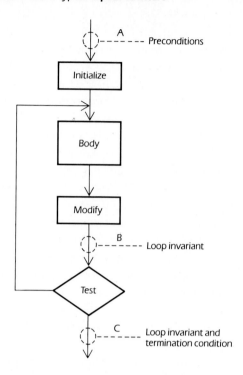

ditions given at point A, we are able to establish that a particular assertion is true each time point B is reached during the repetitive process. (Such an assertion within a loop is known as a loop invariant.) Then, if the repetition should ever terminate, execution would move to point C, where we could conclude that both the loop invariant and the termination condition would hold. (The loop invariant would still hold since the test for termination does not alter any values in the program, and the termination condition would hold since otherwise the loop would not have terminated.) If these combined statements imply the desired output, our proof of correctness can be completed merely by showing that the initialization and modification components of the loop ultimately lead to the termination condition.

You should compare this analysis to our example of the insertion sort shown in Figure 4-11. Indeed, the development of that program was based on the loop invariant:

> Each time the loop body is completed the names in the unshaded portion of the list are sorted.

the termination condition:

> The entire list is unshaded.

and the fact that by repeatedly unshading an additional name the entire list will ultimately be unshaded.

The fact that we informally identified the loop invariant in the process of developing the insertion sort program is not an uncommon phenomenon. Indeed, it turns out that the assertions obtained when proving a program correct are often essentially the insights that led to the program in the first place. This, in turn, has caused many to propose an assertion approach to program development. That is, they propose that the assertions for the various stages of a program be developed first and then the instructions that lead to these assertion be inserted. Note that this is quite similar to our development of the quick sort algorithm represented in Figure 4-17, where we used the assertion approach to establish various relationships among the list entries during program development.

The ultimate goal among researchers working on the problem of program verification is to develop techniques by which the process of proving the correctness of programs can be handled automatically by a computer. Unfortunately, this goal is yet to be achieved, so the process of proving that a program is correct remains a manual task that can become laborious and error prone, especially in the case of large software systems where proof of correctness is most important. Thus, the proof on which our assumption of correctness is based may be no more manageable than the program itself. Consequently, formal proofs of correctness have not yet become popular in the data processing community.

Currently, then, the data processing community must rely on other approaches to software verification, one of which is the use of redundancy. This is the technique of implementing two independent solutions to the same problem. If these solutions disagree, we know that at least one of them is wrong; if they agree, our confidence in correctness is reinforced.

Unfortunately, even the use of redundancy proves to be inefficient in many applications. The result is that in most cases today software is "verified" by applying it to test data—a process that is shaky at best. After all, verification by test data proves nothing more than that the program runs correctly for the test data. Any additional conclusions are merely projections based on statistical analysis. Thus, obtaining test data for use in program verification should be given the same careful consideration as obtaining a random sample in other statistical settings. It is this analogy that clarifies one of the major (yet often violated) rules of thumb in verification by test data—test data should not be designed by a person involved in the software development. After all, a person so involved would tend to overlook the same possibilities when designing the test data that were overlooked when designing the software. Thus, the test data produced would be anything but a random sample, and consequently, errors in the software, just as our error in the gold chain problem, could go undetected.

Questions/Exercises

1. Below is a problem and a proposed answer. Is the proposed answer correct? Why or why not?

> **Problem:** Suppose three cards are contained in a box. One of three cards is painted black on both sides, one is painted red on both sides, and the third is painted red on one side and black on the other. One of the cards is drawn from the box, and you are allowed to see one side of it. What is the probability that the other side of the card is the same color as the side you see?

> **Proposed answer:** One-half. Suppose the side of the card you can see is red. (The argument would be symmetric with this one if the side were black.) Only two cards among the three have a red side. Thus, the card you see must be one of these two. One of these two cards is red on the other side, while the other is black. Thus, the card you can see is just as likely be red on the other side as it is to be black.

2. The following program segment is an attempt to compute the quotient (forgetting any remainder) of two positive integers by counting the number of times the divisor can be subtracted from the dividend before what is left becomes less than the divisor. For instance, 7/3 should produce 2 since 3 can be subtracted from 7 twice. Is the program correct? Justify your answer.

```
assign Count the value 0
assign Remainder the value of the dividend
repeat (assign Remainder the value of Remainder − divisor,
        assign Count the value of Count + 1)
until (Remainder < the divisor)
assign Quotient the value of Count
```

3. The following program segment is designed to compute the product of two nonnegative integers X and Y by accumulating the sum of X copies of Y—that is, 3 times 4 is computed by accumulating the sum of three 4s. Is the program correct? Justify your answer.

```
assign Product the value of Y
assign Count the value 1
while (Count < X) do
   (assign Product the value of Product + Y, and
    assign Count the value of Count + 1)
```

4. Assuming the precondition that the value associated with N is a positive integer, establish a loop invariant that leads to the conclusion that if the following routine terminates then Sum will be assigned the value $0 + 1 + \ldots + N$.

```
assign Sum the value 0
assign I the value 0
while (I < N) do
   (assign I the value I + 1,
    assign Sum the value Sum + I)
```

Give an argument to the effect that the routine will, in fact, terminate.

Chapter 4 Review Problems

1. Does the following program represent an algorithm in the strict sense? Why or why not?

   ```
   assign Count the value 0
   while (Count not 5) do
      (assign Count the value of Count + 2)
   ```

2. In what sense do the following steps not constitute an algorithm?

   Draw a straight line segment between the points with rectangular coordinates (2,5) and (6,11).
   Draw a straight line segment between the points with rectangular coordinates (1,3) and (3,6).
   Draw a circle with radius two and center at the intersection of the previous line segments.

3. Rewrite the following program segment using a repeat structure rather than a while structure. Be sure the new version prints the same values as the original.

   ```
   assign Count the value 2
   while (Count < 7) do
      (print the value assigned to Count and
         assign Count the value Count + 1)
   ```

4. Rewrite the following program segment using a while structure rather than a repeat structure. Be sure the new version prints the same values as the original.

   ```
   assign Count the value 1
   repeat (print the value assigned to Count and
              assign Count the value Count + 1)
   until (Count = 5)
   ```

5. Design an algorithm that, when given an arrangement of the digits 0, 1, 2, 3, 4, 5, 6, 7, 8, 9, will rearrange the digits so that the new arrangement represents the next larger value that can be represented by these digits (or reports that no such rearrangement exists if no rearrangement produces a larger value). Thus, 5647382901 would produce 5647382910.

6. Design an algorithm for determining whether or not the string ACB appears in a given string of letters. You are allowed to compare only single letters to single letters—that is, you can write:

   ```
   if (the first letter in the string is A)
   ```

   but not:

   ```
   if (the first three letters in the string are ABC)
   ```

7. The algorithm represented below is designed to print the beginning of what is known as the Fibonacci sequence. Identify the body of the loop. Where is the initialization step for the loop control? The modification step? The test step? What list of numbers will be produced?

   ```
   assign Last the value 0
   assign Current the value 1
   while (Current < 100) do
      (print the value assigned to Current,
        assign Temp the value of Last,
        assign Last the value of Current, and
        assign Current the value of Last + Temp)
   ```

8. What sequence of numbers will be printed by the algorithm represented below if it is started with input values 0 and 1?

   ```
   procedure MysteryWrite
   assign Last the value of the first input number
   assign Current the value of the second input number
   if (Current < 100)
      then (print the value assigned to Current,
               assign Temp the value of Current + Last, and
               MysteryWrite(Current, Temp))
   ```

9. Modify the procedure MysteryWrite in the preceding problem so that the values are printed in reverse order.

10. What letters would be interrogated by the binary search (Figure 4-13) if it were applied to the list A, B, C, D, E, F, G, H, I, J, K, L, M, N, O when searching for the value J? What about the value Z?

11. What name would be interchanged with the pivot in the first activation of the quick sort (Figure 4-17) if it were applied to the list consisting of only Bill and Carol? What if the list were Carol and Bill?

12. On the average, how many times must two names be compared when searching a list of 6000 entries using the sequential search? What about the binary search?

13. Identify the body of the following loop structure and count the number of times it will be executed. What would happen if the test were changed to read "while (Count not 6)"?

   ```
   assign Count the value 1
   while (Count not 7) do
      (print the value assigned to Count and
         assign Count the value Count + 3)
   ```

14. What problems would you expect to arise if the following program were implemented on a computer? (Hint: Remember the problem of round-off errors associated with floating-point arithmetic.)

```
assign Count the value one-tenth
repeat (print the value assigned to Count and
        assign Count the value Count + one-tenth)
until (Count equals 1)
```

15. Design a recursive version of the Euclidean algorithm (question 3 of Section 4-2).

16. Suppose we applied both test1 and test2 (defined below) to the input value 1. What would be the difference in the printed output of the two routines?

```
procedure test1
    assign Count the value of the input number
    if (Count not 5)
        then (print the value assigned to Count and
              test1(Count + 1))

procedure test2
    assign Count the value of the input number
    if (Count not 5)
        then (test2(Count + 1)
              print the value assigned to Count)
```

17. Identify the important constituents of the control mechanism in the routines of the previous problem. In particular, what condition causes the process to terminate? Where is the state of the process modified toward this termination condition? Where is the state of the control process initialized?

18. Write a program to generate the sequence of positive integers (in increasing order) whose only prime divisors are 2 and 3—that is, your program should produce the sequence 2, 3, 4, 6, 9, 12, 16, 18, 24, 27, ... Does your program represent an algorithm in the strict sense?

19. Redesign the quick sort algorithm using the last name in the list as the pivot entry.

20. The factorial of 0 is defined to be 1. The factorial of a positive integer is defined to be the product of that integer times the factorial of the next smaller nonnegative integer. We use the notation $n!$ to express the factorial of the integer n. Thus, the factorial of 3 (written 3!) is $3 \times (2!) = 3 \times (2 \times (1!)) = 3 \times (2 \times (1 \times (0!))) = 3 \times (2 \times (1 \times (1))) = 6$. Design a recursive algorithm that computes the factorial of a given value.

21. What sequence of steps would be executed if the quick sort algorithm (Figure 4-17) were applied to a list containing only one name?

22. a. Suppose you must sort a list of five names, and you have already designed an algorithm that will sort a list of four names. Design an algorithm to sort the list of five names by taking advantage of the previously designed algorithm.

    b. Design a recursive algorithm to sort arbitrary lists of names based on the technique of part a.

23. The puzzle called the Towers of Hanoi consists of three pegs, one of which contains several rings stacked in order of descending diameter from bottom to top. The problem is to move the stack of rings to another peg. You are allowed to move only one ring at a time, and at no time is a ring to be placed on top of a smaller one. Observe that if the puzzle involved only one ring, it would be extremely easy. Moreover, when faced with the problem of moving several rings, if one could move all but the largest ring to another peg, the largest ring could then be placed on the third peg, and then the problem would be to move the remaining rings on top of it. Using this observation, develop a recursive algorithm for solving the Towers of Hanoi puzzle for an arbitrary number of rings.

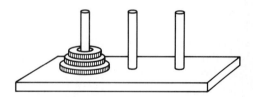

24. Another approach to solving the Towers of Hanoi puzzle (refer to problem 23) is to imagine the pegs arranged on a circular stand with a peg mounted at each of the positions of 4, 8, and 12 o'clock. The rings, which begin on one of the pegs, are numbered 1, 2, 3, etc., starting with the smallest ring being 1. Odd-numbered rings, when on top of a stack, are allowed to move clockwise to the next peg; likewise, even-numbered rings are allowed to move counterclockwise (so long as that move does not place a ring on a smaller

one). Under this restriction, always move the largest numbered ring that can be moved. Based on this observation, develop a nonrecursive algorithm for solving the Towers of Hanoi puzzle.

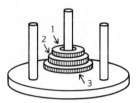

25. Analyze the loop in step 4 of this program for playing craps. Where is the loop initialized? In what sense is its state modified? Is termination guaranteed?

Step 1. Throw two dice and record their sum as "the original value."

Step 2. If the original value is 7 or 11 declare yourself the winner and stop.

Step 3. If the original value is 2, 3, or 12 declare yourself the loser and stop.

Step 4. Continue throwing the dice until their sum is either the original value or 7.

Step 5. If the new sum is 7, declare yourself the loser. Otherwise, declare yourself the winner.

26. Develop two algorithms, one based on a loop structure and the other on a recursive structure, to print the daily salary of a worker who each day is paid twice the previous day's salary (starting with one penny for the first day's work) for a 30-day period. What problems relating to number storage are you likely to encounter if you were to implement your solutions on an actual machine?

27. Design an algorithm to find the square root of a positive number by starting with the number itself as the first guess and repeatedly producing a new guess from the previous one by averaging the previous guess with the result of dividing the original number by the previous guess. Analyze the control of this repetitive process. In particular, what condition should terminate the repetition?

28. Design an algorithm that lists all possible rearrangements of the symbols in a string of five distinct characters.

29. The following program segment is designed to compute the product of two nonnegative integers X and Y by accumulating the sum of X copies of Y—that is, 3 times 4 would be computed by accumulating the sum of three 4s. Is the program segment correct? Explain your answer.

```
assign Product the value 0
assign Count the value 0
repeat (assign Product the value of Product + Y, and
        assign Count the value of Count + 1)
until (Count = X)
```

30. The following program segment is designed to report which of the positive integers X and Y is larger. Is the program segment correct? Explain your answer.

```
assign Difference the value of X − Y
if (Difference is positive)
    then (print "X is bigger than Y")
    else (print "Y is bigger than X")
```

31. The following program segment is designed to find the largest entry in a nonempty list of integers. Is it correct? Explain your answer.

```
assign TestValue the value of the first list entry
assign CurrentEntry the value of the first list entry
while (CurrentEntry is not the last entry) do
    (if (CurrentEntry > TestValue)
       then (assign TestValue the value of CurrentEntry)
    assign CurrentEntry the value of the next list entry)
```

32. a. Identify the preconditions for the sequential search as represented in Figure 4-6. Establish a loop invariant for the while structure in that program that when combined with the termination condition implies that upon termination of the loop the following if statement will report success or failure correctly.

   b. Give an argument showing that the while loop in Figure 4-6 will, in fact, terminate.

33. Based on the preconditions that X and Y are assigned nonnegative integers, identify a loop invariant for the following while structure that combined with the termination condition implies that the value associated with Z upon loop termination must be X − Y.

```
assign Z the value of X
assign J the value 0
while (J < Y) do
    (assign Z the value of Z − 1,
     assign J the value of J + 1)
```

Problems for the Programmer

1. Implement the sequential search and insertion sort algorithms in a language you know.

2. Does your language support recursion? Design a short test program to check your answer. If it does, implement the quick sort algorithm.

3. Identify the statements in your language that are designed for loop control. In each case, identify what parts of the loop control are provided automatically and what parts you must still specify explicitly.

4. Implement your solutions to review problems 5, 6, 18, and 27.

5. If your language supports recursion, implement your solution to review problems 15, 20, 22, and 23.

6. Implement your solutions to review problem 26 so that the length of the pay period can be easily altered. For what length pay period are your answers computed correctly?

5 Programming Languages

5-1 **Historical Perspective**
   Early Generations
   Machine Independence and Beyond
   More Recent Developments
5-2 **Language Implementation**
   The Translation Process
   Translation Versus Interpretation
5-3 **Programming Language Design**
   Semantic Concerns
   Syntactic Concerns
5-4 **Third-Generation Programming Languages**
   Data Description Statements
   Assignment Statements
   Statement-Level Control Statements
   Unit-Level Control Statements
   I/O Statements
   Internal Documentation
   Program Examples
5-5 **Declarative Programming** (optional)
   Logical Deduction
   Prolog

We have learned to appreciate the complexities involved in a software package such as an operating system and to understand the precision with which its algorithmic structure must be expressed. Moreover, this algorithmic structure must ultimately be described within the machine's memory as sequences of instructions coded as bit patterns according to the rules of the machine language. The process of designing software can be tedious enough without this additional error-prone task of expressing it in this coded form.

A technique is needed by which the machine can be made to accept and understand algorithms in a form that is more compatible with humans than is a machine language. With such a system, programmers would be allowed to concentrate their efforts on the design of the software instead of dividing it between design and coding. Such techniques have been developed, with many allowing the program to be expressed in sentence form much like the pseudocode used in Chapter 4. Such a system constitutes a programming language. In this chapter we take a look at some of the features of popular programming languages and briefly evaluate their advantages and disadvantages.

5–1 **Historical Perspective**

We begin by tracing the historical development of today's programming languages.

Early Generations

Before a computer can perform a task, it must be programmed to do so by placing an appropriate algorithm, expressed in machine language, in main memory. Originally this programming process was accomplished by the arduous method of requiring the programmer to express all algorithms in the machine's language. Such a technique added significantly to the already exacting task of an algorithm's design and more often than not led to errors that had to be located and corrected (a process known as debugging) before the job was finished.

The first step toward removing these complexities from the programming process was to do away with the tedious and error-prone use of numeric digits for representing the op-codes and operands found in a machine's language. To this end, it became popular to assign mnemonics to the various op-codes and to use them in place of hexadecimal representation during the design process. Thus, in place of the op-code for loading a register, a programmer might write LD, or to store the contents of a register, ST might be used. In the case of operands, rules were designed by which the programmer could assign names (often called identifiers) to locations in memory and use these names in place of the memory cell addresses in an instruction. A special case of this idea was the assignment of names such as R0, R1, R2, . . . to the registers in the CPU.

By choosing descriptive names for the memory cells and using mnemonics for representing op-codes, programmers could greatly increase the readability of a sequence of machine instructions. As an example of this technique, let us return to the machine language routine at the end of Section 2-2 that added the contents of memory cells 6C and 6D and placed the result in location 6E. Recall that the instructions in hexadecimal notation appeared as follows:

$$
\begin{array}{l}
156C \\
166D \\
5056 \\
306E \\
C000
\end{array}
$$

If we now assign the name PRICE to location 6C, TAX to 6D, and TOTAL to 6E, we can express the same routine as follows using the mnemonic technique:

```
LD R5,PRICE
LD R6,TAX
ADDI R0,R5 R6
ST R0,TOTAL
HLT
```

Most would agree that the second form, although still lacking, does a much better job of representing the purpose and meaning of the routine than does the first. (Note that the mnemonic ADDI is used to represent the add op-code to distinguish it from the op-code for adding floating-point numbers, which might be represented by ADDF.)

When these techniques were first introduced, programmers would use such notation when originally designing a program on paper and later translate it into machine-usable form. It was not long, however, before this translation process was recognized as a straightforward procedure that could be performed by the machine itself. Consequently, the use of mnemonics was formalized into a programming language called an *assembly language,* and a program, called an *assembler,* was developed to translate other programs written in the assembly language into machine-compatible form. (The program was called an assembler because its task was to assemble machine instructions out of the op-codes and operands obtained by translating mnemonics and identifiers. The term *assembly language* followed this lead.)

Today assemblers have become a significant utility program in most computer systems. With such a system, a programmer can type a program at a terminal in mnemonic form using the system's editor and then ask the operating system to use the assembler to translate the program and save the translated version as a file for later execution. Thus, the design of a program can be accomplished using an assembly language, whereas the program is executed from its machine-language form.

At the time assembly languages were first developed, they appeared as a giant step forward in the search for better programming environments. In fact, many considered them to represent a totally new generation of programming languages. Thus, assembly languages came to be known as second-generation languages, the first generation being the machine languages themselves.

Although second-generation languages had many advantages over their machine-language counterparts, they still fell far short of providing the ultimate programming environment. After all, the primitives used in an assembly language are essentially the same as those found in the corresponding machine language. The difference is simply in the syntax used to represent these primitives.

A major consequence of this close association between assembly and machine languages is that any program written in an assembly language is inherently machine dependent. That is, the instructions within the program are expressed in terms of a particular machine's attributes. Thus, a program written in assembly language is not easily transported to another machine. Rather, it must be rewritten to conform to the new machine's register configuration and instruction set.

Another disadvantage of an assembly language is that a programmer, although not required to code instructions in bit pattern form, is still forced to think in terms of the small, incremental steps of the machine's language rather than being allowed to concentrate on the overall solution of the task at hand. The situation is analogous to designing a house in terms of concrete, boards, glass, nails, bricks, etc. It is true that the actual construction of the house will ultimately require a description based on these elementary pieces, but the design process is easier if we think in terms of walls, doors, windows, roofs, chimneys, etc.

In short, the elementary primitives in which a product must ultimately be expressed are not necessarily the primitives that should be used during the product's design. Indeed, the design process is better suited to the use of high-level primitives, each representing a concept associated with a major feature of the product. Once the design is complete, these primitives can be translated to lower-level concepts relating to the details of implementation, just as a contractor ultimately translates a building's design into a bill of materials.

Following this philosophy, computer scientists began developing programming languages that were more conducive to software development than were the low-level assembly languages. The result was the emergence of a third generation of programming languages that differed from previous generations in that their primitives were both higher level and machine independent.

In general, the approach to third-generation programming languages was to identify a collection of high-level primitives (in essentially the same spirit as that in which we developed our pseudocode in Chapter 4) in which software could be developed. Each of these primitives was designed so that it could be implemented as a sequence of the low-level primitives available in machine languages. For example, the statement

assign Total the value Price plus Tax

expresses a high-level activity without reference as to how a particular machine should perform the task, yet it can be implemented by the sequence of machine instructions discussed earlier. Thus, the structure

assign *identifier* the value *expression*

would be a potential high-level primitive.

Once this collection of high-level primitives had been identified, a program could be written to recognize these primitives (a process known as parsing) and translate them into their machine-level equivalents. Such a program was similar to the second-generation assemblers except that the third-generation translators often had to compile several machine instructions into short sequences to simulate the activity requested by a single high-level primitive. Thus, these programs came to be known as *compilers.*

Machine Independence and Beyond

With the development of third-generation languages, the goal of machine independence was largely achieved. Since the statements in a third-generation language did not refer to the attributes of any particular machine, they could be compiled as easily for one machine as for another. Thus, a program written in a third-generation language could theoretically be used on any machine simply by applying the appropriate compiler.

Reality, however, has not proven to be this simple. When a compiler is designed, certain restrictions imposed by the underlying machine are ultimately reflected as conditions on the language being translated. For example, the size of a machine's registers and memory cells places limits on the maximum size of integers that can be manipulated conveniently. Such conditions result in the fact that the "same" language tends to have different characteristics, or dialects, on different machines, and consequently it is often necessary to make at least minor modifications to a program if it is to be moved from one machine to another.

Compounding this problem of portability is the lack of agreement in some cases as to what constitutes the correct definition of a particular language. To aid in this regard, the American National Standards Institute (ANSI) has adopted and published standards for some of the popular languages. In other cases, informal standards have been developed because of the popularity of a certain dialect of a language and the desire of other compiler writers to produce compatible products.

In the overall history of programming languages, the fact that third-generation languages fell short of true machine independence is actually of little significance for two reasons. First, they were close enough to being machine independent that software could be transported from one machine to another with relative ease, and therefore the demand for machine independent languages was essentially satisfied. Second, the goal of machine independence turned out to be only a seed for more demanding goals. Thus, by the time machine independence was within reach, its significance had been diluted in comparison to the loftier ambitions of the time. Indeed, the realization that machines could respond to such high-level statements as

assign Total the value Price plus Tax

led computer scientists to dream of programming environments that would allow humans to communicate with machines in terms of abstract concepts rather than being forced to translate these concepts into machine-compatible data before processing and then to decode the machine's output afterward. Thus, instead of quenching a thirst, the third-generation languages whet an appetite for more advanced languages, each designed to transfer still more of the problem-solving burden onto the machine and away from the user.

More Recent Developments

Two problems arise if we try to continue with the history of programming languages from the generation point of view. One is that after the third generation we bump up against the edge of evolving terminology. The truth is that the lack of a central, definitive source of terminology has resulted in varying definitions of fourth- and fifth-generation languages.

As a general rule, however, the term *fourth-generation language* is used in reference to the numerous software packages that allow users to customize computer software to their applications without needing technical expertise. Programming in such languages normally involves selecting from choices presented on the terminal's screen in sentence or icon form. Such packages include spreadsheet systems that assist in maintaining tables of data in the form of traditional accounting records; database systems that assist in the maintenance and recall of information that might otherwise be stored in a traditional filing cabinet; graphics packages that assist in the development of graphs, charts, and other pictorial representations of information; and powerful word processors that allow documents to be merged, rearranged, and reformatted. Moreover, packages such as these are often bundled (as integrated software) to form one coherent system. With such a system an economist can construct and modify economic models, analyze the effects various changes might have on the economy in general or a given business in particular, and present the results in a written document using graphs and charts as visual aids. Moreover, a small-business manager might customize the same package to develop a system for maintaining inventory and predicting the effects of stocking certain slow-moving items.

Such systems are considered to constitute another generation in programming languages because the programming environment they provide is noticeably closer to that of the application than the environments provided by third-generation languages. For example, instead of describing the details of how data is saved within the machine, how a table of data can be represented on a computer screen, or how entries are actually updated within the machine, a programmer using fourth-generation software merely describes what data items are to appear on the spreadsheet and how they relate to each other. From then on, the software carries out the details of implementation. Thus, the user can customize and use a computerized spreadsheet without concentrating on (or even being aware of) the concepts associated with the technology being used.

The term *fifth-generation language* is being used more and more in reference to the concept of declarative programming, with an emphasis on the more specialized

Figure 5-1 Generations of programming languages

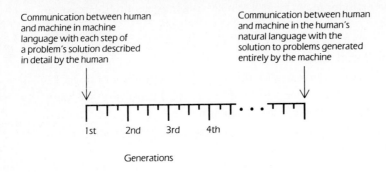

Generations

approach known as logic programming. We define these ideas more thoroughly in the next few paragraphs. For now we merely note that the idea of declarative programming is to allow the computer user to solve a problem by concentrating on what the problem is rather than on how it is to be solved. At this point, such a goal probably seems outrageous to you. How can we hope to solve a problem without ultimately concentrating on how to solve it? The answer is that we do not solve the problem; rather, we let the computer system, with its underlying software, solve it. With this approach, then, our task is merely to declare what the problem is while the machine tackles the issues of its solution.

The concept of declarative programming brings us to the second problem encountered when trying to push the generation analysis of programming languages beyond the third generation. This problem is that the generation approach insists on classifying programming languages on a linear scale (Figure 5-1) according to the degree in which the user of the language must conform to the world of computer gibberish as well as the degree to which the task of solving a problem is placed on the machine as opposed to the user. In reality, the development of programming languages has not progressed in this manner but instead has branched as different approaches to the programming process (different paradigms) have surfaced and been pursued. Thus, the historical development of programming languages is better represented by a branching diagram in which the various paradigms are shown to split from previous developments to form new paths progressing independently from each other (Figure 5-2).

We have represented the ***procedural paradigm*** as the central path in Figure 5-2 because it represents the traditional approach to the programming process. Indeed, the procedural paradigm is the one on which a CPU's fetch-decode-execute cycle is based as well as the paradigm underlying our discussion of program development in Chapter 4. As the name suggests, the procedural paradigm defines the programming process to be the development of procedures that when followed manipulate

Figure 5-2 The nonlinear development of programming languages

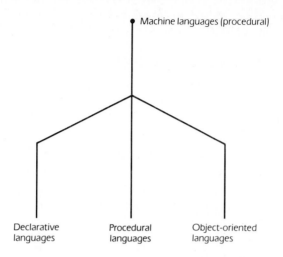

Machine languages (procedural)

Declarative languages

Procedural languages

Object-oriented languages

data to produce the desired result. Thus, the procedural paradigm tells us to approach a problem by trying to find a method for solving it.

In contrast, let us consider the ***declarative paradigm.*** As already mentioned this paradigm emphasizes the question "What is the problem?" rather than "What procedure is required to solve the problem?" The trick here is to discover and implement a general problem-solving algorithm. Once this is done, problems can be solved merely by stating them in a form compatible with this algorithm and then applying the algorithm. In this context, the task of the programmer becomes that of developing a precise statement of the problem rather than of discovering an algorithm for solving the particular problem.

Of course, the major problem in developing a programming language based on the declarative paradigm is the discovery of the underlying problem-solving algorithm. For this reason early declarative languages tended to be special purpose in nature, designed for use in particular applications. For example, the declarative approach has been used for many years in simulation languages with which computer technology is used to simulate a system (economic, physical, political, etc.) in order to test hypotheses. In these settings, the underlying algorithm is essentially the process of simulating the passage of time by repeatedly recomputing values of parameters (gross national product, M1 money supply, etc.) based on the previously computed ones. Thus, to implement a declarative language for such simulations, all one must do is implement an algorithm that performs this repetitive task. Following this, the only task required of a programmer using the language is to describe the relationships among the parameters to be simulated. Then the simulation algorithm merely simulates the passage of time using these relationships to perform its calculations.

More recently, the declarative paradigm has been given a tremendous boost by the discovery that the subject of formal logic within mathematics provides a simple problem-solving algorithm suitable for use in a general-purpose declarative programming system. The result has been increased attention to the declarative paradigm and the emergence of logic programming, a subject discussed in Section 5-5.

Another approach to program development is the *object-oriented paradigm.* Based on this point of view, the components of a problem's environment are thought of as objects that send messages to other objects while responding to messages received. In this context, if one were to construct an economic model involving such indicators as the gross national product, national trade balance, and consumer price index, each of these "measurements" would be implemented as an object. Each object would have an associated value as well as a collection of routines describing how that object should respond to different messages it may receive and what messages it should send to other objects under various conditions. For example, if the value associated with the national trade balance should change, the national trade balance object might send a message to the consumer price index object so that that object could adjust its value accordingly. The result is a system in which the various components of the economic system are modeled like guests at a cocktail party, milling around and interacting with each other.

Many of the advantages of the object-oriented paradigm are consequences of the modular structure that emerges as a natural byproduct of the object-oriented philosophy. Indeed, each object is implemented as a separate, well-defined module whose characteristics are largely independent of the rest of the system. Thus, once an object representing the consumer price index has been developed, it can be reused in other simulations or modified to respond to messages according to a different economic theory without paying attention to other parts of the system. We return to the concept of object-oriented programming in Chapter 7.

Clearly the development of programming languages is an ongoing process. New languages continue to evolve as we search for more convenient ways to communicate with machines. Thus, programming languages that represent the frontier of knowledge today are destined to be criticized as archaic tomorrow.

Questions/Exercises

1. In what sense is a program in a third-generation language machine-independent? In what sense is it still machine-dependent?
2. What is the difference between an assembler and a compiler?
3. We can summarize the procedural programming paradigm by saying that it places emphasis on describing a process that leads to the solution of the problem at hand. Give a similar summary of the declarative and object-oriented paradigms.
4. In what sense are the later-generation programming languages at a higher level than the earlier generations?

5–2 **Language Implementation**

The implementation of high-level programming languages is based on the process of converting programs in these languages into programs in machine language. In this section we discuss the issues of this conversion process. Our motivation is twofold. First, an understanding of this process often helps in understanding the details of a particular programming language since these details are often traceable to concerns that arise during the conversion process. Second, our discussion of the translation of formal programming languages provides a preview to the issues involved in processing natural human languages such as English (an important topic of current research).

The Translation Process

We begin with some terminology. Since both assemblers and compilers perform translation tasks, they are collectively known as **translators.** The program in its original form as presented to a translator is called a **source program,** while the version of the program produced by the translation process is called an **object program.**

From an overall point of view, the translation of a program consists of three activities: lexical analysis, parsing, and code generation (Figure 5-3). Lexical analysis is the process of recognizing which strings of symbols in the source program actually represent a single, elementary object. For example, the string of three symbols 153 should not be interpreted as a 1 followed by a 5 followed by a 3 but should be recognized as representing a single numeric value. Likewise, the identifiers appearing in a program, although composed of several characters, should be interpreted collectively as a name—not as individual characters.

Note that humans perform lexical analysis with apparently little effort. When asked to read aloud, a person pronounces words rather than individual characters. On the other hand, if we expect a computer to perform this analysis, we must take care to describe what we want in an explicit, unambiguous manner. To this end, it is advantageous to design programming languages in a manner that simplifies the task of lexical analysis. Thus, most languages require that names referring to memory

Figure 5-3 The translation process

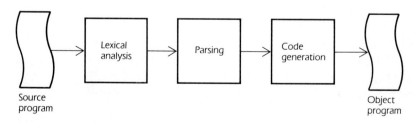

Source
program

Object
program

locations start with an alphabetic character rather than a digit. Such a restriction simplifies the task of distinguishing between a string representing a name and a string representing a numeric value.

The second activity in the translation process, parsing, is the process of analyzing the grammatical structure of a sentence and recognizing the role of its components. It is the technicalities of parsing that cause one to hesitate when reading the sentence

The man the horse that won the race threw was not hurt.

Likewise, it is the parsing process that distinguishes an if-then-else structure from a while structure and determines what statements belong to the then and else clauses. Again the need to request a computer to perform this task dictates that it be expressed to a high degree of precision. Thus, to simplify the parsing task, the collection of statement structures found in a programming language is not as varied as in a natural language but rather is normally restricted to a relatively few and carefully chosen forms. After all, as the variety of statement structures allowed in a programming language increases, so does the complexity involved in distinguishing them from one another and identifying their various components.

The final activity in translating a program, code generation, is the process of constructing sequences of machine-language instructions to simulate the statements recognized by the parser. It is this process, then, that produces the final product of the translation process—the object program.

Unfortunately, the object program produced by the translation process, although expressed in machine language, is rarely in a form that can be executed directly by the machine. One reason is that most programming environments allow the modules of a program to be developed and translated as individual units at different times (which supports the modular construction of software). Thus, the object program produced from a single translation process is often only one of several pieces of a complete program, each piece of which requests services from the other modules in order to accomplish the task of the entire system. In fact, even in cases where a complete program is developed and translated as a single module, its object program is rarely prepared to stand alone at execution time because it most likely contains requests for services from utility software available through the operating system or from the operating system itself. Thus, an object program is actually a machine-language program containing several loose ends that must be connected to other object programs before an executable program is obtained.

The task of making these connections is performed by a utility program called a *linker*. Its job is to link several object modules (the result of previous and separate translations), operating system routines, and other utility software to produce a complete, executable program (sometimes called a load module) that is in turn stored as a file in the machine's bulk storage system.

Finally, to execute the completed program stored as a load module, it must be placed in memory by a utility program called a *loader.* The significance of this step is most pronounced in the case of multiuser, time-sharing systems, in which the exact memory area available to the program is not known until it is time to execute the program (since it must share memory with other programs being executed) and varies from one execution to the next. In this setting, the task of the loader is to place the program in the memory area identified by the operating system and make any last-minute (last-microsecond) adjustments that might be needed once the exact memory location of the program is known. (A jump instruction in the program must jump to the correct address within the program.) It is the desire to minimize these last-minute adjustments by the loader that has encouraged the development of techniques by which explicit references to memory addresses within a program can be avoided, resulting in a program (called a relocatable module) that, without modification, will execute correctly regardless of where it is placed in memory.

In summary, the complete task of preparing a high-level language program for execution consists of the three-step sequence of translate, link, and load, as represented in Figure 5-4. Of course, once the translate and link steps have been completed, the program can be repeatedly loaded and executed without returning to the source version. If, however, a change must be made to the program, it is made to the source program, and then the modified source program is translated and linked to produce a new load module containing the change.

Translation Versus Interpretation

To alleviate the need for translation and linking after each program modification, an alternative to translation known as interpretation has been developed. In contrast to translation, interpretation uses a software package called an *interpreter* to scan the source program and perform the required activities. Thus, unlike a translator, which merely produces a machine-language copy of the program, an interpreter executes the program directly from its source language form. Of course, we realize that because the machine executes only machine-language instructions, a certain translation process must be performed by the interpreter, but this step is hidden from the programmer; thus the program appears to be executed without any required conversions.

Figure 5-4 The complete program preparation process

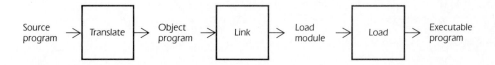

As you might imagine, the major advantage of using an interpreter is that once a program has been submitted to a machine in a high-level language form, it can be executed through a one-step process rather than the multiple translate/link/load/execute sequence required by translation.

The major disadvantage of an interpreter is that no permanent copy of the translation is produced and saved. Rather, the internal translation steps must be repeated each time the program is executed. The result is that a program being interpreted will take longer to execute than will a similar program that is already translated and can be executed from its machine-language form. Thus, translation is often chosen for programs that are to be executed repeatedly, such as a payroll processor or where real-time requirements demand timely execution. However, during program development and debugging or in cases where programs are written on an experimental basis, executed only a few times, and then discarded, interpretation has proven extremely useful.

The terminology within a science is often merely a refinement of the less precise colloquial use of words, and the distinction between translating and interpreting presented here is an excellent example. Indeed, the colloquial concept of translating a book from one language into another is that of producing another copy of the book but in a different language from that of the original (Figure 5-5). Once the translation is complete, anyone who understand only the target language is able to read the book in its translated form. This corresponds to the role of a program translator. In contrast, a diplomat often takes an interpreter along on trips to foreign

Figure 5-5 Translation

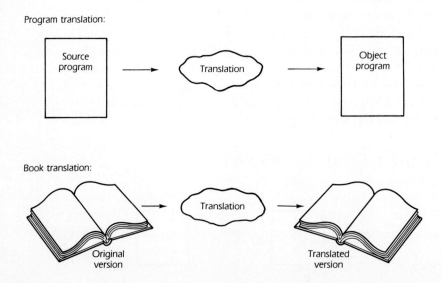

Program translation:

Source program → Translation → Object program

Book translation:

Original version → Translation → Translated version

Figure 5-6 Interpretation

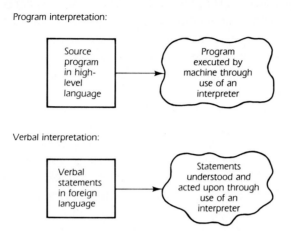

Program interpretation:

Source program in high-level language → Program executed by machine through use of an interpreter

Verbal interpretation:

Verbal statements in foreign language → Statements understood and acted upon through use of an interpreter

countries to assist in interactive conversations. In this setting the interpreter does not produce permanent translations of the conversations but explains to the diplomat what is being said while it is being said (Figure 5-6). Thus, through the interpreter, the diplomat is effectively given the ability to understand and respond to statements in an otherwise unknown language, just as a program interpreter appears to give a machine the ability to understand programs in a high-level language.

Questions/Exercises
1. Summarize the steps in the translation process.
2. a. What is the difference between a translator and an interpreter?
   b. Compare the process of making a change to a program that is translated to the process of making a similar change to a program that is interpreted.
3. In what sense is an object program not ready for execution?
4. What is a relocatable module and how does its relocatable feature simplify the task of a loader?

5–3 Programming Language Design

Before considering detailed aspects of particular programming languages, we should discuss some of the general concerns of programming language design. These concerns center around the choice and implementation of the primitives from which programs in the language must be constructed. Because each primitive consists of a semantic structure and its syntactic representation, our discussion is divided accordingly.

Semantic Concerns

The paradigm on which a language is based goes a long way toward establishing the semantic structures that the language must be capable of expressing. If the paradigm is object-oriented, the language must allow the expression of objects and message passing; if the paradigm is procedural, the language will be called upon to express such control concepts as conditional branching, iteration, and recursion.

Of course, not all the concepts that must be expressible in the language need to be implemented as individual primitives. Instead, many concepts can be described in terms of other, less complex concepts just as ideas that cannot be expressed in a single word of English can be expressed by combining well-established words to form sentences and paragraphs. This, combined with the fact that simple languages make for simple translators and interpreters, encourages the design of languages that are founded on small, well-chosen collections of basic semantic structures from which other, more complex structures can be constructed as needed.

Unfortunately, one cannot predict the applications for which a given programming language may ultimately be used, and one certainly would not want to discover at a later date that the use of the language is restricted because a critical semantic structure was not included in the language's design. (This is especially important in the design of the lowest-level language of the machine itself, because any change in a language at this level would require rebuilding part of the CPU.) Thus, one is faced with conflicting goals. On the one hand, there is pressure to implement a large collection of primitives in hopes of covering all future needs; on the other hand, a cumbersome language is difficult to design, implement, learn, and use.

A major theme of Chapter 11 is that the theoretical foundations of computer science provide a solution to this problem. That is, a surprisingly simple language offers the required expressive power. Indeed, most of the features in today's high-level languages are provided to increase a language's compatibility with the application and ease of use rather than its ultimate capabilities.

In addition to the choice of which semantic structures should be implemented as primitives, the design of a programming language requires that the chosen semantic structures be constructed in a manner that avoids ambiguities. Indeed, the ambiguities occurring in natural languages are totally unacceptable in a programming environment. Anyone who has ever tried to match paint colors knows that the semantics of the statement "The kitchen wall is yellow" is ambiguous when it comes to the task of touching up the discolored area on the wall where an artifact has hung for 10 years. Moreover, some natural language statements have multiple meanings. The semantics of the statement "The better stock ran well ahead of the herd" varies depending on whether one is speaking of a financial market or stampeding cattle.

In the context of programming languages, the precise meaning of each primitive is relatively easy to control. It is when these primitives are combined to form more complex semantic structures that subtle ambiguities can arise. For instance, the semantics of addition and multiplication of integers are well established, yet when combined as in $5 + 7 \times 2$, a potential ambiguity presents itself. Is the value represented 24 (the result of multiplying the sum $5 + 7$ by 2) or 19 (the result of adding 5 to the product 7×2)? This problem is often resolved by accepting the traditional precedence rules associated with numeric operations. In this case, given a numeric expression, all exponentiations are performed first, then multiplications and divisions, and finally additions and subtractions. Another option is to perform the operations as they are encountered from left to right or from right to left.

Other ambiguities arise when combining structures of the if-then-else and if-then variety. Each of these primitives has a well-defined meaning, yet when combined as in the statement

if B1 then if B2 then X else Y

there is the potential for two different interpretations represented by

if B1 then [if B2 then X] else Y

and

if B1 then [if B2 then X else Y]

In the first case, action Y is executed if condition B1 is false, regardless of the condition B2. In the second case, Y is executed only if B1 is true and B2 is false. An example of how this problem might be resolved is to accept the rule that else clauses in a program are assigned to if statements by scanning the program from beginning to end while interpreting each else clause as the alternate activity associated with the nearest preceding if structure that has yet not been assigned an alternative. Thus,

if B1 then if B2 then X else Y

would be assigned the semantics represented by

if B1 then [if B2 then X else Y]

We see, then, that the definition of the semantics within a programming language encompasses more than the meaning of each individual primitive. It also includes the semantics of compound structures formed by combining primitives— a context that has the potential for producing numerous subtle distinctions, all of which must be carefully accounted for.

Syntactic Concerns

Let us now turn to the design issues involving syntax. These include the general structure and layout of a written program, notational conventions for representing the semantics of combined primitives, and the representation of the individual primitives themselves. The overall concern is that a program written in the language should be easily comprehendible by a human as well as by a translator or an interpreter.

We begin with the representation of individual primitives. Here, the symbols used to represent each primitive should reflect the semantics of the primitive in a clear, unambiguous manner. Indeed, examples of awkward syntax/semantic relationships occurring in programming languages are often the source of programming errors, especially for beginning programmers. For instance, consider the statement

$$EXTRA = TAX$$

which represents a common statement structure in the language FORTRAN. Without further explanation of the language, one is left with doubts as to the meaning of this statement. To the layperson it appears to be a declarative statement indicating that the value referred to by EXTRA is the same as the value referred to by TAX. Even when it is explained that the statement is instructing the movement of data from one location to another, the syntax still is ambiguous about which direction the motion is to take place (from EXTRA to TAX or from TAX to EXTRA?).

In contrast, consider the equivalent statement from the language COBOL. It reads like this:

$$MOVE TAX TO EXTRA$$

Most people would agree that the COBOL statement better represents the semantics involved (but might argue that this clarity is at the expense of a slightly more cumbersome syntax).

In addition to representing individual primitives, the syntax of a language should be designed to reflect the semantics of combined primitives. In particular, the syntax should reinforce the manner in which potential ambiguities in the semantics are resolved. As an example, consider the if-then-else and if-then structures in our pseudocode of Chapter 4. There we used parentheses to enclose the various components of the statements. One purpose of these parentheses is to clarify the meaning of combined structures. For example, we could write

$$if (B1) then (if (B2) then X)) else (Y)$$

when activity Y is to be executed if B1 is false and

$$if (B1) then (if (B2) then (X) else (Y))$$

when Y is to be executed only if B1 is true and B2 false.

Similar uses of parentheses are common throughout many programming languages. For instance, parentheses are often used to clarify the interpretation of numerical expressions. The ambiguities inherent in the expression $5 + 7 \times 2$ are easily overcome by writing either $(5 + 7) \times 2$ or $5 + (7 \times 2)$, depending on the interpretation desired.

We turn now to the syntax issues involving the general structure and layout of a written program. One such concern is whether to use a fixed format rather than a free-format design. The term *fixed format* means that the positioning of program statements on the written page must comply with certain rigid rules. For example, in the language COBOL, many statements must start in the eighth position on the line, whereas others must start in the first position. Such restrictions allow a translator to find the beginnings of the statements in a program as well as distinguish between the types of statements found. But, this efficiency in parsing is at the expense of flexibility.

In contrast, newer programming languages tend to be based on a free-format design in which the positioning of statements is not critical. The advantage is that programmers are free to organize the statements on the printed page in a way that enhances a program's readability. Thus, even though the use of parentheses is enough to avoid ambiguity in the statement

if B1 then (if B2 then X) else Y

the use of indentation to produce

if B1
    then (if B2 then X)
    else Y

increases the statement's readability.

Of course, with the advantages of a free-format design also come disadvantages. One is that since more than one statement can appear on a single line while other statements may be spread over several lines, the syntax of a free-format language must include explicit techniques for distinguishing the end of one instruction from the beginning of another. Techniques for resolving this problem include the use of punctuation such as semicolons and periods to separate statements; the use of key words such as if, while, and repeat to mark the beginning of certain structures; and parentheses and brackets for grouping components within statements.

Note that the use of key words for identifying certain components of a program often dictates that such words be used for that purpose only. For example, if ADD were a key word representing the operation of addition, a programmer may experience difficulties if the data relating to an employee's address were referred to in a program as ADD. Thus, key words in a programming language are often also reserved words.

Finally, we note that the development of a parser for a particular programming language relies on a precise definition of the grammatical rules dictating how the symbols in the language can be combined to form programs. One technique for communicating these rules is to use *syntax diagrams.* These diagrams are normally provided as a set of charts, each describing a particular grammatical structure, perhaps in terms of other structures.

A syntax diagram describing the structure of a sentence in a simplified version of the English language is presented in Figure 5-7. By following the arrows, we can quickly determine that a sentence consists of a subject followed by a predicate or

Figure 5-7 A syntax diagram of an English sentence

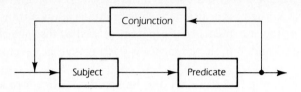

repetitions of this pattern joined by conjunctions. To be more complete, other diagrams describing the structure of a subject, a predicate, or a conjunction would normally accompany the diagram in Figure 5-7 so that the total collection would constitute a detailed description of a sentence. As an example of such a system, a set of syntax diagrams describing the grammar of the Pascal programming language is provided in Appendix D.

Questions/Exercises
1. What ambiguities can arise when combining structures with the conjunctions *and* and *or*? How can parentheses be used to avoid these ambiguities?
2. Give three different values that might be obtained by evaluating the expression $2 \times 4 + 6/2$ and explain how each is obtained.
3. Draw a syntax diagram representing the structure of a subject in an English sentence.
4. What properties of natural languages cause similar problems in both writing legal documents and expressing algorithms? How are these problems resolved in the legal profession? How are they resolved in a programming environment?
5. Give two different meanings for the sentence:

   John ran after the parade.

5–4 Third-Generation Programming Languages

Let us now consider the class of third-generation programming languages in more detail. Our examples will be drawn from the languages Ada, BASIC, COBOL, FORTRAN, and Pascal. Our goal is not to learn how to program in any of these languages. Rather, our goal is to develop an understanding of the programming process dictated by the use of languages in this class.

As indicated earlier, third-generation languages are based on the procedural paradigm, and thus a significant portion of a program written in them consists of a description of the algorithmic process to be executed. However, many of these languages also place a strong emphasis on the description of the data that the algorithm is to manipulate. Thus, a program in a third-generation language tends to be divided into two parts: the declarative part, where pertinent facts about the data to be manipulated as well as other terminology particular to the program (subprogram names and descriptions) are described, and the procedural part, where the algorithmic process itself is described (Figure 5-8). We divide our discussion accordingly, beginning with the issues of the declaration portion of a program.

Data Description Statements

To use descriptive names for data within a program, it is necessary for the programmer to explain the names to the translator or interpreter. This explanation is usually done at the beginning of a program with a collection of data description statements. Such statements provide a means of declaring the data names along with other associated information such as the data type and structure (which we will explain shortly). With this information the translator or interpreter is able to set aside memory cells to hold the data and recall the addresses of these cells when the names are used later in the program.

Data Type

The concept of *type* involves the interpretation that should be given the bit pattern representing the data. Types with which we are already familiar include *integer* (which means that the bit pattern represents a value stored in an integer format such as two's complement notation), *real* (which refers to a numeric value with a fractional part stored perhaps in floating-point notation), and *character* (which means the data is coded according to a system such as ASCII).

Figure 5-8 The traditional organization of a source program

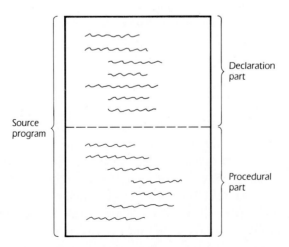

Another popular type is **Boolean** (named in honor of the mathematician George Boole, 1815–1864), which refers to a data item that can take on one of only two values—true or false. A data item of type Boolean can be represented by a single bit. Examples of the occurrence of such a data type include the result of comparisons such as "IS TAX EQUAL TO 5?" or the use of flags as in our proposed solution to the printer access problem of Section 3-6.

Having access to the bit patterns representing data is of little value unless one also knows the type of the data. This is also true for interpreters and translators. For instance, imagine a translator trying to translate the statement:

MOVE PRICE PLUS TAX INTO TOTAL

The object version of this statement will contain a machine-language addition instruction, but as we have seen the translator may have to choose between several such instructions, depending on whether PRICE and TAX are stored in two's complement notation, floating-point notation, or some other form. The translator must know the type associated with PRICE and TAX before completing the translation.

Programming languages provide a means for communicating the type associated with the various elements of data. This communication normally takes place within the same statement in which the name of the data element is first presented to the translator or interpreter. For example, in FORTRAN we find statements such as:

REAL   LENGTH, WIDTH

and

INTEGER   PRICE, TAX, TOTAL

which mean that LENGTH and WIDTH will be used in the program to refer to memory locations containing floating-point values; similarly PRICE, TAX, and TOTAL will refer to cells containing two's complement values. The same message is conveyed in Pascal by the statements:

```
var
    Length, Width:      real;
    Price, Tax, Total:  integer;
```

Other languages may indicate the type of the data elements involved implicitly. If not otherwise stated, a FORTRAN translator will consider data with names beginning with the letters I, J, K, L, M, and N as type integer and all others as type real. The older dialects of BASIC use names consisting of a single letter followed by the symbol $ to represent data of type character and names consisting of a single letter or a letter followed by a digit to represent numeric data. Whether this numeric data is of type integer or type real depends on how the values are used later in the program.

Data Structure

Another major concept associated with data is **structure,** which relates to the conceptual shape of the data. Perhaps the simplest example of this occurs when using a string of characters to represent an employee's name or a part identification number. It is not sufficient to know that the data item is of type character, but one must also know how many characters make up the item. If a translator must generate the machine instructions to move an employee's name from one location in memory to another, it must know how many memory cells to move. Thus, a COBOL program might contain the phrase:

NAME   PICTURE   X(8)

indicating that NAME is to refer to a string of eight characters (X indicates characters, and (8) tells how many). The same information would be expressed in FORTRAN as:

CHARACTER*8   NAME

or in Ada as:

NAME: STRING(1..8);

Another common example of structured data is an **array.** The term *array* refers to a block of values such as a list (often called a vector), a two-dimensional table (a matrix), or tables of higher dimensions (that do not have special names). Elements of an array are normally identified within a program through the use of indices. That is, the third entry in a vector named SALES would be referenced by the expression SALES(3), and the entry from the second row and fifth column of a matrix named SCORES would be identified by SCORES(2,5). Note that it is customary to list the row number before the column number.

To describe an array in the declaration part of a program, most languages use a syntax similar to that used for referring to the array later in the program's procedural part. However, in the description statement the values of the indices indicate the size of the array rather than a position in it. Thus, a matrix of integers containing two rows and nine columns (the shape of a baseball scoreboard as shown in Figure 5-9) named SCORES would be described in FORTRAN by the statement:

INTEGER   SCORES(2,9)

and in BASIC by:

DIM   S(2,9)

(Here DIM is short for DIMension, and the name has been abbreviated to S, since many dialects of BASIC allow names to be only one character long.) The same structure would be described in Pascal by:

```
var
    Scores: array [1..2,1..9] of integer;
```

Figure 5-9 The 2 by 9 array named SCORES

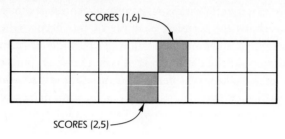

Up to this point we have looked at examples of **homogeneous arrays,** meaning that all the entries of a given array have been of the same type. It is often convenient to deal with **heterogeneous arrays,** which are arrays in which different elements are of a different type. For example, we might consider a block of employee data as a vector whose first entry is NAME (type character), second entry is AGE (type integer), and third entry is RATING (type real) (Figure 5-10). In COBOL such a structure would be described by:

```
01      EMPLOYEE
        02    NAME      PICTURE    X(20).
        02    AGE       PICTURE    9(3).
        02    RATING    PICTURE    9V99.
```

(The notation 9V99 in the definition of RATING indicates the decimal value stored there is to be maintained with one digit to the left of the decimal point and two digits to the right.) A similar array can be described in Pascal by:

```
var
   Employee:    record
                Name:      packed array [1..20] of char;
                Age:       integer;
                Rating:    real
                end
```

The rectangular shape associated with arrays actually exists only in the programmer's mind, not in the machine, and is therefore a virtual structure. In reality,

Figure 5-10 A heterogeneous array named EMPLOYEE

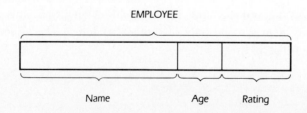

the data contained in the array may be scattered over a wide area of the machine's memory. This is why we referred to structure as being the conceptual shape of data. It is the responsibility of the translator or interpreter to set aside, based on the data descriptions we have been discussing, a suitable block of memory for holding the data and later be able to locate the correct item within this block when an expression in the program such as SCORES(1,4) is reached. In a sense, then, the translator or interpreter simulates the conceptual structure.

Variables Versus Constants

Thus far we have related descriptive names to data by associating the name with the memory cell (or cells) that holds the data. With this arrangement the value associated with a name can be varied as the program executes by changing the bit pattern of the related memory location. The data associated in this manner with the name is said to be variable, and the name is called a variable name or sometimes simply a *variable.* (Note that this terminology does not mean that the name varies but that the value associated with the name can vary.) This terminology is the origin of the key word "var" in the Pascal statements in the preceding paragraphs.

In contrast, it is often helpful to assign a descriptive name to a value that will not be changed later in a program. For instance, in a program for controlling air traffic around an airport, the airport's altitude above sea level might well be used in many computations. If we associate the name AirportAlt with this value, say 645 feet, then this descriptive name can be used when expressing computations instead of the less descriptive value 645. (To anyone reading the program, the name AirportAlt will convey the purpose of a computation in which it appears more readily than the appearance of the actual value 645.) Note that the value associated with AirportAlt will not change during program execution. That is, the value associated with the name would be a constant rather than variable, and thus such a name is referred to as a constant name or simply a *constant.* Many programming languages allow the programmer to specify the use of such constants. For example, AirportAlt could be associated with the constant value 645 in Pascal by:

const   AirportAlt = 645;

or in Ada with the following statement:

AirportAlt: constant INTEGER := 645;

The technique of naming constants is also helpful if the program should ever need to be changed. For example, if our air traffic control program is to be installed at another airport, the altitude of the airport must be changed inside the program. If we had used the value 645 in all the computations requiring this information, we would have to find and change each of these values within the program. The problem would be further complicated if the value 645 should also occur in reference to a quantity other than the airport's altitude. How would we know which occurrences of 645 to change and which to let alone? On the other hand, had we defined the name AirportAlt to refer to the constant 645 as in the preceding statements and used this descriptive name in the program, changing the program for another airport at the altitude 267 feet would simply require changing the preceding statements to:

const   AirportAlt = 267;

or

AirportAlt: constant INTEGER : = 267;

respectively. This simple modification would cause all occurrences of AirportAlt in the associated program to refer to the value 267 rather than 645.

Assignment Statements

When we were discussing machine languages, we separated the instructions for moving data into a different group from those that performed arithmetic or logic operations. However, in high-level languages, these steps are often combined into a single syntactic structure called an assignment statement. For example, although the FORTRAN statement:

EXTRA = TAX

that we discussed earlier is only a data movement statement, the same syntactic structure is used to represent instructions for performing computations. This is done by replacing the right-hand side of the movement statement with an expression describing the operation to be performed and using the left-hand side to indicate the location in which the result is to be stored. Thus, to add PRICE and TAX giving TOTAL in FORTRAN one would write:

TOTAL = PRICE + TAX

Likewise, in Ada and Pascal the preceding assignment statements would be written as:

Extra : = Tax

and

Total : = Price + Tax

respectively. In dialects of BASIC that allow names of multiple characters, one would find:

LET EXTRA = TAX

and

LET TOTAL = PRICE + TAX

COBOL's syntax, however, allows the distinction between computation-oriented statements and simple data movement. Thus, in COBOL the simple movement of TAX to EXTRA can be expressed as:

MOVE TAX TO EXTRA

whereas the computation-oriented process of placing the sum of PRICE and TAX in TOTAL might be expressed as:

COMPUTE   TOTAL = PRICE + TAX

In general, any algebraic expression can be used in place of the expression PRICE + TAX in our examples with the arithmetic operations of addition, subtraction, multiplication, division, and exponentiation represented by the symbols +, −, *, /, and **, respectively, although care should be taken to observe the order in which these operations might be performed. For instance, the expression 2 * 4 + 6 / 2 could be associated with different values depending on the semantic rules of the language (Section 5-3).

Again you should be cautioned not to consider computers as predominately number crunchers (that is, machines that perform numeric computations). In this regard many computations other than the arithmetic operations are expressible in high-level languages. One important group consists of those operations performed on strings of characters. Examples include finding occurrences of one string in another, concatenating two strings to form a single long one, or replacing a part of a string with another. For instance, if FIRST and LAST were names of character strings, the FORTRAN statement:

BOTH = FIRST // LAST

would cause the name BOTH to be associated with the long string formed by concatenating the contents of FIRST and LAST. The equivalent statement in BASIC would read:

LET BOTH = FIRST + LAST

Another example is the selection of a substring from a longer string. In particular, a common syntax is the form LAST(2:5), which refers to the substring consisting of the 2nd through the 5th characters in the string named LAST. Thus, if LAST were assigned the string *microcomputer,* LAST(6:13) would refer to the substring *computer.*

Statement-Level Control Statements

Control statements are those statements that control or alter the execution sequence of the program. Of all the programming statements, those from this group have probably received the most attention and generated the most controversy. The major villain is the simplest control statement of all, the GOTO statement. In general, it provides a means of directing the execution sequence to another location that has been labeled for this purpose by a name or number. It is therefore nothing more than a direct application of the machine-level jump instruction. The problem with such a feature in a high-level programming language is it allows programmers to write rat's nests like:

```
10      GOTO 40
20      LET TOTAL = PRICE + 10
30      GOTO 70
40      IF PRICE < 50 GOTO 60
50      GOTO 20
60      LET TOTAL = PRICE + 5
70      STOP
```

where a two-statement program like:

```
10      IF PRICE < 50 THEN LET TOTAL = PRICE + 5
                ELSE LET TOTAL = PRICE + 10
20      STOP
```

would do.

To avoid such complexities, modern languages are designed with more elaborate control statements, such as the IF-THEN-ELSE, that allow a certain branching pattern to be expressed within a single syntactic structure. The choice of which control structures should be incorporated into a language is a significant design decision. The object is to provide a language that not only allows algorithms to be expressed in a readable form but also assists the programmer in obtaining such readability. This is done by restricting the use of those features that have historically led to sloppy programming while encouraging the use of better designed features. The result is the often misunderstood practice known as *structured programming,* which encompasses an organized design methodology combined with the appropriate use of the language's control statements. The idea is to produce a program that can be readily comprehended and can be easily shown to meet its specifications.

The more common branching structures as they appear in the Pascal language together with their corresponding flowchart representations are listed in Figure 5-11. In each case, the notation S1, S2, etc., has been used to represent arbitrary instructions, and B is used to represent the occurrence of a phrase such as "I < 5" or "NAME = 'SMITH' " that produces a Boolean result. In the CASE statement, N represents the name of a data item, and C1, C2, C3 represent the possible values of that item.

Statements expressing the control structures in Figure 5-11 are found with varying degree in numerous programming languages, especially the newer ones. One control structure, however, that appeared in the early procedural languages has maintained its popularity through the years. This is a form of the loop structure

Figure 5-11 Fundamental Pascal control structures

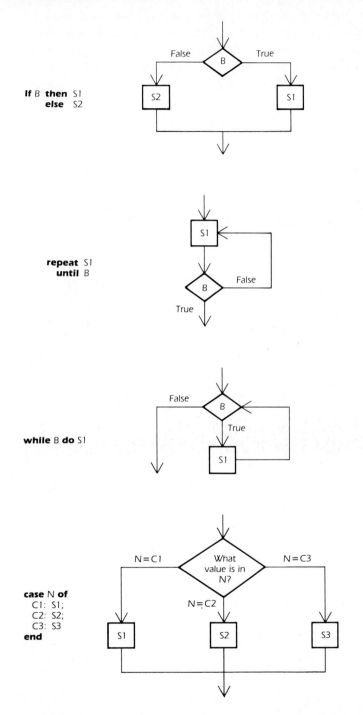

discussed in Chapter 4. Here the repetition of the loop's body is controlled by maintaining an auxiliary data element that is automatically modified each time the loop is traversed in addition to being tested for a programmer-defined termination condition. An example of this structure as it would appear in each of our example languages is shown in Figure 5-12. In each case we have used the name I for the auxiliary data element and requested that the body of the loop (represented by dots) be executed five times.

Although these statements can be thought of as expressing the same semantics, a significant difference exists between the COBOL statement and the others. This

Figure 5-12 Traditional loop control structures

```
Ada:        for I in 1 . . 5 loop
                    .
                    .
                    .

            end loop;


BASIC:      FOR I = 1 TO 5
                    .
                    .
                    .
            NEXT I


COBOL:      PERFORM ...
            VARYING I FROM 1 BY 1
            UNTIL I GREATER THAN 5.


FORTRAN:    DO 10 I = 1,5
                    .
                    .
                    .
         10 CONTINUE


Pascal:     for I := 1 to 5 do
                begin
                    .
                    .
                    .
            end
```

difference is that the statements making up the body of the loop are not placed directly within the loop syntactic structure in COBOL. Instead, this sequence of instructions appears elsewhere in the program as a unit called a paragraph, and it is only the identifying name of this paragraph that replaces the dots in the PER-FORM statement of Figure 5-12. The result is that when it comes time to execute these statements, control is transferred to the paragraph and is then returned to the PERFORM statement after the paragraph is completed.

In a sense, the control implemented by the PERFORM statement is at a higher level than the other control structures we have discussed thus far. That is, rather than controlling the execution of a single instruction or of short instruction sequences within the current program unit, the PERFORM statement is used to control the execution of an entire and otherwise isolated program unit. Control activities of this type are the subject of the next section.

Unit-Level Control Statements

We closed the preceding section by observing that through a transfer/return process, the PERFORM statement of COBOL implements its control in terms of the execution of entire program units rather than individual instructions. This is an elementary form of the more general concept of a subprogram (also known as either a procedure or subroutine) that we encountered in developing our pseudocode in Chapter 4.

Subprograms

In short, a subprogram is nothing more than a sequence of instructions forming a program unit written independently of the main program yet associated with it through the transfer/return process (Figure 5-13). A simplified version of the PERFORM

Figure 5-13 The flow of control involving a subprogram

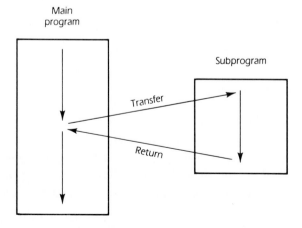

statement is provided in COBOL solely for the exploitation of this subprogram concept. For example, the statement:

PERFORM INSERTION–SORT

would cause the paragraph (subprogram) named INSERTION–SORT to be executed as though it appeared at this location in the program. (Because names of objects in COBOL, as in many languages, cannot contain blanks, dashes are often used to combine several words into a single name such as INSERTION–SORT.)

The syntax used to represent the request of a subprogram varies among the different languages. FORTRAN and BASIC use the key words CALL and GOSUB, respectively. In contrast, Pascal and Ada follow the technique we adopted in our pseudocode of merely identifying the required subprogram by its name alone. Thus, if we wrote subprograms called GET–NAMES (to get a list of names from a person at a terminal), SORT–NAMES (to sort a list of names), and WRITE–NAMES (to write a list of names at a terminal), we could combine them to form a larger program to get a list and write it in sorted order in COBOL with the statement sequence:

PERFORM GET–NAMES.
PERFORM SORT–NAMES.
PERFORM WRITE–NAMES.

or in Pascal with:

GET–NAMES;
SORT–NAMES;
WRITE–NAMES;

The technique used to describe a subprogram itself varies from language to language. In fact, many systems allow such program units to be written in languages other than that of the main program. In such cases the subprograms are translated individually and then their object versions are linked to the object version of the main program, forming a load module containing the entire program package.

Parameters

The simple PERFORM structure in COBOL has one major drawback. It does not provide for explicit communication of data between the main program and the subprogram. For instance, in the preceding example, the statement PERFORM SORT–NAMES does not explicitly state what list is to be sorted. Rather, this information must be conveyed implicitly through the relative structure of the subprogram and the main program. Such obscure implicit communication is known to be a major source of programming errors, just as is the haphazard use of GOTO statements.

A more acceptable technique is to implement the subprogram as though it were a completely separate entity with its own data and algorithm so that an item of data in either the main program or the subprogram is not automatically accessible from within the other. (In fact, data names within the subprogram can be identical to those in the main program without implying any relationship among the data, just as members of different households may have the same name even though no relationship exists between them.) With this arrangement, any transfer of data between the two program parts must be specified explicitly by the programmer. This is usually done by listing the items called *parameters* (or sometimes arguments) to be transferred in the same syntactic structure used to request the subprogram's execution (usually by means of a parenthetical statement).

How the transfer of data between the main program and a subprogram is handled and the repercussions of the various techniques in use today are of major concern to many computer scientists working in the area of programming language design. In its most general form, the transfer takes place in two directions. When execution of the subprogram is requested, the parameters are effectively transferred to the subprogram, the subprogram is executed, the (possibly modified) parameters are transferred back to the main program, and the main program continues. In other cases, the transfer can take place in only one direction—either to the subprogram before it is executed or to the main program after the subprogram's execution. Languages that provide more than one of these transfer techniques also provide a means by which the programmer can specify which option is desired.

Perhaps the most straightforward example of this in our example languages is found in Ada. Here the key words in, out, and in out are used to indicate the direction in which data is transferred. For example, consider a subprogram named LARGER, defined with three parameters named I, J, and K in such a way that, when called, the subprogram compares the numbers assigned to I and J and places the larger one in location K. Such a subprogram could be written in Ada as:

```
procedure LARGER(I,J: in INTEGER; K: out INTEGER) is
begin
  if I < J then K := J
         else K := I
end LARGER;
```

Here the parameters I and J are designated as in parameters, while the parameter K is designated as an out parameter. These designations describe the direction in which data is to be transferred in relation to the subprogram. That is, data is to be transferred into the parameters I and J but out of the parameter K.

Once our subprogram has been defined, it can be used from within a main program to place the larger of the two numbers associated with locations NUM1 and NUM2 in location L by inserting the statement:

```
LARGER(NUM1, NUM2, L);
```

Figure 5-14 An example of parameter passing

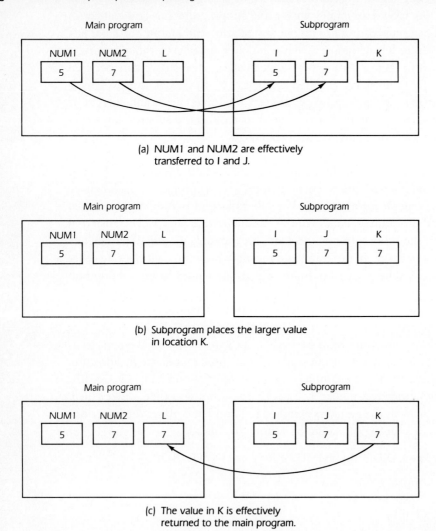

(a) NUM1 and NUM2 are effectively
transferred to I and J.

(b) Subprogram places the larger value
in location K.

(c) The value in K is effectively
returned to the main program.

in the program where this action is desired. To be more precise, when this statement is executed, the following sequence of events will be performed (see Figure 5-14):

1.   The values associated with NUM1 and NUM2 in the main program will be effectively copied into the locations I and J, respectively, in the subprogram.
2.   The subprogram will be executed leaving the larger value in location K.
3.   The value in K (in the subprogram) will be copied into the location L in the main program.

4. Execution of the main program will continue with the statement following the statement that invoked the subprogram.

From this sequence of events we see that the names used for the parameters within the subprogram can be thought of as merely standing in for the actual data that will be supplied when the subprogram is requested. As a result, you will often hear them called *formal parameters,* whereas the data elements supplied from the main program are referred to as *actual parameters.*

A significant benefit of this substitution system is that the same subprogram can easily be asked to perform its task on different sets of data at different points in the main program. In particular, our LARGER subprogram could be used at one point to find the larger of the two values NUM1 and NUM2 with the statement:

LARGER (NUM1, NUM2, L)

and later to find the larger of the values X and Y with the statement:

LARGER (X, Y, L)

Functions

A useful variation from the strict parameter list form of communication between a main program and a subprogram is found in the concept of a *function.* A function is similar to a subprogram in that data being transferred to it is handled through a parameter list. In contrast to a subprogram, however, data is returned from a function to the main program in the form of the "value of the function." That is, a value can be associated with the name of a function in a manner similar to the association between a value and a variable name. The difference is that the value associated with a function name is computed (according to the function's definition) each time it is required, whereas a variable's value is merely retrieved from memory. As an example, by implementing our Ada subprogram LARGER as a function called MAX, we could store the larger of NUM1 and NUM2 in L using the statement:

L := MAX(NUM1,NUM2)

More precisely, the meaning of this statement is that the larger of the values NUM1 and NUM2 will be returned as the value associated with MAX, and this value will then be assigned to L.

A major advantage of a function over a subprogram is that with a function, the value being returned is immediately available for further computation. For example, if MIN were a function that returned the smaller of its two parameters, the statement:

Z := MAX(NUM1, NUM2) − MIN(NUM3, NUM4)

would assign to the variable Z the largest difference that could be obtained by subtracting either NUM3 or NUM4 from one of NUM1 or NUM2. To accomplish this same task using similar subprograms would require a sequence of statements such as:

$$\text{LARGER(NUM1, NUM2, L)}$$
$$\text{SMALLER(NUM3, NUM4, S)}$$
$$\text{Z: = L } - \text{ S}$$

String Processing Functions

The use of functions often provides a convenient way of implementing the features of a language or adding features not available in a language's original design. For instance, BASIC and FORTRAN as well as many dialects of Pascal provide a collection of ready-to-use functions to assist a programmer in manipulating strings of characters. One such function is called LEN (short for LENgth). It accepts one parameter (a character string) and returns a numeric value equal to the parameter's length (the number of characters in it). Thus, LEN('ABC') would return 3, and LEN('BILL') would return 4.

Another common function is INDEX (called POS for POSition in BASIC). It accepts two parameters (both character strings), checks to see if the second one occurs as a part of the first, and if so returns a numeric value indicating the position of the first such occurrence. Thus, INDEX('CALL', 'ALL') would return the value 2 since ALL begins at the second character of CALL, and INDEX('ABCDCBA','C') would return 3. If the second parameter does not appear in the first one, INDEX will return the value 0.

As an example, observe that the following FORTRAN statement assigns to the variable A that part of the character string associated with B that follows the first occurrence of the string associated with C (remember that the notation B(M:N) extracts the Mth through the Nth characters from the string assigned to B):

$$\text{A = B(INDEX(B,C) + LEN(C): LEN(B))}$$

Thus, if B were *microcomputer* and C were *cro,* A would be assigned the string *computer.*

Implicit Subprogram Activation

Until now our discussion of the control of program units has centered around explicit control techniques. That is, when using these techniques we must explicitly request the execution of the desired program unit. In contrast numerous implicit techniques exist by which program units can be activated. One example is the interrupt routine discussed earlier in terms of time-sharing operating systems, where we saw that the execution of the dispatcher is initiated by the expiration of a program's time slice rather than by an explicit request by the program. In fact, the program whose time slice has terminated would probably prefer to keep running and not call the dispatcher. Thus, we have an example of a program unit being activated by the occurrence of an event rather than by an explicit request.

Ada has numerous features that provide for such unit control. With them, programs can be developed as individual units, each of which essentially waits in the background until the occurrence of the particular event that activates it. Since this might happen in the case of several units at the same time, programs of this nature are excellent candidates for parallel processing environments and promise to be quite popular in the coming years.

I/O Statements

We learned earlier that operating systems contain prewritten routines for controlling the peripheral devices attached to a machine. From the high-level language point of view, these routines are nothing more than subprograms that can be invoked by the program being written simply by requesting their execution where needed. For this the programmer merely needs to know the correct subprogram names and any special syntax rules associated with them. For example, to receive a value from the keyboard of a terminal and place it in a location named Value, a Pascal programmer would write:

readln (Value)

and to write the value on the screen of the terminal:

writeln (Value)

would be used (readln indicates "read line" and writeln indicates "write line"). In the same manner COBOL uses the terms ACCEPT and DISPLAY, BASIC uses INPUT and PRINT, FORTRAN uses READ and WRITE, and Ada uses GET and PUT.

A bit more needs to be said in the case of FORTRAN since it uses formatted input and output. Simply translated this means that the programmer explicitly describes the form that the data will have when it is read or that it should have when it is written. As an example, a request to read the character strings called NAME and ADDRESS from the keyboard of a terminal might appear as follows:

READ (5,100) NAME, ADDRESS
100   FORMAT (A8,X,A25)

The 5 identifies the device to be used (the keyboard in this case), and the 100 indicates the label of the associated FORMAT statement. The FORMAT statement itself indicates (in a form reminiscent of the PICTURE clause in COBOL) that the operating system's routine should expect to receive a pattern of eight characters (A8), followed by an ignored symbol (X), which is followed by a string of 25 characters (A25). The first string is to be placed in memory location NAME and the last string in location ADDRESS.

Internal Documentation

Experience has shown that no matter how well the syntax of a language is designed or how well the language's features are used, additional information is either helpful or mandatory when trying to understand a program that someone else has written. For this reason, languages are designed to allow additional comments to be inserted within a program for documentation purposes. This is done by providing a syntactic structure that informs the translator or interpreter to ignore certain parts of the written program. Any remarks placed in this ignored portion will be available to a human reading the program but not to the translator or interpreter.

Two popular syntax structures are used for inserting comments. One is to enclose the comment within special characters. For example, the beginning of a comment in Pascal is indicated by the symbol { and the end of the comment is marked by the symbol }. The other technique is to mark the beginning of the comment with a special character and end the comment by starting a new line. Using this technique, Ada starts comments with a double hyphen (--); FORTRAN with the letter C; COBOL with the asterisk; and BASIC with the key word REM, which is short for REMark.

A few words are in order about what constitutes a meaningful comment. For some reason beginning programmers, when told to use comments for internal documentation, end up following a program statement such as:

MOVE PRICE PLUS TAX TO TOTAL

with a comment such as "Calculate TOTAL by adding PRICE and TAX." Such redundancy adds length rather than clarity to the program. Remember that the purpose of internal documentation is to enhance the meaning of the program, not to repeat it. A more appropriate comment associated with the preceding statement might be to explain why the total is being calculated if that is not obvious. For example, the comment "TOTAL is used later to compute GRANDTOTAL and not needed after that" would be more helpful than the previous one.

Program Examples

We close this section by showing how the insertion sort algorithm can be implemented in Ada, BASIC, COBOL, FORTRAN, and Pascal. In each case you will observe that the list to be sorted is defined as a one-dimensional array. The procedural part of each program consists of three smaller routines. The first gets the names to be sorted from the terminal, the second is the sort routine itself, and the third writes the names in alphabetical order at the terminal.

Ada Example

Ada is the newest of the languages presented in this text, with its design finally being established as recently as 1979. Ada translators are only now becoming available to the programming public in any meaningful quantity.

Ada, named after Augusta Ada Byron (1815–1851) who was an assistant of Charles Babbage and the daughter of poet Lord Byron, was developed at the initiative of the U.S. Department of Defense in an attempt to obtain a single, general purpose language for all its software development needs. A major emphasis during Ada's design was to incorporate features for programming real-time computer systems used as a part of larger machines such as missile guidance systems, environment control systems within buildings, and control systems in automobiles and small home appliances. Ada thus contains features for expressing activities in parallel processing environments as well as convenient techniques for handling special cases (called exceptions) that might arise in the application environment.

Because it is so new, Ada is still at the center of much debate—a stage through which every new language must pass. Many computer scientists argue that Ada is too big to become an efficient and useful language. On the other hand, the Department of Defense has committed significant resources to Ada's development, and its influence alone may well overcome the obstacles to the language's acceptance.

The insertion sort routine expressed in Ada is shown in Figure 5-15. Although not a feature in the actual language, our example adopts the convention of writing Ada's reserved words in boldface to enhance readability.

BASIC Example

BASIC was developed at Dartmouth College and announced in 1965 by John Kemeny and Thomas Kurtz as an introductory programming language. Its name is an acronym for Beginners' All-purpose Symbolic Instruction Code. Because of its simplicity, it has become quite popular and is now one of the leading languages in the microcomputer field. Since it was designed for use by beginning programmers, early versions of the language were not well endowed with the more advanced programming features. The result has been a somewhat ad hoc enhancement process through which numerous dialects of the language have emerged. Consequently, BASIC is probably the least standardized among the languages presented here, although this problem is being actively pursued by the American National Standards Institute.

The insertion sort routine implemented in BASIC is shown in Figure 5-16. In coding this example, we have tried to remain faithful to the original BASIC syntax. Note that all statements are labeled numerically. These labels indicate the order of execution (unless otherwise altered by a control statement) and serve as identification for use in GOTO statements.

COBOL Example

COBOL is an acronym for COmmon Business Oriented Language. Its business orientation is clearly evident from its comparatively conversational tone and lack of emphasis on numerical computations. Created in the late 1950s, COBOL has benefited from early standardization efforts by the American National Standards Institute.

Figure 5-15 The insertion sort in Ada

```
-- Insertion sort in Ada
with TEXT __ IO;
use TEXT __ IO;
procedure MAIN is
      subtype NAME __ TYPE is STRING (1 .. 8);
      LIST __ LENGTH: constant := 10;
      NAMES: array (1 .. LIST __ LENGTH) of NAME __ TYPE;
      PIVOT: NAME __ TYPE;
      HOLE: INTEGER;
begin
-- First, get the names from the terminal.
      for K in 1 .. LIST __ LENGTH loop
          GET(NAMES(K));
      end loop;
-- Sort the list   (HOLE contains the location of the
--                 hole in the list from the time
--                 the pivot is removed until it
--                 is reinserted.)
      for N in 2 .. LIST __ LENGTH loop
          PIVOT := NAMES(N);
          HOLE := N;
          for M in reverse 1 .. N - 1 loop
              if NAMES(M) > PIVOT
                  then NAMES(M + 1) := NAMES(M);
                  else exit;
              end if;
              HOLE := M;
          end loop;
          NAMES(HOLE) := PIVOT;
      end loop;
-- Now, print the sorted list.
      for K in 1 .. LIST __ LENGTH loop
          NEW __ LINE;
          PUT(NAMES(K));
      end loop;
end MAIN;
```

Figure 5-16 The insertion sort in BASIC

```
100  REM  Insertion sort in BASIC.
110        DIM N$(10)

200  REM  Get the names from the terminal.
210        FOR K = 1 TO 10
220        INPUT N$(K)
230        NEXT K

300  REM  Now, sort the list.
310        FOR J = 2 TO 10
320        LET P$ = N$(J)
330        FOR K = J - 1 TO 1 STEP - 1
340        IF (N$(K) < P$) GOTO 370
350        LET N$(K + 1) = N$(K)
360        NEXT K
370        LET N$(K + 1) = P$
380        NEXT J

400  REM  Print the sorted list.
410        FOR K = 1 TO 10
420        PRINT N$(K)
430        NEXT K

500        END
```

COBOL's separation of programs into four distinct divisions (the first two of which are mainly for documentation purposes), the outline form of its data declarations, and its paragraph structure make it conducive to well-organized and well-written programs. In fact, COBOL's design was promoting the concept of structured programming well before that term was defined and popularized.

The insertion sort routine implemented in COBOL is shown in Figure 5-17. Observe that the complete routine is expressed in the paragraph MAIN–PROGRAM. Here the casual reader sees that the program consists of three steps: READ–NAMES, POSITION–PIVOT, and WRITE–NAMES. The details of how each routine actually does its job need not be considered unless they are of interest.

Figure 5-17 The insertion sort in COBOL

```
*      Insertion sort in COBOL

IDENTIFICATION DIVISION.
PROGRAM-ID. INSERTSORT.

ENVIRONMENT DIVISION.
CONFIGURATION SECTION.
SOURCE-COMPUTER.      VAX-11.
OBJECT-COMPUTER.      VAX-11.

DATA DIVISION.
WORKING-STORAGE SECTION.
01   LIST.
     02   NAMES OCCURS 10 TIMES      PICTURE X(8).
01   PIVOT      PICTURE X(8).
01   I     PICTURE 9(2).
01   J     PICTURE 9(2).
01   K     PICTURE 9(2).

PROCEDURE DIVISION.

MAIN-PROGRAM.
        PERFORM READ-NAMES VARYING I FROM 1 BY 1
            UNTIL I GREATER THAN 10.
        PERFORM POSITION-PIVOT VARYING I FROM 2 BY 1
            UNTIL I GREATER THAN 10.
        PERFORM WRITE-NAMES VARYING I FROM 1 BY 1
            UNTIL I GREATER THAN 10.
        STOP RUN.
READ-NAMES.
        ACCEPT NAMES (I).

WRITE-NAMES.
        DISPLAY NAMES(I).

*      The following routine removes the pivot and
*      reinserts it in its proper position.
```

```
POSITION-PIVOT.
    COMPUTE K = I + 1.
    MOVE NAMES(K) TO PIVOT.
    PERFORM MOVE-DOWN VARYING J FROM I BY − 1
        UNTIL J EQUAL 1 OR NAMES(J) LESS THAN PIVOT.
    COMPUTE K = J + 1.
    IF NAMES(J) LESS THAN PIVOT
        THEN MOVE PIVOT TO NAMES(K)
        ELSE MOVE NAMES(J) TO NAMES(K)
            MOVE PIVOT TO NAMES(J).


MOVE-DOWN.
    COMPUTE K = J + 1.
    MOVE NAMES(J) TO NAMES(K).
```

FORTRAN Example

FORTRAN is an acronym for FORmula TRANslator. This language was one of the first high-level languages developed (announced in 1957) and the first to gain wide acceptance within the computing community. Over the years its official description has undergone numerous extensions, and thus you may hear computer scientists mention FORTRAN II or FORTRAN IV. The latest in the series is FORTRAN 77, which extended FORTRAN IV to include such features as character data types and the IF-THEN-ELSE control structure. Although criticized by many, FORTRAN continues to be a popular language within the scientific community. In particular, many numerical analysis and statistical packages are, and will probably continue to be, written in FORTRAN. The insertion sort routine implemented in FORTRAN is shown in Figure 5-18.

Pascal Example

Pascal is named after the French mathematician and inventor Blaise Pascal (1623–1662). Announced by Niklaus Wirth in 1971, it incorporates many of the later design features such as an emphasis on data type in addition to structure, a free-format syntax, and numerous control structures. Today, Pascal is used extensively in computer science education, and as students complete their education and move into the applied computing community, the language is rapidly becoming a popular commercial language as well.

The insertion sort routine implemented in Pascal is shown in Figure 5-19. As with Ada, we have adopted the convention of writing the reserved words in boldface to increase our program's readability.

Figure 5-18 The insertion sort in FORTRAN

```
C               Insertion sort in FORTRAN

        INTEGER J,K
        CHARACTER*8 NAMES(10),PIVOT

C               First, get the names from the terminal.

        READ(5,100)(NAMES(K),K = 1,10)
100     FORMAT(A8)

C               Now, sort the list.

        DO 300 J = 2,10
        PIVOT = NAMES(J)
        DO 200 K = J − 1,1, − 1
        IF (NAMES(K) .GT. PIVOT) THEN
            NAMES(K + 1) = NAMES(K)
        ELSE
            GOTO 250
        ENDIF
200     CONTINUE
250     NAMES(K + 1) = PIVOT
300     CONTINUE

C               Now, print the sorted list.

        WRITE(6,400)(NAMES(K),K = 1,10)
400     FORMAT(' ', A8)
        END
```

Figure 5-19 The insertion sort in Pascal

```
        { Insertion sort in Pascal }
program InsertSort(Input, Output);
Const
        Blanks = '          ';
        ListLength = 10;
type
        NameType = packed array [1 .. 8] of char;
var
        Names: array [1 .. ListLength] of NameType;
        Pivot: NameType;
        LocationFound: Boolean;
        J,M,N: Integer;
{GetName is a procedure for reading an entire name.}
procedure GetName(var Name: NameType);
var J: Integer;
begin J := 1;
        repeat read(Name[J]); J := J + 1; until (J > 8) or eoln;
        readln
end;
begin
{ First, get the names from the terminal. }
        for J := 1 to ListLength do
            begin Names[J] := Blanks; GetName(Names[J]) end;
{ Sort the list. }
        N := 2;
        repeat
            Pivot := Names[N];
            M := N − 1;
            LocationFound := false;
            while (not LocationFound) do
                if Names[M] > Pivot
                    then begin Names[M + 1] := Names[M];
                    M := M − 1;
                    if M = 0 then LocationFound := true
                        end
                    else LocationFound := true;
            Names[M + 1] := Pivot;
            N := N + 1
        Until N > ListLength;
{ Now print the sorted list. }
        for J := 1 to ListLength do writeln (Names[J])
end.
```

Questions/Exercises

1. What syntax would you expect to use in a third-generation programming language to refer to the entry in the third row and fifth column of a 10-by-6 matrix named XYZ?

2. What would be the result of assigning 26.1 to a variable of each of the following types:

   a. integer   b. real   c. character

3. What structure is associated with the following data examples:

   a. The individual daily sales of five employees for a one-week period.

   b. The data from part a for 52 weeks.

   c. The attendance for each of six football games.

   d. The block of information pertaining to an item in a store's stock such as name, quantity, stock number, supplier, or cost.

4. What is the difference between a constant and a variable?

5. When moving data as a result of an assignment statement from a location of type integer to a location of type real, what action must take place in addition to the transfer of data?

6. If B were assigned the string *abab* and C were assigned *ab,* what would be obtained by the following expressions:

   a. LEN(B)   b. INDEX(B,C)   c. INDEX(C,B)   d. LEN(B(1:INDEX(B,C)))

7. In each of the sample programs in this section, identify the point where the declaration part ends and the procedural part begins.

8. In each of the sample programs in this section, identify the statements that would be ignored by a translator or an interpreter. Why are these statements included if they do not affect the program's performance?

5–5 Declarative Programming (optional)

Earlier we claimed that formal logic provides a general problem-solving algorithm around which a declarative programming system can be constructed. In this section we investigate this claim by first introducing the rudiments of the algorithm and then taking a brief look at a declarative programming language based on it.

Logical Deduction

Suppose we already know that either John is at school or John is sick. If we are then told that John is not sick, we could conclude that John is at school. This is an example of a deductive-reasoning principle called resolution. To better understand this principle, let us first agree to represent statements by single letters and the negation of a statement by preceding the letter representing the statement with the symbol $\neg$. For instance, we might represent the statement "John is at school" by P, the statement "John is sick" by Q, and the statement "John is not sick" by $\neg$Q. Then, the reasoning described above could be summarized as:

$$\left. \begin{array}{l} P \text{ or } Q \\ \neg Q \end{array} \right\} \text{imply } P$$

In a more general form, the *resolution* principle says that if P, Q, and R are statements, then the statements:

$$P \text{ or } Q$$

and

$$R \text{ or } \neg Q$$

collectively imply the statement:

$$P \text{ or } R$$

as represented in Figure 5-20. In this case we say that the two original statements resolve to produce the third statement, which is called the *resolvent.* (You may wish to stop here while you convince yourself that the resolvent is, in fact, a logical consequence of the parent statements. However, you should also keep in mind that the process of computing the resolvent once the original statements have been formulated is independent of the semantics represented. Indeed, the computation of a resolvent, being the process of essentially canceling contradictory portions of statements while combining what is left, is performed at a totally syntactic level.)

Figure 5-20 Resolving the statements (P or Q) and (R or ⌐Q) to produce (P or R)

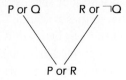

P or R

Of course, resolution is only one rule of inference used by logicians. (For example, the rule called *modus tollens* states that the statements:

If P then Q

and

⌐Q

collectively imply ⌐P.) But there is something special about resolution. Logicians have shown that a deductive system applying only resolution is complete in the sense that any statement that logically follows from an initial collection of statements can be obtained by repeatedly applying resolution and only resolution.

For our purpose, this means that an algorithm based on the mere repetition of resolution has the potential to be a general problem-solving algorithm—the only major obstacle being the question as to whether problems in general can be stated in a form compatible with the application of resolution. Indeed, resolution is applicable only to statements written in clause form—that is, statements whose elementary components are connected by the word *or*. The fact that this potential problem poses no serious concern is a consequence of a theorem in formal logic to the effect that any statement expressed in the first-order predicate calculus (a syntactic system for representing statements with extensive expressive power) can be expressed in clause form. We will not prove this important result here, but for future reference, we do note that the statement:

if P then Q

is equivalent to the clause form statement:

Q or ⌐P

We summarize our thoughts so far with a simple example. Suppose a university offers two history courses, History 1 and History 2, with the following requirements:

A.   Each student must complete History 1 before taking History 2.
B.   Each student must take one of the history courses unless both have been completed.

These rules can be stated in clause form by first establishing the following notational system:

P = The student should register for History 1.
Q = The student should register for History 2.
R = The student has completed History 1.
S = The student has completed History 2.

Then, requirement A can be expressed by the two clauses:

$$R \text{ or } \neg Q$$

and

$$R \text{ or } \neg S$$

(the clause form of "if (Q or S) then R"), while requirement B can be expressed as:

$$P \text{ or } Q \text{ or } S$$

We now wish to decide what effect these rules have on Sue, a student who has not completed History 1. Note that Sue's status can be expressed by:

$$\neg R$$

Thus, Sue's situation can be summarized by the four clauses (R or $\neg Q$), (R or $\neg S$), (P or Q or S), and $\neg R$, which when resolved produce the resolvent P as indicated in Figure 5-21. Indeed, Sue should register for History 1.

Figure 5-21 The resolution pattern producing P from the statements (P or Q or S), (R or $\neg Q$), (R or $\neg S$), and $\neg R$

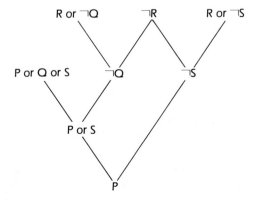

Having established the theoretical foundations of our problem-solving algorithm, we should now consider some of the issues of practicality that arise from its application. For instance, although an algorithm based on the repetition of resolution can ultimately find any logical consequence of the initial statements, in a particular application it may take a long time to produce the consequence we are looking for. For example, Figure 5-22 presents several logical consequences of a given collection of initial statements. If our task is to decide whether or not the collection implies the statement P, we would not want the deductive system to spend time finding and reporting all these other results. What we need is a way of giving the general problem-solving algorithm direction.

With this as our goal, let us consider what will happen if we apply resolution to a collection of statements that are inconsistent—that is, a collection of statements that contradict one another. The fact that the statements contradict one another implies that although some of the statements imply some result P, others imply the opposite—¬P. Thus, if we apply repeated resolution to the collection, we will ultimately obtain both P and ¬P, which when resolved will produce the empty statement. Conversely, if repeated resolution produces the empty statement, that statement must have been produced by resolving two contradictory statements, each of which was obtained from the original collection, meaning that the initial collection of statements must have been inconsistent. We conclude that repeated resolution will produce the empty statement if and only if the initial collection of statements is inconsistent.

Let us now suppose that we have a collection of consistent statements and wish to determine if P is a consequence of them. One approach would be to apply repeated resolution and wait to see if P is ever produced. However, a better approach is to add ¬P to the collection of initial statements and apply repeated resolution to the expanded collection. Then, if the empty statement is ever produced, we can conclude that the expanded collection must be inconsistent, which means that the original

Figure 5-22 Some logical consequences of a collection of statements

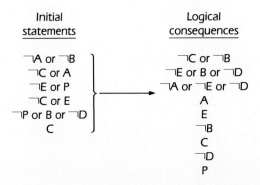

Initial statements	Logical consequences
¬A or ¬B	¬C or ¬B
¬C or A	¬E or B or ¬D
¬E or P	¬A or ¬E or ¬D
¬C or E	A
¬P or B or ¬D	E
C	¬B
	C
	¬D
	P

collection must imply P since the only opportunity for inconsistency is through a conflict with the added statement ¬P. This approach is better because in this case the application of resolution can begin with the process of resolving the statement ¬P with other statements in the collection. This in turn will tend to focus the resolution process on those statements involving P and thus produce a process geared toward the task at hand rather than the production of arbitrary consequences of the original collection of statements.

One final point remains to be discussed before we are ready to apply resolution in an actual programming environment. Suppose we have the two statements

<blockquote>if Mary is at X then Mary's lamb is at X</blockquote>

and

<blockquote>Mary is at home</blockquote>

where X is intended to represent any location. In clause form the two statements become

<blockquote>(Mary's lamb is at X) or ¬(Mary is at X)</blockquote>

and

<blockquote>(Mary is at home)</blockquote>

which at first glance do not have components that can be resolved. On the other hand, the components (Mary is at home) and ¬(Mary is at X) are quite close to being opposites of each other. The problem is to recognize that X, being a statement about all locations in general, is a statement about home in particular. Thus, a special case of the first statement is

<blockquote>(Mary's lamb is at home) or ¬(Mary is at home)</blockquote>

which can be resolved with the statement

<blockquote>(Mary is at home)</blockquote>

to produce the statement

<blockquote>(Mary's lamb is at home)</blockquote>

The process of assigning values to variables (such as assigning the value home to X) so that resolution can be performed is called unification. It is this process that allows general statements to be applied to specific applications in a deduction system. It also provides a technique for extracting information from the system. For example, it is by means of unification that we are able to conclude that Bill is a grandparent of Tom from the statements

<blockquote>
Bill is a parent of Joan.
Joan is parent of Tom.
If Y is a parent of X and Z is a parent of Y,
   then Z is a grandparent of X.
</blockquote>

Prolog

The language Prolog (short for PROgramming in LOGic) is a declarative programming language whose underlying problem-solving algorithm is based on repeated resolution. A program in Prolog consists of a collection of initial statements upon which the underlying algorithm bases its deductive reasoning. The components from which these statements are constructed are called predicates. A predicate consists of a predicate identifier followed by a parenthetical statement listing the predicate's arguments. A single predicate represents a fact about its arguments, and its identifier is usually chosen to reflect this underlying semantics. Thus, if we wanted to express the fact that Bill is Mary's parent, we might use the predicate form

parent(bill, mary).

(Note that the arguments in this predicate start with lower-case letters even though they represent proper nouns. This is because Prolog distinguishes between constants and variables by insisting that constants begin with lower-case letters and variables begin with upper-case letters.)

Statements in a Prolog program are either facts or rules (each of which must be terminated by a period). A fact consists of a single predicate. For example, the facts that Bob is taller than Carol and Carol is taller than Sue could be represented by the Prolog statements

taller(bob, carol).

and

taller(carol, sue).

A Prolog rule is an if-then statement. (Prolog accepts the responsibility of converting if-then statements into clause form.) An if-then statement in Prolog (such as "if X then Y") is represented with the consequence first (as in "Y if X"). The symbol :- is used in place of the word *if*. Thus, the rule "Z is taller than X if Z is taller than Y and Y is taller than X" could be expressed as

taller(Z,X) :- taller(Z,Y), taller (Y,X).

The comma separating taller(Z,Y) and taller(Y,X) represents the conjunction *and*.

Keep in mind that the Prolog system does not know the meaning of the predicates in a program; it simply manipulates the statements in a totally symbolic manner according to the resolution inference rule. Thus, it is up to the programmer to describe all the pertinent features of a predicate in terms of facts and rules. In this light, Prolog facts tend to be used to identify specific instances of a predicate whereas rules are used to describe general principles. This is the approach followed by the preceding statements regarding the predicate taller. The two facts describe particular instances of "tallerness" while the rule describes a general property. Note that the fact that Bob is taller than Sue, though not explicitly stated, is a consequence of the two facts combined with the rule.

Most Prolog implementations are designed to be used interactively. In this context, the task of a programmer is to develop the collection of facts and rules that constitute the set of initial statements to be used in the deductive system. Once this collection of statements is established, conjectures (called *goals* in Prolog terminology) can be proposed to the system by typing them at a terminal's keyboard. When such a goal is presented to a Prolog system, the system tries to confirm it as a consequence of the initial statements. Based on our collection of statements describing the relationship taller, each of the goals

```
taller(bob, carol).
taller(carol, sue).
taller(bob, sue).
```

could be so confirmed since each is a logical consequence of the initial statements. (The first two are identical to facts appearing in the initial statements, whereas the third requires a certain degree of deduction by the system.)

More interesting examples are obtained if we provide goals whose arguments are variables rather than constants. In these cases, Prolog will try to derive the goal from the initial statements while keeping track of the unifications required to do so. Then, if the goal is obtained, Prolog will report these unifications. For example, consider the goal

```
taller(W, sue).
```

In response to this, Prolog would report

```
taller(carol, sue).
```

Indeed, this is a consequence of the initial statements and agrees with the goal via unification. Furthermore, if we asked Prolog to tell us more, it would find and report the consequence

```
taller(bob, sue).
```

In contrast, we could ask Prolog to find people shorter than Carol by proposing the goal

```
taller(carol, W).
```

In fact, if we started with the goal

```
taller(V, W).
```

Prolog would ultimately report all the height relationships that could be derived from the initial statements. Thus, a single Prolog program can be used to confirm that a particular person is taller than another given person, to find those who are taller than a given person, to find those who are shorter than a given person, or to find all height relationships. This versatility is one of the features that has captured the imagination of computer scientists.

Let us now consider the Prolog program in Figure 5-23 for sorting a list of numbers. Although it uses some features that we have not discussed, such as the use of square bracket notation for representing lists, we can still grasp the main structure of the program—an understanding that will provide insight into the power of declarative programming. Let us look at the purpose of the program's statements.

The first statement:

sort(L,S) :- permutation(L,S), ordered(S).

represents the rule that a list S is the sorted version of the list L if S is a permutation of L and S is ordered. However, the Prolog system does not know the meaning of the predicates permutation and ordered, so the remaining statements are provided to define these predicates. Thus, the next two statements represent the fact that the empty list is a permutation of itself and the rule that a nonempty list is a permutation of another list if the two contain the same entries.

The next three statements define the predicate ordered. The first states that the empty list is ordered; the next states that a list with only one entry is ordered; and the third is the rule stating that a list with at least two entries is ordered if its first entry is less than its second and the entries after the first are in order.

Finally, the statements regarding the predicate append describe the condition of one list being the result of appending two other lists. (This concept was required in the definition of permutation.)

To use our sort program to sort the list 8, 2, 4, 3, we enter the goal

sort([8,2,4,3],X).

to which the Prolog system will respond

sort([8,2,4,3],[2,3,4,8]).

With this example behind us, we are now in position to appreciate the power of declarative programming. Note that our sort program says nothing about how the sort process is to be done. Rather, the program concentrates on expressing what a sorted list is. Thus, the process of developing the program is one of describing the problem to be solved, not describing a sequence of events that will solve the problem. The significance of this distinction is enormous. It says that when developing a program under the declarative paradigm, many of the concerns discussed in Chapter 4 regarding the development and expression of algorithms become superfluous.

With such strong credentials behind the declarative approach to programming, you may be wondering why it has not revolutionized the programming process throughout the programming community. The answer lies in the question of efficiency. Although significant progress has been made, the underlying algorithms on

Figure 5-23 A Prolog program for sorting a list of numbers

```
sort (L,S) :− permutation(L,S), ordered(S).

permutation([],[]).
Permutation(Q,[X|T]) :−  append(A, [X|B],Q),
                         append(A,B,P),
                         permutation(P,T).

ordered([]).
ordered([_|[]]).
ordered([A|[B|T]]) :− A  < B, ordered([B|T]).

append([],Z,Z).
append([X|L],M,[X|N]) :− append(L,M,N).
```

which general-purpose declarative languages are based continue to produce systems that are quite slow when compared to their procedural counterparts. For instance, the process of deciding which clauses to resolve and finding unifiers when clause components do not exactly agree can consume a lot of time. Whether or not these problems can be overcome is a current question and provides an active area of research in computer science. On the other hand, even with its sluggish performance in terms of execution speed, declarative programming continues to gain converts.

Questions/Exercises

1. Describe the pattern of resolutions required to derive statement P from the initial statements in Figure 5-22.

2. Which of the statements R, S, T, U, and V are logical consequences of the collection of statements ($\neg$R or T or S), ($\neg$S or V), ($\neg$V or R), (U or $\neg$S), (T or $\neg$U), and (S or V).

3. Is the following collection of statements consistent? Explain your answer.

$$P \text{ or } Q \text{ or } R$$
$$\neg R \text{ or } Q$$
$$R \text{ or } \neg P$$
$$\neg Q$$

4. Suppose a Prolog program consisted of the statements:

```
smaller(carol, john).
smaller(bill, sue).
smaller(sue, carol).
smaller(X,Z) :- smaller(X,Y), smaller(Y,Z).
```

List the results that could be produced from each of the following goals:

a. smaller(sue,V).

b. smaller(U, carol).

c. smaller(U,V).

Chapter 5 Review Problems

(Asterisked problems are associated with optional sections.)

1. a. Using our pseudocode, design a program for simulating the interaction between the fox and rabbit populations in a certain region over a 10-year period. Make the following assumptions:
   1. The initial fox population is $F_0 = 18,000$ and the initial rabbit population is $R_0 = 98,000$.
   2. If the fox and rabbit populations at the end of one month are F_i and R_i, respectively, then the populations at the end of the next month are given by:

   $$F_{i+1} = F_i + (.038 \times R_iF_i - .218 \times F_i)/12$$

   and

   $$R_{i+1} = R_i + (.934 \times R_i - .041 \times R_i \times F_i)/12$$

   b. Circle the portions of your program that are specific to this particular simulation problem. Then, modify your program so that these portions can be easily altered.

   c. In what sense does your modified program constitute a general-purpose simulation system?

2. Suppose your checking account was to be represented as an object in an object-oriented program for maintaining your financial records. What data would be stored inside this object? What messages might that object receive and how should it respond to each? What are other objects that might be used in the program?

3. Translate the high-level statement:

   MOVE LENGTH PLUS WIDTH INTO HALFWAY

   into the machine language of Appendix B assuming that LENGTH, WIDTH, and HALFWAY are all represented in floating-point notation.

4. Translate the high-level statement:

   IF X EQUALS 0 THEN MOVE Y PLUS W INTO Z
   ELSE MOVE Y PLUS X INTO Z

   into the machine language of Appendix B assuming that W, X, Y, and Z are all represented as binary values occupying one byte of memory each.

5. Why was it necessary to identify the type of data associated with the variables in problem 4 in order to translate the statements? Why do many high-level programming languages require the

programmer to identify the type of each variable at the beginning of a program?

6. Common data types include integer, real, and character. Describe a likely technique for representing data of each of these types inside a machine.

7. Draw a syntax diagram representing the grammar of a predicate in an English-language sentence.

8. State a sentence in the English language that does not conform to the syntax diagram of Figure 5-7. Modify the syntax diagram to allow for sentences having the structure of your example.

9. Suppose the following rectangular array is named BOX:

   $$\begin{array}{cccc} 1 & 2 & 3 & 4 \\ 5 & 6 & 7 & 8 \\ 9 & 10 & 11 & 12 \end{array}$$

   What will BOX look like after executing (independently) each of the following statements:
   a. LET BOX(2,1) = 16
   b. LET BOX(1,2) = BOX(1,1) + BOX(2,2)
   c. LET BOX(3,4) = BOX(3,3) − BOX(3,2)

10. Draw a picture of the array described by each of the following Pascal statements:
    a. var
       xxx: array [1..4,1..2] of integer;
    b. var
       yyy: array [3..6,1..3] of integer;
    c. var
       zzz: array [1..3,1..4,1..3] of integer;

11. What ambiguities could be introduced in a program if a function with two parameters of type integer were given the same name as a two-dimensional array? What subtle technique is used in Pascal to avoid this problem?

12. What is the difference between a homogeneous array and a heterogeneous array?

13. Summarize the following rat's-nest routine with a single IF-THEN-ELSE statement:

    ```
    50   IF X > 5 GOTO 80
    60   LET X = X + 1
    70   GOTO 90
    80   LET X = X + 2
    90   STOP
    ```

14. Summarize the following nested IF-THEN-ELSE structure with a single CASE-OF-END statement:

    IF X = 4
       THEN LET X = X + 1
       ELSE IF X = 5
               THEN LET X = X + 2
               ELSE IF X = 6
                       THEN LET X = X + 3

15. Using the case statement structure to handle the opponent's possibilities, design an algorithm to play tic-tac-toe (naughts and crosses). Your algorithm should take the first move by placing an X in the upper left-hand corner. (Use symmetry to reduce the number of options.)

16. If your tic-tac-toe algorithm in problem 15 were changed to always select the middle square for its first move, how could the use of symmetry reduce the rest of the algorithm to one large IF-THEN-ELSE structure?

17. In what way is the "for . . ." loop structure in Pascal less flexible than its "repeat . . ." and "while . . ." counterparts?

18. The following Ada program sequence is designed to make use of the subprogram LARGER discussed in this chapter. What values will be assigned to the variables A, B, and C at the end of the routine?

    A := 5;
    B := 6;
    C := 7;
    LARGER(A, B, C);
    LARGER (C, B, A)

19. Using the subprogram LARGER from the text, describe a sequence of instructions that accomplishes the same objective as the single statement:
    Z = MAX(I,J) + MAX(A,B)
    where MAX is the function introduced in the text.

20. Suppose you have access to a subprogram REVERSE that reverses the letters in a character string. The subprogram has two parameters. The first is the string to be reversed; the second is used to transfer the reversed string back to the main program. Using a Pascal-like syntax, write the statement needed to request this subprogram to reverse the character string assigned to the variable STRG and assign the result to the variable REVSTRG.

21. Suppose REVERSE in problem 20 were implemented as a function rather than as a subprogram. (The function form has only one parameter representing the string to be reversed.) Again using a Pascal-like syntax, write the statement needed to apply the function to the string assigned to the variable STRG and assign the result to the variable named REVSTRG.

22. Using such string manipulation functions as LEN and such operations as concatenation, design an algorithm that will reverse a string of characters.

23. Suppose the value assigned to LAST is the character string Smith and the value assigned to FIRST is the string Mary. In each of the following cases, identify the value of NAME or LONG after the corresponding instruction has ben executed:
    a. LET NAME = FIRST + LAST
    b. LET NAME = FIRST + ' ' + LAST
    c. LET NAME = LAST + ', ' + FIRST
    d. LET LONG = LEN(FIRST + " + LAST)
    e. Let NAME =
            LAST(1:2) + FIRST(2:3) + LAST(4:4)
    f. LET NAME = LAST(4:4) + FIRST(3:4)
    g. LET LONG = POS(LAST,'ith')

24. What ambiguity exists in the assignment statement:
    LET X = 3 + 2 * 5

25. Suppose a small company has five employees and is planning to increase the number to six. The following are excerpts from two equivalent programs used by the company that must be altered to reflect the change in the number of employees. Both programs are written in a Pascal-like language. Indicate what changes must be made to each program. What complications arise in the case of program 1 that are avoided by the use of constants in program 2?

    Program 1
                .
                .
                .

    DailySalary := TotalSal/5;
    AvgSalary := TotalSal/5;
    DailySales := TotalSales/5;
    AvgSales := TotalSales/5;
                .
                .
                .

Program 2

.
.
.

```
const
    NumEmpl = 5;
    DaysWk = 5;
```

.
.
.

```
DailySalary : = TotalSal/DaysWk;
AvgSalary : = TotalSal/NumEmpl;
DailySales : = TotalSales/DaysWk;
AvgSales : = TotalSales/NumEmpl;
```

.
.
.

*26. Draw a diagram (similar to Figure 5-21) representing the resolutions needed to derive P from the collection of statements (Q or ¬R), (T or R), (P or ¬T), and (P or ¬Q).

*27. Is the collection of statements ¬R, (T or R), (P or ¬Q), (Q or ¬T) and (R or ¬P) consistent? Explain your answer.

*28. What conclusions would Prolog be able to find if faced with the goal

bigger(X, lassie).

and the initial statements

bigger(rex, lassie).
bigger(fido, rex).
bigger(spot, rex).
bigger(X,Z) :- bigger(X,Y), bigger(Y,Z).

*29. What conclusions would Prolog be able to find if faced with the goal

eq(X,Y).

and the initial statements

grteq(a,b).
grteq(b,c).
grteq(c,a).
grteq(U,W) :- grteq(U,V), grteq(V,W).
eq(X,Y) :- grteq(X,Y), grteq(Y,X).

Problems for the Programmer

1. Pick a third-generation language and identify any reserved words in it. If there are reserved words, identify statements in the language that would become ambiguous if these words were not reserved.

2. What features are present in your third-generation language that allow a translator to isolate the various statements in a program?

3. Which statements in your third-generation language are really calls to subprograms in the operating system?

4. What data types and structures are available in your programming language? What syntax is provided for declaring these characteristics? Are any of these characteristics declared implicitly?

5. Implement your own version of the functions LEN and INDEX in the language of your choice. (If your language already has these functions, ignore them for the purpose of this exercise.)

6. Implement the algorithm to reverse a character string that you designed in review problem 22.

7. Write a program that will search for the value five within a two-dimensional array of integers. What control structures does the language you are using provide for stopping the search process once this value is found?

8. Suppose that a savings and loan association determines the maximum amount it will loan to an individual for a home mortgage using the following system. The individual's job and the home being purchased are each rated on a scale from 1 to 10. If the job rating is 1, no loan is given. If the job rating is greater than 1 but less than 7, the loan limit is determined by the formula:

((job rating)/10)(annual salary)(2)((home rating)/10)

If the job rating is 7 or more, the mortgage limit is determined by:

((job rating)/10)(annual salary)(3)((home rating)/10)

Write a program that computes the loan limit based on a customer's ratings and annual salary.

9. A palindrome is a character string that appears the same when read backward as when read forward such as madam or noon. Write a program that accepts a character string and reports whether or not it is a palindrome.

10. Design a set of mnemonics for the machine language in Appendix B and write an assembler to translate the programs expressed with these mnemonics into hexadecimal form.

11. Implement your solution to review problem 1.

6 Software Engineering

6–1 **The Software Life Cycle**

6–2 **Modular Design**
  A Design Example
  An Alternate Approach
  Advantages of Modular Design

6–3 **Coupling**
  Data Coupling in Perspective
  Side Effects

6–4 **Cohesion**

6–5 **Design Methodologies**
  Top-Down Design
  Data Flow Diagrams

6–6 **Documentation**

We began our study of the human/machine interface with the software operating system that creates the environment in which interaction between a human and a machine is conducted. We then turned our attention to the subject of algorithmic processes and the programming techniques that we as humans have developed for communicating these processes to machines. However, the development and actual programming of algorithms is only a small part of the overall process of developing and maintaining software. Indeed, large software systems must be engineered in the same sense as automobiles, bridges, and television sets.

It is important to recognize that we are discussing large software systems, the complete comprehension of which exceeds the short-term memory capabilities of the human mind. For this reason the issues involved are more than merely enlarged versions of those faced when writing small programs. For instance, the development of large systems inherently requires the efforts of more than one person. In turn, the subject of software engineering encompasses much more than algorithm design and representation. Also included are such issues as personnel management, project management, and communication skills. In fact, many topics within the subject of software engineering are closely associated with business management. In this chapter, however, we restrict our attention to those topics traditionally associated with computer science.

6–1 **The Software Life Cycle**

To appreciate the importance of software engineering, it is helpful to understand the *software life cycle,* which refers to the various phases through which software passes from the time its need is first recognized until it is discarded. The major phases in this cycle are development, use, and modification (Figure 6-1).

The diagram in Figure 6-1 depicts the fact that once software is developed it enters a cyclic pattern of being used and modified that continues for the rest of the software's life. Such a pattern is common for many manufactured products as well. The difference is mainly that in the case of other products the modification phase would be more accurately called a repair or maintenance phase. That is, other products tend to move from being used to being modified because their parts become worn.

Software, on the other hand, does not wear out. Instead, a piece of software in the use phase might move into the modification phase because errors that were not discovered earlier in the development phase force changes to be made, because changes in the program's application occur that require corresponding changes in the software, or because changes made during a previous modification are found to induce problems elsewhere in the software. For example, changes in tax laws will often require modifications to payroll programs that calculate withholding taxes, and all too often these changes have adverse effects in other areas of the program that may not be discovered until sometime later.

Our major motivation for introducing the software life cycle is to discuss the relationship between the development phase and the modification phase. With this goal, let us take a closer look at what takes place within the modification phase. Regardless of the reason for a piece of software entering this phase, the modification process requires that a person (often not the original author) study the program and its documentation until the program, or at least the pertinent part of the program, is understood. Otherwise, any modification could introduce more problems than it solves. Acquiring this understanding can be a difficult task even when the software is well designed and documented. In fact, it is often within this phase

Figure 6-1 The software life cycle

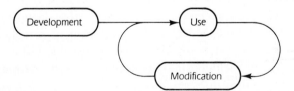

that a piece of software is finally discarded under the pretense (too often true) that it is easier to develop a new system from scratch than to modify the existing package successfully.

To understand how this modification process can be greatly affected by apparently insignificant decisions made during software development, consider the use of descriptive names to represent constant values in a program. In particular, in our discussion of data description statements in Chapter 5, we saw how the name AirportAlt might be used in lieu of the nondescriptive value 645 in a program and reasoned that if a change became necessary, it would be easier to change the value associated with the name instead of finding and changing numerous occurrences of the value 645.

The point is that a little effort during the development phase can make a tremendous difference in the modification phase. This is emphasized by the fact that the effort during the development phase is expended only once, whereas the modification phase will be repeated numerous times throughout the software's life. Studies have shown that approximately two-thirds of the total effort on a piece of software during its life is expended within the modification phase (Figure 6-2).

Since the effort expended in modifying large software systems is typically twice that of the system's development, you might expect most cost-reduction efforts to be directed toward the modification stage of the life cycle. This is, in fact, the case,

Figure 6-2 A typical disposition of effort during the life of a large software system

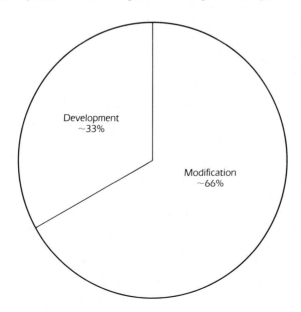

except the approach taken is an indirect one. That is, instead of attacking the problems of modification in the context of the modification phase, the approach is to take advantage of the leverage provided by the relationship between the development and modification stages. Thus, a significant amount of work in the area of software engineering has been directed toward the development phase and its effects on later modifications.

The development phase is therefore the major subject of this chapter so before leaving this section, we will describe the major components within this part of the software life cycle. To a large degree, the components listed here are actually the steps traversed during the development process. On the other hand, these steps often overlap one another to the point that it would be inaccurate to say that the development phase consists of these steps in the following strict order:

1. *Formalize the system requirements*. It is within this step that the decision is made regarding whether or not computer technology is applicable and should be applied to the problem at hand. This is done by isolating the requirements of the application and comparing a variety of possible solutions. These requirements are stated in terms of the application. For instance, a requirement might be that access to data must be restricted to authorized personnel. The requirements are then refined into specifications stated in terms of the technology under consideration. That is, the previous requirement might become the specification that a program will not run until an approved five-digit password is typed at the terminal. With such specifications one can decide whether current technology is sufficient for the job and, if so, whether its use would be cost-effective.

It is also during this step that the goals of the proposed system are established. In the case of a system being developed at the request of the ultimate user (for example, if the data-processing department is charged with the task of developing an inventory maintenance system for the company's purchasing department), this requires a thorough understanding of the user's needs and expectations. In the case of a system that will be marketed to a variety of users (such as a general-purpose student records system that is expected to meet the needs of a large number of university registrars), this requires a substantial amount of market research.

2. *Design the system structure*. Once the goals of the system have been established, the decision has been made to apply computer technology to the problem, and the system specifications have been defined, the proposed software system is broken into manageable units called modules. It is by means of this decomposition that the implementation of large systems becomes a possibility. Indeed, without such a breakdown of the overall task, the details of the implementation would exceed a human's short-term memory capabilities, and hence the final product would be destined to internal errors, malfunctions, and catastrophic maintenance costs. In fact, it is in the design of a system's modular structure that we obtain control over

the future maintenance of the software. Thus, it is this design process that will attract our attention in the next four sections of this chapter.

3. *Implement the system.* This step involves the actual writing of programs. With a good modular design it can be accomplished by several programmers working independently on different modules in the system without interfering with one another.

4. *Test and debug the system.* This step is closely associated with the previous one and is extremely important. Again a good modular design allows the various modules to be tested both individually and together as a complete system.

5. *Document the system.* In the past, because this step in the software development process was considered as the final stage, it was often hurriedly done to meet a deadline or took place merely as an afterthought. Today with a better understanding of the software life cycle, the documentation of software is considered one of the most important steps in the development phase. With this in mind, design techniques have been developed that result in documentation being produced as the software is designed and written.

You will notice a similarity between these steps and the problem-solving phases identified by Polya (Section 4-3). After all, to develop a large software system is to solve a problem. On the other hand, there are also significant differences between the two processes. Whereas it is acceptable for an individual problem solver to try various solutions in an effort to learn more about the problem being attacked, it is mandatory that a thorough understanding of a large software system's goals be understood before one commits resources to its development. Moreover, the development of a large software system is a team project, and hence it is imperative that the efforts of everyone involved be coordinated. However, truly creative problem solving is more of an individual, "free wheeling" process in which such constraints as identifying and reporting various stages of progress to others can be devastating. Thus, whereas software engineering seeks to establish a highly structured environment in which progress can be monitored, creative problem solving seeks a nonstructured environment in which one can drop previous plans of attack to pursue sparks of intuition without explaining why.

Questions/Exercises
1. At what phase or phases in the software life cycle are the advantages of high-level languages most pronounced?
2. Which steps within the development phase of the software life cycle would be applicable in the development of a nonautomated system?
3. Which steps within the development phase of the software life cycle would not appear in the development of a small automated system?
4. Which steps within the development phase of the software life cycle are combined by the use of comments within the source program?

6–2 Modular Design

One of the key statements in Section 6-1 was that to modify software one must understand the program or at least the pertinent parts of the program. Such an understanding is often difficult enough to obtain in the case of small programs and would be close to impossible when dealing with large software systems if it were not for the concept of *modular design.* This refers to the practice of dividing the software into manageable units, with each unit designed to perform only a part of the overall task.

Note that we introduced this technique during the discussion of algorithms. There we observed that by isolating the details of certain activities within subprograms, we could obtain a main program that more readily expresses its purpose and methods than would be available if we insisted on including complete descriptions of the activities in a single program unit.

A Design Example

We illustrate the modular concept further by applying it to a problem involving an airline schedule system. Suppose a software package is desired that will allow airline agents to retrieve schedule information about the current routes by means of a terminal. Information about the flight in question is to be obtained by providing the flight number. Observe that two levels of access are involved in this system. One is a retrieve-only level that should be given to all the agents so that they are able to get information from the system. The other is a modify level that allows the schedule information within the system to be changed. Clearly the latter access level must be controlled to maintain the validity of the system. In our example this control is to be implemented by means of passwords. Each user of the system will be given a password that will be also stored in the software. The software's response to some of these passwords should be to provide the user modify privileges; in the remaining cases, it would allow data retrieval only.

We begin our design by observing the need to maintain an interactive dialogue between the computer and the user. For this, the program must be able to write messages on the terminal screen and accept messages from the keyboard. We might therefore begin with a program module whose job it is to handle such dialogue. It will prompt the user at the terminal with the appropriate message, analyze the user's response, and invoke other modules based on such analysis. Thus, we envision this module as playing the role of a control module that requests actions of the other modules in the system according to the instructions of the user.

Next we consider what modules are needed to support the dialogue module. Once the user has typed a password it will be necessary to check the validity of what was typed and obtain the privileges associated with any valid password. We therefore provide a module in our design for checking passwords. This module is subordinate to the dialogue module in that it is executed by request of the dialogue module. More precisely, once the dialogue module has obtained a password from the user, it hands the password (most likely as a parameter of a subprogram) to the password-checking module. The password is checked for validity, and a report is sent back to the dialogue module (again through a parameter) indicating that the password is not valid, is good for access only, or is good for modification (Figure 6-3). Through use of this subordinate module, the dialogue module is able to respond intelligently to the entry of a password. For instance, if the password were found invalid, the dialogue module would know to terminate the conversation with the user.

In the case of a valid password, the dialogue module should be able to respond to instructions to display, delete, or insert schedules. We might therefore design a separate module for performing each of these actions. If the dialogue module receives a request to display a schedule, it should first ask the user for the number of the flight in question and then request the display module to display the requested schedule. At the time of this request the dialogue module must provide the display module with the flight number obtained from the user. In return, once the display module has performed its task, it should report the degree of success to the dialogue module (Figure 6-4). Such a report allows the dialogue module to continue its conversation with the user in an intelligent manner. For example, if the display module were unable to find the requested schedule, the dialogue module would know to send the message NO SUCH FLIGHT NUMBER EXISTS to the user.

The relationship between the delete module and the dialogue module is similar to the display case, except that a higher privilege is required by the user. In addition to providing the flight number, the dialogue module will provide the delete module with the privilege level obtained earlier from the password-checking module. Knowing this privilege level, the delete module can block any unauthorized activities. In this manner the duties of the dialogue module remain communication oriented while the task of protecting the schedules against illegal deletions is delegated to the subordinate delete module. (We return to this concept of distribution of duties in Section 6-3.) Again to allow the dialogue module to continue intelligent commu-

Figure 6-3 A password validation by a separate module

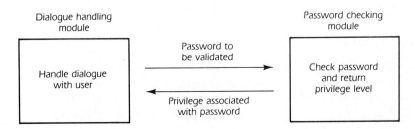

Figure 6-4 A schedule displayed by a separate module

nication with the user after executing the delete module, we will design a success reporting system in the delete module similar to the one in the display module. The dialogue module may ultimately report to the user with the message DELETION COMPLETE or, if the user's password does not allow modification privileges, YOU ARE NOT ALLOWED TO DELETE DATA—NO ACTION TAKEN, or perhaps FLIGHT NUMBER NOT FOUND—NO ACTION TAKEN.

The insert module is similar in its relation to the dialogue module in that the exchange of the modification privilege and a success report is involved. However, when inserting a new schedule, more information than just the flight number is required. The entire schedule must be provided. Since this information must come from the user at the terminal, we include the collection of this data in the dialogue module and have the collected data handled as a single unit to the insertion module along with the privilege information.

The diagram in Figure 6-5 is a **structure chart** of our design of the airline schedule software. Such charts provide a pictorial representation of the software organization. In such a chart, each module is represented by a rectangle surrounding the module's name. These rectangles are connected by arrows indicating which modules are subordinate to which other modules. In this case we have designed a hierarchical system with the modules CHECK PASSWORD, DISPLAY, DELETE, and INSERT subordinate to DIALOGUE. Note the technique used in the structure chart to indicate the information that is passed among the modules. For example, the arrow pointing from DIALOGUE to CHECK PASSWORD (labeled "password") indicates that the password is given to CHECK PASSWORD when this module is executed, and the arrow going the other way (labeled "privilege") means that the privilege level is reported back to DIALOGUE when the submodule terminates.

An Alternate Approach

Do not assume that there is only one modular design for a given system. In fact, we will shortly consider several flaws in the preceding design that would lead one to hope that a better design exists. For this reason, let us look at the following alternative to the previous design. This alternative is obtained by placing initial emphasis

Figure 6-5 A structure chart of the airline schedule system

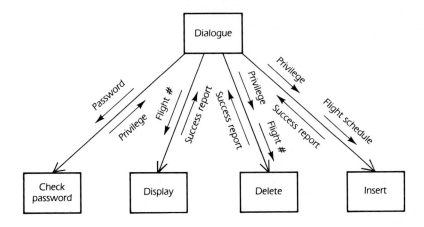

on access control rather than on the dialogue with the user. We begin with a module called CONTROL ACCESS that controls the user's access to the schedules depending on the password provided. This module uses its subordinate GET PRIVILEGE to obtain the privilege level of the current user. The subordinate's job is to get the password from the user and check its validity. When CONTROL ACCESS receives this report, it either terminates the conversation in the case of a nonvalid password or executes another of its subordinates depending on the privilege level associated with the password.

The other subordinates are called CONTROL DISPLAY ACTIVITIES and CONTROL MODIFICATION ACTIVITIES. The former module provides communication dialogue with the user in relation to the display of schedules only and is executed when a password is valid for access-only privileges. A user who is not allowed to modify the schedules will see only the access dialogue and may never be aware that other options exist. On the other hand, the CONTROL MODIFICATION ACTIVITIES module will be executed in those cases where the password entered is associated with modification privileges. It therefore controls communication with the user pertaining to displaying, deleting, and inserting schedules.

To accomplish the actual display, delete, or insert activities, we again use three separate modules (DISPLAY, DELETE, and INSERT). In this design these modules are allowed to carry on a dialogue with the user. Thus, they can report error conditions such as invalid flight numbers directly to the user rather than indirectly through their superior modules. Such a design eliminates the need for the success reports found in the previous system.

A structure chart for such a design appears in Figure 6-6. Observe that the module DISPLAY is used by both CONTROL MODIFICATION ACTIVITIES and CONTROL DISPLAY ACTIVITIES. At first glance this may appear to provide a

Figure 6-6 A structure chart of an alternate airline schedule system

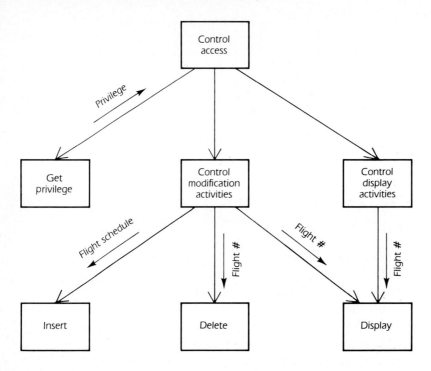

link through which a user without modify privileges could obtain access to the modification routines. Recall, however, that once a subprogram is completed, control is returned to the original routine where the execution request was made. Consequently, the two modules CONTROL MODIFICATION ACTIVITIES and CONTROL DISPLAY ACTIVITIES can use the same DISPLAY submodule without complications.

Advantages of Modular Design

In conclusion, we should point out the benefits provided by a modular design during the implementation of a system. For example, consider the problem of writing and debugging the main module DIALOGUE in our first design in relation to doing the same for the module CHECK PASSWORD. The development of neither of these depends on the other. To write and test DIALOGUE, all that is needed in place of the completed CHECK PASSWORD is a short subprogram called CHECK PASSWORD that accepts a password and returns a privilege. Since, for initial test purposes, the privilege returned does not have to actually correspond to the password in any special way, this test version of CHECK PASSWORD need be only a few instructions long. Such a subprogram that does nothing but allow another routine to run for test purposes is called a *stub.* To write and test the module DIALOGUE, one needs only four stubs (CHECK PASSWORD, DISPLAY, DELETE, and INSERT).

In the same manner, we see that to write and test the module CHECK PASSWORD we do not need the completed control module but need only a routine to request the execution of CHECK PASSWORD and at the same time provide a password to be checked. Such a routine is easily provided and allows CHECK PASSWORD to be developed without first developing other modules in the system.

We see, then, that once the interface between the modules in a modular design is established, development of the modules can proceed simultaneously and independent of each other. This is a tremendous asset when developing large software systems with numerous programmers.

Questions/Exercises
1. Does the design of a modular structure for a system involve programming?
2. Do modular systems always have a hierarchical-like structure?
3. Which of the two modular designs in this section requires less communication among its modules?
4. What stubs are required to write and test the CONTROL ACCESS module in our second design of the schedule system? What about to write and test CONTROL MODIFICATION ACTIVITIES?

6–3 Coupling

We have introduced the concept of modular design as a way of obtaining modifiable software. The idea is that a future modification will likely require changes to only a few of the modules so that one's attention can be restricted to this portion of the system during the modification process. The success of this greatly depends on the assumption that changes in one module will not unknowingly affect other modules in the system. Consequently, one's goal when designing the original system should be to maximize the independence between modules.

Working against this objective is the fact that there must be some connection between modules for them to form a coherent system. This connection is referred to as *coupling.* The goal of maximizing independence therefore corresponds to minimizing coupling. The importance of such minimization is illustrated in Figure 6-7, which graphically depicts the explosion of possible coupling paths as the number of modules in a system increases. Each of these paths, if exploited, decreases one's ability to comprehend the role of a give module and increases the chance that a change in one module will affect the activities in another.

Intermodule coupling actually occurs in several forms. One is *control coupling,* which occurs when one module passes control to another as in the transfer/return

Figure 6-7 The explosion of possible coupling paths as the number of modules increases

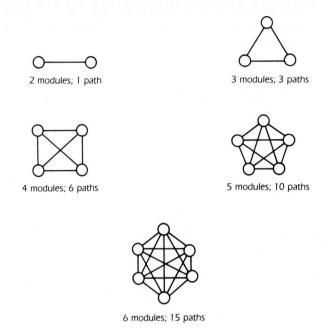

2 modules; 1 path

3 modules; 3 paths

4 modules; 6 paths

5 modules; 10 paths

6 modules; 15 paths

relationship associated with subprograms. Another is ***data coupling,*** which refers to the sharing of information, or data, between modules. For introductory purposes, it will suffice to restrict our discussion to the latter form. On the other hand, our conscience would not be clear if we did not at least point out how well our hierarchical five-module design of the schedule system in Section 6-2 (with only four control coupling paths) compares to the potential maze of 10 paths represented in Figure 6-7.

Data Coupling in Perspective

We begin our study of data coupling by comparing the relationship between DIALOGUE and CHECK PASSWORD in our first design in Section 6-2 with that of CONTROL ACCESS and GET PRIVILEGE in our second. Although different in design, these interfaces provide the controlling module with the user's privilege level. In the first case, however, we require that the dominant module DIALOGUE get the password before calling on the services of its subordinate. The result is that we see the password being transferred to the submodule in the structure chart. In contrast, our second design places the job of getting the password from the user within the submodule GET PRIVILEGE; consequently, no need exists for the modules to exchange this password between them since the password is obtained and digested within

GET PRIVILEGE. The data coupling within this second interface is therefore less complex than in the first.

You might argue at this point that the actual transfer of the password from DIALOGUE to CHECK PASSWORD is simple enough that no harm should come from it. After all, parameter passing is quite straightforward in high-level languages. However, the problem in this case, as in many others, is not the coupling itself. The increased coupling is only a symptom, and the problem lies in the necessity of transferring the password in the first place. To appreciate this, consider what would be involved if it later became necessary to modify the software to accommodate longer passwords. In the first example, two modules, DIALOGUE and CHECK PASSWORD, must be changed, whereas in the second case only GET PASSWORD need be considered. The difference is that the modification effort required in the first case is at least twice that of the second.

Along these same lines, but on a broader scale, note the difference between our two designs in the amount of coupling associated with the privilege information. In the first design four different modules deal with this data. In the second, the information is required by only two. To reduce the coupling in the first design, we could modify the design so that the module DIALOGUE becomes DIALOGUE WITH ACCESS CONTROL, which checks the user's privilege before calling on the services of DELETE or INSERT. With this change, the modules DELETE and INSERT no longer need access to the user's privilege level since they will not be activated unless their services have already been approved. Interest in the user's privileges is thus restricted to the modules DIALOGUE WITH ACCESS CONTROL and CHECK PASSWORD, resulting in a structure chart like the one in Figure 6-8.

Figure 6-8 Our initial airline schedule system after modification to reduce data coupling

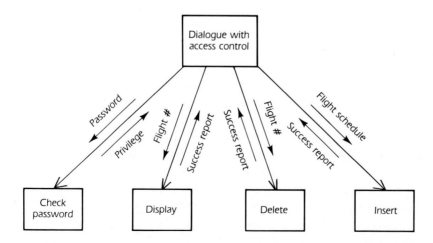

Side Effects

In addition to being concerned with minimizing the coupling between modules, we should consider how this coupling should ultimately be implemented in a programming context. We have already alluded to the correspondence between a modular structure and the use of subprograms. Indeed, the use of subprograms is the most popular technique for implementing modular systems, and the use of parameters provides a natural method for implementing any data coupling between the main module and its subordinates. Such a coupling technique is explicit in that its existence is readily recognizable in the high-level language version of the program.

A different, and potentially more dangerous, form of module interaction is implicit coupling. Such interaction falls under the broad collection of software goblins known as side effects. More precisely, a *side effect* is an action performed by a program element that is not directly represented by the syntax. This program element can range from a single instruction to a complete subprogram. For example, consider the single statement:

MOVE PRICE PLUS TAX TO TOTAL

Judging by the syntax one would not be surprised to find that the value associated with TOTAL is altered as a result of executing this statement. On the other hand, one would be shocked if the values of PRICE and TAX were also changed since there is no indication by the syntax that this should occur. Such an unexpected alteration of PRICE or TAX would be a (completely unacceptable) side effect.

To understand how implicit coupling can be introduced through side effects, first recall that subprograms are often implemented as separate entities so that data within one subprogram is not available to other units of the program. Such data along with any associated names are said to be *local* elements, meaning that they are available only within a certain locality. On the other hand, most high-level languages also provide for *global* elements. Such data can be accessed by means of the same name throughout the program and is therefore implicitly passed to any subprogram in the system.

With this in mind, consider again our modular design for the airline schedule system in Figure 6-5. As mentioned before, four modules use the privilege information. One might therefore be tempted to implement this information as a global data element. With such an arrangement the module CHECK PASSWORD would place the appropriate information in the memory cell reserved for this global data, and from then on the data would be available to the other modules without further actions. At first glance this may seem to be superior to passing the information explicitly through parameters. However, there are still four modules that use the data and thus still four modules that must be considered if changes relating to the privilege levels are ultimately made to the system. Thus, no work during the modification phase has been saved. In fact, more work has most likely been generated since we have essentially hidden the fact that these four modules are exchanging this information from anyone reading the program.

To appreciate this hiding effect more fully, consider the statement one would find in the module DIALOGUE that requests CHECK PASSWORD to validate the user's password. Without the use of local data the statement would look something like:

CHECKPASSWORD (PASSWORD, PRIVILEGE)

rather than:

CHECKPASSWORD (PASSWORD)

which would occur if PRIVILEGE were global. Note that the first statement clearly indicates that something is happening to PRIVILEGE, whereas the second gives no warning that the data element PRIVILEGE is in any way involved in the action of CHECK PASSWORD. The use of global data has demoted the major action of the subprogram (the calculation of PRIVILEGE) to the status of a side effect. You can imagine the complications this could inject into the modification phase of the software life cycle and should therefore appreciate the fact that any implicit coupling between modules should be well documented within the program itself. This, then, is an example where the comment statements, which are ignored by the translator or interpreter, can be considered as important as the statements that contribute directly to the execution of the program.

It is important to realize that passing information through parameter lists does not completely remove the threat of side effects since a program that calls a subprogram has little control over which parameters in the list will actually be changed. Thus, a poorly designed subprogram could alter values in the main program in an unintentional manner. For example, suppose a subprogram named FINDADR is given the task of finding and returning an employee's address having been given the employee's name. This routine might be called by the statement:

FINDADR (NAME, ADDRESS)

with the expectation that the employee's name will be passed to the subprogram and later returned along with that employee's address. However, FINDADR might need to rearrange the name to find the address. For instance, it might need to drop first names in favor of initials before searching through a table of names and addresses. As a result, the name ultimately returned to the main program could be an altered version of the one originally passed, and if not accounted for, this alteration could have adverse effects later in the program.

In this case, we see that finding an employee's address could have the side effect of changing the format of the name under consideration. In the context of our airline schedule system in Figure 6-5, the potential for a similar problem exists with the privilege level. Imagine, for instance, the resulting havoc if the DELETE module inadvertently lowered the privilege level it was originally passed in such a way that later deletions and insertions would be denied.

The need to protect main programs from such side effects is the primary reason many high-level programming languages provide techniques by which various parameter-passing systems can be selected by the programmer. (Refer to the discussion on parameter passing in the section on unit-level control statements in Chapter 5.)

Questions/Exercises

1. How does a novel differ from an encyclopedia in terms of the degree of coupling between its units such as chapters, sections, or entries?
2. What courses in a college curriculum traditionally have a high degree of coupling between them? Identify how they are coupled.
3. To what extent is there coupling between the programs being run by different users in a time-sharing system?
4. What are some side effects of taking certain medication? How is this use of the term *side effect* similar to its use in a programming context?
5. A hand of bridge is divided into two phases: the bidding and the actual playing of the cards. Analyze the coupling between these phases by identifying the information that is passed from the first phase to the second explicitly. What is passed implicitly?

6–4 Cohesion

Just as important as minimizing the coupling between different modules is maximizing the internal binding within each individual module. To appreciate this importance, we must look beyond the initial development of the system and consider the entire software life cycle. If it becomes necessary to make changes in a module, the existence of a variety of activities within it can easily confuse what would otherwise be a simple process. The term *cohesion* has been adopted for referring to this internal binding, or the degree of relatedness of a module's internal parts. Thus, in addition to seeking low intermodule coupling, software designers strive for high intramodule cohesion.

In an effort to achieve higher intramodule cohesion, some researchers in computer science have directed their energies toward a better understanding of cohesion itself. This has resulted in the isolation and classification of various types of cohesion found in software modules. One such class has been identified as *logical cohesion,* one of the weaker forms that refers to the cohesion within a module induced by the fact that its internal elements perform activities logically similar in nature. An example is the DIALOGUE module found in our original solution to the airline schedule problem. There, the "glue" that holds the module together is the fact that all the activities taking place deal with communication with the user. Note that although these activities are logically similar, their actual functions vary greatly. Some of the dialogue centers around obtaining the user's password, while another section is concerned with finding out which flight schedule is to be deleted, and yet another part deals with reporting errors.

A stronger form of cohesion is known as *functional cohesion,* which means that all the parts of the module are geared toward the performance of a single activity. Unfortunately, the use of the phrase "single activity" results in our definition being somewhat vague since what constitutes a single activity depends on one's point of view. In the broad sense, the entire airline schedule software package can be considered as performing the single activity of maintaining the flight schedules. On the other hand, from the machine's viewpoint anything requiring more than one machine instruction would consist of more than one activity. In our discussion of module cohesion, however, the meaning of "single activity" falls between these two extremes. We will rely on the following examples to clarify the issue.

We first note that the DIALOGUE module discussed previously is not functionally cohesive since it consists of several activities as already mentioned. On the other hand, the CHECK PASSWORD module in the same design is functionally cohesive since all its parts contribute to the checking of the password for validity.

In Section 6-3, we modified the first airline schedule system to reduce its intermodule coupling caused by widely distributed use of the user's privileges. In doing so we created the module DIALOGUE WITH ACCESS CONTROL. This module has little cohesion at all. Even its name implies that it deals with two distinct concepts: communication with the user and control of access. To improve the design in terms of cohesion this module should be divided. A natural way of doing this is to separate the control of access from that of the dialogue. This can be done by dividing the dialogue into two modules: one for display purposes only and the other for both display and modify purposes. The module controlling the user's access can then activate the appropriate dialogue module depending on the current user's privilege. The resulting design is described in the structure chart in Figure 6-9.

Since the modules constructed around the dialogue activities are only logically cohesive, it is reasonable to further divide the dialogue to obtain modules with a higher form of cohesion. One approach would be to place the control of any dialogue in the same module that performs the activity relating to that dialogue. Following this idea, the dialogue required to obtain the password from the user would be placed in the module that checks the validity of the password, and the dialogue that reports the success or failure of the delete, insert, and display operations would be

Figure 6-9 Our airline schedule system after modification to increase cohesion

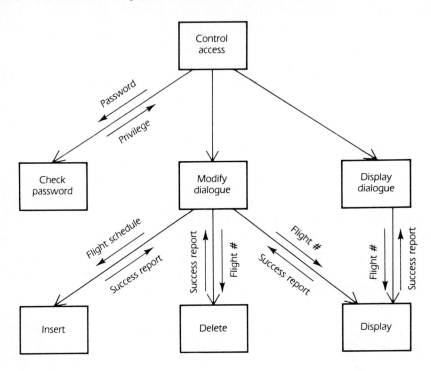

placed in the module responsible for performing the corresponding action. Note that such a distribution of the dialogue activities does not destroy the cohesion of the modules, but rather has the effect of pulling the activities relating to each operation together into one individual package.

In closing, observe that adding these last changes to the design of Figure 6-9 results in the second design of Section 6-2.

Questions/Exercises

1. How does a novel differ from an encyclopedia in terms of the degree of cohesion within its units such as chapters, sections, or entries?
2. Is the goal of maximizing cohesion compatible with minimizing coupling? (That is, as cohesion increases, does coupling naturally tend to decrease?)
3. Identify the cohesive property that binds the various parts together in each of the following settings. Also identify how the natural divisions in each setting are related to cohesion:

    a. a club
    b. a department store
    c. a university registration system
    d. a newspaper

6–5 **Design Methodologies**

Now that we have discussed the concept of modular design and its advantages, we should say a few words about how such designs are obtained. The development of design techniques is a major topic within software engineering, and its study has resulted in the development of design strategies general enough to be applied uniformly over a wide range of applications. In fact, the concepts discussed in this section are applicable whether the system being designed is to be automated or not. In large systems the overall design is often first constructed and then used in deciding whether or not automation is applicable and, if so, for what activities.

Top-Down Design

Perhaps the most common concept associated with system design is that of top-down analysis, which we met in Chapter 4 as stepwise refinement. The point of this concept is that one's first step when performing a task, such as a system design or the programming of a module, should not be to produce a final detailed version of the solution but rather a short, undetailed summary of the solution. This summary often takes the form of little more than a restatement of the problem itself. (For instance, faced with the problem of maintaining the airline schedule system, one might first write the solution in the form MAINTAIN AIRLINE SCHEDULES.)

The next step is to refine the solution produced in the preceding step. Here one considers the solution in slightly more detail and divides the preceding summarized activity into its major units. (For example, one might envision MAINTAIN AIRLINE SCHEDULES as consisting of three major units: VALIDATE PASSWORDS, DISPLAY SCHEDULES, and MODIFY SCHEDULES.) The important point is that each of these units, although being more detailed, encompasses only a part of the overall task. The original problem thus gets divided into several smaller and simpler problems whose solutions collectively provide a solution to the original problem. This refinement process continues successively until problems with manageable solutions are obtained.

The result of top-down analysis is a hierarchical system of refinements that often can be translated directly into a modular structure. That is, the smallest units in the hierarchy (such as VALIDATE PASSWORDS or DISPLAY SCHEDULES) become modules that perform single tasks while the superior units (such as MAINTAIN AIRLINE SCHEDULES) become modules that control the execution of their subordinates.

In Chapter 4 we discussed the use of top-down techniques as applied to the design and expression of algorithms. In that setting our concern was to find both the activities required to solve a problem and the order in which these activities should be performed. With the modular design of large systems, however, the concern of order is best left until the overall modular structure has been developed and one is ready to design the algorithms to perform the tasks within the individual modules. Thus, the development of a modular structure consists mainly of identifying the tasks required without concern for their order of execution or how each task will actually be performed.

Data Flow Diagrams

The separation of task identification from execution order has resulted in the emergence of numerous design strategies to aid in the initial modular design phase. One is to place the emphasis on the data involved and the changes this data undergoes as it passes through the system. The reasoning is that a change in the data indicates the need for a module. Moreover, a clear understanding of the relationship between the data entering a module and the data leaving it is a significant aid toward understanding the activities required within the module itself.

As a result of this philosophy, techniques have been developed for designing systems that concentrate on the data, or information, that will flow through the proposed system as opposed to the procedures, or algorithms, that will be executed. One such technique centers around the use of *data flow diagrams,* which are pictorial representations of the data paths in the system. The idea behind the use of such diagrams is that by following the data paths through the proposed system, we discover where data units merge, split, or are otherwise altered. Because computational activity is needed at these locations in the system, such activities, or groupings of activities, should form the modules of the system. Consequently, we see that the use of data flow diagrams helps us discover a modular structure for the system instead of forcing us to break it into pieces according to intuition.

The various symbols in data flow diagrams have specific meanings. A data path is represented by an arrow, sources and sinks of data by rectangles, locations of data manipulation by circles (also called bubbles), and data in a stored form (for example, a file on a disk) by heavy straight lines. In each case the symbol is labeled with the name of the object represented either within it or alongside it.

As an example, let us apply the use of data flow diagrams to the airline schedule problem. This will also provide an opportunity to show how top-down analysis can be incorporated in a different design strategy. Our approach will be to develop a data flow diagram for the airline schedule problem by means of a top-down process. We begin by stating the initial problem in the form of a simple data flow diagram (Figure 6-10). In this diagram, the only data source, USER, also serves as a data sink; the only location of data manipulation is represented by the circle labeled MAINTAIN SCHEDULES. The data moving within the represented system consists of passwords, requests (consisting of a command such as delete, display, or insert and the identifying flight number), new-schedules, and retrieved-schedules.

Figure 6-10 Our initial data flow diagram

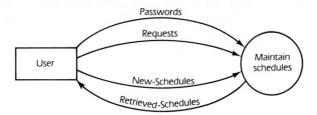

Starting with such a simple, undetailed level has allowed us to identify the major data paths in the system and to translate the overall problem into terms of a data flow diagram. We can now continue by taking a closer look at the interior of the circle MAINTAIN SCHEDULES in Figure 6-10 to obtain the more detailed diagram in Figure 6-11. Note that passwords have the form of short strings of characters when they enter the system but are changed into one of three privilege levels (non-valid, valid for access only, or valid for update) for use within the system. In Figure 6-11, this alteration takes place at the location indicated by the circle labeled

Figure 6-11 Our refined data flow diagram

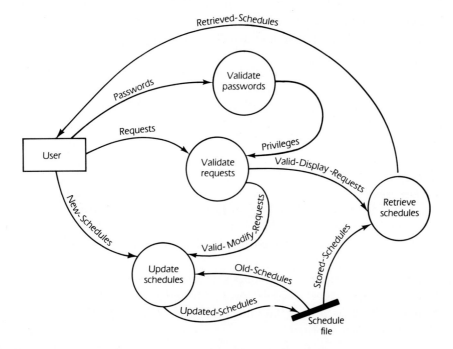

VALIDATE PASSWORDS. From here the privileges are passed on to the location called VALIDATE REQUESTS where they are needed for request validation. If we now follow the flow of requests coming from the USER, we find they also enter the VALIDATE REQUESTS circle and exit as either valid-modify-requests or valid-display-requests. Following the valid-display-requests we find they enter the circle labeled RETRIEVE SCHEDULES along with stored-schedules that flow from the file called SCHEDULE FILE. Leaving the circle RETRIEVE SCHEDULES is the flow of retrieved-schedules going back to the USER.

Returning to the valid-modify-requests, we observe that they join the incoming new-schedules at the location UPDATE SCHEDULES along with old-schedules coming from storage. Exiting this location are updated-schedules, which flow back to the storage file.

We could, of course, continue refining the program. For example, our next step might be to look more closely at the circle labeled UPDATE SCHEDULES, where we would find that the entering valid-modify-requests are separated into insertion and deletion requests that follow different paths. For our purposes, however, it suffices to stop here and see how a modular design might be obtained from the present diagram.

One technique for doing this essentially reduces to identifying the circle (or circles) from which the major control module will be formed. The other circles (or groups of circles) then become the subordinate modules in the system. Numerous guidelines have been proposed for selecting the components of this control module. One is to select those circles at which incoming data becomes outgoing data. Another is to identify and select those circles that serve as clearinghouses for data units which, upon entering other circles, serve to trigger actions. VALIDATE REQUESTS in our example is a case of the latter concept. It is here that requests become valid requests that are used to generate activities in other circles. Following this lead, we might construct a control module from the VALIDATE REQUESTS circle and arrive at the final structure chart in Figure 6-12. Observe that this design is similar in many ways to the second design in Section 6-2.

Questions/Exercises

1. Draw a data flow diagram depicting the flow of information between an instructor, a student, and a textbook. Include the fact that quizzes are given.
2. In the data flow diagrams of the airline schedule system, have we indicated that a password must be entered before a request for schedule information can be made?
3. Suppose that a certain receptionist receives requests for appointments. Response to these requests may be either a schedule for a future appointment or an immediate appointment. Draw a data flow diagram representing the overall flow of data handled by the receptionist.

Figure 6-12 A structure chart based on our refined data flow diagram

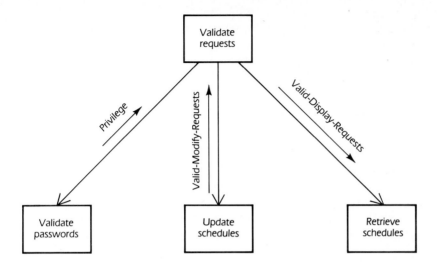

6–6 **Documentation**

A software package is of little use unless people can learn to use it and maintain it. Hence, documentation is an important part of the total package, and in turn its development is an important topic in software engineering. We close this chapter by considering some of the issues relating to this subject.

Documentation of a software package is normally produced for two purposes. One is to explain the features of the software and describe how to use them. This is known as user documentation in that it is designed to be read by the user of the software system. Hence, user documentation tends to be nontechnical.

User documentation is normally packaged in the form of a user's manual. Most agree that the ideal format for such a manual follows a top-down approach in which the user is given an introduction to the major, most commonly used features of the system, followed by a reference section that contains a detailed description of all the system features in a reference format. In addition, user documentation often contains a simple installation section (especially in the case of software for personal computers, where the user must install the system) and a description of the hardware configuration required to support the software.

The other purpose for documentation is to describe the software itself so that the system can be modified later in its life cycle. Documentation of this type is known as system documentation and is inherently more technical than user documentation. The one universal item of documentation in this category is the collection of written programs making up the system. In fact, if it were not for the efforts of software engineers, these programs might constitute the entire documentation package in many cases. (Writing documentation has never been a popular undertaking.)

On the other hand, even software engineers must admit that the programs within a system provide the final definition of what the system will do in different settings. It is therefore important that these programs be presented in a readable format, which is why software engineers support the use of well-designed, high-level programming languages, the use of comment statements for annotating a program, and a modular design that allows each module to be written on a single printed page.

In addition to the programs themselves, the system documentation should contain such items as a narrative description of the software structure, the specifications by which the system is verified, the data flow diagrams from which the software was designed, and the structure charts representing the modular structure of the system. In this sense, then, the documentation of a software system is carried out in parallel with the development of the system itself. (Along these lines, many designers have found that writing a rough draft of the user's manual is an excellent way to begin the design of a software system, since such a process forces one to identify the system requirements and specifications.)

This observation leads us to one of the conflicts between the goals of software engineering and human nature. It is highly unlikely that the initial specifications, flow diagrams, or structure charts will remain unchanged as the system development progresses. Instead, it is more likely that changes will be made as the people involved in the project recognize problems that were not foreseen. (This phenomenon is essentially what we observed in the case of creative problem solving, in which one gains a better understanding of the problem by trying to solve it.) At issue in this case is the temptation to make ongoing changes in the system's design without going back to update the earlier design documents. The result is a high possibility that these documents will be incorrect, and hence their use in the final documentation will be misleading.

(The previous example is only one of many instances in which software engineering must encompass both the cold, hard facts of a science and a realistic understanding of human nature. Others include the inevitable personality conflicts, jealousies, and ego clashes that arise when people work together. Indeed, a project manager must be versed in both the latest design methodologies and the realities of personnel management.)

Still another important item in a system's documentation is the data dictionary—a central depository of information about the data items in a software system, which in the case of an integrated system might include all data items throughout the entire organization. One goal of these dictionaries is the standardization of data formats and the elimination of redundant data within the organization. Without a data dictionary, it is quite common to find organizations maintaining the same information in different forms for use by different programs. For instance, a company might well have separate employee files for payroll, announcement mailings, and employment history. Clearly, these three files contain repeated copies of the same information. In contrast, with a data dictionary available, each time a new software package is developed the designer can easily find out what items of data are already available and avoid such duplication.

Looking more closely at the contents of data dictionaries, we find that they consist of a record of each data item name along with its structure, where it is stored, and how it is used. Thus, in an organization using the airline schedule system discussed earlier, we could look up the data item PASSWORD and find that it consists of a string of no more than five characters and is used to control access to the airline schedule records. Moreover, we would find that a file of the legal passwords is maintained within the airline schedule system.

From this example, we can see that the maintenance of the data dictionary can quickly become a major undertaking. It is not enough merely to keep the dictionary's information up-to-date as new programs are written, but security problems are involved as well. For instance, where and how the passwords to the airline schedule system are maintained should be guarded as closely as the passwords themselves. The maintenance of the data dictionary in an organization represents a significant and complex computer application in itself, and in recent years the design of data dictionaries has begun to receive a corresponding degree of attention.

Questions/Exercises
1. In what forms can software be documented?
2. At what phase (or phases) in the software life cycle is documentation prepared?
3. Which is more important, a program or its documentation?

Chapter 6 Review Problems

1. Which of the following statements is an argument for coupling and which is an argument for cohesion:
   a. For a student to learn, the subject should be presented in well-organized units with specific goals.
   b. A student doesn't really understand a subject until the subject's overall scope and relationship with other subjects has been grasped.
2. Does the major role of the part previews in this book deal with interchapter coupling or intrachapter cohesion?
3. In what manner is the first half of a basketball game explicitly coupled to the second half? What about implicit coupling?

4. In the text, we mentioned control coupling but did not pursue it. Contrast the coupling between two program units obtained by a simple GOTO statement with the coupling obtained by a subprogram call.
5. Answer the following questions in relation to the accompanying structure chart:
   a. To which module does module Y return control?
   b. To which module does module Z return control?
   c. Are modules W and X linked via control coupling?
   d. Are modules W and X linked via data coupling?

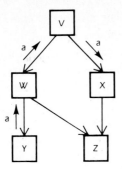

e. What data is shared by both module W and module Y?

f. In what way are modules Y and X related?

6. In relation to the structure chart in problem 5, what stubs would be necessary to test module V? What characteristics might these stubs have?

7. Here are sketches of some subprograms expressed in a Pascal-like syntax. Draw a structure chart representing the control and data coupling indicated by these sketches. Within which module is a person's address apparently determined? What about a person's age? The skills required for a job?

```
procedure A(Name: String; var Addr: String);
    .
    .
    .
end;
procedure B(Job: String);
    .
    .
    .
F(Job, Skills);
    .
    .
    .
end;
procedure C(Name: String);
    .
    .
D(Name, Age);
    .
    .
A(Name, Addr):
    .
    .
    .
end;
procedure D(Name: String; var Age: int);
    .
    .
    .
end;
procedure E(EmplID: String);
    .
    .
C(Name);
    .
    .
    .
```

```
B(Job);
    .
    .
    .
end;
procedure F(Job: String; var Skills: SkillType);
    .
    .
    .
end;
```

8. Modify the structure chart in Figure 6-6 to include the activities associated with maintaining reservations for the flights in the system.

9. Design a modular structure for an on-line inventory/customer records system for a mail-order business and represent it with a structure cart. What modules in your system must be modified because of changes in tax laws? What if the length of the postal system's ZIP code changes?

10. Suppose we referred to the collection of modules that share a common data item as a module unit. If a software system contains four modules, how many different module units of two or more modules might potentially be formed by data coupling? What if there were five modules? Six? What does this say about the potential ramifications of a change in a single module as the size of the software system increases?

11. Suppose you are about to change the type associated with the variable TOTAL in a FORTRAN program containing the statement:

    CALL GETTAX (RATE, PRICE, TAX, TOTAL)

    What warning does this statement give you about additional changes you should make?

12. Suppose the function HANDICAP were designed to compute and return the handicap of the golfer identified in the parameter list, but in so doing suppose it also adds one to the value of a global variable called PAR. If the value of PAR is initially 4 and BILL's handicap is 2, how will the result of the computation

    PAR + HANDICAP(BILL)

    vary depending on the order in which the values needed in the computation are obtained?

13. What potentially disastrous side effects are lurking in a software system whose modules use global rather than local variables?

14. What side effects does the order of execution have in performing the calculation $4 / 2 + 6$?

15. Refer to the answer for question 1 of Section 6-5 and identify the medium used to transfer the data along each flow path in the diagram.

16. Expand question 3 of Section 6-5 to include the preparation and mailing of bills for services during past appointments.

17. A major role of the personnel department of a medium-size manufacturing business is the filling of vacancies as they occur on the shop floor. Draw a data flow diagram depicting the flow of data through the portion of a personnel department charged with this responsibility.

18. Draw a data flow diagram depicting the registration process at a university.

19. Contrast the information represented in data flow diagrams with that given in structure charts.

20. Draw a simple data flow diagram representing the activities in a bank.

21. Suppose that 100 errors were intentionally placed in a large software system before the system was subjected to final testing. Moreover, suppose that a total of 200 errors were discovered and corrected during this final testing of which 50 errors were from the group intentionally placed in the system. If the remaining 50 known errors are then corrected, how many unknown errors would you estimate are still in the system?

22. Why would it not be desirable for the same person who wrote a program to also design the test data?

Problems for the Programmer

1. Using stubs for the other modules, design and implement a simple version of the CONTROL ACCESS module (Section 6-2).

2. Implement a simple version of the DIALOGUE and CHECK PASSWORD modules (Section 6-2). Use stubs for the other modules.

3. Does the programming language you are using provide for both global and local data elements? Using a function similar to the handicap function of review problem 12, write a test program to find out if your language evaluates expressions from right to left or left to right.

4. Extend your simple operating system of programming problem 6 in Chapter 3 to include a resource allocator and a dispatcher. Assume that the system has access to four nonshareable resources. Modify the file manager so that it randomly associates a collection of these resources to each file when it is CREATEd to simulate that program's resource requirement list. Then to execute a program the resource allocator must approve that program's resource request. After a suitable amount of time, the dispatcher in your system should report to the scheduler that the program has completed. Design your system so that more than one program could be under control of the dispatcher at the same time.

3 Part Three

Data Organization

Chapter 7   Data Structures

Chapter 8   File Structures

Chapter 9   Database Structures

Part Three Preview
Data Organization

We have seen that the data residing inside a machine is represented in a coded form and stored either in memory cells, in sequential strings on magnetic tape, or perhaps on the circular tracks of a disk pack. However, the information when viewed in this form is rarely conducive to use in an application where it is needed. Rather, the application normally suggests that we imagine the data as being organized in some structure other than its actual form inside the machine. For example, data representing the weekly sales of a company's sales force might be envisioned in tabular form with a separate column for each day of the week and a separate row for each member of the sales force, the names and positions of a company's employees might be pictured in the form of an organization chart, or a company may wish to view its inventory records organized by part number for one application but arranged by cost for another. The subject of Part Three is the study of how a machine can be programmed to present the data to the user as though it were stored in these conceptual and more useful organizations and how this goal affects the way the data is actually stored within the machine.

We will see that the gap between the actual and the conceptual storage organizations is bridged by software routines that allow the user of the stored information to request activities in terms of the conceptual structure. For example, the user may request the next item of data as though the information were stored in a sequential arrangement, and the software would respond by retrieving the correct item even though the information may not be stored sequentially. With such a system the machine becomes much more useful in the application.

A significant concept used by software systems in these cases is the idea of a pointer. This is nothing more than a storage cell used to hold the location of data rather than the data itself. Such a cell is similar to a page in an address book in which we record a friend's address or phone number. That is, just as we can contact a person by referring to an address book, a software system can find an item of data by first referencing a pointer in which the data's location has been stored.

In general, pointers are used to provide a link between related items of information even though the items may be stored in separate locations inside the machine. For instance, a list of names may have its entries scattered as individual items throughout a machine's memory (for perhaps the sake of storage efficiency). In such a case each item would be accompanied by a pointer that contained the address of the next item in the list. Thus, the list (in this case called a linked list) could be retrieved in its proper order by hopping from one item to the next as directed by the pointers. Of course, in a final application this hopping would be done by a software package so that the user of the information would be given the illusion of the data actually being stored in a sequential order.

Thus, although the actual storage system within a machine might not be conducive to the application at hand, techniques are available that allow the user to manipulate stored data as though it were. Most of Chapter 7 consists of a discussion of those data organizations that are commonly found in applications and are therefore often imitated by software systems. In particular, the structures covered in addition to lists are arrays, stacks, queues, and trees.

An array is a (perhaps multidimensional) block of entries in which items are located by identifying their position in terms of rows, columns, or planes. An example of a two-dimensional array would be the tabular sales record discussed earlier in this preview.

A stack is an ordered collection of objects on which all alterations are performed at one designated end known as the top of the stack. This corresponds to the normal use of the word *stack* as in a stack of books, a stack of cafeteria trays, or a stack of coins. Inherent in such a structure is the fact that objects are ultimately removed from a stack in the opposite order from which they were inserted. Thus, a stack is referred to as a last-in-first-out (LIFO) structure. This LIFO property is paramount in a stack's application. In particular, stacks are used when it is necessary to retrieve objects in the opposite order from which they were set aside. Thus, if we are to enter a system from which we must later back out, a stack provides a perfect system in which we can record the "sign posts" we pass during entry. To back out of the system (a process known as backtracking) we merely visit the sign posts in the order in which we recall them from the stack.

A queue is similar to a stack except that objects are inserted and deleted from opposite (yet fixed) ends. The result is that objects are ultimately removed in the same order in which they were inserted. Hence, queues are known as first-in-first-out (FIFO) structures and are used for the storage of objects waiting to be served by priority of arrival time. A typical application of queues in computing is found in a time-sharing operating system when allocating time slices to competing users. In effect, the users wait in a queue to be given a slice of time.

A tree structure is exemplified by a company's organization chart. The president of the company is at the top with lines leading down to the vice-presidents. Below each vice-president we might find a variety of regional managers or department heads, each of whom has lines leading on down the chart to his or her subordinates, etc. We will see that tree organizations are quite useful when storing data that will be subjected to the demands of rapid data retrieval.

The concepts involved in implementing and maintaining such structures as arrays, lists, stacks, queues, and trees in a machine's main memory form the core of the subject known as data structures. Such topics represent the foundation on which more varied and complex data organizations are often constructed. For example, when organizing data for retention on bulk storage devices, additional techniques are blended with those used for implementing more traditional data structures. This is largely a consequence of the comparative slowness of bulk storage devices and the fact that data stored on these devices is accessed in relatively large blocks called records rather than individual small units such as bytes. The study of these additional techniques is often isolated under the heading of file structures even though it is merely an extension of data structure concepts.

The discussion of file structures in Chapter 8 concentrates on the distinction between sequential and direct access files along with a look at how each of these systems might be implemented. Conceptually, a sequential file is much like a list in that its entries must be accessed in a particular sequential order starting from the beginning. The main difference between a sequential file and the traditional list is that the entries in a list are normally thought of as being single items (or at least simple organizations), whereas the entries (the records) in a file are normally collections of data items, called fields. For example, a sequential file containing data about the employees of a business would conceptually appear as a sequential list, with each entry (or record) consisting of all the information about a single employee.

Sequential files are useful for applications in which the data they contain will always be processed in the order compatible with their sequential organization. However, when other access orders are required, the sluggishness of bulk storage systems further emphasizes the time-consuming problems encountered with sequential lists. Consequently, structures known as direct access files are quite common when random access to records is important. These are files whose records can be accessed independently of their storage order.

One popular way of implementing a direct access file is to maintain an index for it in much the same way that an index is supplied with a book. In particular, an item of information in each record called a key field is first specified for record identification. In the case of an employee file, this field might be the employee identification number since that piece of information would uniquely identify a record. Next, a special record called the file's index is constructed containing a listing of the key field entries appearing in the file together with each corresponding record's location in bulk storage. In the case of the employee file, we could access a particular employee's record by finding that employee's identification number in the index and then retrieving the record stored at the indicated location. In this manner rapid retrieval of individual records is available but at the expense of maintaining an index.

A direct access technique that avoids the overhead of index maintenance is called hashing, which results in a file system called a hashed file. Here, instead of referring to an index to find the location of a record with a particular key field value, one computes the location directly from the bit pattern representing the key field value.

Just as file structures can be considered an extension of the subject of data structures, the concept of a database, which we analyze in Chapter 9, is essentially an extension of file structures. The subject arises from the need to reduce redundancy of stored information in situations where several applications require similar yet different data files. Thus, a database is essentially a file (or collection of files) designed to appear in different forms to different users. For instance, a database maintained by a company might appear as a sequential file of employee salary records for processing payroll, a direct access file of employee work histories for the personnel department, and a collection of files containing the employee positions within each department for management purposes.

The actual storage structure required to support this flexibility can be rather complex and involves technical concerns that are of no interest to the ultimate user of the information in the database. Consequently, databases are normally implemented through a series of conceptual layers in which each layer allows the person working on the database to concentrate on the problems involved at that level while ignoring the more technical details. In particular, the ultimate user of the database is able to interact with the system using terminology associated with the application. This interaction is handled by a program written by a programmer (the application programmer) who understands the ultimate user's needs. Since this programmer needs to concentrate on the system's interaction with the user, methods are used by which the technicalities of the database itself are simplified in the form of a database model. This simplified model is produced by another software package called the database management system, which actually maintains the database itself.

Figure A The relational model

Course	Professor	Semester
Theory of mouse traps	Jones	Fall
Theory of mouse traps	Jones	Spring
Theory of mouse traps	Brown	Summer
Underwater finger painting	Jones	Summer
Underwater finger painting	Smith	Spring

Figure B The network model

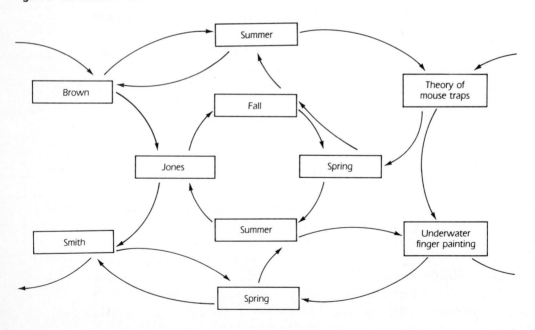

Figure C The hierarchical model

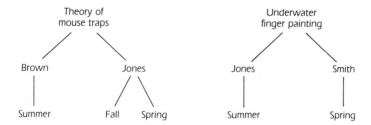

The concept of a database model is quite important since it is in terms of this model that the application software must be developed. Several such models have been proposed, and some have been standardized in the same manner as high-level programming languages. The three major models in use today are the relational model (which allows the programmer to imagine the database as being in tabular form), the network model (which allows the database to be envisioned as a collection of data items in which those with common properties are linked together in a way similar to a linked list), and the hierarchical model (which allows the database to be imagined as a collection of tree structures).

Figures A, B, and C represent the same database (about courses and the professors who teach them) as it would appear using each of these popular models. As a testimonial to the success of these approaches, you will probably be able to interpret the semantics of this database by just looking at these diagrams even though we have not yet discussed the details of the models themselves. For instance, it is clear from the diagrams that Professor Jones teaches Theory of Mouse Traps in the Fall and Spring.

7 Data Structures

7–1 **Arrays**
  One-Dimensional Arrays
  Multidimensional Arrays
7–2 **Lists**
  Pointers
  Dense Lists
  Linked Lists
  Supporting the Conceptual List
7–3 **Stacks**
  Stack Applications
  Stack Implementation
  A Particular Stack Application
7–4 **Queues**
  Queue Implementation
  A Particular Queue Application
7–5 **Trees**
  Terminology
  Tree Implementation
  A Binary Tree Package
7–6 **Abstract Data Types**
7–7 **Object-Oriented Programming** (optional)

We have used the terms *virtual* and *conceptual* several times in reference to properties that, although appearing to belong to the hardware, are actually simulated through a combination of hardware and software. In particular, we saw that a single machine can appear to be many machines through the use of a time-sharing system or that a machine can appear to understand the words in a high-level programming language by means of an interpreter. This chapter is concerned with another conceptual feature, the structure (or organization) of data.

To be more precise, we first note that any information stored in a machine's memory must be organized to fit into a row of memory cells, each of which can be individually referenced by means of its address. However, the information being stored may be more conveniently considered in terms of another organization such as a rectangular table of values. Our problem, then, is to simulate this rectangular shape using the tools provided by the machine. The goal is to allow the user of the data to think of the data as having this simulated shape without being concerned with the data's actual organization within the machine.

7–1 **Arrays**

We begin our study of data structures by considering the organizations known as arrays encountered earlier in our discussion of high-level programming languages. There we saw that many high-level languages allow a programmer to express an algorithm as though the data being manipulated were stored in a rectangular arrangement. Thus, one might refer to the fifth element in a one-dimensional array or the element in the third row and sixth column of a two-dimensional array. Of course, the data is actually stored in a row of memory cells within the machine, and thus it becomes the job of either the translator or the interpreter to convert such references into the terminology of memory cells and addresses.

One-Dimensional Arrays

Suppose an algorithm for manipulating a series of 24 hourly temperature readings is expressed in a high-level language. It is likely that the programmer would find it convenient to think of these readings arranged as a one-dimensional array, that is, a list called READINGS whose various entries are referenced in terms of their position in the list. The first reading might be referenced by READINGS[1], the second by READINGS[2], etc.

In this case the conversion from the conceptual one-dimensional array organization to the actual arrangement within the machine can be rather straightforward. For instance, the actual data can be stored in a sequence of 24 memory cells in the same order envisioned by the programmer. Knowing the address of the first cell in this sequence, an interpreter or translator could then easily convert terms such as READINGS[4] into the proper memory terminology. To find the actual address one merely needs to subtract one from the position of the desired entry and then add the result to the address of the first cell in the sequence. (If the first cell in the sequence were at address 13, the reading referenced by READINGS[4] would be located at location $13 + (4 - 1) = 16$ as shown in Figure 7-1.)

Multidimensional Arrays

The conversion is not quite so simple with multidimensional arrays. Consider, for example, a record of the sales made by a company's sales force during a one-week period. We could think of this data arranged in tabular form with the names of the sales personnel listed down the left side and the days of the week listed across the top. Hence we think of the data being arranged in rows and columns; the values

Figure 7-1 The array READINGS stored in memory starting at address 13

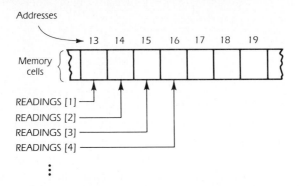

across each row indicate the sales made by a particular employee while the values down a column represent all the sales made during a particular day. Extracting information from the table therefore involves finding the value common to both a given row and a given column.

A machine's memory is arranged not in a rectangular fashion but rather as a row of memory cells; thus, the rectangular structure required by the sales table must be simulated. To do this we first recognize that the size of the array will not vary as updates are made. We can therefore calculate the amount of storage area needed and reserve a block of contiguous memory cells of that size. Next, we store the data in the cells row by row. That is, starting at the first cell of the reserved block, we copy the values from the first row of the table into consecutive memory locations; following this we copy the next row, then the next, etc. (Figure 7-2). Such a storage system is said to use *row major order* in contrast to *column major order,* where the array is stored column by column.

With the data stored, the problem now becomes locating particular entries as they are requested. Recall that because the user will be thinking in terms of rows and columns a request will be in the form of wanting, for example, the contents of the entry in the third row and fourth column (that is, the sales made by the third employee on Thursday). To find this entry we first envision ourselves as being at the first location in the reserved block of the machine's memory. The cells following this location contain the data in the first row of the array followed by the second, then the third, etc. To get to the data in the third row, we must jump over both the first and second rows. Since each row contains five entries (one for each day from Monday through Friday), we must jump over a total of 10 entries to reach the first entry of the third row. From the beginning of the third row, we must jump over another three entries to reach the entry in the fourth column of the array. Altogether, to reach the entry in the third row and fourth column, we must jump over 13 entries from the beginning of the block.

Figure 7-2 A two-dimensional array with 4 rows and 5 columns stored in row major order

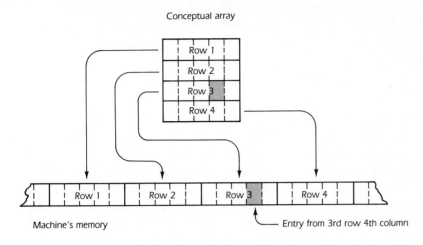

Conceptual array

Machine's memory

Entry from 3rd row 4th column

The preceding calculation is a special case of a general process that can be used for finding entries in a two-dimensional array when it is stored by rows as just discussed. In particular, if we let C represent the number of columns in the array (which is the number of entries in each row), to find the entry in the Ith row and Jth column we must jump over:

$$(C \times (I - 1)) + (J - 1)$$

entries from the beginning of the array. That is, we must jump over $I - 1$ rows, each of which contains C entries, to reach the Ith row and then $J - 1$ more entries to reach the Jth entry in this row. In our prior example, C was equal to 5, I to 3, and J to 4: $(5 \times (3 - 1)) + (4 - 1)$ equals 13.

With this information, software routines can be written to convert requests in terms of rows and columns into locations within the block of memory containing the array. A translator, for example, would use this technique to convert a reference such as SALES[2,4] into an actual memory address. Thus, a programmer can enjoy the luxury of thinking of the data in tabular form (the conceptual structure) even though it is actually stored in a single row (the actual structure) within the machine.

Questions/Exercises

1. Show how the array $\begin{matrix} 5 & 3 & 7 \\ 4 & 2 & 8 \\ 1 & 9 & 6 \end{matrix}$ would appear in memory when stored in row major order.

2. Give a formula for finding the entry in the Ith row and Jth column of a two-dimensional array if it were stored in memory column by column rather than row by row (that is, in column major order rather than row major order).

3. If a two-dimensional array of 8 rows and 11 columns were stored in row major order beginning at memory address 25, what would be the address of the entry in the third row sixth column if each entry occupied two memory cells?

7–2 **Lists**

An important property of arrays is that their size and shape are constant, and thus simulating them in a machine's memory is essentially a process of converting the conceptual location of an element into the actual location. In contrast are dynamic structures that vary in size and shape. For instance, a club's membership list grows as new members join and shrinks as old members leave. In such cases we find that in addition to locating elements in the structure, we are required to accommodate variations in the structure itself.

Pointers

A prominent concept in the maintenance of dynamic structures is that of a *pointer,* so let us introduce this idea before proceeding. Recall that the various storage locations in a machine's memory are identified by numeric addresses. If we knew the address of a piece of data, we could find that data with little difficulty. Being merely numeric values, these addresses themselves are easily stored in a machine's memory. Thus, having stored an item of data in one cell of memory we could store the address of that data in another memory cell. Later, if we wanted to retrieve that data item and we had access to the cell containing its address, we could find the data by referring to its address.

In a sense, then, a memory cell containing the address of a data item can be thought of as pointing to that data item. Such cells are called *pointers.* (Note that we have already encountered the idea of a pointer in our discussion of a machine's fetch-decode-execute cycle, in which a program counter is used to hold the address of the next instruction to be executed. In fact, another but somewhat outdated term for program counter is *instruction pointer.*)

Many programming languages today allow for the declaration, allocation, and manipulation of pointers just as they allow for such operations for integers or character strings. Using such a language, a programmer can design elaborate networks of data items within a machine's memory. For example, suppose a library had its holdings represented in a machine's memory in alphabetical order by title. Although convenient in many applications, this arrangement would make it difficult to find all the books by a particular author since the books would be scattered throughout the list. To solve this problem we could reserve an additional memory cell of type pointer within the block of cells representing each book. In each of these pointer

Figure 7-3 Library holdings arranged by title but linked according to authorship

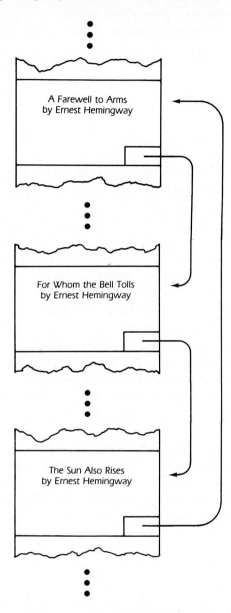

cells we could place the address of another block representing a book by the same author so that each collection of books with common authorship would be linked in a loop (Figure 7-3). That is, once we found one book by a given author, we could find all the others by following the pointers from one book to another in the same way we would follow a sequence of clues in a treasure hunt. Thus, the use of pointer data types can be very important when organizing data that must be accessible in a variety of contexts. This, in fact, is a major theme of this chapter.

We begin our discussion of dynamic data structures and the role of pointers by considering two methods of maintaining a list of names within a machine's memory. The first of these methods (dense list) is similar to array storage systems and does not use pointers; the other method (linked list) takes advantage of pointer techniques to overcome some of the disadvantages encountered with a dense list.

Dense Lists

One technique for storing a list of names in a machine's memory is to store the entire list in a single block of consecutive memory cells. Assuming that each name is no longer than eight letters, we could divide this large block of cells into a collection of subblocks, each containing eight cells. Into each subblock we could store a name by recording its ASCII code using one cell per letter (Figure 7-4). If the name alone does not fill all the cells in the subblock allocated to it, we could merely fill the remaining cells with the ASCII code for a space. Using this system would require a block of 80 consecutive memory cells to store a list of 10 names.

Such an organization is referred to as a **dense list** and appears to be straightforward and convenient. It is really nothing more than a one-dimensional array in which each element consists of eight memory cells. However, problems can easily arise when we try to modify a list stored in this way. For example, suppose we need to delete a name. If this name is currently toward the beginning of the list and we need to keep the list in the same (possibly alphabetical) order, we must move all the names occurring later in the list forward in memory to fill the hole left by the deleted name.

A more serious problem can occur if we need to add a name since this requires not only moving names to create a hole for the new entry but also checking that there is room in memory to make this extension. In particular, if we originally reserved a block of 80 memory cells for our list of 10 names, the addition of one name would create the need for a block of 88 cells. If we are lucky, there will be

Figure 7-4 Names stored in memory as a dense list

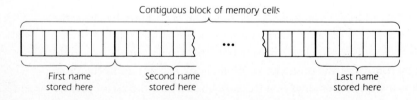

Contiguous block of memory cells

First name stored here Second name stored here Last name stored here

eight unused cells adjacent to the current block. However, if there are not, the addition of a single name would force us to move the entire list to a new area of memory where there is room.

Linked Lists

Such problems can be avoided if we allow the individual names in the list to be stored in different areas of memory rather than together in one large, contiguous block. To do this, we store each name in a string of nine memory cells. The first eight of these cells are used to hold the name itself, and the last cell is used as a pointer to the next name in the list. In this form the list can be scattered among several small nine-cell blocks linked together by pointers. Because of this linkage system such an organization is called a *linked list.*

To keep track of where the first entry of a linked list is located, we set aside a memory cell in which we save the address of the first entry. This cell points to the beginning of the list and is normally called the *head pointer.* To read the list we start at the location indicated by this head pointer and find the first name along with the pointer to the next entry. Following this pointer we can find the second entry and so forth throughout the list. In this manner, we can traverse the entire list by hopping from one name to the next. (Searching a linked list for a particular entry is similar to a treasure hunt. The head pointer provides the first clue that directs us to another location. If we do not find the treasure there, we follow the next clue, etc.)

At this point, we have considered the problem of moving from one member of the list to the next but have ignored the problem of detecting the end of the list. This problem is easily solved by using a *NIL pointer* (or *NULL pointer*). This is nothing more than a special bit pattern appearing in the pointer cell of the last entry that indicates that no further entries appear in the list. For example, if we agreed never to start an entry at address zero, the value zero would never appear as a legitimate pointer value, and we could use it as the NIL pointer in the list storage. Thus, we would place the value zero in the pointer cell of the last entry in the list. Later when the list is traversed, this special value can be interpreted as marking the end of the list rather than as being the address of yet another entry.

The final linked list storage organization is represented by the diagram in Figure 7-5. We depict the scattered blocks of memory used for the list by individual rectangles. Each rectangle is labeled to indicate its composition. Note that the information stored in each pointer is represented by an arrow that leads one from the pointer itself to the pointer's addressee.

Let us return now to the problems of deleting and inserting entries in the list to see how the use of pointers alleviates the movement of names encountered when storing the list in a single contiguous block. First we note that a name can be deleted

Figure 7-5 The structure of a linked list

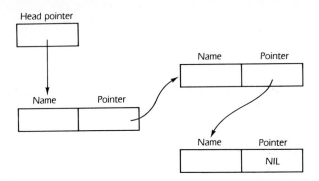

merely by changing a single pointer. This is done by changing the pointer that formerly pointed to the name being deleted so that it points to the name following the deleted entry (Figure 7-6). From then on, when the list is traversed the deleted name will be passed by since it is no longer a part of the chain.

Inserting a new name is only a little more involved. We first find an unused block of nine memory cells, store the new name in the first eight cells, and fill the ninth cell with the address of the name in the list that should follow the new name. Finally we change the pointer associated with the name that should precede the new name so that it points to the new name (Figure 7-7). Observe that after this is done, the new entry will be found in the proper place anytime the list is traversed.

(In reality, the deletion or insertion of an entry in a linked list is not quite as simple as our previous description implies, since one might want to keep track of those blocks of cells that have been removed from the list. Indeed, since the data in these blocks is no longer important, these blocks of cells can be reused at a later date to hold new entries in the list. One technique for keeping track of blocks

Figure 7-6 Deleting an entry from a linked list

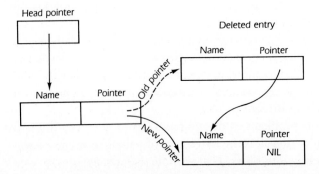

Figure 7-7 Inserting an entry into a linked list

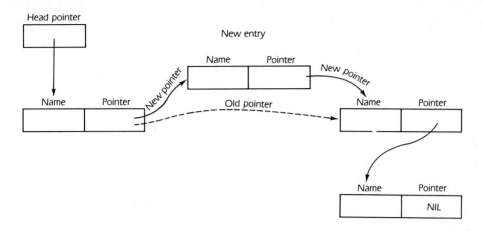

available for reuse is to maintain a record of pointers to reusable blocks or perhaps maintain another linked list consisting of these blocks. Thus, as a block is removed from the main list, it would be added to the list of available storage blocks, and as new entries are needed, blocks to contain them can be removed from the list of available blocks and inserted in the list. Computer scientists refer to the process of collecting reusable memory space as garbage collection.)

Supporting the Conceptual List

Regardless of whether one chooses to implement a list as a dense structure or as a linked one, the user of the list should not have to consider the technicalities of the implementation each time a list access is required. Rather, the user should be able to forget about these details and merely use the list as though the storage system was actually organized in the same way as the conceptual structure (just as a programmer is allowed to refer to a particular element in an array without being concerned with the technicalities of how the array is actually stored).

For example, consider the task of developing a software package for maintaining the class enrollments for a university registrar. The person developing this package might approach the problem by establishing a separate list structure for each class, with each list containing an alphabetically ordered list of the students in that class. Once this is done, the programmer's attention should be allowed to shift to the more general concerns of the problem and not be repeatedly distracted by the details of how data might be moved within a dense list or what shifting of pointers is required in a linked list.

What is needed is a collection of subprograms for performing the activities, such as inserting a new entry, deleting an old entry, searching for an entry, or

Figure 7-8 A subprogram for printing a linked list

procedure print list

assign Current Pointer **the value** in the head pointer
while (Current Pointer is not NIL) **do**
    (print the name in the entry pointed to by Current Pointer
    and move the value in the pointer cell in the entry pointed
    to by Current Pointer to Current Pointer)

printing the list, that would otherwise require an understanding of the underlying list structure. These routines together with the actual storage cells being used would then fill the needs of the remaining software package while hiding the technicalities of how the list is actually implemented. Indeed, to insert an entry the programmer could write a statement such as

insert (Brown, J. W.) in class (Physics 208)

and rely on the subprograms to carry out the details of the insertion.

As an example of such a routine, a subprogram named print list for printing a linked list of names is shown in Figure 7-8. Recall that the first entry of the list is pointed to by a pointer called the head pointer and each entry in the list consists of two pieces: a name and a pointer. Note that once this subprogram has been developed, it can be used by a programmer to print the list without concern for how the list is actually stored. For example, to obtain a printed class list for Economics 301, the programmer need only write

print list (Economics 301)

Questions/Exercises

1. If you knew the address of the beginning of the first entry in a dense list, how could you find the address of the fifth entry? What about the case of a linked list?
2. What condition indicates that a linked list is empty?
3. Modify the subprogram in Figure 7-8 so that it stops printing once a particular name has been printed.
4. Design an algorithm for finding a particular entry in a linked list and then deleting it.

7–3 Stacks

One of the properties of a list that makes the overhead of a linked structure more inviting than a contiguous block for its storage is the need to insert and delete entries inside the list. You will recall that it was such operations that had the potential of forcing the massive movement of names in order to fill or create holes in the case of a dense list. If we restrict such operations to the ends of the structure, we find that the use of a contiguous block becomes a more convenient system. An example of this phenomenon is a *stack,* which is a list where all insertions and deletions are performed at the same end of the structure. The end at which these operations occur is called the *top* of the stack. The other end is sometimes called the stack's base.

To reflect the fact that access to a stack is restricted to the topmost entry, we use special terminology when referring to the insertion and deletion operations. The process of inserting an object on the stack is called a *push* operation, and the process of deleting an object is called a *pop* operation. Thus, we speak of pushing an entry onto a stack and popping an entry off a stack.

We are quite familiar with stack structures in everyday life. For example, consider a stack of books on a table. Such an organization yields itself to the particular insertion and deletion operations of placing books on top of the stack (a push operation) and lifting books off the top (a pop operation). Disaster could result, however, from an attempt to remove or insert a book in the middle of a tall stack. Indeed, the structure of a stack dictates that the last object inserted must be the first one removed. This observation results in a stack often being referred to as a *last-in-first-out (LIFO)* structure.

Stack Applications

Before considering how a stack can actually be implemented in a computer's memory, let us take a moment to see where such structures might be useful. A common example is found within an interpreter for a high-level programming language where a stack is used to manage the execution of subprograms. Recall that when the execution of a subprogram is requested by a program, the machine must transfer its attention to the subprogram; yet later, when the subprogram is completed, it must return to continue the original program (Figure 7-9). Thus, when the initial transfer is made, there must be a mechanism by which the location in the original program can be remembered.

The situation is further complicated by the fact that the subprogram may itself request the execution of another subprogram, which may request still another, etc. Consequently, the return locations being remembered will begin to pile up. Later, as each of these subprograms is completed, execution must be returned to the proper place within the program unit that called the completed subprogram. Thus, a system is needed by which the return locations can be saved and later retrieved in the proper order.

A stack is an ideal structure for such a system. As each subprogram is called, the interpreter merely pushes a pointer to the pertinent return location on the top of a stack, and as each subprogram is completed, the interpreter extracts the top entry from the stack with the assurance of obtaining a pointer to the proper return

Figure 7-9 Nested subprograms terminating in the opposite order to that in which they were requested

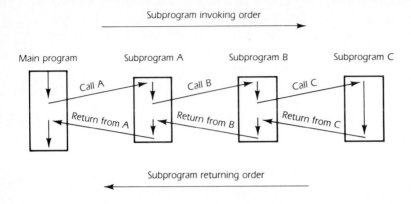

location. The return locations are required in exactly the opposite order from the order in which the subprogram calls were made. (The last subprogram called will be the first one finished.)

This example is representative of stack applications in general in that it demonstrates the relationship between stacks and the process of backtracking. Whether one recognizes it or not, the concept of a stack is inherent in any process that entails backing out of a system in the opposite order from that in which the system was entered.

Stack Implementation

We turn now to the problem of implementing a stack structure in a computer's memory. It is customary to reserve a block of contiguous memory cells large enough to accommodate the stack as it grows and shrinks. (Determining the size of this block can often be a critical design problem. If too much room is allocated, the result is a waste of memory space, whereas if too little room is reserved, the stack will ultimately exceed the allotted storage space.) Having reserved a block of memory, we select one end to serve as the stack's base. This is where we place the first entry that is pushed on the stack, with each additional entry being placed next to its predecessor as the stack grows toward the other end of the reserved block.

One additional tool is needed in our system—a way of keeping track of the top of the stack. After all, as entries are pushed and popped, the stack top will move back and forth within the reserved block of memory cells. To find the top entry when needed, it is therefore necessary to maintain a record of its location. For this purpose we set aside another memory cell in which we store the address of the cell currently residing at the top of the stack. This additional cell is known as the **stack pointer.** The complete system, as illustrated in Figure 7-10, works as follows: To push a new entry on the stack, we first adjust the stack pointer to point to the

Figure 7-10 A stack in memory

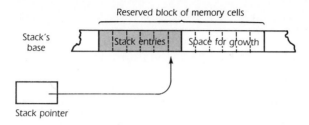

vacancy just beyond the top of the stack and then place the new entry at this location. To pop an entry from the stack, we first read the data pointed to by the stack pointer and then adjust the pointer to point to the next entry down on the stack.

Note that when a stack is organized in memory as previously described, there is little difference between the conceptual structure and the actual structure of the data in memory. This does not have to be the case. For example, suppose it is impossible to estimate the maximum size to which a particular stack may grow so that a fixed block of memory cannot be reserved with assurance that the stack will always fit. A solution is to implement the stack as a linked structure similar to that discussed in Section 7-2. This avoids the limitations of restricting the stack to a fixed-size block since it allows the entries in the stack to be stuffed into small pieces of available space anywhere in memory. (The expense, however, is the need for a more complex overhead.) In such a situation the conceptual stack structure will be quite different from the actual arrangement of the data in memory.

To complete the implementation of a stack, one must develop subprograms to perform the push and pop operations as well as a subprogram to test whether or not the stack is empty. These three routines would allow the stack to be used by a programmer without demanding that the programmer pay attention to the internal implementation of the stack itself.

A Particular Stack Application

As a closing example, we return to the list-printing problem considered at the end of Section 7-2. Now, however, we suppose that the names in the linked list are to be printed in the order opposite the order in which they appear in the list. The problem is that the only way we can access the names is by following the linked structure; thus the first name accessed must be the last one printed. We need a way of holding each name retrieved until all the following names have been retrieved and printed. Our solution is to traverse the list from its beginning to its end while pushing the names we retrieve onto a stack (Figure 7-11). After reaching the end of the list, we print the names as we pop them off the stack. A more formal description of this process is presented in Figure 7-12.

Figure 7-11 To print a linked list in reverse order: (a) push the entries on a stack while traversing the list, then (b) print them as they are popped off the stack

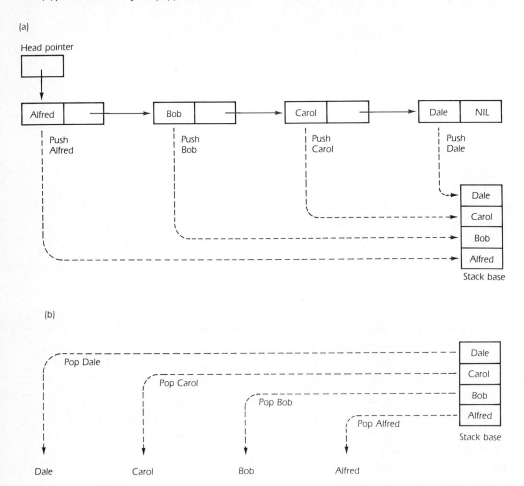

Figure 7-12 A subprogram (using an auxiliary stack) for printing a linked list in reverse order

> **assign** Current Pointer **the value** in the list's head pointer
> **while** (Current Pointer is not NIL) **do**
>   (push the name pointed to by Current Pointer onto the stack
>   and move the value in the pointer cell of the entry pointed
>   to by Current Pointer to Current Pointer)
> **while** (the stack is not empty) **do**
>   (pop a name off the stack and print it)

Questions/Exercises

1. List some additional occurrences of stacks in everyday life.
2. Suppose a main program calls subprogram A, which in turn calls subprogram B, and after B is completed, subprogram A calls subprogram C. Follow this scenario maintaining the stack of return locations.
3. Based on the technique of this section for implementing a stack in a contiguous block of cells, what condition indicates that the stack is empty?
4. Design an algorithm for popping an entry off a stack that is implemented with a stack pointer. Your algorithm should print an error message if there is no entry on the stack to pop.
5. Describe how a stack could be implemented in a high-level language in terms of a one-dimensional array.

7–4 Queues

A queue is another form of a restricted access list. In contrast to a stack in which both insertions and deletions are performed at the same end, a queue restricts all insertions to one end while all deletions are made at the other. The result is analogous to rolling marbles through a pipe. The marbles are dropped into one end and exit from the other end in the same order in which they entered. We have already met and discussed this structure in relation to waiting lines in Chapter 3 where we recognized it as being a first-in-first-out (FIFO) storage system. Actually, the concept of a queue is inherent in any system in which objects are served in the same order in which they arrive.

The ends of a queue get their names from this waiting-line relationship. More precisely, the end at which entries are removed is called the *head* (or sometimes the front) of the queue just as we say that the next person to be served in a cafeteria is at the head (or front) of the line. Similarly, the end of the queue at which new entries are added is called the *tail* (or rear). The terminology associated with the addition and deletion of entries in a queue is not as standard as for a stack. You will hear some speak of put and pull operations but insert and remove seem to win the majority of votes today.

Queue Implementation

With these observations behind us, let us consider how we might implement a queue in a computer's memory. We will do this within a block of contiguous cells in a way similar to our storage of a stack. Since we will need to perform operations at both ends of the structure, it makes sense to set aside two memory cells to use as pointers instead of just one as we did for a stack. Thus, we will establish one pointer, called the *head pointer,* which will always point to the head of the queue, and another

Figure 7-13 A queue implemented with head and tail pointers

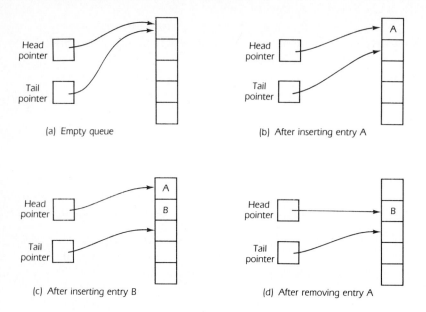

(a) Empty queue

(b) After inserting entry A

(c) After inserting entry B

(d) After removing entry A

pointer, called the ***tail pointer,*** which will keep track of the tail. We begin with an empty queue by setting both these pointers to the same location (Figure 7-13). Each time an entry is inserted, we will place it in the location pointed to by the tail pointer and then adjust the pointer to point toward the next unused location. In this manner we see that the tail pointer will always be pointing to the first vacancy at the tail of the queue. To remove an entry, we will extract the object occupying the location pointed to by the head pointer and then adjust this pointer to point toward the entry that followed the removed one.

A major problem remains with the storage system as described thus far. If left unchecked, the queue will crawl slowly through memory like a glacier, destroying any other data in its path (Figure 7-14). This movement is the result of the rather egocentric policy of inserting each new entry by merely placing it next to the previous one and repositioning the tail pointer accordingly. Thus, if we added enough entries, the tail of the queue could ultimately extend all the way to the end of the machine's memory.

This greed for memory is not the result of the queue's size but rather is a side effect of the queue's access procedure. (A small yet active queue could easily require more of a machine's memory resources than could a large, inactive one.) One solution to this memory space problem is to move the entries in a queue forward as the leading ones are removed in the same manner as people waiting to buy theater tickets step forward each time a person has been served. However, it was exactly

Figure 7-14 A queue "crawling" through memory, shown here containing entries A, B, and C and later containing C, D, E, and F

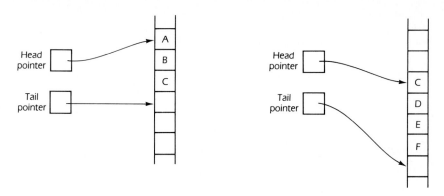

such mass movement of data that drove us to the concept of linked structures in the discussion of lists. What we want is a way of confining the queue to one area of memory without being forced to perform major rearrangements of data.

A popular solution to this dilemma is to set aside a block of memory for the queue, start the queue at one end of the block, and let the queue migrate toward the other end of the block. When the tail of the queue reaches the end of the block, we merely start inserting additional entries back at the original end of the block, which by this time is vacant. Likewise, when the last entry in the block finally becomes the head of the queue and is removed, we adjust the head pointer back to the beginning of the block where other entries are by this time waiting. In this manner the queue will chase itself around within the block rather than wander off through memory.

Such a technique results in an implementation called a **circular queue** since the effect is that of forming a loop out of the block of memory cells allotted to the queue (Figure 7-15). That is, as far as the queue is concerned, the last cell in the block is adjacent to the first cell.

Once again we should recognize the difference between the conceptual structure envisioned by the user of a queue and the actual cyclic structure implemented in the machine's memory. As in the case of the previous structures, these differences are bridged by software. That is, along with the collection of memory cells used for data storage, the queue implementation includes a collection of subprograms that interpret the stored data according to the rules of a queue. These subprograms would consist of routines to insert and remove entries from the queue as well as routines to test whether the queue is empty or full. Then, by means of these routines a programmer can request that entries be inserted or removed by executing prewritten software routines that perform these operations without reflecting the details of the actual storage system in memory.

Figure 7-15 (a) A circular queue containing the letters F through O as actually stored in memory, and (b) in its conceptual form in which the last cell in the block is "attached" to the first cell

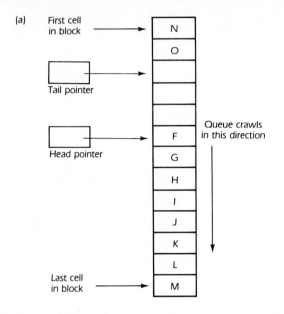

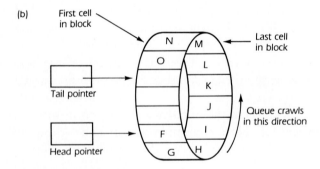

A Particular Queue Application

In closing, we return to the idea of manipulating a linked list of names, but this time we assume the list represents a combined alphabetized listing of both undergraduate and graduate students at a university. Moreover, we assume that with each name in the list is an additional item of data indicating whether the student is an undergraduate or a graduate student. Our task is to produce an alphabetized listing of the undergraduate students followed by an alphabetized listing of the graduate students.

One technique would be to traverse the linked list twice—producing the undergraduate list the first time and the graduate list the second. On the other hand, such a procedure could be very inefficient since the second pass through the list would repeat the same separation process already done during the first pass.

A more efficient system would temporarily store the names of the graduate students that were found during the first pass (while the undergraduate names are being printed) and then produce the graduate list from the auxiliary storage instead of searching through the linked list a second time. Note that once we are ready to produce the list of graduate students, we will want to retrieve the names from the auxiliary storage system in the same order in which they were inserted so that the final listing will be in alphabetical order. Thus, this auxiliary system should be organized as a queue. An algorithm for solving the printing problem would therefore take the form shown in Figure 7-16.

Questions/Exercises

1. Using paper and pencil, keep a record of the circular queue structure described in this section during the following scenario (assume the block reserved for the queue can contain four entries):

   Insert entry A.
   Insert entry B.
   Insert entry C.
   Remove an entry.
   Remove an entry.
   Insert entry D.
   Insert entry E.
   Remove an entry.
   Insert entry F.
   Remove an entry.

2. When a queue is implemented in a circular fashion as described in this section, what is the relationship between the head and tail pointers when the queue is empty? What about when the queue is full? How can one detect whether a queue is full or empty?

3. Design an algorithm for inserting an entry in a circular queue.

Figure 7-16 A program (using an auxiliary queue) for printing separate listings of undergraduates and graduates

```
assign Current Pointer the value in the list's head pointer
while (Current Pointer not NIL) do
        (if (the name pointed to by Current Pointer represents
              an undergraduate)
            then (print the name)
            else (insert that name in the queue called Graduates)
         assign Current Pointer the value in the pointer cell of the
              entry pointed to by Current Pointer)
while (the queue Graduates is not empty) do
        (remove an entry from the queue and print it)
```

7–5 **Trees**

The last data structure that we will consider is the *tree,* which is the structure reflected by an organization chart of a typical company (Figure 7-17). Here, the president is represented at the top, with lines branching down to the vice-presidents, who are followed by regional managers, etc. To this intuitive definition of a tree structure we impose one additional constraint, which (in terms of an organization chart) is that no individual in the company reports to two different people. That is, different branches of the organization do not merge at a lower level.

Terminology

In the terminology of tree structures, each position in the tree is called a *node.* The single node at the top is called the *root node* (since if we turned the drawing upside down, this node would represent the base or root of the tree). The nodes at the other extreme are called *terminal nodes* (or *leaf nodes*). A line connecting two nodes is called an *arc.*

If we position ourselves at any node in a tree, we will find that this node together with those nodes below it again have the structure of a tree. This, in fact, is a major advantage of such an organizational structure since it divides a company into different suborganizations, each of which has the same type of structure. (A regional manager is effectively the president of that region.) We call these smaller structures *branches.*

Additional terminology has its origins in the concept of each node giving birth to those nodes immediately below it. Thus, we often speak of a node's immediate subordinates as its *children,* and from the point of view of the subordinate nodes, we refer to their immediate superior as the *parent* node. Moreover, we speak of nodes with the same parent as being *twins* or *siblings.*

Finally, we often refer to the *depth* of a tree, which is nothing more than the

Figure 7-17 An example of an organization chart

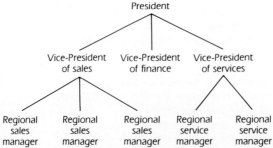

number of nodes in the longest path from the root to a leaf. In other words, the depth of a tree is the number of horizontal layers within it.

We will encounter tree structures repeatedly in subsequent chapters, so rather than elaborate on applications now, we will simply mention the uses that will be discussed later. In Section 7-6 as well as in our discussion of index organization in Chapter 8, we will find that information that must be searched quickly for data retrieval is often organized as a tree; in Chapter 9, we will see that records themselves are often envisioned as trees; and in Chapter 10, we will see how games can be evaluated in terms of trees.

Tree Implementation

As for the storage of a tree structure in a machine's memory, we will restrict our attention to what are called *binary trees,* which are trees in which each node has at most two children. Such trees are normally stored in memory using a linked structure similar to that of linked lists. However, rather than each entry consisting of two components (the data followed by a next-entry pointer), each entry (or node) of the binary tree contains three components: the data, a pointer to the node's first child, and a pointer to the node's second child. Although there is no left or right inside a machine, it is helpful to refer to the first pointer as the *left child pointer* and the other pointer as the *right child pointer* in reference to the way we would draw the tree on paper. Thus, each node of the tree will be represented by a short, contiguous block of memory cells with the format shown in Figure 7-18.

Storing the tree in memory involves finding available blocks of memory cells to hold the nodes and linking these nodes according to the desired tree structure. That is, each pointer must be set to point to the left or right child of the pertinent node or assigned the NIL value if there are no more nodes in that direction of the tree. Thus, a terminal node is characterized by having both of its pointers assigned NIL. Finally we set aside a special memory location in which to store the address of the root node. We call this the *root pointer.*

An example of this linked storage system is presented in Figure 7-19, where a conceptual binary tree structure is exhibited along with a representation of how that tree might actually appear in a computer's memory. With this system we can always find the root node by means of the root pointer and then trace any path down the tree by following the appropriate pointers from node to node.

Figure 7-18 The structure of a node in a binary tree

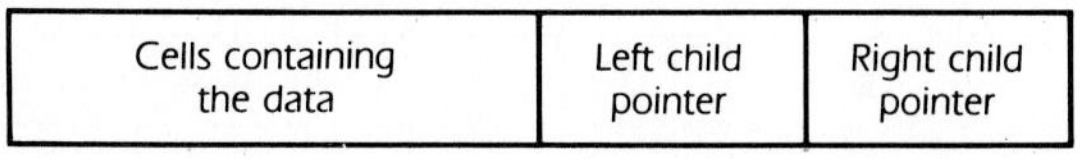

Cells containing the data	Left child pointer	Right child pointer

Figure 7-19 The conceptual and actual organization of a binary tree using a linked storage system

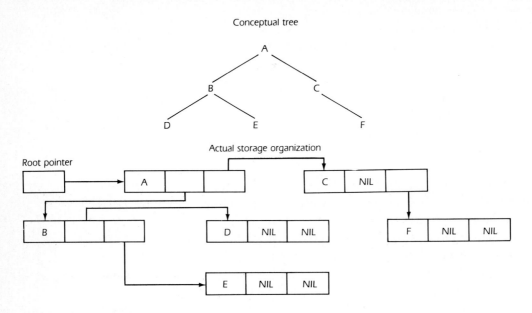

An alternative to a linked storage system for binary trees is the technique of setting aside a contiguous block of memory cells, storing the root node in the first of these cells (for simplicity we assume that each node of the tree requires only one memory cell), storing the left child of the root in the second cell, storing the right child of the root in the third cell, and in general storing the left and right children of the node found in cell n in the cells $2n$ and $2n + 1$, respectively. Following this technique, the conceptual tree shown in Figure 7-19 would be stored as shown in Figure 7-20. Note that the system is essentially that of storing the nodes across successively lower levels of the tree as segments, one after the other. That is, the first entry in the block is the root node, followed by the root's children, followed by the root's grandchildren, etc.

In contrast to the linked structure described earlier, this alternate storage system provides a convenient method for finding the parent or sibling of any node. (Of course, this could be done in the linked structure at the expense of additional pointers.) Indeed, the location of a node's parent can be found by dividing the node's

Figure 7-20 The tree of Figure 7-19 stored without pointers

1	2	3	4	5	6	7
A	B	C	D	E		F

Figure 7-21 A sparse, unbalanced tree shown in its conceptual form and as it would be stored without pointers

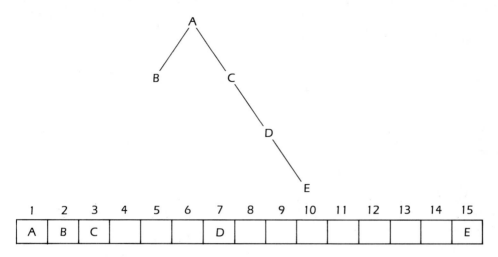

position in the block by two while discarding any remainder (the parent of the node in position 7 would be the node in position 3), and a node's sibling can be found by adding one to the location of a node in an even-numbered position or subtracting one from the location of a node in an odd-numbered position (the sibling of the node in position 4 is the node in position 5, while the sibling of the node in position 3 is the node in position 2). Moreover, this storage system makes efficient use of space in the case of binary trees that are approximately balanced (in the sense that both subtrees tend to have the same depth) and full (in the sense that they do not have long, thin branches). For trees without these characteristics, though, the system can become quite inefficient, as shown in Figure 7-21.

We see then that, as in the case of the other structures we have studied, there are a variety of systems for storing binary trees, each with its advantages and disadvantages, and once again we find it advantageous to shield the user of the tree from the technicalities of the implementation chosen. Consequently, one normally identifies the activities that will be performed on a tree by the external software and then writes subprograms to accomplish these activities while hiding the technicalities of the actual storage system. These subprograms together with the storage area would then form a package that would allow a programmer to use the tree without being distracted by the details of the implementation.

A Binary Tree Package

To demonstrate such a package, let us return to the problem of storing a list of names in alphabetical order. We assume that the operations to be performed on this list are the following:

search for the presence of an entry,
print the list in alphabetical order, and
insert a new entry

Our goal is to develop a storage system along with a collection of subprograms to perform these operations.

We begin by considering options regarding the subprogram for searching the list. If the list were stored according to the linked list model in Section 7-2, we would be forced to search the list in a sequential fashion, a process that, as we discussed in Chapter 4, could be very inefficient if the list should become long. Thus, we might try to find an implementation that would allow us to use the binary search algorithm (Chapter 4) for our search subprogram. However, to apply this algorithm, our storage system must allow us to find the middle entry of successively smaller portions of the list. Such an operation is possible when using a dense list, since we could compute the address of the middle entry in much the same manner as we can compute the locations of entries in an array. But using a dense list would introduce problems when making insertions, as observed in Section 7-2.

Our problem can be solved by implementing the "list" as a binary tree rather than using one of the traditional list systems. We merely make the middle list entry the root node, the middle of the remaining first half of the list the root's left child, and the middle of the remaining second half the root's right child. The middle entries of each remaining fourth of the list become the children of the root's children and so forth. For example, under this process the tree in Figure 7-22 could be used to represent the list of letters A, B, C, D, E, F, G, H, I, J, K, L, and M. (We have taken the larger of the middle two entries as the middle when the part of the list in question contains an even number of entries.) Binary trees with this underlying order are often called **search trees.**

To search the "list" stored as a search tree, we merely compare the target value to the root node. If the two are equal, our search has succeeded. If they are not equal, we move to the left or right child of the root, depending on whether the target is less than or greater than the root, respectively. There we find the middle of the portion of the list necessary to continue the search. This process of comparing and moving to a child should continue until the target is found (meaning that our search

Figure 7-22 The letters A through M arranged in a search tree

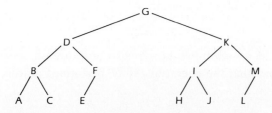

was successful) or the bottom the tree is reached without finding the target (meaning that our search was a failure). Figure 7-23 shows how this search process could be implemented in the case of a linked tree structure. (Annotative comments are bracketed by asterisks.)

Having altered the natural sequential order of our stored list for the sake of search efficiency, you may think that the process of printing the "list" in alphabetical order would now be difficult. This hypothesis, however, proves to be false. Indeed, to print the "list" in alphabetical order, we need merely print the left subtree in alphabetical order, print the root node, and then print the right subtree in alphabetical order (Figure 7-24). After all, the left subtree contains those elements that are less than the root node, while the right subtree contains the elements larger than the root. Thus, a sketch of our print routine would look like:

> if (tree not empty)
> then (print the left subtree in alphabetical order,
>   print the root node,
>   print the right subtree in alphabetical order)

You may argue that this outline achieves little toward our goal of developing a complete print subprogram since it involves the tasks of printing the left subtree and the right subtree in alphabetical order, both of which are essentially the same as our original task. Indeed, the only difference in the task of printing the entire tree and that of printing the left or right subtree is in the size of the trees involved. Thus, solving the problem of printing a subtree should be just as difficult as solving the original problem. However, from a more optimistic point of view, this means that the same algorithm can be used for all three problems, which in turn suggests a recursive system in which our subprogram is applied to smaller and smaller trees.

Figure 7-23 The binary search applied to a linked binary tree

```
        ***  Current Pointer is used to hold a pointer to the current  ***
        ***  position in the tree. The node at this location is        ***
        ***  called the current node.                                  ***

        assign Current Pointer the value found in the tree's root pointer
        assign Found the value false
        while (Found is false and Current Pointer is not NIL) do
                (select the applicable case from those listed below and
                perform the associated activity:
                target value = current node: (assign Found the value true)
                target value < current node: (assign Current Pointer the
                    value of the current node's left child pointer)
                target value > current node: (assign Current Pointer the
                    value of the current node's right child pointer))
        if (Found is false) then (declare the search a failure)
                        else (declare the search a success)
```

Figure 7-24 Printing a search tree in alphabetical order

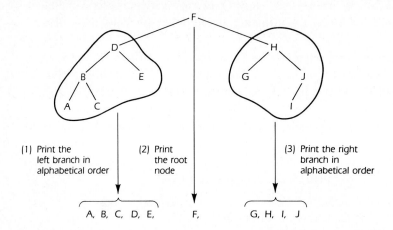

(1) Print the left branch in alphabetical order

(2) Print the root node

(3) Print the right branch in alphabetical order

A, B, C, D, E,   F,   G, H, I, J

Following this lead, we can expand our outline into the complete pseudocode subprogram for printing a linked search tree in alphabetical order shown in Figure 7-25. You will observe that in addition to assigning the routine the name Print Tree and then requesting the services of Print Tree for printing the left and right subtrees, we have modified references to the tree structure to conform with the pointer system found in our search tree implementation. Moreover, you should confirm for yourself that the termination condition of the recursive process (reaching an empty subtree) is guaranteed to be reached, since each activation of the routine operates on a smaller tree than the one causing the activation.

The task of inserting a new entry in the tree is also easier than it may at first appear. You may guess that certain insertions would require cutting the tree open to allow room for the new entry, but actually the new node can always be attached to the bottom of the tree as a leaf, regardless of the value involved. To find the proper place for this new leaf, we merely move down the tree along the path that would be followed if we were searching for the value to be inserted. Then, when the

Figure 7-25 A subprogram for printing a linked search tree in alphabetical order

```
procedure Print Tree

if (root pointer not NIL)
    then (Print Tree (the tree whose root is the left child of
                        the current root node),
          print root node,
          Print Tree (the tree whose root is the right child of
                        the current root node))
```

bottom of the tree is reached, we have found the proper location for the new node. Indeed, we have found the location to which a search for the new data would lead.

A program segment expressing this process in the case of a linked tree structure is shown in Figure 7-26. It first searches the tree for the value being inserted and then places the new node at the proper location. Note that a slightly special case occurs if the tree is empty in the first place. This case is detected by testing for the condition of Current Pointer still being the same as the root pointer after the search

Figure 7-26 A subprogram for inserting an entry in a linked search tree

```
***   Current Pointer is used to hold a pointer to the current    ***
***   position in the tree. The node at this location is          ***
***   called the current node. Likewise, Previous Pointer         ***
***   holds a pointer to the parent of the current node, which    ***
***   is called the previous node.                                ***

***   First, find the correct location for the new node.          ***

assign Current Pointer the value found in the tree's root pointer
assign Found the value false
while (Found is false and Current Pointer is not NIL) do
        (select the applicable case from those listed below and
        perform the associated activity:
        target value = current node: (assign Found the value true)
        target value < current node:
                (assign Previous Pointer the value of Current Pointer,
                and assign Current Pointer the value of the current
                node's left child pointer)
        target value > current node:
                (assign Previous Pointer the value of Current Pointer,
                and assign Current Pointer the value of the current
                node's right child pointer))

***   Now, insert the new node as a child of the current node.  ***
***   A special case occurs if Current Pointer is still the     ***
***   same as the root pointer, meaning that the original tree  ***
***   is empty.                                                 ***

if (Found is false)
        then (create a new node containing the target value, and
                if (Current Pointer equals root pointer)
                        then (establish the new node as the root node)
                        else (if (target value < the Previous Node)
                                then (establish the new node as the left
                                        child of the previous node)
                                else (establish the new node as the right
                                        child of the previous node)))
```

process has been completed. Moreover, if the data being inserted is actually found in the tree during the search, no insertion is made.

We see, then, that a software package consisting of a linked search tree together with our subprograms for searching, printing, and inserting provides an excellent system for implementing the list required by our hypothetical application.

Questions/Exercises

1. Identify the root and leaf nodes in the following tree:

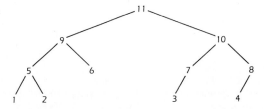

2. What condition indicates that a linked tree in a machine's memory is empty?

3. Draw a diagram representing how the tree:

would appear in memory when stored using the left and right child pointers as described in this section. Then, draw another diagram showing how the tree would appear in storage using the alternate storage system described in this section.

4. Draw the binary tree structure you would use to store the list R, S, T, U, V, W, X, Y, and Z for future searching.

5. Indicate the path traversed by the binary search algorithm in Figure 7-23 in the search tree in Figure 7-22 when searching for the entry J. What about the entry P?

6. Draw a diagram representing the status of activations of the recursive tree-printing algorithm in Figure 7-25 at the time node K is printed within the search tree in Figure 7-22.

7–6 Abstract Data Types

In Chapter 5 we said the term *type* refers to the interpretation given to stored data. We also found that programming languages tend to allow for a small collection of types such as integer, real, character, Boolean, and pointer. In these languages a programmer can easily declare an object named quantity to be of type integer and another object weight to be of type real. But what if the programmer wants to establish an object known as membership list to be a list of names maintained in alphabetical order? Conceptually there is nothing different here. The only distinction is that the interpretation desired is not a primitive in the language.

To allow for these additional declarations, some programming languages provide a method of developing and using types other than those implemented as primitives in the basic language. These additional types are known as **abstract data types.** In general, an object having an abstract data type (which we call an instance of the abstract data type) is implemented as a software package consisting of stored data and a collection of program segments that are charged with the task of interpreting this data according to the desired type. In particular, an object of type "alphabetically ordered list of names" could be implemented as a linked list structure along with the collection of routines insert, delete, search, and print, as discussed in Section 7-2. Similarly, an object of type "stack of integers" could be implemented as a block of contiguous memory cells along with push and pop routines.

You will note that the idea of using a software package to represent an otherwise abstract object is a recurring theme in this chapter. Indeed, we have continually emphasized the role of subprograms for supporting conceptual interpretations of the underlying data, although the implementation of an abstract data type is normally associated with a feature that we have yet to point out. This is the idea that the use of the subprograms provided in a package is not a luxury but a necessity. After all, it is through these program segments that the proper image of the data is projected, and thus it is important that all transactions between an object of the given type and the object's environment be performed by these routines. To do otherwise would be to open the doors to unforeseen complications.

The situation is analogous to a bank teller who also has a checking account with the bank. The system works well as long as the teller makes deposits and withdrawals through accepted procedures. But the stage is set for disaster if the teller decides to borrow lunch money from the teller drawer with the idea of replenishing the drawer later in the afternoon.

Likewise, in the case of software development it is often tempting to circumvent the established protocol of an abstract data type for the sake of short-sighted efficiency. For example, if an object is assigned the abstract type "stack of integers" and one step in the application should require a reference to the third entry on the stack, a programmer might be tempted to violate the stack's integrity by extracting the third entry from the stack package without going through the formal process of popping the first two entries. Such a tactic has been found to lead to complications later in the software's life cycle and is considered to be one of the worst of evils by software engineers. The problem is simply that future maintenance programmers, seeing that the object is described as a stack of integers, will not be aware of any nonstandard operations and could easily make changes that are not compatible with these anomalies.

A more precise example would be an alphabetically ordered list that in the software's development phase was implemented as a linked list yet later in maintenance must be replaced by a linked tree structure to provide for faster searching. Such a change would not be compatible with any "clever" shortcuts that rely on the linked list structure. Thus, any such nonstandard references to the list would have to be tracked down and changed before the otherwise straightforward modification would prove successful. Even worse, these shortcuts may not be discovered until the software has been placed back in use and found to produce erroneous results at the expense of a large financial loss (and perhaps a "clever" programmer's job).

To prevent such circumvention of abstract data types, newer programming languages, such as Ada, provide techniques by which a software package can be *encapsulated,* meaning that the package is constructed in such a manner that its internal structure can be accessed only by means of the approved package routines. If instances of the abstract data types occurring in a software system are encapsulated, the integrity of these data types will be protected from poorly conceived modifications that might otherwise be made under the pressure of meeting a completion deadline or from any short-sighted efforts of maintenance personnel who may be tempted to implement a modification by means of a nonstandard reference to the object.

Of course, if the abstract data type is properly selected and its implementation accurately simulates the type, one will not need to violate the integrity of the object or even be aware of its internal features. Thus, although an alphabetically ordered list of names could be implemented as a dense list, a linked list, or even a tree, the user of the abstract list need not be concerned with the pros and cons of these options. Rather, these concerns would have been evaluated and resolved during the development of the package. The user of the package would in turn be free to envision the list in any conceptual manner desired. Indeed, the result of the statement

insert(Tom)

would be the same from the point of view of the package user regardless of the underlying structure.

In closing, we observe that the ability to extend the collection of primitives in a programming language through the use of abstract data types is an extremely important feature. Through the use of such types, a general-purpose programming language can be customized to a particular application. Consider, for example, an architect whose job requires the construction and modification of computer models of traffic flow patterns in large buildings. Given a general-purpose programming language that allows the implementation of abstract data types, the architect could develop a collection of abstract types such as entrance, lobby, hallway, etc. Then, programming a new model would consist merely of declaring objects of the appropriate types, followed by a brief description of how these objects should interact with one another. Indeed, the design and implementation of the pertinent data types would be the major part of the programming task—an observation that leads to the next section.

Questions/Exercises

1. In what way is a checking account at a bank encapsulated?
2. What is the difference between an abstract data type and an instance of that type?
3. What is the difference between a traditional program module and an instance of an abstract data type?
4. Describe two underlying structures that might be used to implement an object of type "queue of integers."

7–7 **Object-Oriented Programming** (optional)

Although it may seem odd to return to our discussion of programming paradigms at this time, the truth is that our discussion of data structures and their implementation provides an extremely good foundation on which to understand the object-oriented approach to programming. Indeed, the process of implementing instances of abstract data types as individual packages is essentially the same process as implementing objects under the object-oriented approach to software design.

As an example, let us return to our problem of printing the entries in a linked list in reverse order. We solved this problem in Section 7-3 by pushing the entries onto a stack as we traversed the list and then popping them from the stack after reaching the end of the list (Figure 7-11). Thus, our solution involved two structures—a list and a stack—that we manipulated to obtain the desired results.

The important point here is that, in addition to the data structures involved, we had to provide an algorithm for moving the data from one structure to another. This is the procedural paradigm—objects such as data structures are constructed as passive commodities that require additional algorithmic procedures to move information among them. We represent this approach in Figure 7-27.

In contrast, let us approach the list-printing problem by constructing two abstract objects called NameList and NameStack. Each object is a software package consisting of an internal data structure and a collection of subprograms that define how the object is to react to receiving external stimuli in the form of messages (Figure 7-28). In particular, the object NameList contains a linked list structure and "knows" that, upon receiving the message "print your entries backward," it should send its list entries to NameStack and then request NameStack to send its entries to the printer. In turn, the object NameStack contains a stack structure along with program

Figure 7-27 The procedural approach to our list-printing problem

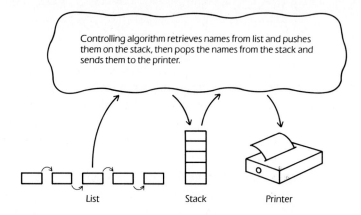

Controlling algorithm retrieves names from list and pushes them on the stack, then pops the names from the stack and sends them to the printer.

List   Stack   Printer

segments telling it how to receive names and how to respond to such messages as "send our entries to the printer." Roughly speaking, then, the objects are "intelligent" data structures.

Once these objects are established, the task of printing the list backward can be accomplished merely by sending the object NameList the message "print our entries backward." This, then, is the object-oriented paradigm—objects are active commodities that interact with one another without direction from some external controlling algorithm.

Of course, this example has been a rather simplistic one, consisting of only two objects that interact to perform a rather straightforward task. The advantages of object-oriented software are more prominent in the case of larger software systems

Figure 7-28 The object-oriented approach to our list-printing problem

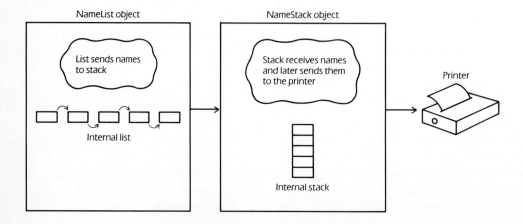

NameList object   NameStack object

List sends names to stack

Stack receives names and later sends them to the printer

Printer

Internal list

Internal stack

where numerous objects are required. In this setting each object represents a highly cohesive module containing those activities and only those activities required to simulate the actions of that object. Thus, a software system designed on the object-oriented philosophy has a natural and very well-defined modular structure—the dream of any software engineer.

As a final example, consider an object-oriented approach to a business accounting system. The journal and each ledger account (such as cash on hand, accounts payable, accounts receivable, dividends payable, and retained earnings) could be implemented as an object with the ability to react to messages received from other objects as well as to send messages to other objects in the system. Thus, as entries are posted in the journal, the journal object would send appropriate debit and credit messages to the ledger accounts so that the total ledger would remain up to date and balanced.

Questions/Exercises

1. Identify the objects that might be used in an object-oriented simulation of the pedestrian traffic in a shopping mall. What actions should each of these objects be able to perform?
2. In what sense are the objects in an object-oriented system functionally cohesive?
3. In what sense is a single object in an object-oriented system divided into submodules?
4. Must each object in an object-oriented system contain only one data structure?

Chapter 7 Review Problems

(Asterisked problems are associated with optional sections.)

1. Draw pictures showing how the following array would appear in a machine's program when stored in row major order and in column major order:

A	B	C	D
E	D	G	H
I	J	K	L

2. Suppose an array with 6 rows and 8 columns is stored in row major order starting at address 20 (decimal). If each entry in the array requires only one memory cell, what is the address of the entry in the third row and fourth column? What would your answer be if each entry required two memory cells?

3. Work problem 2 assuming column major order rather than row major order.

4. Suppose the list of letters A, B, C, E, F, and G is stored in a contiguous block of memory cells. What activities are required to insert the letter D in the list if the alphabetical order is to be maintained?

5. The following is a table representing the contents of some cells in a computer's main memory along with the address of each cell represented. Note that some of the cells contain letters of the alphabet and each such cell is followed by an empty cell. Place addresses in these empty cells so that each cell containing a letter together with the following cell form an entry in a linked list in which the letters appear in alphabetical order. (Use zero for the NIL pointer.) What address should the head pointer contain?

Address	Contents
11	C
12	
13	G
14	
15	E
16	
17	B
18	
19	U
20	
21	F
22	

6. Below is a table representing a portion of a linked list in a computer's main memory. Each entry in the list consists of two cells: the first contains a letter of the alphabet; the second contains a pointer to the next list entry. Alter the pointers so that the letter N is no longer in the list. Then replace the letter N with the letter G and alter the pointers so that the new letter appears in the list in its proper place in alphabetical order.

Address	Contents
30	J
31	38
32	B
33	30
34	X
35	46
36	N
37	40
38	K
39	36
40	P
41	34

7. Below is a table representing a linked list using the same format as in the preceding problems. If the head pointer contains the value 44, what name is represented by the list? Change the pointers so that the list contains the name Jean.

Address	Contents
40	N
41	46
42	I
43	40
44	J
45	50
46	E
47	00
48	M
49	42
50	A
51	40

8. Which of the following routines correctly inserts NEW ENTRY immediately after the entry called PREVIOUS ENTRY in a linked list? What is wrong with the other routine?

Routine 1

1. Copy the value in the pointer field of PREVIOUS ENTRY into the pointer field of NEW ENTRY.

2. Change the value in the pointer field of PREVIOUS ENTRY to the address of NEW ENTRY.

Routine 2

1. Change the value in the pointer field of PREVIOUS ENTRY to the address of NEW ENTRY.

2. Copy the value in the pointer field of PREVIOUS ENTRY into the pointer field of NEW ENTRY.

9. John Programmer thinks he has discovered a clever way of saving space when the same entry must appear more than once in a linked list. His idea is to store the repeated entry only once in memory and merely "point to it" from each of its predecessors. What is the flaw in John's thinking?

10. Design an algorithm for concatenating two linked lists (that is, placing one before the other to form a single list).

11. Design an algorithm for combining two sorted dense lists into a single sorted dense list. What if the lists were linked?

12. Design an algorithm for reversing the order of a linked list.

13. In Figure 7-12 we presented an algorithm for printing a linked list in reverse order using a stack as an auxiliary storage structure. Design a recursive algorithm to perform this same task without making explicit use of a stack. In what form is a stack still involved in your recursive solution?

14. Sometimes a single linked list is provided with two different orders by following each entry with two pointers rather than one. Fill in the following table so that by following the first pointer after each letter one finds the name Carol, but by following the second pointer after each letter one finds the letters in alphabetical order. What values belong in the head pointer of each of the two lists represented?

Address	Contents
60	O
61	
62	
63	C
64	
65	
66	A
67	
68	
69	L
70	
71	
72	R
73	
74	

15. The following table represents a stack stored in a contiguous block of memory cells as discussed in the text. If the base of the stack is at address 10 and the stack pointer contains the value 12, what value will be retrieved by a pop instruction? What value would then be in the stack pointer?

Address	Contents
10	F
11	C
12	A
13	B
14	E

16. a. Draw a table showing the final contents of the memory cells if the instruction in problem 15 had been to push the letter D on the stack rather than to pop it. What would the value in the stack pointer be after the push instruction?

    b. How would your answer to part a change if the base of the stack had been at address 14 rather than 10 (that is, if the cells used for the stack precede the stack rather than follow it)?

17. Design an algorithm to remove the bottom entry from a stack.

18. Design an algorithm to compare the contents of two stacks.

19. Suppose we wished to create a stack of names that vary in length. Why would it be advantageous to store the names in separate areas of memory and then build the stack out of pointers to these names rather than allowing the stack to contain the names themselves?

20. Does a queue crawl through memory in the direction of its head or its tail?

21. Suppose the entries in a queue require one memory cell each, the head pointer contains the value 11, and the tail pointer contains the value 17. What will be the values of these pointers after one entry has been inserted and two have been removed?

22. a. Suppose a queue implemented in a circular fashion is in the state shown below. Draw a diagram showing the structure after the letters G and R have been inserted, three letters have been removed, and the letters D and P have been inserted.

    b. What error would have occurred in part a if the letters G, R, D, and P had been inserted before any letters were removed?

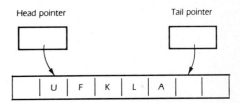

23. Describe how an array could be used to implement a queue in a high-level language.

24. The following table represents a tree stored in a machine's memory. Each node of the tree consists of three cells. The first cell contains the data (a letter), the second contains a pointer to the node's left child, and the third contains a pointer to the node's right child. A value of zero represents a NIL pointer. If the value of the root pointer is 55, draw a picture of the tree represented.

Address	Contents
40	G
41	0
42	0
43	X
44	0
45	0
46	J
47	49
48	0
49	M
50	0
51	0
52	F
53	43
54	40
55	W
56	46
57	52

25. The table following represents the contents of a block of cells in a computer's main memory. Note that some of the cells contain letters of the alphabet and each such cell is followed by two blank cells. Fill in the blank cells so that the memory block represents the tree following the table. Use the first cell following a letter as the pointer to that node's left child and the next cell as the pointer to the right child. Use zero for NIL pointers. What value should be in the root pointer?

Address	Contents
30	C
31	
32	
33	H
34	
35	
36	K
37	
38	
39	E
40	
41	
42	G
43	
44	
45	P
46	
47	

26. Design a nonrecursive algorithm to replace the recursive one represented in Figure 7-25. Use a stack to control any backtracking that may be necessary.

27. Apply the recursive tree-printing algorithm of Figure 7-25 to the tree represented in problem 24. Draw a diagram representing the nested activations of the algorithm (and the current position in each) at the time node X is printed.

28. While keeping the root node the same and without changing the physical location of the data elements, change the pointers in the tree of problem 24 so the tree-printing algorithm of Figure 7-25 will print the nodes alphabetically.

29. Draw a diagram showing how the binary tree below would appear in memory when stored without pointers using the alternate storage system presented in this chapter.

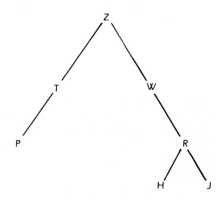

30. Describe a data structure suitable for representing a board configuration during a chess game.

31. Describe a data structure suitable for representing a Rubik's cube. What subprograms should be provided to support the conceptual image?

32. Modify the subprogram in Figure 7-25 to print the list in reverse order.

33. Design an algorithm for searching a search tree that is stored in the alternate tree storage system presented in this chapter.

34. Describe a tree structure that might be used to store the genealogical history of a family. What operations would be performed on the tree? If the tree were implemented as a linked structure, what pointers should be associated with each node? Design subprograms to perform the operations you identified above assuming that the tree is implemented as a linked structure with the pointers you just described.

35. Design an algorithm for finding and deleting a given value from a search tree.

*36. Design an object-oriented model of an automobile.

*37. Design an object-oriented model of a computer.

Problems for the Programmer

1. Does your language provide statements for requesting and releasing pieces of memory as entries of a linked list are added and deleted? If so, what are they?

   What garbage-collection features must be provided in the underlying software to support these dynamic memory allocation requests?

2. How could you simulate a stack using the data types and structures available in your programming language? Write routines to perform the push and pop operations.

3. Extend your solution to the token problem of Chapter 3 (programming problem 4) to store the token requests made while the tokens are not available and then grant those requests later as their turns come.

4. How could you simulate a tree structure using the data types and structures available in your programming language? Implement the tree-printing algorithms using this technique.

5. Implement your solutions to review problems 10, 11, 12, 17, and 18.

8 File Structures

8–1 **Sequential Files**
 Rudiments of Sequential Files
 Sorted Files
 Programming Concerns
8–2 **Indexed Files**
 Index Fundamentals
 Index Organization
 Programming Concerns
8–3 **Hashed Files**
 A Particular Hashing Technique
 Distribution Problems
 Handling Section Overflow
 Programming Concerns
8–4 **The Role of the Operating System**
 Data Control Blocks
 Opening Files
 Closing Files

In Chapter 7 we discussed various ways of organizing data. In terms of actual implementation, we focused on how those organizations might be simulated within a machine's main memory. In this chapter we will concentrate on data storage techniques used in bulk storage.

Recall that a collection of data stored in bulk storage is called a file, which in turn is subdivided into records. The subject of this chapter concerns how these records can be organized in bulk storage to provide convenient access by the user. As in the case of data structures, we will find that the organization ultimately presented to the user may not be the same as the actual storage system. Thus, as in Chapter 7, we will find ourselves discussing and comparing both conceptual and real organizations.

As a preview, we can summarize the major subject of this chapter as being a study of the relationship between the way in which the file is to be used and the way in which it should be stored. That is, some storage systems allow individual records to be retrieved in an arbitrary order but at the expense of additional overhead, whereas other systems require little overhead yet force the file to be accessed as though it were simply a list of records that must always be retrieved in the order in which they were originally stored.

8–1 **Sequential Files**

Let us begin with an example of a file application. Suppose we wish to maintain information about the employees in a business. The information would consist of such items as name, address, employee identification number, Social Security number, pay scale, hours worked, date hired, and job title.

We may want this employee information stored in bulk storage rather than in main memory for several reasons. One is that there probably would not be enough space in main memory. Another might be that the memory in our machine is volatile and the data would be lost if power were disconnected. Still another would be that we want to keep a copy of our data in off-line storage (perhaps even at another location) for backup purposes.

For whatever reason, we assume that the information about the employees is to be recorded in bulk storage with one logical record for each employee. Each record in turn consists of units called **fields** containing the individual items of information about the employee.

Suppose our employee file were to be used for payroll processing where the entire file must be accessed each pay period. As each employee record is retrieved, that employee's pay will be calculated and the appropriate check produced. Since all records will be processed, it makes little difference in this application which records are processed first. The most straightforward technique would therefore be to consider the records as organized in a list and then to retrieve and process them one at a time from the beginning to the end. Such an organization is called a *sequential file*.

Rudiments of Sequential Files

This sequential organization may, of course, be only conceptual in nature. That is, depending on the physical characteristics of the storage device being used, we may choose to store the file in another form and present it to the user as a sequential system (Figure 8-1). For example, if the storage device were a tape system, we would most assuredly remain faithful to the conceptual sequential order because of the sequential nature of the tape itself. However, if the device were a disk system, we might choose to disperse the records of the file over the disk to take advantage of unused portions. In this case we could link the records with a pointer system very similar to the linked list system in Chapter 7, except that here the pointers would represent locations on the disk rather than in main memory.

Figure 8-1 A sequential file storage

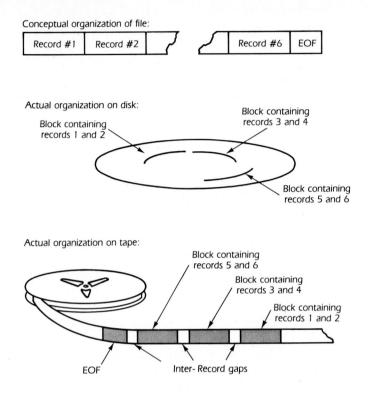

Conceptual organization of file:

| Record #1 | Record #2 | | | Record #6 | EOF |

Actual organization on disk:

Block containing
records 3 and 4

Block containing
records 1 and 2

Block containing
records 5 and 6

Actual organization on tape:

Block containing
records 5 and 6

Block containing
records 3 and 4

Block containing
records 1 and 2

EOF   Inter- Record gaps

The pros and cons of these approaches to sequential file storage are quite similar to those of dense versus linked lists. However, in the case of files, the type of bulk storage system being used plays an important role in determining manipulation techniques and efficiency. For instance, to insert a new record in a file on tape we would have to move the records following it backward to create a hole, or to delete a record we would have to move records forward to fill the hole. Such movement of records would result in a seemingly endless task of winding and rewinding a magnetic tape. As a consequence, updating a file stored on magnetic tape is almost always accomplished within the context of copying the information from one tape to another. For this application, if a record is to be deleted, it is simply skipped during the copy process; or if a record is to be inserted, it is written to the output tape before copying the rest of the file.

In contrast, a linked system on a disk medium allows sequential files to be updated within themselves. That is, old records can be deleted or new ones added with little more effort than adjusting pointers. (We say "little more effort" in recognition of the fact that several logical records are normally stored in a single physical record block and this block usually constitutes a very short physically sequential file all by itself. Thus, a certain movement of logical records within the physical record might be necessary.)

In addition to selecting a storage technique, we must adopt a method of indicating the end of the file with what is commonly called an *EOF (End Of File) mark*. In the linked structure this mark might be similar to the NIL pointer in a linked list. In other cases a special record, called a *sentinel*, may be written as the last record of the file to mark the end. Of course, to avoid confusion, the fields in such a record must contain values that will never occur as data in the application.

Sorted Files

Regardless of which techniques are chosen when implementing a sequential file, the ultimate result is that the user of the file is allowed (or from another point of view, forced) to view the records in a simple sequential order. The only way to retrieve records is to start at the beginning of the file and extract them in the order provided.

Although convenient for the actual processing of payroll checks, this procedure nonetheless has some undesirable aspects. For example, note that before processing the payroll from the employee file, we must update all the records to reflect the amount of time worked by each employee during the current pay period. To accomplish this we could note the time worked by a particular employee, search through the file to find the employee's record, and update the record. Next we could select another employee and search for that corresponding record. If we knew this record was beyond the record of the previous employee, we could start the second search from the current location in the file. Otherwise, we would be forced to return to the beginning of the file and search from there. We can see, then, that an attempt to update the records in a random order forces us to constantly return to the beginning of the file to search the file over and over again.

Our task would be greatly simplified if we were always assured that the next record to be updated was beyond the current position in the file. This can be accomplished by selecting the records to be updated in the same order as their file sequence, which, of course, requires knowing the order of the file. For this reason sequential files are normally stored in alphabetical or numerical order according to the contents of a selected field known as the *key field*. For example, we might choose to store the employee file in alphabetical order by last name or, since two employees may have the same last name, we may choose numerical order by Social Security number or employee identification number. Using such a technique, we could then arrange the update information in the same order and thus remove the necessity of returning to the beginning of the file during the update process.

Having seen the advantage of order, you will probably not be surprised to learn that a lot of sorting takes place in relation to sequential files. For instance, the collection of update information (normally stored in a file known as the transaction file) is rarely collected in the order required for the updating process and must therefore be sorted before updating begins. This is one reason why sort routines are popular utility programs associated with most operating systems.

Programming Concerns

Now that we have discussed the rudiments of sequential files, we need to take a brief look at how such files (or, more accurately, their records) are manipulated from the programmer's point of view. This we do in the context of programming in a high-level language. A variety of key words such as READ and WRITE, GET and PUT, or INPUT and PRINT is used to identify the operation of retrieving and depositing (respectively) a record in bulk storage. These identifiers are normally followed by syntactic structures that identify the target file and the area of main memory that is to receive or supply the data in the record being manipulated. For example, in Pascal, statements such as:

readln (MailList, Name, Address)

and

writeln (MailList, Name, Address)

would be used to retrieve and deposit information relative to a sequential file named MailList. Note that along with the file name within the parentheses we find the names of the data items to be transferred. Similar statements in FORTRAN would be:

READ (10,150) NAME, ADDRESS

and

WRITE (10,150) NAME, ADDRESS

Here, the file being referenced is indicated by the number 10 (which would have been assigned as the file identifier earlier in the program), the organization of the record itself is defined by the number 150 (which is a reference to another instruction in the program where the record structure is described), and the individual fields in the record are identified as NAME and ADDRESS.

Note that there is no explicit information in these statements as to the location in the file of the record being manipulated. Because it is a sequential file, there is no choice to be made: the record being read will be the one immediately following the current position in the file or the record being written will be placed immediately following the current position.

In addition to instructions for the manipulation of records in a sequential file, most high-level languages provide features that assist with the problem of detecting the EOF mark. This may appear as a special condition within the retrieve statement itself or as a test to be performed independently of actual record retrieval.

In particular, FORTRAN uses the former system, allowing an extra parameter in the READ statement to indicate where control should be transferred if the record retrieved is, in fact, the EOF mark rather than a regular record. Thus, a statement to retrieve an employee record might have the following form:

READ (10,150,END = 900) NAME, ADDRESS, . . .

where the phrase END = 900 means that if the record obtained is the EOF mark, control should be transferred to the instruction labeled 900.

In contrast to this FORTRAN system of combining the EOF test with the retrieval statement, Pascal essentially uses a flag whose interrogation is independent of record retrieval. With this system one can test for the EOF mark on the file named EmplData with the syntax eof(EmplData). The result will be the value true if the EOF mark has been reached and false if not. Thus, a program sequence of the form:

```
while (not eof(EmplData)) do
       (read the next record and
        process the appropriate check)
```

would be used to process the payroll from the employee file. The result is that the process and retrieve statements will be repeated as long as there are employee records to be processed. However, once the last employee record is processed, execution will go on to the next part of the program. Such an application typifies the while loop structure.

The traditional merge algorithm provides an excellent medium in which to observe the need for EOF detection while at the same time presenting a classical example of sequential file processing. The setting is that new records have been collected that are to be inserted into an existing sequential file. This insertion will be done in the context of producing a totally new copy of the sequential file with the updates inserted. The new records are stored in a file called the transaction file, the file to be updated is called the old master file, and the updated file will be called the new master file (Figure 8-2). Both the transaction file and the old master file are assumed to be sorted according to a field referred to as the key field. We assume that all new records are indeed new; that is, no record in the transaction file will be found with an identical key field to that of a record in the old master file.

Observe that with these assumptions the problem becomes one of merging the two existing files, which we call the input files, into one large output file (the new master file). The algorithm accomplishes this by starting at the beginning of the two input files, accessing a record from each file, comparing the records, writing the smaller one into the new master file, and then reading another record from the appropriate input file before returning to compare again.

Within this basic framework we must also maintain a vigil for the end of either input file and, if found, respond accordingly. For our example here we adopt the

Figure 8-2 The traditional merging of two sequential files

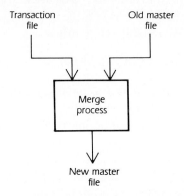

use of a sentinel for marking the end of files. This leads to the algorithm represented in Figure 8-3.

Questions/Exercises

1. Follow the merge algorithm presented in Figure 8-3 assuming that the transaction file contains records with key field values equal to B and E while the old master file contains A, C, D, and F.
2. It may surprise you to learn that the merge algorithm is the heart of a popular sort algorithm called the merge sort. Can you discover this algorithm? (Hint: A file containing only one record is sorted.)
3. Identify the tape motions involved in inserting a new record into a sequential file stored on tape if the file is to remain on the same tape. (Assume all records are the same size. Why is this assumption important?)

8–2 Indexed Files

Let us suppose now that in addition to processing payroll with the employee file, we want to use the file in an interactive query system. For instance, we may want to have a terminal available in the personnel office on which the records of employees could be displayed as questions surfaced as to time in service, available skills, past promotions, etc. In this atmosphere, records in the file would be requested in an arbitrary order throughout the day.

This is a significant departure from the naturally sequential payroll application of Section 8-1. If we store the employee data as a sequential file and attempt to use it in this interactive application, we could easily find a lengthy delay between a request for a record and the displaying of that record at the terminal. To satisfy each

Figure 8-3 The sequential file update (or merge) algorithm represented in pseudocode

```
read a record (called the current transaction record)
      from the transaction file.
read a record (called the current master record)
      from the old master file.
while (neither current record is the sentinel) do
      (if (the key field of the current transaction record is
            less than that of the current master record)
            then (write the current transaction record on the new
                  master file and read the next record from the
                  transaction file)
            else (write the current master record on the new
                  master file and read the next record from the old
                  master file))
while (current master record is not the sentinel) do
            (write the current master record on the new master file
            and read the next record from the old master file)
while (current transaction record is not the sentinel) do
            (write the current transaction record on the new master
            file and read the next record from the transaction file)
write the sentinel on the new master file
```

request, the program handling the retrieval must start at the beginning of the file and consider each record until it finds the one requested.

We have already discussed the disadvantages of such a process in relation to searching a list data structure. Compounding the problem in the present application is that the accessing of records from bulk storage requires the additional time-consuming mechanical motion associated with the particular device being used. The result is that sequential search techniques are even more sluggish when applied to bulk storage than when applied to main memory.

What we need is a way of storing the employee file that reduces this search time. One possibility is suggested from the study of data structures where we found that by storing information in a tree structure, we were able to apply binary search techniques that resulted in a significant reduction in search time. Such an organization is sometimes used as a file storage system, although a major drawback in many applications is that the maintenance of the required pointer system is significantly more time consuming in bulk storage than in main memory. (Again, manipulating data in bulk storage requires relatively slow mechanical motion.) Other techniques are thus often applied when storing files that are to be accessed in the random fashion inherent in the interactive employee information system.

One common technique is to copy the idea used in most textbooks where an index allows a topic to be located more directly than through a sequential search of the entire book. The index consists of a list of the topics along with the page numbers on which each corresponding topic appears.

The index concept is easily applied to file storage, resulting in what is called an *indexed file*. In this case the index consists of a listing of the key field values occurring in the file along with the location in bulk storage of the corresponding record. For example, in an employee file we might build an index listing all the employee identification numbers. Finding the record for a particular employee would require searching for that particular employee number in the file's index and then retrieving the record stored in the indicated bulk storage location.

Index Fundamentals

We should mention several fine points regarding indexed files. First note that finding a record by means of an index requires knowing a part of the information stored in the desired record. For instance, in the preceding example we must know the employee identification number of the employee in question. One should therefore give serious consideration during a file's design regarding the choice of the key field. It would be disappointing to construct the index of an employee file based on employee numbers and then learn that we will need to access records based on Social Security numbers.

If, however, a file must really be accessed by two different key fields, a multiple index system is often the solution. In particular, in addition to constructing an index listing employee identification numbers, we might build a second index based on the key field being Social Security number (Figure 8-4). Then, regardless of whether one starts with an employee number or a Social Security number, the desired record could be accessed quickly by interrogating the appropriate index. (You will often

Figure 8-4 An inverted file

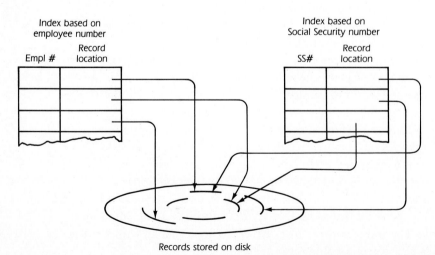

Records stored on disk

hear such a file referred to as an *inverted file*, with one key field designated as the *primary key* and the other as the *secondary key*.) The luxury of multiple indexes is not without its disadvantages, however. In particular, as records are inserted and deleted, all indexes must be updated, and the existence of additional indexes can greatly increase the time required to update the file.

Other points we should discuss relate to the organization of the index itself. Keep in mind that the index is stored in bulk storage along with the file. To access a record, we first retrieve the index into main memory where we search through it for the desired entry before returning to bulk storage for the record in question. Because the index must be dealt with during each file access, it is not surprising that design decisions relating to its organization can have significant repercussions. The points we are about to discuss deal with the size and internal structure of the index together with how such characteristics relate to the search process.

The preceding retrieval scenario points out that the mere introduction of an index has transferred the stage for the search process from the file in bulk storage to the index, which can be searched in main memory. This transfer alone has significantly increased the efficiency of the search. In the case of a simple sequential file, the search must involve the time-consuming retrieval of records from bulk storage as each is considered in the search process. In contrast, the search of an index involves retrieving only the index from bulk storage and then searching through its entries within main memory. Consequently, the use of an index results in a significant reduction in the number of bulk storage accesses required during the search.

Index Organization

Consider now the question of index size. Since the index must be moved to main memory to be searched, it (or perhaps sections of it) must remain small enough to fit within a reasonable memory area. This requirement could produce problems if the number of records in the file were to become large. One popular technique used to overcome such a growth problem is based on the idea of using the index to find an approximate, rather than the precise, location of the desired record. This can be accomplished by first organizing the file in a sorted sequential order and then chopping it into short, multirecord segments. The index is then built to direct a search to the proper file segment rather than to an individual record. Note that this approach requires only one index entry per file segment rather than one per record, resulting in what is sometimes called a *partial index* (in contrast to a full index). In such cases, it is common for each segment to be represented in the index by its largest, and consequently its last, key field entry.

The partial-index structure is summarized in Figure 8-5 in which we have indicated only the key field entry in each record and have assumed that these entries are single, alphabetic letters. The retrieval of a record from this partial-index system

Figure 8-5 A file with a partial index

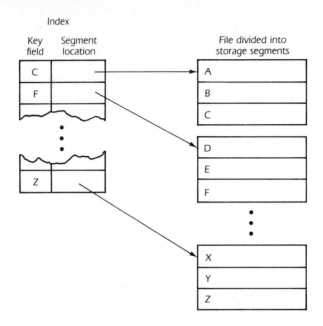

would consist of finding the first entry in the index that is equal to or greater than the desired entry and then searching the corresponding sequential segment for the target record. For example, to find the record with key field entry E in the file in Figure 8-5, we would follow the pointer associated with the index entry F and then search that segment to find the desired record.

A popular implementation of the partial-index idea is based on the physical characteristics of disk storage systems where the size of the file segments is chosen so that each segment fits on a separate track of the disk being used. When retrieving a record, one uses the index to determine which track contains the target record after which that track can be searched as a short, sequential file. You might expect that since larger segments mean a smaller index, the segment size should be chosen to fill the tracks completely. This is true if no records will be added to the file in the future. However, if file growth is anticipated, only a fraction (called the **load factor**) of each track is initially filled. This leaves room to insert new records where they properly belong. Of course, even a very small load factor does not guarantee that a segment will not ultimately outgrow its track. Thus, provisions are normally made to either split large segments into smaller ones or store the overflow records on a separate part of the disk.

Another approach to the large-index problem is to divide the index into pieces using the concept of an index to the index. Thus, the overall index would take on a layered or tree structure. We might envision such a system as an extension of the partial-index idea previously discussed. More precisely, if the sequential segments represented by the index entries were to become inefficiently large, we could construct a separate index for each of them. Thus, the original index would no longer direct the search to a file segment but rather to the correct segment index, which would then be used to find the location of the record in question.

We now turn from the concerns of index size to the topic of an index's internal structure. The efficiency obtained by transferring the search process from bulk storage to main memory through the use of an index does not mean that gains cannot be achieved by properly organizing the index internally. This, in fact, is an excellent example of data structure application. In particular, if the index is small, it might well be implemented as a sorted list as represented in Figure 8-5. However, for larger indexes it is common to use a tree structure, which allows the application of binary search techniques. The question ultimately becomes one of the anticipated use of the file (will it be static or constantly modified) and a case of search efficiency versus index maintenance.

Note that both index structures allow the file to be processed sequentially by properly traversing the index while retrieving the corresponding records. This property is important in our employee information example since we will still want to produce paychecks via a sequential process.

Programming Concerns

Just as with sequential files, many high-level languages provide instructions for manipulating records in an indexed file. By using such techniques, programs can be written without the programmer being concerned with the actual structure of the index system being applied. As an example, in FORTRAN a record in an indexed version of the employee file could be retrieved with a statement of the form:

> READ (10,150,REC = EMPLID,ERR = 950) NAME, ADDRESS, . . .

which is similar to the sequential file statement presented in Section 8-1. We have simply deleted the END phrase (since an EOF mark has no meaning when retrieving a particular record from an indexed file) and inserted the phrases REC = EMPLID and ERR = 950. The first phrase indicates that the RECord being sought is one with its key field entry equal to the value currently assigned to the variable EMPLID; the second phrase states that if such a record is not found (an ERRor condition), execution of the program should be transferred to the statement labeled 950.

In a similar manner the FORTRAN statement:

> WRITE (10,150,REC = EMPLID) NAME, ADDRESS, . . .

is used to store a record in the file. If a record already exists with a key field equal to the current value of EMPLID, the new record replaces the old one. However, if no record currently exists with that key field, a new record is inserted along with any updates needed in the index.

Questions/Exercises

1. Within a partial index, why is it advantageous to represent each segment of the file with its largest key field rather than its smallest? (Hint: Compare the algorithms needed to search the index in each case.)
2. The concepts of sequential and indexed files are often combined by supplying an index to an otherwise sequential file, producing what is called an indexed sequential file. What advantages does such an organization have?
3. Identify some pros and cons to organizing a file's index as a list rather than as a tree.
4. In the case of an inverted file, could both the primary and secondary indexes be organized as partial indexes using the technique presented in this section?

8–3 Hashed Files

Recall that the indexed file structures discussed in Section 8-2 can actually allow either of two file access techniques: sequential and direct. The first, which we have already discussed several times, refers to a file in which the method of accessing records is to start at the beginning and retrieve the records in a predetermined order. The second refers to a file in which any individual record can be retrieved without interrogating other records in the file. Files of this type are called *direct access* (or *random access*) files. Note that an indexed file can provide direct access characteristics yet allow the records to be processed in their sequential order by properly traversing the index.

As you might imagine, there is a price to pay for this duality. In particular, the overhead of maintaining the index can become a noticeable burden if the file is frequently modified. It is reasonable, therefore, to seek a more efficient means of obtaining the direct access feature in those situations that do not require sequential processing as well.

A popular structure that does exactly this is called a *hashed file*. In short, the idea is to compute the location of a record in bulk storage by applying some algorithm (the *hash algorithm*) to the value of the key field in question. The result is a system that (knowing the desired key field) can quickly determine the location of a record without the use of any auxiliary tables that would otherwise have to be maintained.

A Particular Hashing Technique

Let us take a more detailed look at the hashing concept by applying it to our employee file. First we divide the bulk storage area allotted to the file into several disjoint sections. How many sections we use is a design decision that we will return to later. For now let us assume that we have divided the storage region into 40 sections.

Next, assuming that records in the file will always be requested in terms of the employee identification number, we establish that field in each record as the key field.

Our first task is to convert any key field value into a numeric value. This step may seem meaningless to you since the key field is, in fact, the employee identification number. However, the actual value of this field may not be numeric. That is, identification "numbers" may take the form 25X3Z or J2–X35. On the other hand, recall that any information stored in the machine is represented in terms of a string of 0s and 1s. Thus, we can always interpret an item of data simply as a binary number whether or not that was the original intention when the data was coded.

Using this numeric interpretation we can divide any key field value stored in memory by the number of bulk storage sections, which in our case is 40. Note that the result of this division process will be an integer value called the quotient along with another integer value known as the remainder. The important point is that this remainder will always be in the range from 0 to 39. That is, if we consider only the remainder from the division, we will always find one of the 40 possible values 0, 1, 2, 3, . . . 39. Thus, we can relate exactly one of the bulk storage sections to each of these possible remainders (Figure 8-6).

With this system we can quickly convert any key field value into an integer (the remainder of the division) that identifies one of the sections of bulk storage, and we can use this system to determine the section in which to store the corresponding record. That is, we can consider each record individually, convert its key field value to an integer identifying a section of bulk storage through the division process, and then store the record in that section (as summarized in Figure 8-7). Later, if we needed to retrieve the record with a certain key field value, we could simply trans-

Figure 8-6 The rudiments of a hashing system

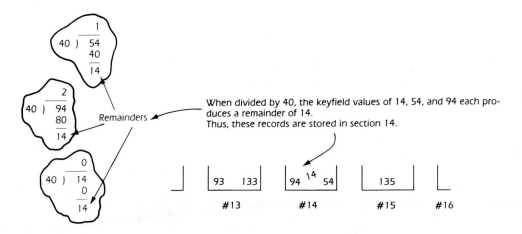

When divided by 40, the keyfield values of 14, 54, and 94 each produces a remainder of 14.
Thus, these records are stored in section 14.

Figure 8-7 Hashing the key field value 25X3Z to one of 40 storage sections

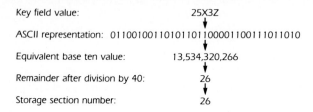

form this value to a section number as before, retrieve the records in that section, and then search the retrieved records for the one in question.

Distribution Problems

Our simplified explanation has thus far overlooked a few complications inherent in a hashed file. At the root of these complications is the fact that once we have chosen the hash algorithm, we have no more control over which sections of bulk storage will contain which records. In particular, if we were to use the divide-by-40 algorithm previously presented and if the numeric interpretation of the key field values tended to be multiples of 40, a disproportionate number of the records would be placed in the section assigned to the remainder zero. The result would be that when retrieving a record the search through the selected section could approximate a search through the entire file. Thus, we would have gained little advantage over a sequential file structure. Moreover, unless the storage sections are extremely large, some system must be provided for handling sections that overflow.

As a result of these potential problems, it is to our advantage to select a hash algorithm that will evenly distribute the records among the sections provided in bulk storage. However, the selection process is complicated by the fact that we normally do not know in advance exactly what the key field values will be (because of employee turnover, the employee identification numbers used today will not be those used tomorrow). Thus, the choice of a hash algorithm must be based on a combination of one's artistic abilities, statistical analysis, and rules of thumb.

One such rule of thumb concerns our decision to divide bulk storage into 40 sections, which is generally not a good choice. To see why, recall that if a dividend and a divisor both have a common factor, this factor will be present in the remainder. Thus, the numbers produced by the division process will tend to be multiples of this common factor while other values are ignored. We have already seen this effect when we conjectured the possibility of the key fields being multiples of 40 (which consistently produced remainders of zero). However, a similar problem would exist if the key fields were multiples of five. Since 40 is also a multiple of five, the factor of five would appear in the remainder of our division process, and the records in the file would cluster in those sections associated with the remainders 0, 5, 10, 15, 20, 25, 30, and 35.

Similar situations could occur in the case of key field values that are multiples of 2, 4, 8, 10, and 20 since they are all also factors of 40. Of course, the observation of this fact suggests a partial solution. That is, the chance of clustering due to this phenomenon could be minimized by selecting the number of sections to have as few factors as possible. Thus, one usually selects the number of bulk storage sections to be a prime number. For instance, the chance of clustering in the employee file example could be greatly reduced by dividing bulk storage into 41 sections rather than 40 since the only factors of 41 are 1 and 41.

Other attempts to reduce clustering involve the choice of hash algorithms based on principles other than division. For example, one technique (the midsquare method) is to multiply the key field value by itself and select the middle digits from the product to represent the section number. Still another (the extraction method) is to select the digits appearing in certain positions within the key field and construct the section number by combining these selected digits using some predetermined process. In any case one often tests the performance of several hash algorithms on sample records before settling on a final choice.

Unfortunately, regardless of the hash algorithm we ultimately use, clustering of records will most likely occur as a file is modified over a period of time. We can gain an understanding of how quickly this might occur by considering what would happen as we initially insert records into the modified 41-section employee file.

Assume that we have found a hash algorithm that arbitrarily distributes records among the sections, that our file is empty, and that we are going to insert records one at a time. When we insert the first record, that record must go into an empty section. However, when we insert the next record, only 40 of the 41 sections will be empty. Thus, the probability that the second record will be placed in an empty section is only 40/41. Assuming that the second record was placed in an empty section, the third would find only 39 empty sections, and the probability of its being placed in one of them is 39/41. Continuing this process we would find that if the first seven records were placed in empty sections, the eighth record would then have a 34/41 probability of being placed in one of the remaining empty sections.

This analysis allows us to compute the probability of all first eight records being placed in empty sections since it is the product of the probabilities of each record being placed in an empty section assuming that the preceding records were so placed. This probability is therefore

$$(41/41)(40/41)(39/41)(38/41)\dots(34/41) = .482$$

The point is that the result is less than one-half. That is, it is more likely than not that clustering will occur even with only eight records and 41 sections from which to choose.

Handling Section Overflow

We have seen that a hashed file should never be implemented under the assumption that clustering will not occur, thus some plan must be established for handling the problem. Our first approach might be to divide our allotted bulk storage into large sections that could accommodate numerous records before problems arise. But as already mentioned, this can result in an inefficient search when trying to retrieve a record; furthermore, such sections could still fill up over a period of time.

Ultimately, the file organization must allow for the fact that certain sections might fill up and that records that our hash algorithm says should go into these sections must then be placed elsewhere. A typical technique for handling this is to reserve an additional area of bulk storage to hold overflow records. With this arrangement, if a section fills up, future records that would normally be placed in it would be placed in the overflow area and linked to the appropriate section through an organization analogous to a linked list. With such a system a hashed file stored in five sections might ultimately have the structure as in Figure 8-8 in which the storage area actually occupied by records is indicated by shading. (Note that sections 1 and 4 have spilled into the overflow area, whereas one additional record in section 2 will cause section 2 to do the same.)

Observe that when trying to retrieve a record from a hashed file, one would first extract the proper section using the hash algorithm. If, however, the desired record was not found in that section, one would search the overflow records linked to that section.

We conclude that if a lot of overflowing takes place, the efficiency of searching the file can drop off significantly. Thus, the design of a hashed file requires a careful analysis involving the choice of the hash algorithm, the number and size of the

Figure 8-8 Handling section overflow

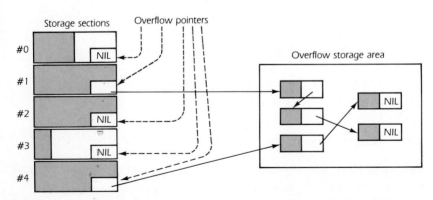

sections in bulk storage, and the size and structure of the overflow area to produce a file whose access will remain efficient over a long period of insertions and deletions of records.

Programming Concerns

We close our discussion of hashed files by considering their appearance to a programmer when using a high-level language. Once again we find that most of the technicalities are handled by the software system rather than by the programmer. In most cases all the programmer must do is provide a statement to the effect that a record having a particular key field value is to be retrieved or inserted relative to a particular file and, in the case of a retrieval, that program execution should be transferred to another location if such a record is not found. As with indexed files, the other details will be handled automatically. Thus, a high-level language statement instructing the retrieval or insertion of a record in a hashed file might look exactly like the corresponding statement for an indexed file.

The use of such automatic handling of hashed files does not give the programmer control over the hash algorithm being used but rather results in the use of some general-purpose algorithm provided by the software system. For this reason it is often advantageous to forgo the convenience of established hash systems and develop one's own routines. It is therefore more common to find indexed files than hashed files supported by high-level languages.

Questions/Exercises

1. Suppose an employee record system were to be implemented as a hashed file using 1000 sections of bulk storage with the Social Security number field as the key field. Observe that one possible hash algorithm would be to select the first three digits from the Social Security number since this would always result in a value between 0 and 999 inclusive. Why would this not be a good choice?
2. Explain how a poorly chosen hash algorithm could result in a hashed file system becoming little more than a sequential file.
3. Suppose a hashed file were constructed using the division hash algorithm as presented in the text but with six bulk storage sections. For each of the following key field values, identify the section in which the record with that key field value would be placed. What goes wrong and why?

    a. 24   c. 3   e. 15   g. 9   i. 27
    b. 30   d. 18   f. 21   h. 39   j. 0
4. How many people must be gathered together before the odds are that two members of the group will have birthdays on the same day of the year?
5. How might the concepts of a hashed file blend with the physical characteristics of disk storage?

8–4 **The Role of the Operating System**

We have seen that associated with each file structure is a variety of details relating to the retrieval or insertion of records. However, we concluded our discussion of each structure by indicating that such details are normally of no real concern when accessing the file by means of a high-level programming language. In this section we take a brief look at how this simplification is achieved.

Data Control Blocks

The manipulation of records in a file is normally handled by routines within the operating system. Indeed, a file is essentially an instance of an abstract data type— the underlying data structure being in bulk storage and the routines supporting the abstract image being a part of the operating system. Thus, those statements appearing in a programming language that request the manipulation of a file are really nothing more than calls to these routines.

Because different routines must be used for different file structures, it is necessary for the operating system to know what kind of file is being manipulated. In addition, the operating system must know such things as the blocking factor that was used in storing the file, the maximum record size, which item within a record is the key field (if applicable), and whether the file is to be saved after the program using it is finished. Furthermore, some items of information must be remembered by the operating system between the retrieval of one record and the next. Depending on the type of file being manipulated, this may include the current position in the file, which physical record is currently in memory, and whether any abnormal conditions occurred during the previous access (for example, in an indexed file, was the requested record actually found?).

To manage this information, the operating system maintains a table, often called a *data control block (DCB)* or file control block, for each file being processed. Here all the information relating to the processing of a single file is kept in an organized manner and made available to the various routines in the operating system as needed. Thus, if a program involves the processing of three files, the operating system must construct three data control blocks to assist in the file management.

Opening Files

You may have noticed that some of the items of information in a data control block are not supplied by the high-level language statements such as the READ and WRITE mentioned previously. It is therefore clear that the operating system must get information from another source. Moreover, the operating system must be told to construct the data control block in the first place.

For this purpose many programming languages provide a statement for requesting the construction of a data control block in addition to conveying the information that will not be supplied later in other statements and cannot be foreknown by the operating system. Such statements are often identified by the key word OPEN. For example, a typical statement would have a form similar to:

> OPEN "EMPLFILE" FOR INPUT AS FILE #10,
>   ORGANIZATION IS INDEXED,
>   ACCESS IS UPDATE,
>   KEY IS EMPLID

which requests the operating system to construct a data control block for the file named EMPLFILE. The information conveyed by this statement is that the file already exists in bulk storage (FOR INPUT), it will be referred to as file number 10 later in the program (AS FILE #10), it is an indexed file (ORGANIZATION IS INDEXED), it will be both read from and written to (ACCESS IS UPDATE), and the key field is the item named EMPLID (KEY IS EMPLID).

Options not explicitly described in the OPEN statement are normally given default values by the operating system. That is, most operating systems are programmed to assume certain values if not otherwise instructed. For example, it is common to assume that a file is sequential unless told otherwise. Thus, a request to open a sequential file named EMPLDATA might appear as the shortened statement:

> OPEN "EMPLDATA" FOR INPUT AS FILE #5

rather than stating what would be assumed anyway. One should note, however, that such use of defaults has the effect of removing some of the internal documentation from the written program, and thus care should be taken to ensure the program is readily readable by humans as well as by the machine.

Closing Files

Having been directed to construct a data control block, the operating system must also be told when it is no longer needed. After a file has been processed, most programming languages require the use of a CLOSE statement. Basically this statement informs the operating system that the memory space used for the data control block can be used for something else; however, in some settings the statement initiates more than this simple release of memory space. For instance, in the case of a sequential file that has been created by the program, the CLOSE statement often causes the operating system to write an EOF mark at the end of the file. In any case the syntax of the CLOSE statement is rarely anything more than a simple instruction such as:

> CLOSE #10

which means the file identified as file number 10 will no longer be used in the program (or if it is used again, it will be reOPENed).

Questions/Exercises

1. Identify the sequence of events followed by an operating system when retrieving a record from a partially indexed file.

2. What might be added to your answer to exercise 1 if the operating system is also controlling a time-sharing system?

3. Could a file that was originally built as a sequential file be OPENed as an indexed file?

Chapter 8 Review Problems

1. Suppose a sequential file is stored on a magnetic tape using a blocking factor of 5. If each of the physical blocks actually contained five logical records, what would be the ramifications (in terms of the following physical block structures) of adding another logical record to the early part of the file? (Why do you think files that will be expanded later are sometimes initially stored with only partially filled blocks?)

2. If the merge algorithm in Figure 8-3 is to be applied to two sequential files, does it matter which file plays the role of the master file and which plays the transaction file?

3. List the steps that would be executed in the merge algorithm in Figure 8-3 if the transaction file were actually empty at the start.

4. Modify the algorithm in Figure 8-3 to handle the case where a transaction record may have a key field value equal to a record already in the old master file. In this case, the transaction record should appear in the new master file and the old master record should be omitted.

5. Why must a high-level programming language statement for reading a record from a direct access file require more information than it would for reading a sequential file? What is this additional information?

6. How is processing a file on a tape similar to manipulating data in a queue? (Hint: Where is it most convenient to add a new record to the tape? From where is it most convenient to read a record?)

7. Would it be practical to use a sequential access storage device to implement a direct access file? How about a direct access device for a sequential file?

8. Explain how a single file could be implemented on a disk pack so that it could be processed as a sequential file with either of two different sequential orderings.

9. Why would a company-assigned employee identification number be a better choice for a key field than the last name of each employee?

10. In what sense is the advantage of an index lost if, to keep the index small, the segments used for a partial-index system are made extremely large?

11. Below is a table representing the contents of a partial index. Indicate which segment should be retrieved when searching for the record with each of the following key field values:
   a. 24X17   b. 12N67   c. 32E75   d. 26X28

Key field	Segment number
13C08	1
23G19	2
26X28	3
36Z05	4

12. Based on the index in problem 11, what is the largest key field value in the file? What do you know about the smallest?

13. If the only way to extract information from a hashed file is by actually hashing the key of each record, what information would be required to obtain a complete listing of all the records?

14. If a hashed file were partitioned into 10 storage sections, what would be the probability of at least two of three arbitrary records hashing to the same section? (Assume the hash algorithm gives no section priority over the others.) How many records must be stored in the file until it is more likely for clustering to have occurred than not?

15. If we are using the division technique discussed in this chapter as a hash algorithm and the file storage area is divided into 23 sections, which section should we search to find the record whose key field value, when interpreted as a binary value, reduces to the integer 124?

16. If the division hash algorithm as presented in the text is being used, why is clustering more likely to occur when the file storage space is divided into 60 sections rather than 61?

17. Why might it be advantageous to keep the list of overflow records (from a section in a hashed file) sorted according to key field values?

18. If we divided the storage area for a hashed file into 41 sections that could each hold exactly one record, we would expect at least one section to overflow after only 8 records had been stored. On the other hand, if we combined the same storage area into one section that could hold 41 records, we could always store 41 records before overflow would occur. What keeps us from deciding to implement hashed files using this latter configuration?

19. Suppose a record's key field value is XYZ. Using the division technique for hashing discussed in the text, convert this value into the section number that should contain the record in a hashed file consisting of 41 sections. (Assume characters are stored using ASCII.)

20. List three items of information that an operating system might store in a data control block.

Problems for the Programmer

1. Assume the existence of a sequential file pertaining to airline flights with three fields: the first is the flight number (used as the key field), the second is the three-letter code of the origin airport, and the third is the three-letter code for the destination airport. Write a program that accepts an origin code and a destination code from the terminal, searches the file, and either prints the flight numbers of all flights between those airports or reports that there are no such flights, if such is the case.

2. Write a program based on the merge algorithm that allows the addition of flights to the airline file of programming problem 1.

3. Using the record structure of programming problem 1, modify the merge algorithm to allow both the addition of new flights and the modification of the information about existing flights.

4. Assume that the airline file described in programming problem 1 is indexed by the key field flight number. Write a program that will accept a flight number from the terminal and respond by printing the information about that flight or respond with a message that there is no such flight.

5. Extend the program written for programming problem 4 so that once the correct flight is found a search is made to print all other flight numbers of flights between the same airports as the requested flight.

6. Write a program to check the spelling of words. That is, your program should accept a word typed at the terminal, compare the word to its dictionary, and report whether or not the word was found. Do not search the dictionary sequentially but use a hashing system to narrow the search to a section of the dictionary. (Use a dictionary of at least 100 words.)

7. Write a program to perform the hash algorithm discussed in Section 8-3. Using this program, experiment with the effects of dividing the available bulk storage area into 40 versus 41 sections.

9 Database Structures

9–1 **The Database Concept**
9–2 **Conceptual Versus Physical Organization**
9–3 **The Relational Model**
    Relational Design
    Relational Operations
9–4 **The Network Model**
    Network Design
    Network Operations
9–5 **The Hierarchical Model**
    Hierarchical Design
    Hierarchical Operations

This final chapter regarding data organization represents a combination of the techniques of data structures and file structures discussed previously. Indeed, a database is formed by combining techniques from both these more traditional areas to obtain a single bulk storage data system that can appear to have a multitude of organizations for serving a variety of applications. Such structures eliminate the redundancy (providing separate data systems for each application even though these applications may require much of the same information) found in the more traditional file-oriented approach.

9–1 The Database Concept

The term *database* has evolved through its use in the popular press, in the business world, and among computer scientists. It is not surprising therefore to find varying definitions of the term, depending on whom you ask. Loosely speaking, any collection of data could be considered a database, although the term is usually reserved to mean a collection of data stored in bulk storage that can take on a variety of appearances depending on the requirements at the time and can thus serve as the data source for a variety of applications.

We have already seen an elementary example of this phenomenon in our discussion of employee records in Chapter 8. For example, we envisioned times such as during payroll processing when we would want the information involved to appear as a sequential file, while on other occasions, as in general employee information retrieval, a direct access configuration would be more convenient. We discovered that record storage based on an indexed system could provide this dual appearance, and some would argue that such indexed files are simple databases. Others, citing the diversity achievable through large modern databases, would say that this example is merely an amoeba in the evolution of databases. After all, databases in use today contain information encompassing the full spectrum of business activities and can provide access to selected portions of this data in a variety of formats.

To grasp a fuller meaning of the term *database,* we might look at the concept from the opposite direction. That is, we have just introduced a database as a data collection injected with the ability to emulate a variety of organizational forms depending on the needs of the application. From the other point of view, one often considers a database as the result of combining a variety of data collections (each of which was originally designed for a particular application) into a single integrated collection.

Again we find an elementary example in an employee data system where the information requirements of a business might be handled initially by two independent systems: one based on a sequential file from which payroll could be processed and the other built around a hashed file to support the requirements of the personnel department. Redesigning the two systems as specialized applications of a single indexed file structure captures much of the flavor of the database concept but this time as a consolidation technique.

The consolidation approach to the database concept is perhaps the more popular point of view since it reflects the historical development of automated data storage and maintenance. As computing machinery found wider and wider uses in information management, each application tended to be implemented as a separate system with its own collection of data. Typically, the need to process payroll gave rise to a sequential file, and later the need for on-line data retrieval produced an entirely different system using a direct access file.

Although each of these systems represented an improvement over the corresponding manual techniques previously used, taken as a whole the collection of individual automated systems still constituted a limited and inefficient use of resources when compared to the possibilities of a combined database system. For example, different departments were not able to share data needed by both, and thus much of the information required by an organization was duplicated in storage. The result was that when an employee moved, visits were required to numerous departments throughout the organization where address change cards were filed. Typographical errors, misplaced cards, and employee apathy could soon result in erroneous and conflicting data within the various data systems. Thus, after a move, an employee's newsletter might begin to arrive at the new address but with the wrong name while

Figure 9-1 A file versus a database organization

File-Oriented information system:

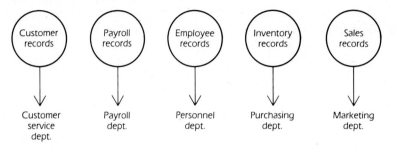

Database-Oriented information system:

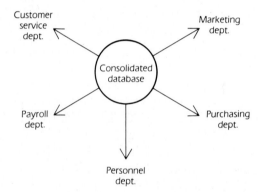

the payroll records could continue to reflect the old address. In this atmosphere, database systems emerged as a means of consolidating the information stored and maintained by a particular organization (Figure 9-1). With such a system both payroll and the mailing of newsletters could be processed from a single integrated data system.

Although such consolidation does not totally remove the possibility of incorrect data, it significantly reduces the chance of error (since the update process is not diversified) and simplifies the correction of those errors that do occur (since any incorrect information is stored in only one location in the overall system).

Another major advantage of a consolidated data system is the control achieved by an organization when the information it owns is placed in one common pot. As long as each department has complete control over its own data, that data tends to be used for the good of the department rather than for the good of the organization. In contrast, when database systems are implemented in a large organization, the control of data is normally concentrated in the administrative position known as *database administrator (DBA)*, which may or may not consist of a single individual. This central administrator (or administrative position) is cognizant of both the data available within the organization and the needs of the various departments. It is thus within this structure that decisions regarding data organization and access can be made with the entire organization in mind.

Along with the benefits of data consolidation come disadvantages as well. One significant concern is the control of access to sensitive data. For example, someone working on the organization's newsletter might need access to employee names and addresses but should not have access to payroll data; similarly an employee processing payroll should not have access to the other financial records of the corporation. The ability to control access to the information in the database is often as important as the ability to share it.

In recognition of the advantages of consolidated systems, data storage in terms of simple file organizations is giving way to integrated database systems. Such consolidated systems together with interactive techniques have given rise to an explosion in administrative use of computing along with a corresponding proliferation of terminology to reflect the variations in applications. Today one hears of management information systems, decision support systems, and business support systems, all of which are becoming major topics in business administration. Since our purpose, however, is the study of the database systems themselves, we do not pursue these additional topics here.

Questions/Exercises
1. Identify two departments in a manufacturing plant that would have different uses for the same or similar inventory information.
2. Identify a variety of data collections found in a university environment that might be collected into one common database.

9–2 Conceptual Versus Physical Organization

To give you a proper perspective for the database models discussed in the following three sections, we reserve this section for a discussion of the overall picture of a database implementation. The major theme here involves the distinction between a conceptual organization and the actual organization, which plays an important role in disguising the complexities of the actual data storage system. The ultimate goal is to make the information contained in the database readily accessible to a person without requiring that person to have computer expertise.

We will refer to this person as the user, or at times as the end user. You may imagine this person being an airline reservation clerk who interrogates the database from a terminal at an airport counter or perhaps an executive who retrieves information from the database at a CRT terminal in an office. (Database systems are also used in batch processing environments, but for our purposes we concentrate on the increasingly popular interactive systems.) In either case, the user is most likely not trained in computer science and should not be required to consider the details of computer technology and techniques but rather should be allowed to concentrate on the problems of the application at hand. It is therefore the duty of the overall database system to present its information in terms of the application and not in computer gibberish.

To accomplish this goal in an organized manner, a database installation is constructed from layers (Figure 9-2). The image of the data given to the end user is produced by the *application software*, which is normally a system of programs, often written by the programming staff within the business itself, that communicates with the user in an interactive manner and in the application's terminology. It is in the design of this software that the overall system is given its personality. It may, for example, communicate with the user through such means as a question-and-answer dialogue or a fill-in-the-blank scenario. Regardless of the user interface ultimately adopted, the application software communicates with the user to learn what information is required and later, having obtained the requested information, presents it to the user in a meaningful format.

Note that we did not say that the application software retrieves the information from the database. The actual manipulation of the database is accomplished by another software package called the *database management system (DBMS)*. This dichotomy has several benefits. One is that the division of duties simplifies the design process. Just as the end user's task would be complicated by the requirement to consider computer concepts along with the task of solving a problem in the application world, the application programmer's task would be more complex if the actual data manipulation were a part of the application software.

Another and perhaps more important reason for separating the user interface and actual data manipulation into two different software packages is the goal of *data independence*. This refers to the ability to change the organization of the data-

Figure 9-2 The conceptual layers of a database

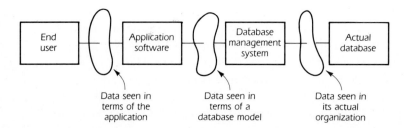

base itself without changing the application software. For example, the personnel department might need to add an additional field to each employee's record to indicate whether or not the corresponding employee chose to participate in the company's new health insurance program. If the application software dealt directly with the database, such a change in the data's format would be reflected in the need to modify all other application programs dealing with the same database. Thus, the change required by the personnel department would cause changes to the payroll program as well as to the program for printing mailing labels for the company's newsletter. In contrast, database management systems are designed so that changes to the actual database structure can be reflected in some application programs while being hidden from others.

We can see that the data organization presented to the application program by the database management system is not the actual organization but a modified, or conceptual, version of it. Although this modified version could take on a number of different forms, it is customary to present the database to the application software in the form of one of the popular database models that we discuss in the following sections. These models allow the application software to be written as though the data were stored in tables with rows and columns (the *relational model*), grouped according to common characteristics (the *network model*), or presented as a sequence of trees (the *hierarchical model*).

We have seen similar disguises in several instances. For example, we have seen that a row of main memory cells can be made to appear as a rectangular array, a stack, a queue, or a tree. In such cases software routines are used to translate requests in terms of the conceptual structure (such as push and pop) into the proper activities in the actual storage organization. In a similar manner, a database management system consists of a collection of similar routines that can be used as subprograms in the application software to convert commands in terms of the database model into the terms of the actual data storage. Thus, a database is essentially an instance of a very elaborate abstract data type.

More precisely, application software is normally written in general purpose programming languages such as those discussed in Chapter 5. These languages provide the basic ingredients for algorithm expression but lack the operations that make manipulation of the database convenient. The routines provided by the database management system in effect extend the capabilities of the language being used (as we see in the following sections). This concept of the general purpose language being the original system to which the capabilities of the database management system are added results in the original language being referred to as the *host language*. (Many commercial database management system packages today are actually combinations of the traditional database system and a host language. This tends to disguise the two as one, although the distinction still exists within.)

Figure 9-3 An onion-skin diagram of a database system

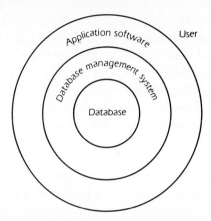

In summary, a database system is constructed from layers in much the same manner as an operating system. In fact, the onion-skin diagram used to describe the architecture of an operating system is also quite applicable here (Figure 9-3). We envision the outer layer in a database system as consisting of the application software since this software unit communicates with the user in much the same manner as does an operating system's command processor. Within this layer is the database management system, which in turn communicates with the database itself.

To develop application software for a database installation, a programmer must understand the features provided by the database management system being used. This is the subject of the remaining sections of this chapter. We will be looking through the eyes of the application programmer at the database models available from popular database management systems. Our goal is to develop an elementary understanding of the features provided, the consequences of these features, and how they simplify the task of designing the application software.

Questions/Exercises

1. Does the use of a common indexed file for both payroll processing and interactive data retrieval provide data independence?

2. In a form similar to Figure 9-2, draw a diagram representing the machine language, high-level language, and end-user views of a computer.

3. Summarize the roles of the application software, the database management system, and the actual data-manipulating routines in retrieving information from a database.

4. Is it possible to build hardware so that the database is actually stored in the form of the database model, thereby removing the need for the database management system?

9–3 The Relational Model

The first data model we discuss is the relational model, which is the most popular database model today. Its popularity stems from the simplicity of its structure. It portrays data as being stored in tables called *relations*, which are the formats often chosen for use in precomputer manual systems. More precisely, the relational model allows information regarding the employees of a firm to be represented by a relation such as that in Figure 9-4.

A row in a relation is called a *tuple*. Thus, in the relation of Figure 9-4, tuples consist of the information about a particular employee. Columns in a relation are referred to as *attributes* since each entry in a column describes some characteristic, or attribute, of the entity represented by the corresponding tuple.

Relational Design

The design of a database in terms of the relational model centers around the design of the relations making up the database. Although this may appear to be a simple task, many subtleties are waiting to trap the unwary designer. Because the identification and understanding of these subtleties is a major concern in computer science today, we should take a moment to touch on the problems involved.

We begin by supposing that in addition to the information contained in the relation of Figure 9-4 we wish to include information about the jobs held by the employees. Thus, associated with each employee we may want to include a job history consisting of such attributes as job title (secretary, office manager, floor supervisor), a job identification code (unique to each job), the skill code associated with each job, the department in which the job exists, and the period during which the employee held the job in terms of a starting date and termination date. (We use an asterisk as the termination date if the job represents the employee's current position.)

One approach to this problem is to extend the relation in Figure 9-4 to include these attributes as additional columns in the table, as shown in Figure 9-5. However, close examination of the result reveals several problems. One is a significant lack of efficiency.

Figure 9-4 A relation containing employee information

EMPL–ID	NAME	ADDRESS	SSNUM
25X15	Joe E. Baker	33 Nowhere St.	111223333
34Y70	Cheryl H. Clark	563 Downtown Ave.	999009999
23Y34	G. Jerry Smith	1555 Circle Dr.	111005555
.	.	.	.
.	.	.	.
.	.	.	.

Figure 9-5 A relation containing redundancy
(Note: The personal information about Baker and Smith is repeated because they have held more than one job. Also duplicated is the description of the floor manager job because it has been held by more than one person.)

EMPL–ID	NAME	ADDRESS	SSNUM	JOB–ID	JOB–TITLE	SKILL–CODE	DEPT	START–DATE	TERM–DATE
25X15	Joe E. Baker	33 Nowhere St.	111223333	F5	Floor manager	FM3	Sales	9-1-81	9-30-83
25X15	Joe E. Baker	33 Nowhere St.	111223333	D7	Dept. head	D2	Sales	10-1-83	*
34Y70	Cheryl H. Clark	563 Downtown Ave.	999009999	F5	Floor manager	FM3	Sales	10-1-83	*
23Y34	G. Jerry Smith	1555 Circle Dr.	111005555	S25X	Secretary	T5	Personnel	3-1-81	4-30-82
23Y34	G. Jerry Smith	1555 Circle Dr.	111005555	S25Z	Secretary	T6	Accounting	5-1-82	*
.	.	.	.	.	.	.	.	.	.
.	.	.	.	.	.	.	.	.	.
.	.	.	.	.	.	.	.	.	.

In particular, the relation would no longer contain one tuple for each employee but rather one tuple for each assignment of an employee to a job. Thus, if an employee had advanced in the company through a sequence of several jobs, several tuples in the new relation would be dedicated to that single employee. The problem with this is that the information contained in the original relation (each employee's name, address, identification number, and Social Security number) must be repeated. Moreover, if a particular job has been held by numerous employees, the department associated with that job along with the appropriate skill code must be identified in each tuple representing an assignment of the job. Of course, this repetition of data need not be present in the actual storage system since it could be simulated from a single source by the database management system. But if the need for this repetition could be avoided in the first place, the overall database system would be more efficient.

Another, perhaps more serious problem with our extended relation surfaces when we consider deleting information from the database. Suppose, for example, that Joe E. Baker has been the only employee to hold the job with JOB–ID D7. If he were to leave the company and be deleted from the database represented in Figure 9-5, we would lose the information about job D7. Indeed, the only tuple containing the fact that job D7 requires a skill level of D2 is the tuple relating to Joe Baker. Thus, if we deleted all references to Joe Baker and then returned to the database to retrieve information about the job D7, we would not find the needed data.

You might argue that the ability to erase only a portion of a tuple could solve the problem, but this would in turn introduce other complications. (Should the information relating to job F5 also be retained in a partial tuple or does this data reside elsewhere in the relation?) Moreover, the temptation to use partial tuples is a strong indication that the design of the relation is not compatible with the application.

The source of these problems is that we are trying to combine more than one concept into a single relation. More precisely, the extended relation would contain information dealing directly with employees (name, identification number, address, Social Security number), information about the jobs available in the company (job identification, job title, department, skill code), and information regarding the relationship between employees and jobs (start date, termination date). Having made this observation, we find that our problems can be solved by redesigning the system in terms of three relations—one for each of the preceding topics. Thus, we might keep the original relation (which we now call the EMPLOYEE relation) as it was and insert the additional information in the form of the two new relations called JOB and ASSIGNMENT, which produces the database in Figure 9-6.

Note that a database consisting of these three relations contains the pertinent information about employees through the EMPLOYEE relation, about available jobs through the JOB relation, and about job history through the ASSIGNMENT relation. Additional information is implicitly available by combining the information from different relations. For instance, we can find the departments in which a given employee has worked by first finding all the jobs that employee has held using the ASSIGNMENT relation and then finding the departments associated with these

Figure 9-6 An employee database consisting of three relations

EMPLOYEE relation

EMPL–ID	NAME	ADDRESS	SSNUM
25X15	Joe E. Baker	33 Nowhere St.	111223333
34Y70	Cheryl H. Clark	563 Downtown Ave.	999009999
23Y34	G. Jerry Smith	1555 Circle Dr.	1110055555
.	.	.	.
.	.	.	.
.	.	.	.

JOB relation

JOB–ID	JOB–TITLE	SKILL–CODE	DEPT
S25X	Secretary	T5	Personnel
S26Z	Secretary	T6	Accounting
F5	Floor manager	FM3	Sales
.	.	.	.
.	.	.	.
.	.	.	.

ASSIGNMENT relation

EMPL–ID	JOB–ID	START–DATE	TERM–DATE
23Y34	S25X	3-1-81	5-1-82
34Y70	F5	10-1-83	*
23Y34	S26Z	5-1-82	*
.	.	.	.
.	.	.	.
.	.	.	.

Figure 9-7 A three-attribute relation of employees, jobs, and departments

jobs by means of the JOB relation. Through processes such as this any information that could have been obtained from the single large relation can be obtained from the three smaller relations without the problems previously cited.

Unfortunately, dividing information into various relations is not always as trouble free as in the preceding example. For instance, consider the relation in Figure 9-7 having attributes EMPL–ID, JOB–TITLE, and DEPT as compared to its decomposition into the two relations in Figure 9-8.

At first glance, the two-relation system may appear to contain the same information as the single-relation system, when in fact it does not. Consider, for example, the problem of finding the department in which a given employee works. This is easily done in the single-relation system by interrogating the tuple containing the employee identification number of the target employee and extracting the corresponding department. However, in the two-relation system the desired information is not necessarily available. We can find the job title of the target employee and a department having such a job, but this does not necessarily mean that the target employee works in that particular department since several departments may have jobs with the same title.

Thus, at times a relation can be decomposed into smaller relations without losing information (called a ***nonloss decomposition***); and at other times information will be lost. The classification of such characteristics has been, and still is, a concern in computer science. Questions concerning the properties of relations have resulted in a hierarchy of relation classes called first normal form, second normal form, third normal form, etc., with the relations in each class being more conducive to use in a database than those in the preceding class.

Relational Operations

Now that you have a basic understanding of the structure involved in the relational model, it is time to see how such an organization can be used from a programmer's

Figure 9-8 Two relations containing information about employees, jobs, and departments

point of view. We begin with a look at some operations that we may wish to perform on a relation or relations.

First note that there will be times when we will need to select certain tuples from a relation. For example, to retrieve the information about an employee we would need to select the tuple with the appropriate identification attribute value from the EMPLOYEE relation, or to obtain a list of the job titles in a certain department we must select the tuples from the JOB relation having that department as their department attribute. Note also that the result of this selection will be another relation (another table) consisting of the tuples selected from the parent relation. (The outcome of selecting information about a particular employee results in a relation containing only one tuple from the EMPLOYEE relation. The outcome of selecting the tuples associated with a certain department probably results in several tuples from the JOB relation.)

Consequently, one operation we may wish to perform on a relation is to select from one relation those tuples possessing certain characteristics and to place these selected tuples in a new relation. To express this operation, we adopt the COBOLish syntax of the form:

SELECT FROM EMPLOYEE WHERE EMPL–ID EQUALS "25Y64" GIVING NEW

The semantics of this statement is to create a new relation called NEW containing those tuples (there should be only one in this case) from the relation EMPLOYEE whose EMPL–ID attribute equals 25Y64.

In contrast to the SELECT operation that extracts rows from a relation is the PROJECT operation that extracts columns. Suppose, for example, that in searching for the job titles in a certain department we had already SELECTed the tuples from the JOB relation that pertained to the target department and placed these tuples in a new relation called NEW1. The list we are seeking is the JOB–TITLE column within this new relation. The PROJECT operation allows us to extract this column (or columns if required) and place the result in a new relation. Again, in our CO-BOLish syntax, we might write:

PROJECT JOB–TITLE FROM NEW1 GIVING NEW2

The result would be the creation of another new relation (called NEW2) that contains the single column of values from the JOB–TITLE column of relation NEW1.

As another example of the PROJECT operation, the statement:

PROJECT NAME, ADDRESS FROM EMPLOYEE GIVING MAIL–REL

could be used to obtain a listing of the names and addresses of all employees. This list would be in the newly created (two-column) relation called MAIL–REL.

The third operation is used to combine different relations into one. Let us call it the MULTIPLY operation. By way of introduction, suppose we wished to obtain a listing of all employee identification numbers along with the department in which each employee works. Our first observation might be that in contrast to the previous examples, the data required this time is distributed over more than one relation, and thus the process of retrieving the information must entail more than SELEC-Tions and PROJECTions.

The operation of MULTIPLYing the ASSIGNMENT relation by the JOB relation turns out to be the weapon we need, so let us look at what the product of two relations actually is. First we consider the smaller example of MULTIPLYing a relation A with attributes W and X by a relation B with attributes Y and Z to obtain a relation C (Figure 9-9).

Observe that the attributes of the product are in fact the attributes from the original relations, except that we have used the original relation names as prefixes to indicate which relation initially contributed which attribute. (This naming convention is designed to assure that the attributes in the product have unique names even though the original relations may have common attribute names.) The actual entries in the product relation are formed by combining each tuple from the first relation with each of the tuples from the second relation. Thus, if one relation had 4 attributes and 2 tuples and another had 3 attributes and 5 tuples, their product would contain 7 attributes and 10 tuples.

To express the multiplication of A by B as just defined, we use the syntax:

MULTIPLY A BY B GIVING C

(In reality, the word MULTIPLY is rarely used in an actual programming syntax since it may conflict with the more traditional use of the term. In fact, most database

Figure 9-9 A relation multiplication where relation C is the product of relations A and B

Relation A

W	X
1	2
3	4

Relation B

Y	Z
5	6
7	8
9	10

Relation C (the product of A times B)

A.W	A.X	B.Y	B.Z
1	2	5	6
1	2	7	8
1	2	9	10
3	4	5	6
3	4	7	8
3	4	9	10

systems use several variations of the MULTIPLY operation to obtain the capabilities provided by the single, more general-purpose MULTIPLY.)

Returning now to the problem of obtaining a list of all employee identification numbers along with their corresponding departments, we see that the following sequence will do the trick. That is, the final relation LIST will be the list we want. (Recall that a termination date of * indicates an employee's current job.)

```
MULTIPLY ASSIGNMENT BY JOB GIVING NEW1.
SELECT FROM NEW1 WHERE ASSIGNMENT.JOB–ID EQUALS
   JOB.JOB–ID GIVING NEW2.
SELECT FROM NEW2 WHERE ASSIGNMENT.TERM–DATE EQUALS "*"
   GIVING NEW3.
PROJECT ASSIGNMENT.EMPL–ID, JOB.DEPT FROM NEW3 GIVING LIST.
```

Before closing this section, we return to the overall picture of a database system to see where the relational model fits. Remember that the data in a database is actually stored in terms of a bulk storage system. To relieve the application programmer from these concerns as well as for other reasons, a database management system is provided that allows the application software to be written in terms of a database model such as the relational system we have been discussing. It is the duty of the database management system to accept commands in terms of the relational model and convert them into actions relative to the actual storage structure. This is done by providing a collection of subprograms that can be used within the application software. Normally one subprogram is provided for each operation that may need to be performed on the model. Thus, a database management system using the relational model would include routines to perform the SELECT, PROJECT, and MULTIPLY operations, which could then be called from the application software using a syntactic structure compatible with the host language. In this manner, the application software can be written as though the data were actually stored in the simple tabular form of the relational model.

Questions/Exercises

1. Answer the following questions based on the partial information given in the EMPLOYEE, JOB, and ASSIGNMENT relations in Figure 9-6:
   a. Who is the secretary in the accounting department with experience in the personnel department?
   b. Who is the floor manager in the sales department?
   c. What job does G. Jerry Smith currently hold?
2. Based on the EMPLOYEE, JOB, and ASSIGNMENT relations presented in Figure 9-6, write a sequence of commands in our COBOLish syntax to obtain a list of all job titles within the personnel department.
3. Based on the EMPLOYEE, JOB, and ASSIGNMENT relations presented in Figure 9-6, write a sequence of commands in our COBOLish syntax to obtain a list of employee names along with the employees' departments.

4. How does the relational model provide for data independence?
5. How are the different relations in a relational database tied together?

9–4 **The Network Model**

The second database model for consideration is the network model, which, having undergone extensive standardization efforts, probably shows more consistency among its implementations than the other models available in commercial database management systems. Most of the terminology introduced in this section is a result of this standardization effort as it originates in the proposals of the Data Base Task Group (DBTG) of the Conference on Data Systems Languages (CODASYL). Many refer to the database model presented here as the DBTG model. (CODASYL is the same group responsible for the standardization of COBOL.)

The basic building block in a network database is the structure referred to as a *set*, which consists of a collection of information called the *owner* of the set and a varying number of other collections called *members* of the set. These member collections are attached to the owner via a linkage system similar to that of a linked list. Set structures are used to represent such relationships as found between a magazine (owner) and its subscribers (members), a business (owner) and its departments (members), or a course (owner) and its prerequisites (members).

In contrast to the structure of a simple linked list in which the last pointer is NIL, the last pointer in a set structure points back to the owner of the set where the head pointer is stored. Thus, beginning at a set's owner, one can easily find all the members of the set and return to the owner.

The result of this set structure approach to data storage is a database that contains a network of paths that can be followed by the user to find the information required at the time. Such a model closely reflects the way data is actually stored in bulk storage, which is, no doubt, why the network model was developed well before the more conceptual relational model.

Network Design

As in Section 9-3, we will discuss the network model in the context of constructing a database containing information about employees and their job histories within a company. Our first task is to identify the items of information about employees (name, address, identification number, Social Security number) that we wish to have in the database. If we were going to store this information on paper in a traditional filing cabinet, we might at this point design a form, called the EMPLOYEE form, with a space in which to record each of these items and have the print shop print several copies of it. As each employee joined the company, we could fill out an EMPLOYEE form and file it in the cabinet.

The process when creating a network database is quite similar, except that a form is called a **group** and it is not an organization on paper but rather an organization in a machine's bulk storage. We distinguish between this mere organization (or a blank form) and a collection of data having this organization (a filled-in form) by referring to the latter as an occurrence of the group or sometimes a **group occurrence.**

At this point, our concept of the database is that of several occurrences of the EMPLOYEE group (one for each employee) scattered over bulk storage. Since there will most likely be times that we will need to interrogate each of these group occurrences systematically, we will link them together as a linked list, except that we adjust the last pointer to point back to the head pointer rather than being NIL. The result is an example of the set structure described earlier, with the head pointer playing the role of the set owner and the occurrences of the EMPLOYEE group being the members. This example of a set owner is a special case since it does not constitute a collection of data in the same sense as the EMPLOYEE group occurrences. However, we will see in a moment that this special case serves as an entry point to the database. For now we note that the network model allows for such a special set owner and refers to it (or to collections of them) by the term **area.**

The database as designed thus far is represented in Figure 9-10. Rectangles represent group occurrences (with the group name nearby) and arrows represent the pointers. (The dots indicate that the picture is not complete.) As well, you will note that we have named the set EMPLOYEE–SET and placed this name in the diagram.

Our next step might be to incorporate each employee's job history in the database. One approach to this would be to design another group called JOB–ASSIGNMENT to contain information about a job and its assignment (job identification number, job title, skill code, department, start date, termination date), store one occurrence of this group for each job assignment made in the company,

Figure 9-10 Employees as members of a set

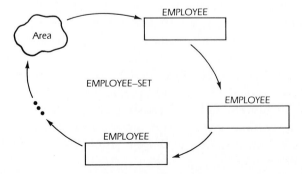

Figure 9-11 Employees as members of the EMPLOYEE–SET and owners of ASSIGNMENT–SETs

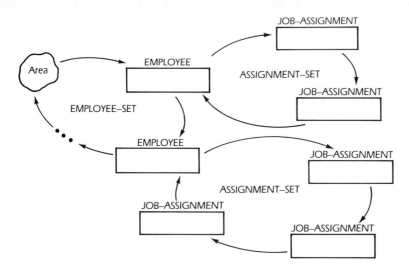

and link the occurrences with the appropriate EMPLOYEE to form several ASSIGN-MENT–SETs, each consisting of an EMPLOYEE as owner and JOB–ASSIGNMENTs as members. The result would be a structure as shown in Figure 9-11.

This arrangement, however, results in a significant amount of repetition. If a job has been assigned to several employees over the years, information about it will appear in the job history of each of these employees. Moreover, if we deleted all the employees who had held a given job, we would lose the information about that job as well.

Consequently, designers of network databases would never adopt this approach. Rather, they would divide the JOB–ASSIGNMENT group into two groups called perhaps JOB and ASSIGNMENT, with the JOB group containing information relating only to the job (job identification, job title, skill code, department) and the ASSIGNMENT group containing information relating to the assignment of an employee to a job (start date, termination date). An occurrence of the JOB group would be stored for each job in the company, and these group occurrences would be linked together forming a set called JOB–SET owned by the area. At this point the database would have the structure shown in Figure 9-12.

With this arrangement established, EMPLOYEEs and JOBs would be associated by means of the ASSIGNMENT group. This would be done by allowing each EMPLOYEE to own a set of ASSIGNMENTs via a set structure we will call the WORK–HISTORY set, while at the same time each JOB is given ownership to a set of ASSIGNMENTs through a set structure we will call the FILLED–BY set. Each

Figure 9-12 A database containing employees and jobs

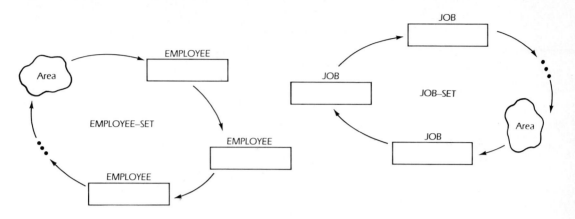

time an employee is assigned a job, a new occurrence of the ASSIGNMENT group would be stored with the appropriate date information. This new group occurrence would then be placed in the WORK–HISTORY set owned by the EMPLOYEE involved and in the FILLED–BY set owned by the JOB being assigned. The result would be a database with the structure shown in Figure 9-13.

Network Operations

To gain an understanding of the operations required to interrogate a network database, consider the question of finding the job history of the second EMPLOYEE in the EMPLOYEE–SET of Figure 9-13. We begin by noting that this EMPLOYEE has held two positions in the company as indicated by the fact that there are two ASSIGNMENTs in its WORK–HISTORY set. We can also see that these JOBs are the first and second JOBS in the JOB–SET since these are the JOBs that own those ASSIGNMENTs also owned by the target EMPLOYEE. Intuitively, we found this information by traversing the WORK–HISTORY set owned by the EMPLOYEE in question while stopping at each member to find the owner of that corresponding FILLED–BY set. This suggests that the operations we need to interrogate a network database include the ability to move to the next entry in a set and the ability to move directly to the owner of a set.

These operations are traditionally implemented in the form of two commands called FIND–NEXT and FIND–OWNER. The first is used to advance one entry in the identified set. In particular, we use the syntax

FIND–NEXT set name

where in place of set name we will insert the actual name of the set in question.

Figure 9-13 The structure of the complete database

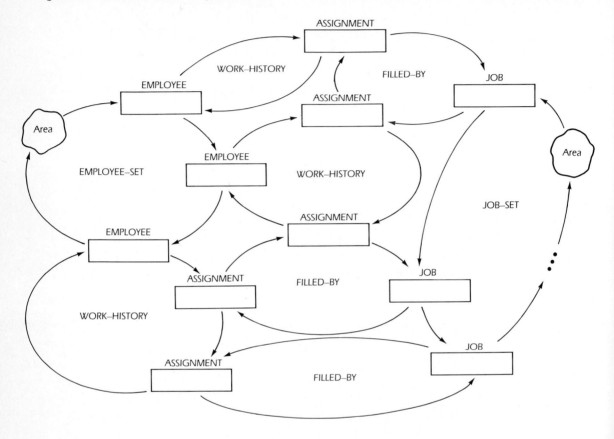

The second operation is used to advance directly to the owner of the target set. We will use the syntax:

FIND–OWNER *set name*

where again an actual name of a set is to be substituted in place of *set name*.

To understand how these two commands can actually be used to maneuver within a database, it is important to realize that both commands request action relative to a previously established position. A request to find the next entry in a set implies the existence of a current entry (which may be the owner or a member). Moreover, a request to find the owner of a set requires more specification than just the set name. For example, the command FIND–OWNER FILLED–BY alone would be ambiguous in the database of Figure 9-13 since there are several instances of the FILLED–BY set in the database.

Figure 9-14

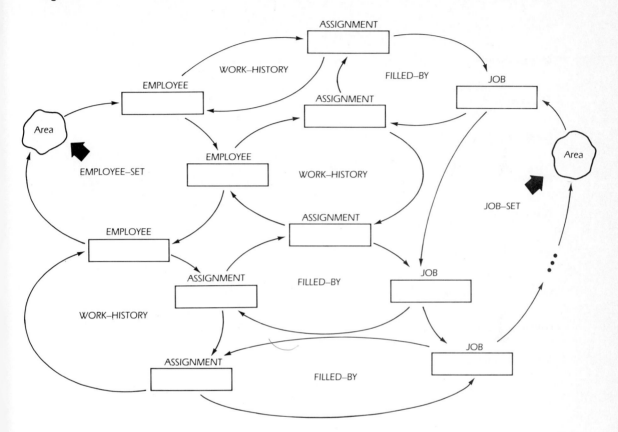

To resolve these problems, one's position in a database is initially considered to be at the areas that we recognized earlier as being special examples of set owners. Thus, any initial request is interpreted relative to this position. Later, any command referring to a set is interpreted relative to the last position established in a set occurrence of that name.

To demonstrate these ideas, let us use the FIND–NEXT and FIND–OWNER commands to retrieve the job history of the second employee in the example database of Figure 9-13. We begin with our current position established at the areas in the database, as shown by the bold arrows in Figure 9-14.

From this starting configuration, we see that executing the sequence:

FIND–NEXT EMPLOYEE–SET
FIND–NEXT EMPLOYEE–SET

will move our position in the EMPLOYEE–SET to the second EMPLOYEE. Having done this, our position within the network would be as shown in Figure 9-15.

Figure 9-15

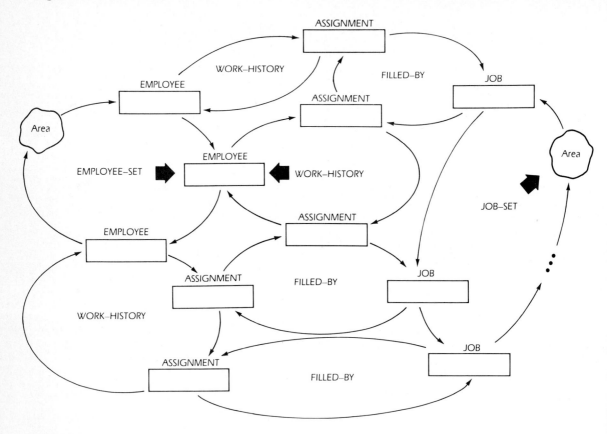

Note that the current EMPLOYEE group occurrence, being associated with a WORK–HISTORY set, provides a reference from which motion in this latter set can now be made. Thus, we can find the first ASSIGNMENT for this EMPLOYEE by executing the command:

FIND–NEXT WORK–HISTORY

which will shift our reference positions in the database to the configuration in Figure 9-16.

At this point the dates stored in the current ASSIGNMENT group occurrence are available to us, but the information about the job itself is stored in the JOB group occurrence owning the current ASSIGNMENT. To reach this JOB we can use the command:

FIND–OWNER FILLED–BY

Figure 9-16

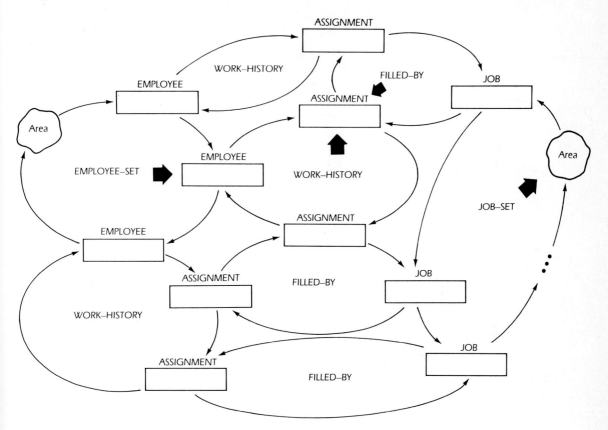

which establishes a position at the owner of the current FILLED–BY set. (Note that this command would have been ambiguous before we reached an ASSIGNMENT group occurrence.) Following this command our situation will be as in Figure 9-17.

The next step is to move on to the next ASSIGNMENT owned by the EMPLOYEE in question. You may have noticed that as we shifted attention from one set to another we left bold arrows in the diagrams marking the last entry visited in each type of set. These arrows mark our current position in each of the appropriate sets. Consequently, we can move to the next ASSIGNMENT owned by the EMPLOYEE in question with the command:

FIND–NEXT WORK–HISTORY

which will produce the situation represented by Figure 9-18.

It is important to note that the new ASSIGNMENT is a member of another

Figure 9-17

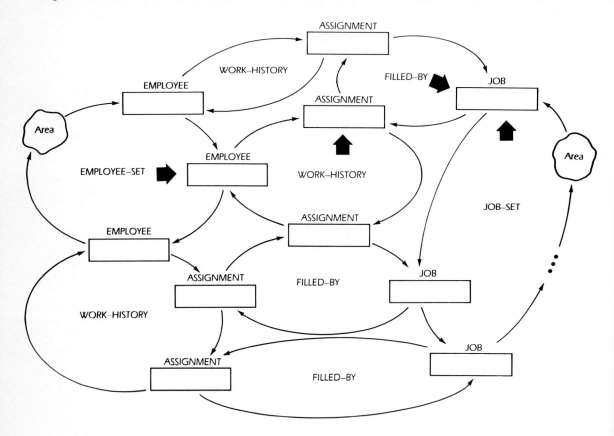

FILLED–BY set, and moving to it has shifted our position from the old FILLED–BY set to the new one. Consequently, executing the command:

FIND–OWNER FILLED–BY

will lead us to the JOB that owns this other FILLED–BY set (Figure 9-19). At this point, we can extract information about the second and final job in the target employee's job history.

In closing, we should note that operations such as FIND–NEXT and FIND–OWNER are provided as a part of a network database management system in the form of subprograms that can be called by the application software when needed. Consequently, the application programmer is allowed to pretend that the data in the database is actually stored in the network structure rather than being scattered over the tracks of a disk bulk storage device.

Figure 9-18

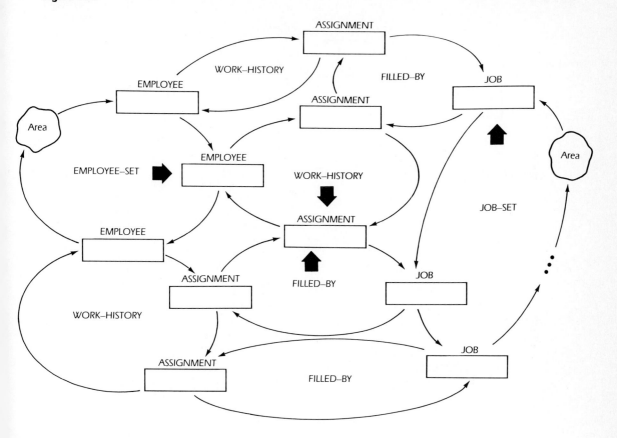

Questions/Exercises

1. How does retrieving information from a set in a network database compare with reading records from a sequential file?

2. Write a sequence of steps to direct the printing of the names of those employees who have held the second job represented in the database of Figure 9-13.

3. Could the first operation after opening the database of Figure 9-13 be FIND–NEXT WORK–HISTORY?

4. If information that is stored in the middle of a large network database were needed, would it be necessary to start from the area and "walk" all the way into the structure using FIND–NEXT and FIND–OWNER commands?

5. Would you expect an airline representative at the airport counter to be able to tell you whether the database being used for reservations is based on either the relational or network model?

Figure 9-19

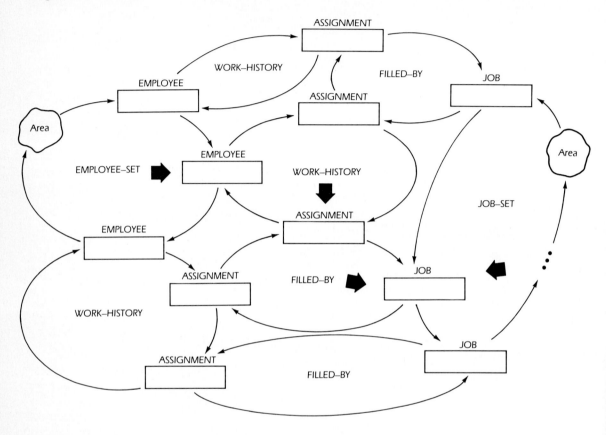

9–5 The Hierarchical Model

The third database model for our discussion is the hierarchical model and is based on the idea of making the data appear to be organized in a sequence of tree structures. Much of the terminology in this section is based on the very popular hierarchical database system IMS (Information Management System) marketed by IBM. The central theme of the hierarchical model is that data in its natural habitat is normally viewed in a hierarchical fashion. For example, consider the collection of information about the physicians practicing in a certain clinic, each physician's patients, and the records of each patient's visit to the clinic. The information ultimately relating to each physician is easily pictured as having the structure of the tree in Figure 9-20. We envision the information about each patient being attached to the information about that patient's physician and the information about each visit being attached to the pertinent patient.

Figure 9-20 A hierarchical structure containing information about a physician's patients

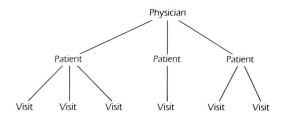

From this point of view, the total database takes on the appearance of a collection of trees (a forest) with one tree for each physician in the clinic. Each tree in the database is the same in the sense that each has the information about a physician as its root, patients as intermediate nodes, and visits as its leaves. But, just as real trees of the same type differ, each tree in the database is different in the sense that each contains different information and therefore takes on its own unique shape depending on the number of patients and the patients' visits.

In the terminology of popular hierarchical databases the nodes of the trees are called *segments*, each of which is divided into parts called *fields* according to the items of information held in the segment. We might observe that the database previously proposed would contain three types of segments: physician, patient, and visit. In turn, the physician segment might be composed of such fields as name, specialty, and office number; the patient segment may contain fields relating to name, address, and next of kin; and the visit segment may contain date, reason for visit, and diagnosis.

Hierarchical Design

We turn now to the problem of building a database containing information about the employees of a company and the job history of each employee. In this case we might readily consider building the database from trees of the form represented by Figure 9-21 where we envision the root of each tree containing the information about an employee and the nodes below the root representing the job history of that employee. Each root node would be an occurrence of the segment named EMPLOYEE containing the fields such as NAME, ADDRESS, EMPL–ID, and SSNUM, while each leaf node would be an occurrence of the segment named JOB–ASSIGNMENT containing such fields as JOB–ID, SKILL–CODE, DEPT, START–DATE, and TERM–DATE.

Such an organization may disturb you since it gives the impression of a lot of repeated information. This organization, in fact, is quite similar to the one we rejected in Section 9-4 as being too redundant because of repetition of information pertaining to each job. (The same job may have been assigned to many employees over its history and therefore may be repeated in many trees.) Now, however, removing this

Figure 9-21 A hierarchical structure representing an employee's job history

redundancy would destroy the tree structure since it would require the existence of a node with two parents. (Each occurrence of the ASSIGNMENT group in the final network of Section 9-4 was owned by both an EMPLOYEE and a JOB.) Thus, the database management system is forced to simulate the repeated occurrence of job information in the case of the hierarchical model.

Hierarchical Operations

To assist in data retrieval, the trees in a database are normally assigned a sequential order according to the value in some field of the root node. The children of each node are likewise assigned an order. In this case we use the value of EMPL–ID to arrange the trees themselves, and within each tree we arrange the JOB–ASSIGNMENTs in descending order by START–DATE. Thus, the database can be considered as a row of trees with the EMPL–ID values increasing as we move down the row, and within each tree the job history of the employee is presented with the most recent job first. Note that with this sequential organization it makes sense to talk about the first EMPLOYEE segment or the second JOB–ASSIGNMENT appearing under the EMPLOYEE segment with EMPL–ID equal to 25X56.

With this sequential order established, we are in a position to present the operations used to interrogate a hierarchical database. Our discussion will include two such operations, which we will call GET–FIRST and GET–NEXT. Each of them will be accompanied by segment name and an optional WHERE clause. For example, we use the syntax:

GET–FIRST EMPLOYEE

to retrieve the information from the first root node in the database, or:

GET–FIRST EMPLOYEE WHERE NAME EQUALS "Joe Smith"

to retrieve the first root segment pertaining to an employee named Joe Smith. When more than one segment is involved in the command, we precede the field name with the corresponding segment name and a period (in case different segments have fields of the same name). Thus, the command:

GET–FIRST JOB–ASSIGNMENT WHERE EMPLOYEE.EMPL–ID EQUALS "24S17"

would retrieve the data relating to the most recent job assigned to employee 24S17.

The GET–FIRST command is essentially used to establish a current position within the database. Once this has been established, the GET–NEXT command can be used to move this position farther through the database. For example, to retrieve the information about all employees with identification numbers greater than 24S17, we could first execute the command:

GET–FIRST EMPLOYEE WHERE EMPL–ID GREATER THAN "24S17"

and then repeat the command:

GET–NEXT EMPLOYEE

until the end of the database is reached.

A similar technique could be used to retrieve the entire job history of the employee with identification number 24S17. We could start with:

GET–FIRST JOB–ASSIGNMENT WHERE EMPLOYEE.EMPL–ID EQUALS "24S17"

and then repeat:

GET–NEXT JOB–ASSIGNMENT

until all the JOB–ASSIGNMENTs have been retrieved relative to the target EMPLOYEE. The only problem here is detecting when the last JOB–ASSIGNMENT under the target EMPLOYEE has been retrieved. Unless this EMPLOYEE is the last in the database, most likely more JOB–ASSIGNMENTs will occur farther down the sequential order (but under other EMPLOYEEs). Taken literally the GET–NEXT JOB–ASSIGNMENT command should continue extracting JOB–ASSIGNMENTs until the end of the database is reached.

To solve this problem, we add another optional clause to the GET–NEXT command of the form UNDER PARENT. This clause indicates that the next target segment is to be retrieved only if it is under the current parent (where the current parent is the last segment retrieved by a GET–FIRST or GET–NEXT command not having an UNDER PARENT clause). With this option the search for the entire job history of the employee with identification number 24S17 would begin with the command:

GET–FIRST EMPLOYEE WHERE EMPL–ID EQUALS "24S17"

to establish this EMPLOYEE as the current parent. Following this we would repeat:

GET–NEXT JOB–ASSIGNMENT UNDER PARENT

until we were informed that all the JOB–ASSIGNMENTS under the current parent had been retrieved.

You may have noticed that the hierarchical model as presented thus far does not offer the symmetry provided in the other employee/job history databases. In the previous models it was just as easy to find the job history of any employee as it was to find the employee history of any job. However, in the current hierarchical imple-

Figure 9-22 A hierarchical structure representing the assignment history of a job

mentation finding those employees who have held a certain job would result in a much longer search process.

Because of this problem, hierarchical database management systems allow several different tree structures to be applied to the same physical database. Thus, if we were faced with the task of finding the employee history of a certain job, we might choose to view the database as constructed from trees of the form represented by Figure 9-22. Here each JOB segment contains information about a job, and each EMPL–ASSIGNMENT contains information about the assignment of the parent job to an employee. The ability of the database management system to produce different images of the database depends on a pointer system being initially implemented in the actual data storage system to supply the required links between the various data objects. Thus, the selection of a tree structure is not an arbitrary decision but must be planned during the original design of the database.

Questions/Exercises

1. How might the database management system inform the application software when the end of the database is reached when executing a GET–NEXT command or when the last segment under the current parent is reached when executing a command with the UNDER PARENT clause?
2. Using the view of the employee/job database having the JOB segment as the root of each tree, describe a sequence of steps to retrieve the list of all employees who have held the job with JOB–ID equal to T25.
3. Draw the hierarchical (tree) structure you would use in relation to information about parts and their manufacturers.
4. How does the parent/child relationship in the hierarchical database model differ from the owner/member relationship in the network model?

Chapter 9 Review Problems

1. Summarize the distinction between a simple file and a database.
2. What is meant by data independence in the setting of a database system?
3. Compare the role of an operating system when manipulating a sequential file with that of a database management system when manipulating a database.

4. Identify the level within a database system (end user, programmer of application software, designer of the database management system software) at which each of the following concerns or activities would occur:
   a. How should the data be stored on a disk to maximize efficiency?
   b. Is there a vacancy on flight 243?
   c. Should the owner of the set be found through consecutive FIND–NEXT commands or should a FIND–OWNER be used?
   d. Should set owners be stored close to the set members on the disk?
   e. Could a relation be stored as a sequential file?
   f. How many times should a user be allowed to mistype a password before the conversation is terminated?
   g. Should the user/machine interface be menu driven?
   h. How can the PROJECT operation be implemented?
   i. How many packages of sardines were accidentally shipped without ice?

5. For each of the database models we have discussed, draw a diagram representing the conceptual image of the following information about airlines, flights (for a particular day), and passengers:
   Airlines: Clear Sky, Long Hop, and Tree Top
   Flights for Clear Sky: CS205, CS37, and CS102
   Flights for Long Hop: LH67 and LH89
   Flights for Tree Top: TT331 and TT809
   Smith has reservations on CS205 (seat 12B), CS37 (seat 18C), and LH89 (seat 14A).
   Baker has reservations on CS37 (seat 18B) and LH89 (seat 14B).
   Clark has reservations on LH67 (seat 5A) and TT331 (seat 4B).

6. In terms of the following relations, what would be the appearance of the relation RESULT after executing each of these instructions:

   X relation   Y relation

U	V	W
A	Z	5
B	D	3
C	Q	5

R	S
3	J
4	K

   a. PROJECT U, W FROM X GIVING RESULT.

   b. SELECT FROM X WHERE W EQUALS 5 GIVING RESULT.
   c. PROJECT S FROM Y GIVING RESULT.
   d. MULTIPLY X BY Y GIVING RESULT.

7. Using the commands SELECT, PROJECT, and MULTIPLY, write a sequence of instructions to answer each of the following questions about parts and their manufacturers in terms of the database shown below:

   PART relation

Part-Name	Weight
Bolt 2X	1
Bolt 2Z	1.5
Nut V5	0.5

   MANUFACTURER relation

Company-Name	Part-Name	Cost
Company X	Bolt 2Z	.03
Company X	Nut V5	.01
Company Y	Bolt 2X	.02
Company Y	Nut V5	.01
Company Y	Bolt 2Z	.04
Company Z	Nut V5	.01

   a. Which companies make bolt 2Z?
   b. Obtain a list of the parts made by Company X along with each part's cost.
   c. What companies make a part with weight 1?

8. What redundancy would be introduced if the information in the PART and MANUFACTURER relations in problem 7 were combined into one single relation?

9. Using commands such as SELECT, PROJECT, and MULTIPLY write sequences to answer the following questions about the information in the EMPLOYEE, JOB, and ASSIGNMENT relations in Figure 9-6:
   a. Obtain a list of the names and addresses of the company's employees.
   b. Obtain a list of the names and addresses of those who have worked or are working in the personnel department.
   c. Obtain a list of the names and addresses of those who are working in the personnel department.

10. What is the difference in the information supplied by the single relation:

Name	Department	Telephone-Number
Jones	Sales	111–2222
Smith	Sales	111–3333
Baker	Personnel	111–4444

and the two relations:

Name	Department
Jones	Sales
Smith	Sales
Baker	Personnel

Department	Telephone-Number
Sales	111–2222
Sales	111–3333
Personnel	111–4444

11. In terms of the relational model, design a database containing information about automobile parts and their subparts. Be sure to allow for the fact that one part may contain smaller parts while at the same time it is contained in still larger parts.

12. Redesign the database in problem 11 using the network model.

13. In the setting of the network database model, what is the difference between the commands FIND–NEXT and FIND–OWNER?

14. In the network database following, what ambiguity would exist if we were to start a query with the command FIND–NEXT B–SET:

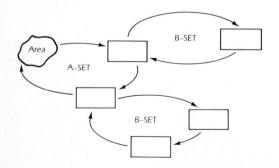

15. Draw a diagram representing the current positions in the database of problem 14 after executing the following sequence of commands:

```
FIND–NEXT A–SET
FIND–NEXT B–SET
FIND–NEXT A–SET
FIND–NEXT B–SET
```

16. Suppose we were to start from the areas in the employee/job database of Figure 9-13 and execute the following sequence of commands:

```
FIND–NEXT EMPLOYEE–SET
FIND–NEXT EMPLOYEE–SET
FIND–NEXT EMPLOYEE–SET
FIND–NEXT WORK–HISTORY
FIND–OWNER FILLED–BY
```

Which JOB group occurrence would be the current one?

17. Suppose we were to start from the areas in the employee/job database of Figure 9-13 and execute the following sequence of commands:

```
FIND–NEXT JOB–SET
FIND–NEXT FILLED–BY
FIND–OWNER WORK–HISTORY
FIND–NEXT EMPLOYEE–SET
```

Which EMPLOYEE group occurrence would be the current one?

18. Using the commands FIND–NEXT and FIND–OWNER, write a sequence of instructions that will lead to the EMPLOYEEs that have held the second JOB in the employee/job database of Figure 9-13.

19. In a hierarchical database relating cars and their parts, which of the following tree structures would be most efficient if one needed to obtain a list of all the cars using a certain part:

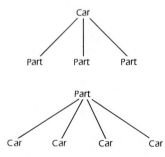

20. Based on the physician/patient/visit hierarchical structure of Figure 9-20, write a sequence of GET–FIRST and GET–NEXT instructions that

could be used to obtain a list of the patients of John W. Baker, MD.

21. Based on the physician/patient/visit hierarchical structure of Figure 9-20, write a sequence of GET–FIRST and GET–NEXT instructions that could be used to find out if John W. Baker is a patient at the clinic.

22. Sketch a tree structure that might be used in a hierarchical database that contains the names of the employees who work in each of various departments within a company along with the office telephone number of each employee.

Problems for the Programmer

1. Using sequential files to represent relations with each record representing one tuple, write a system of subprograms to perform the operations of SELECT, PROJECT, and MULTIPLY appearing in the relational model.

2. Using the routines developed in programming problem 1, write a program to answer a specific question about the information in the database. What part of this complete software system would be classified as part of a database management system? What part would be classified as application software?

3. Suppose the data in a hierarchical database is stored in a sequential file using the pattern of storing the children of any node immediately after the node itself. Write subprograms to perform the operations of GET–FIRST and GET–NEXT in this system.

4. Write an application software package that understands a limited number of questions (from a user) about the information in the network employee database of Figure 9-13 and activates the appropriate sequence of FIND–NEXT and FIND–OWNER commands to generate the answer to each. Use stubs for the FIND–NEXT and FIND–OWNER routines.

Part Four

The Potential of Algorithmic Machines

Chapter 10.   Artificial Intelligence

Chapter 11.   Theory of Computation

Part Four Preview
The Potential of Algorithmic Machines

In light of the attention given to computers by the popular press, it is important to take the time to consider the potential of algorithmic machines from a scientific rather than a science fiction perspective. With this as our goal, we study in Chapter 10 the dreams and aspirations of many computer scientists in the area of artificial intelligence, and in Chapter 11 we turn to the more sobering study of the inherent limitations of algorithmic machines.

Although the popular press would like to create the image of computer scientists wearing white laboratory coats as they pore over a mass of wires and spark gaps in hopes of bringing it to life, the truth is that the field of artificial intelligence is merely an extension of continuing efforts to develop machines that can perform tasks in increasingly unpredictable environments. To do this, computer science has turned to other sciences such as psychology and biology to find out how humans are able to perform "intelligent" tasks in hopes of simulating these findings with machines. The result has been machines that appear to possess intelligent characteristics.

The mystique surrounding these machines results from the fact that intelligence is an interior characteristic whose presence cannot be measured directly. Thus, we are forced to detect intelligence indirectly by observing responses to stimuli. Consequently, if a machine happens to respond in an apparently intelligent manner, we are easily caught in the trap of assuming that the machine is intelligent. The debate over whether such an assumption is valid has added a high degree of romanticism to an otherwise sound science.

In Chapter 10 we attempt to unravel some of the mystery surrounding this science. Because the field is too broad for us to discuss all its topics, we will concentrate on the task of building machines that can "reason" in the sense that they can draw conclusions from given information.

Our approach to the process of deductive reasoning centers around the concept of production systems. A production system is merely a collection of conditions called states in which the object of the reasoning might be found at a given time, a collection of rules (or productions) that can be applied to the object to move it from one state to another, and a control system charged with deciding which rule should be applied at each stage of the process. For example, we consider the problem of solving the 8—puzzle, a game consisting of equal square tiles in a three-by-three frame. Each tile has a digit from 1 through 8 written on it. The tiles are initially positioned as shown below. The problem is to return the tiles to these starting positions after they have been arbitrarily moved around the frame.

1	2	3
4	5	6
7	8	

In this context, the states of the production system are the various arrangements of the tiles, a production is the movement of a single tile, and the control system decides which tile to move at each step in the solution.

A common strategy that a control system might adopt is to consider systematically where each of the available productions will lead and then apply the production providing the best prospects for the future. To decide which production provides the best prospects, the control system normally looks well into the future. That is, it normally pretends to apply each of the available productions, records the states that would be reached by each, and continues its analysis as though it were actually at each of these states. The result is that each of the various options available is expanded in turn to form a tree structure representing all the future states to which a current action might ultimately lead. The control system then selects the production that looks the best in terms of this analysis.

The major problem associated with such an approach involves the multiplicity of options that the control system must keep track of as it projects the results of each possibility into the future. This is reflected in both time and memory space requirements. For example, if at each state there were only two possible productions, to evaluate the ramifications of a current choice five steps into the future would require the control system to consider a total of 62 (2 + 4 + 6 + 8 + 16 + 32) different future states. Moreover, if the control system wished to consider the ramifications of a sixth step, a total of 64 additional states would have to be considered.

Because of the explosive nature of the problem, control systems are normally designed to imitate intuition. For this purpose they are supplied with a way of guessing which possibility will prove to be best at each stage. They can then pursue these paths first. The other paths are considered only if the guessed ones turn out to be nonproductive. This latter situation can, of course, happen since the guess, being based on unproven heuristic information, is exactly a guess and could be wrong just as with our intuition. On the other hand, just as our intuition proves advantageous when solving a problem, heuristic techniques prove helpful when implemented in control systems.

We see then that machines can be programmed to exhibit intelligent characteristics such as perception and reasoning. Whether or not these characteristics represent the actual existence of intelligence, however, is frequently debated. Nonetheless, the appearance of intelligence alone is significant enough to raise many questions of ethics and to allow the layperson's imagination to extend today's capabilities well into the world of science fiction. Thus to get a grasp on reality, we should consider a scientific investigation of the ultimate power of computers as algorithmic machines. This is the goal of Chapter 11.

Since a variety of computers is available today, an investigation of a computer's ultimate abilities requires our establishing a uniform characterization of the properties of a computer. Surprising as it may seem, this was done by Alan M. Turing in the 1930s, well before today's technology evolved. Today, Turing's abstract machines, called Turing machines, are accepted as capturing the essence of a computational process. That is, any problem that can be solved by an algorithmic process can be solved by a Turing machine. Moreover, being an algorithmic machine, a Turing machine can perform only those things accomplished by algorithms.

Thus, by demonstrating a problem that no Turning machine can solve, we will have established a problem that no algorithmic machine (and thus no modern computer) can solve. With this as our goal, we will describe a simple language (called Bare Bones) in which an algorithm for solving any problem solvable by a Turing machine can be expressed and proceed to exhibit a problem whose solution cannot be described in that language.

The problem is known as the halting problem and is essentially the following:

> Detect whether or not programs written in Bare Bones
> will result in an infinite loop when executed.

The logic involved in proving that a program for solving this problem does not exist is basically an argument that if such a program did exist it would lead to a paradox.

After showing that algorithmic machines cannot solve all problems, we will turn to the collection of solvable problems. Our goal is to investigate the more practical issue of how long it might take to solve a solvable problem using an algorithmic machine. We will see that although a problem may be theoretically solvable by an algorithmic process, the complexity of its solution may dictate that an exorbitant amount of time (measured in hundreds of years and more) would be required to compute its solution. Moreover, this time requirement is a property of the algorithmic approach and not of today's technology. Consequently, our dilemma cannot be overcome by merely building faster machines.

We must conclude that not only are there problems that computers cannot solve but there are also problems that, although theoretically solvable, require such complex algorithms that their solution by a computer is, and will remain, impractical.

10 Artificial Intelligence

10–1 **Some Philosophical Issues**
   Machines Versus Humans
   Performance Versus Simulation
   Intelligence as an Interior Characteristic
   An "Intelligent" Machine
10–2 **Image Analysis**
   Character Recognition
   General Image Analysis
10–3 **Reasoning**
   Production Systems
   Other Applications
10–4 **Control System Activities**
   Control Strategies
   Search Trees
   Problems of Efficiency
10–5 **Using Heuristics**
   Designing Heuristics
   Applying Heuristics
10–6 **Applications of Artificial Intelligence**
   Language Processing
   Robotics
   Database Systems
   Expert Systems

A major goal among computer scientists is the development of machines that communicate with their environments through traditionally human sensory techniques and proceed intelligently without human intervention. Such a goal often requires that the machine "understand" the input received and be able to draw conclusions through some form of a reasoning process.

Both understanding and reasoning fall within the category of common-sense activities that, although natural for the human mind, are apparently quite difficult for machines. The result is that the area of research associated with this pursuit, known as artificial intelligence, is still in its infancy when compared to its goals and expectations. This is not to say that successes have not been achieved. The efforts of many have resulted in well-founded theories and techniques.

In this chapter we look at some of these theories in the context of designing a puzzle solving machine that possesses elementary perception and reasoning abilities. As a side effect, we have an opportunity to see how such concepts as trees and stacks are used as tools in actual applications.

10–1 **Some Philosophical Issues**

Perhaps one of the more difficult tasks for a beginner in computer science involves the separation of science fiction from science, and nowhere is this distinction more clouded than in the area of artificial intelligence. Although the major thrust behind the subject is merely to build machines that are able to forge ahead in uncontrolled environments without relying on human backup (and thus better serve the human race), the popular press would have us believe that computer scientists are striving to build mechanical humans.* Of course, the aura of mystery is only enhanced by calling the subject artificial intelligence. Let us begin then by considering the distinction between today's algorithmic machines and human minds.

Machines Versus Humans

Although the computer is often personified, an important distinction exists between its properties and the properties of the human mind. Algorithmic machines are designed to perform precisely defined tasks with speed and accuracy, and they do this extremely well; however, machines are not gifted with common sense. When faced with a situation not foreseen by the programmer, a machine's performance is likely to deteriorate rapidly. The human mind, although often floundering on complex computations, is capable of understanding and reasoning. Thus, whereas a machine might outperform a human in computing solutions to problems in nuclear physics, the human is much more likely to understand the problem and to comprehend the meaning of the results.

We see, then, that if we are to build machines that are able to continue when faced with unforeseen or unpredictable situations, the machines must become more humanlike in the sense that they must possess (or at least simulate) the ability to reason. Recognizing this requirement, computer scientists have turned to psychologists and their models of the human mind in hopes of finding principles that can

---

*There are those, of course, who dream of building models of the human mind. Early researchers such as von Neumann often thought along these lines and even discussed the components of early machines in terms of organs. However, major breakthroughs must still be made before such dreams have even a chance of becoming realities.

be applied to the construction of more flexible programs. The result is that it is now often difficult to distinguish between the research of a psychologist and that of a computer scientist. The distinction is not in what they do but rather in their goals. The psychologist is trying to learn more about the human mind, and the computer scientist is trying to build more useful machines. Let us consider this distinction in more detail.

Performance Versus Simulation

To explain the two approaches we might hypothesize that a mathematician and a psychologist each embark on separate projects to develop a poker-playing program. The mathematician would most likely design a program based on the foundations of probability and statistics. The result would therefore be a program that would play the odds, bluff at random, show no emotion, and consequently maximize its chances of winning. The psychologist, on the other hand, would probably develop a program based on theories of human thought and behavior. The project might even result in the production of several different programs (for example, one might play aggressively while another might be easily intimidated). In contrast to the mathematicians's program, the psychologist's program might become emotionally involved in the game and lose everything it owned.

Reconsidering, we hypothesize that the mathematician's main concern while developing the program would be the program's final performance. Such an approach is said to be *performance oriented*. In contrast, the psychologist would be more interested in understanding the processes of natural intelligence, and thus the project would be approached as an opportunity to test theories by building computer models based on those theories. From this point of view the development of the "intelligent" program is actually a side effect of another pursuit—progress in understanding human thought and behavior. This approach is said to be *simulation oriented.*

Both approaches are sound and make significant contributions to the field of artificial intelligence. However, they also raise elusive philosophical questions within the discipline. Consider, for example, the discussion that might ensue if a group were asked to decide if the programs possess intelligence and if so which program is more intelligent. (Is intelligence measured by the ability to win or the ability to be humanlike?)

Intelligence as an Interior Characteristic

The difficulty in determining whether or not a program possesses intelligence is rooted in the difficulty of distinguishing between the mere appearance of intelligence and its actual existence. In the final analysis, intelligence is an interior characteristic whose existence is detected from the outside only indirectly in the context of a stimulus/reaction dialogue.

This illusive nature of intelligence was recognized by Alan Turing in 1950 when he proposed a test (now known as the *Turing test*) for detecting intelligence within a machine. Turing's proposal was to allow a human, whom we call the interrogator, to communicate with a test subject by means of a typewriter system without being told whether the test subject was a human or a machine. In this environment, a machine would be declared intelligent in the event that the interrogator was not able to distinguish it from a human. As yet, machines have not been able to pass the Turing test, although surprising results have been achieved.

A well-known example arose as a result of the program DOCTOR (a version of the more general system called ELIZA) developed by Joseph Weizenbaum in the mid-1960s. This interactive program was designed to project the image of a Rogerian analyst conducting a psychological interview; the computer played the role of analyst while the user played the patient. Internally, all that DOCTOR did was restructure the statements made by the patient according to some well-defined rules and direct them back to the terminal screen. For example, in response to a statement such as "I am tired today," DOCTOR might have replied with "Why do you think you're tired today?" If DOCTOR was unable to recognize the sentence structure, it merely responded with something like "Go on" or "That's very interesting."

Weizenbaum's purpose in developing DOCTOR dealt with the study of natural language communication. From this point of view, the subject of psychotherapy played the secondary role of providing an environment (or a domain of discourse) in which the program could function. To Weizenbaum's dismay, however, several psychologists proposed using the program for actual psychotherapy. (The Rogerian thesis is that the patient, not the analyst, should lead the discussion during the therapeutic session, and thus, they argued, a computer could possibly conduct a discussion as well as a therapist could.) Moreover, DOCTOR projected the image of comprehension so strongly that many who "communicated" with it found themselves relating intimate thoughts and feelings and, in many cases, actually becoming subservient to the machine's question-and-answer dialogue. The result was that moral, as well as technical, issues were raised.

An "Intelligent" Machine

With such philosophical questions residing at the very foundation of the subject, it is not surprising that much of the research in artificial intelligence is accompanied by controversy and an aura of mystery often exploited by both the news media and fiction writers. In an effort to get our feet firmly on the ground, let us consider the design of a machine having elementary "intelligent" properties.

Our machine will take the form of a large metal box with two mechanical arms attached to opposite sides (Figure 10-1). One arm will be equipped with a gripper, the other with a single finger with a rubber end so that it doesn't slip when pushing

Figure 10-1 Our puzzle solving machine

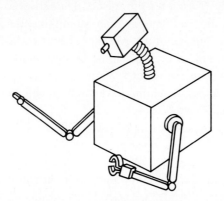

something. On top of the box will be a camera resembling those used with home video systems.

Imagine such a machine next to a table holding an 8–puzzle. Recall that this puzzle consists of eight square tiles labeled 1 through 8 mounted in a frame capable of holding a total of nine such tiles in three rows and three columns. Thus, among the tiles in the frame is a hole into which any of the adjacent tiles can be pushed. The tiles are currently arranged as shown in Figure 10-2.

We begin by picking up the puzzle and rearranging it by repeatedly pushing arbitrarily chosen tiles into the hole. We then turn on the machine, and the gripper begins to open and close as if asking for the puzzle. We place the puzzle in the gripper, and the gripper closes on the puzzle and lifts it up to the camera. After a short time the finger raises and begins pushing the tiles around in the frame (in an orderly fashion) until they are back in their original order. At this point the machine places the puzzle back on the table and turns itself off. Because such a machine involves elementary perception as well as reasoning abilities, its design provides a basis for presenting the topics of the following four sections.

Questions/Exercises
1. A plant placed in a dark room with a single light source will grow toward the light. Is this an intelligent response? Does the plant possess intelligence?
2. Suppose a vending machine is designed to dispense various products depending on which lever is pulled. Would you say that such a machine is "aware" of which lever is pulled?

10–2 Image Analysis

The first real intelligent behavior required by our puzzle solving machine is the extraction of information through a visual medium. The opening and closing of the

Figure 10-2 The 8-puzzle in its solved configuration

1	2	3
4	5	6
7	8	

gripper presents no serious problem, and the ability to detect the presence of the puzzle in the gripper during this process is straightforward since our application requires very little precision. (Automatic garage door openers are able to detect and react to the presence of an obstacle in the doorway when closing.) Even the problem of focusing the camera on the puzzle could be handled simply by designing the arm to position the puzzle at a particular predetermined position for viewing.

It is important to realize that the problem faced by our machine when looking at the puzzle is not that of merely producing and storing an image. Technology has been able to do this for years as in the case of traditional photography and television systems. Rather, the problem is to understand the image in order to extract the current status of the puzzle (and later to monitor the movement of the tiles). This is a significant distinction from the activity of a television receiver that simply transforms the image from one medium to another with no conceptual understanding of whether the image represents a horse or a politician.

Character Recognition

In the case of our puzzle solving machine, the options as to what the images might be are relatively limited. We can assume that what appears will always be an image of the puzzle containing the digits 1 through 8 in a well-organized pattern. The problem is merely to extract the arrangement of these digits. For this we imagine that the picture of the puzzle has been coded in terms of ones and zeroes in the computer's memory, with each bit representing the brightness level of a particular part of the picture called a *pixel* (short for picture element). Assuming a uniform size of the image (the machine will hold the puzzle at a predetermined location in front of the camera), we can detect which tile is in which position by comparing the different sections of the picture to prerecorded templates consisting of the bit patterns produced by the individual digits used in the puzzle. As matches are found, the condition of the puzzle will be revealed.

This technique of recognizing images is one method used in modern optical character readers. It has the drawback, however, of requiring a certain degree of uniformity among the style, size, and orientation of the symbols being read. In particular, the bit pattern produced by a physically large character would not match the template for a smaller version of the same symbol even though the shapes are the same, and you can imagine how such problems would increase when trying to process hand-written material.

Another approach to the problem of character recognition is based on matching the geometric characteristics rather than the exact appearance of the symbols. In such cases the digit 1 might be characterized as a single vertical line, 2 might be an opened curved line joined with a horizontal straight line across the bottom, etc. Thus, recognition of the symbols turns out to be the process of extracting the features from the image being processed (called *feature extraction*) and comparing them to those of known symbols (*feature evaluation*). This technique is not foolproof either since minor errors in the image can produce a set of entirely different geometric features as in the case of distinguishing between an O and a C or, in the case of the 8–puzzle, a 3 and an 8.

General Image Analysis

We are fortunate in our puzzle application that we do not need to recognize and understand images of general three-dimensional scenes since the complexities could become enormous. Consider, for example, the advantage gained in our application by being assured that the shapes to be recognized (the digits 1 through 8) are isolated in different parts of the picture rather than presented as overlapping images common in more general settings. In a general photograph for instance, one is faced not only with the problem of recognizing a chair as a chair regardless of the angle from which it is viewed but also with the fact that some portions of the chair may be hidden from view by other objects.

Before we could even begin to identify the objects in such a picture, the light and dark (or perhaps color) portions of the picture would have to be recognized and grouped to form the patterns for identification. Essentially two approaches to such region analysis have been investigated: *region growing* and *region splitting*. Region growing refers to the process of first considering each pixel in the image as an individual region and then repeatedly combining adjacent regions that have the same intensity or color to obtain larger regions until no further consolidation is possible. In contrast, the process of region splitting first considers the image to be one region and then proceeds to divide it along boundaries where pixel intensity changes until all the regions obtained are homogeneous. Both approaches leave numerous opportunities for error. For instance, consider the problems introduced by the occurrence of shadows in a two-dimensional picture of a three-dimensional scene. Here, a pattern of light and dark areas may be more closely related to an object elsewhere in the picture than to the objects on which it is located.

The shadows that cause problems in object recognition can, however, turn out to be of assistance once identified for what they are. In particular, they can be used to solve positioning ambiguities that might otherwise persist. For instance, we may wonder whether the long beam pictured in Figure 10-3a is actually hanging from

Figure 10-3 Line drawings of a beam: (a) without shadows, (b) with shadows

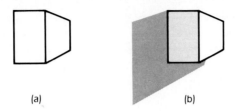

(a)   (b)

the ceiling or resting on the floor, but by introducing the shadow in Figure 10-3b, we discover that neither of these hypotheses is true. In fact, the left side of the beam is apparently glued to a wall on which the shadow appears.

Since simple character-recognition techniques are sufficient for our puzzle solving machine, we adopt this approach for the visual input system and move on to the problem of solving the puzzle itself.

Questions/Exercises

1. What is the difference in the requirements of a video system used on a robot for sending pictures back to the earth from the moon and a video system used by the same robot for controlling its own maneuvers without intervention?

2. What tells you that the following drawing is nonsense? How can this insight be programmed into a machine?

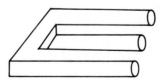

3. Suppose the following three lines represent the junction of three flat surfaces in a line drawing. What orientations are possible for the surfaces?

4. Combining two copies of the pattern in question 3 produces the following pattern. Suppose this new pattern represents flat surfaces that meet at right angles. What interpretations can be given to the drawing?

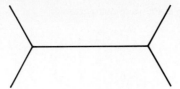

10–3 **Reasoning**

Once our puzzle solving machine has deciphered the positions of the tiles from the visual image, its task becomes that of actually solving the puzzle. One technique that might come to mind is to preprogram the machine with solutions to all possible arrangements of the tiles. Then, the machine's task would merely be the selection and execution of the proper program. However, because even this simple puzzle provides a total of 181,440 different configurations, the idea of exhaustively providing an explicit solution for each is certainly not inviting and probably not even possible when time and storage constraints are considered.

We are thus forced to approach the problem in terms of programming our machine to solve the problem itself. Consequently, the program we develop must provide the machine with the ability to make decisions, draw conclusions, and in short perform elementary reasoning activities.

Production Systems

The development of such abilities within a machine is the goal of much research today, and as with any subject of current research a high degree of debate exists over which technique or theory is the correct one to pursue. For our purposes, we will approach the subject in the context of production systems. A **production system**, in its most general sense, is a system in which each condition that might occur in the application's environment (each arrangement of the tiles) is associated with an appropriate action taken by the machine when that condition is detected. From a more precise viewpoint, we consider a production system to consist of three main components:

1. *A collection of states.* Each **state** is a situation that might occur in the application environment. The beginning state is called the **start** (or initial) **state**; the desired state (or states) is called the **goal state.** (In our case the state start is the configuration of the puzzle when handed to the machine; the goal state is the configuration of the puzzle before we rearranged it.)
2. *A collection of productions (or rules).* A **production** is an operation that can be performed in the application environment to move from one state to another. Each production may be associated with preconditions; that is, conditions may

exist that must be present in the environment before a production can be applied. (Productions in our case are the movements of tiles. Each movement of a tile has the precondition that the hole must be next to the tile in question.)

3. A *control system*. The **control system** consists of the logic that decides which of those productions whose preconditions are satisfied should be applied next. (Given a particular state in our 8–puzzle example, there would be several tiles next to the hole and therefore several applicable productions. The control system must decide which tile to move.)

From the point of view of production systems, the task of developing an intelligent machine is to implement the control system as a program stored in the machine. This program will inspect the current state of the target system, develop a program that leads to the goal state by selecting available productions in the correct order, and initiate the execution of that program. Thus, the control system constructs an algorithm to solve the initial problem using productions as building blocks. The main obstacle to designing our puzzle solving machine is the development of this control program. This we do in the following sections.

For now we should present the concept of a **state graph**, which is a convenient way of representing, or at least conceptualizing, all the states, productions, and preconditions in a production system. Here we are using the term **graph** in its mathematical sense meaning a collection of locations called **nodes** connected by arrows called **arcs.** A state graph consists of a collection of nodes representing the states in the system connected by arcs representing the productions that produce movement from one state to another. Thus, two nodes would be connected by an arc in the state graph if and only if there is a production in the system that could be used to transform the system from the state at the origin of the arc to the state at the destination of the arc. Preconditions are implicitly represented by the absence of arcs between certain nodes.

We might emphasize here that just as the number of possible states prevented us from explicitly providing predesigned solutions to the 8–puzzle, the problem of magnitude prevents us from explicitly representing the entire state graph. Thus, a state graph is a way of conceptualizing the problem at hand but not something that we would consider expressing in its entirety. Nonetheless, you may find it helpful to consider (and possibly extend) the portion of the state graph for the 8–puzzle actually displayed in Figure 10-4.

Note that in terms of the state graph, the problem faced by the control system becomes one of finding a sequence of arcs that leads from the start state to the goal state since this sequence of arcs will represent a sequence of productions that will solve the original problem. This is the context in which our control system will function. Moreover, observe that there is nothing unique about the 8–puzzle that allows us to conceptualize the production system in terms of a state graph. Such a

Figure 10-4 A small portion of the 8-puzzle's state graph

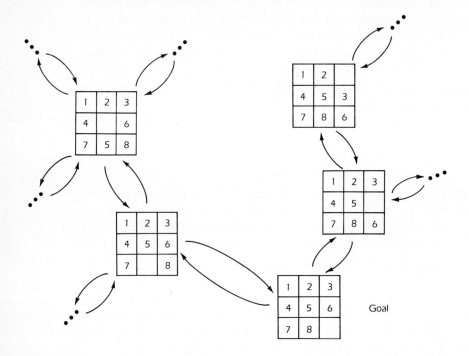

representation is applicable in any production system, and thus the formulation of problems in terms of production systems provides a uniform approach to the problem-solving process. That is, regardless of the application, the control system involved always reduces to the problem of finding a path through a state graph. To emphasize this point we close this section by observing how some popular tasks can be formulated in terms of production systems and thus of state graphs.

Other Applications

One of the old standbys in the area of artificial intelligence is the playing of games such as chess. Here, the states are the possible board configurations, the productions are the moves of the pieces, and the control system is embodied in the players (human or otherwise). The start node of the state graph represents the board with the pieces in their initial positions. Branching from this node are arcs leading to those board configurations that can be reached after the first move; branching from each of these nodes one finds those configurations reachable by the next move; etc. With this formulation, we can imagine a game of chess as consisting of two players, each trying to find a path through a large state graph to a goal node of his or her own choosing.

Perhaps a less obvious example is the problem of drawing logical conclusions from given facts. The productions in this context are the rules of logic that allow new statements to be formulated from old ones. For example, the statements "All students work hard" and "John is a student" can be combined to produce "John works hard," or "Mary and George are smart" can be reworded as "Neither Mary nor George is not smart." States in such a system consist of collections of statements known to be true at particular points in the deduction process: the start state is the collection of given statements (often called axioms), and a goal state is any collection of statements that contains the proposed conclusion. Consequently, the problem becomes that of finding a path through the state graph from the axioms to the proposed conclusion.

Questions/Exercises

1. What is the significance of production systems in artificial intelligence?
2. Draw a portion of the state graph for the 8–puzzle surrounding the node representing the following state:

4	1	3
	2	6
7	5	8

3. Formulate the problem of traversing the following maze in terms of a production system:

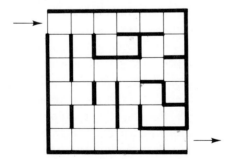

10–4 **Control System Activities**

A major point of Section 10-3 is that the problem of finding the proper sequence of productions in a production system can always be formulated in terms of finding a path through a state graph. This is important to computer scientists since it means that any knowledge gained about finding paths through graphs has immediate application in the solution of a multitude of problems. Thus, by designing control systems from the state graph point of view, one is effectively working on numerous applications at the same time.

Our consideration of control systems will therefore center around the problem of graph traversals along with a look at how paths in a state graph (or actually in what we call the search tree) can be converted into solutions to the original problem and executed. In terms of the graph traversal problem, we present in this section a rather brute-force technique and see in the next section how a degree of intuition can be added to provide a more efficient (or more intelligent) system.

Control Strategies

It may be helpful if we begin by considering how our control system will execute the final solution in the outside world since this will clarify what activities will or will not be taking place while the graph search is being done. This outside world communication might be handled in two ways. One is to execute each production as soon as it is thought to be the next step in the target problem's solution. This means that the problem solver becomes committed to these steps and, if the steps are later found to be incorrect, cannot simply drop them from consideration. (Players of games are rarely allowed to recall moves that prove to be to their opponents' advantage.) Consequently, the strategy used by the control system for selecting productions in such a system is said to be an ***irrevocable strategy*** and requires a rather demanding design. Humans often attempt to use this form of interface to the outside world when trying to solve a maze problem in the Sunday paper by marking each path as it is considered with a pencil or pen. Of course, the mental strategy being used rarely supports the demands of this irrevocable interface, and as a consequence one often finds a collection of eraser holes where "irrevocable" marks were revoked after all.

The other approach available to a control system is to delay any action in the outside world until a correct solution is completely determined. This relaxes the demand of getting it right the first time since incorrect decisions are easily discarded and new ones investigated. Thus, the less demanding strategies applicable here are said to be ***revocable strategies*** (in contrast to the irrevocable ones).

Returning to the problem of solving a maze in the Sunday paper, we can relate this approach to a human trying to search the maze mentally for a path and marking with a pencil only after success is obtained. In this case, however, humans suffer because they are prone to forget the early part of the solution by the time they find the latter part. In contrast, a control system within a computer can easily store records of the previously considered actions for later retrieval. In fact, the orderly maintenance of these records turns out to be a major activity of a control system.

For our purposes we concentrate on revocable strategies. Thus, only after our control system finds a complete solution internally will it consider applying the solution to the outside world.

Search Trees

The major part of the control system's job of developing a solution to the target problem requires little more than an algorithm for searching the state graph to find a path from the state node to the goal. A popular method of performing this search is to first traverse individually each of the arcs leading from the start state and in each case record the destination state, then traverse those arcs leaving these new states and again record the results, etc. This process continues until one of the new states is the goal state, at which point a solution has been found.

Observe that the effect of this strategy is to build a tree called a *search tree*, with the root node being the start state and the children of each node being those states reachable by applying one production. Each arc between nodes in a search tree represents the application of a single production, and each path from the root to a leaf in the search tree represents a path between the corresponding states in the state graph. In particular, if the 8–puzzle were originally configured as in Figure 10-5, the tree of Figure 10-6 would represent the search tree that might result.

Note that the left-most branch of this tree represents an attempt to solve the problem by first moving the 6 tile up, the center branch represents the approach of moving the 2 tile to the right, and the right-most branch represents moving the 5 tile down. Furthermore, the search tree shows that if we do begin by moving the 6 tile up, the only production allowable next would be to move the 8 tile to the right. (Actually, at that point we could also move the 6 tile down but that would return us to the state represented by the root node and thus be an extraneous move.)

Close inspection shows that the goal state occurs in the last level of the search tree of Figure 10-6. Since this represents the completion of the search, the control system would not need to construct additional levels of the tree once this point is reached. As soon as this node is discovered, the control system could terminate its search procedure and begin constructing the instruction sequence that will be used to solve the puzzle in the external environment. This turns out to be the simple

Figure 10-5 An unsolved 8-puzzle

1	3	5
4	2	
7	8	6

Figure 10-6 A sample search tree

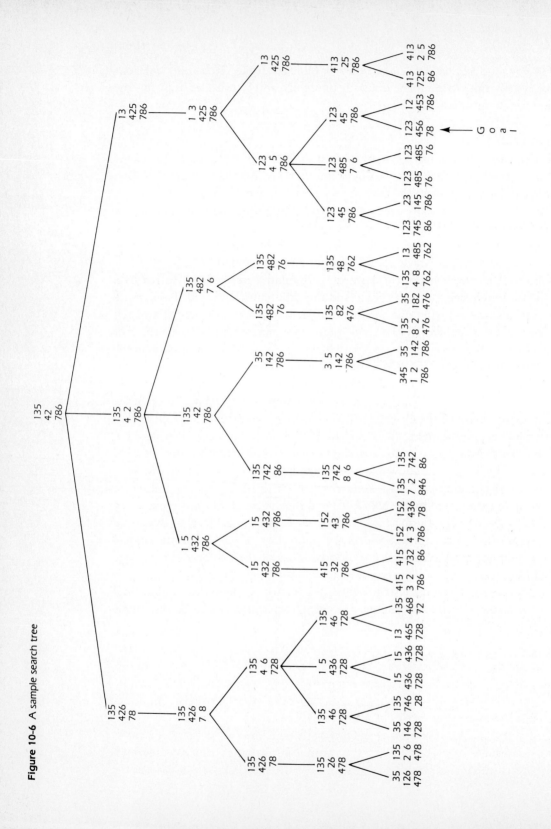

Figure 10-7 Productions stacked for later execution

Top of stack

Move the 5 tile down.
Move the 3 tile right.
Move the 2 tile up.
Move the 5 tile left.
Move the 6 tile up.

process of walking up the search tree from the location of the goal node while pushing the productions represented by the tree arcs on a stack as they are encountered. Applying this technique to the search tree in Figure 10-6 produces the stack of productions in Figure 10-7. Note that the control system can solve the puzzle in the outside world by merely executing the instructions as they are popped from this stack.

One unusual yet important property of a search tree that needs pointing out relates to the need of the control system to walk up the tree once the goal node is produced. Recall that the trees we discussed earlier use a pointer system that points down the tree, thereby allowing us to move from a parent node to its children. In the case of a search tree, however, we must be able to move a child to its parent. Such trees are constructed with their pointer systems pointing up rather than down (or in some cases with two sets of pointers that allow movement in the tree in both directions).

Problems of Efficiency

We pointed out earlier that the size of the state graph normally precludes its actual representation in a machine's memory. Thus, the control system usually stores only the search tree as it is created while analyzing the available productions. After all, the search tree represents that part of the state graph considered pertinent to the task at hand and is therefore all that is required by the control system. Moreover, it is necessary that the search tree be recorded since it is through later reference to it that the control system builds the final solution.

For our example in this section we have chosen a problem that produces a manageable search tree. In contrast, you can imagine that the search tree generated in an attempt to solve a more complex problem would grow much larger than the preceding one because of a larger number of options at each stage and the greater depth required in the tree before the goal is found. For example, because a game of chess has 20 possible first moves, the root node of the search tree in such a case would have 20 children rather than the 3 in the case of the 8–puzzle; and a game of chess can easily consist of 30 to 35 pairs of moves rather than the 5 straightforward ones in our example. Even in the 8–puzzle example the search tree could become quite large if the goal node is not quickly reached. Thus, it is not surprising that developing a full search tree in most applications becomes just as impractical as representing the entire state graph in terms of both time and memory in space.

With this in mind, we should find a more economical approach to the construction of a search tree than that just presented. One technique is to remove the redundancy inherent in the preceding inefficient policies. There is, for example, no need for the same state to have multiple occurrences in the tree since the occurrence of a node in the search tree indicates that the search process has discovered a path in the state graph leading to that node and little is gained by maintaining records of several ways to reach the same node. Yet had we not reached the goal in our example early in the search process, we would have soon found many duplications in the tree, and ultimately the search tree would have become plagued with repetitions. Thus, we should consider changing our search procedure so that the search tree retains records of only one path to each node.

In the case of the 8–puzzle this can be accomplished simply by adopting the policy of not attaching a new node to the tree if that state is already represented elsewhere. This would certainly remove the chance for repeated entries but would be too simplistic as a general rule in other applications. For instance, in other problems it might well be the case that the new occurrence of the node in some way represents a more advantageous or efficient solution than the previous one and consequently should be added while the older occurrence is removed. In a game of chess, for example, trying to reach a certain board configuration via one path of moves may rely on the opponent's overlooking an opportunity to take control of the game, whereas pursuing another path might assure that the advantage would remain at home. Thus, the more conservative path should be kept in the search tree regardless of whether or not it was the first one discovered.

Consequently, many control systems use more complex methods for eliminating redundancy in the search tree than the simple technique previously proposed. These systems normally associate a cost to the various paths represented in the tree and pursue those paths whose cost is the smallest. Thus, redundancy in the search tree is eliminated since as repetitions of states are encountered, only the occurrence associated with the smallest cost is retained.

We could adopt this cost-evaluating approach in the 8–puzzle by considering the cost of any path to be the number of moves in the path. As repetitions of states occur in the search tree, we would always keep the occurrence on the less expensive path. Because the less expensive path would be the shorter one, we would always keep the occurrence of the state appearing highest in the tree. If we develop the tree level by level as previously discussed, the node retained would always be the older one, and the effect of adopting this cost system for our application would be the same as applying the rule of always retaining the older node.

Questions/Exercises

1. In this section we suggested building the search tree level by level (commonly known as a **breadth-first search**). Another technique (a **depth-first search**) is to pursue one branch continuously until either the goal is reached or a predetermined depth is obtained without finding the goal. If this second option occurs, the search returns to a higher node and again follows a single branch down the tree. More precisely, if we agree that to "expand a node" means to attach its children to it, a standard depth-first procedure consists of expanding the root node, expanding its left-most child, expanding that child's left-most child, etc., until a certain depth is reached. At this point, the search proceeds by repeatedly looking back up the tree for a downward path not yet pursued and expanding the nodes along that path. Draw a sketch to indicate how the search tree might develop if this depth-first technique were applied to the problem of solving the 8–puzzle from the configuration in Figure 10-5.

2. In what way is a depth-first search similar to a system in which the productions are irrevocably executed as they are selected by the control system?

3. Suppose the depth-first search technique were applied to the 8–puzzle system along with the technique of defining the cost of each path as being the number of steps in it. Would the rule of retaining the oldest occurrence of a duplicate state still be equivalent to retaining the state associated with the lesser cost?

4. From the point of view of constructing our puzzle solving machine, why would it be better to express the productions on the stack as shown below rather than with the method used in the text:

   MOVE THE TILE IN THE UPPER RIGHT CORNER DOWN.   (Top of stack)
   MOVE THE TILE IN THE CENTER OF THE TOP ROW RIGHT.
   MOVE THE TILE IN THE CENTER UP.
   MOVE THE TILE IN THE CENTER OF THE RIGHT COLUMN LEFT.
   MOVE THE TILE IN THE BOTTOM LEFT CORNER UP.

10–5 Using Heuristics

We closed Section 10-4 by briefly discussing ways in which the size of a search tree could be controlled through the use of elementary techniques. In this section we look at this problem in more detail and discover that the equivalent of intuition can be added to our system to increase efficiency.

We might begin by considering how we as humans would proceed when faced with the 8–puzzle. We would rarely pursue several options at the same time but would select the option that appeared most promising and follow it. Note that we said "appeared" most promising. After all, we usually do not know for sure which option is best at a particular point but rather follow our intuition, which may, of course, lead us into a trap. Nonetheless, the use of such intuitive information seems to give humans an advantage over the brute-force methods of Section 10-4 where each option was considered equally. It therefore makes sense to incorporate intuition into our system if possible.

In this section we alter the search procedure (or the way in which we construct the search tree) to take advantage of intuition in the hopes of obtaining a system that spends less time developing nonproductive (and space-occupying) branches in the search tree. Unfortunately, the term *intuition* conjures up personified images and introduces a degree of magic or preconceived impressions into our discussion, and although coveted by the popular press, such extraneous connotations are not desirable for our purposes. It is therefore customary to refer to such untested and empirical information (which humans gain by the use of intuition) as heuristic information. More specifically, we define a **heuristic** policy as one that leads in a direction that appears to be the best without assurance that it will turn out to be the correct direction. Thus, whereas a human might follow a rule of thumb, we speak of a program applying a heuristic policy.

Designing Heuristics

The first step is to identify those characteristics for which we as humans look when deciding which option to pursue. In general, we could argue that humans tend to keep the goal state in mind and pick the option that appears to lead toward that state. In the case of the 8–puzzle this means that a human, when given a choice, would tend to select the option that moves a tile toward its final position.

To apply this technique in a programming environment we must first develop a system by which a program can determine which of several states should be considered closest to the goal. One approach might be to associate with each state the value equal to the number of tiles out of position and consider the state with the smallest value to be closest to the goal. However, this value does not take into account how far out of position the tiles are. Thus, we might want to adopt a slightly more complicated measure that accounts for this distance as well. One technique would be to measure the distance each tile is from its destination and add these values to obtain a single quantity. The distance in this case could be taken as the minimum number of moves a given tile must make to reach its goal position disregarding any complexities introduced by the location of the other tiles. Thus, a tile immediately adjacent to its final destination would be associated with a distance of one, whereas a tile whose corner touches the square of its final destination would be associated with a distance of two (since it must move at least one position vertically and another position horizontally).

Adopting this system, we observe that the quantity associated with each state is actually an approximation of the number of moves required to reach the goal

Figure 10-8 An unsolved 8-puzzle

from that state, which we refer to as the projected cost. For instance, the projected cost associated with the configuration in Figure 10-8 would be seven (since tiles 2, 5, and 8 are each a distance of one from their final destinations while tiles 3 and 6 are each a distance of two from home), and in fact it would actually taken seven moves to return it to the solved configuration.

The projected cost has two important characteristics. First, as just noted, it constitutes a reasonable estimate of the amount of work remaining in the solution if that state were reached. This means that it should be helpful in decision making. Second, it can be calculated easily and independently of the actual puzzle solution. This means that its use has a chance of benefiting the search process rather than of becoming a burden. (In contrast, although an excellent piece of information to have when making decisions would be the actual number of moves required to reach the goal from the given state, computing this information would involve finding the actual solution first.)

Applying Heuristics

Now that we have a quantitative measure for the heuristic information, the next step is to incorporate it into our decision-making process. To this end we recall that a human faced with a decision tends to select the option that appears closest to the goal. Thus, we will alter our search procedure of Section 10-4 to consider the projected cost of each leaf node in the tree and pursue the search from a leaf node associated with the smallest such cost. Based on this principle, we present the algorithm of Figure 10-9 for developing a search tree and executing the solution obtained.

As an example, let us walk through this algorithm as it applies to the 8−puzzle starting from the initial configuration in Figure 10-5. First, we establish this initial state as the root node and record its projected cost, which is five. Then, the first pass through the body of the while loop instructs the addition of the three nodes, as in Figure 10-10. Note that we have recorded in parentheses the projected cost of each leaf node beneath it.

Since the goal node has not been reached, we again pass through the body of the while loop, this time extending our search from the left-most node ("the left-

Figure 10-9 A pseudocode program for a control system using heuristics

Establish the start node of the state graph as the root of the
search tree and record its projected cost.
while (the goal node has not been reached) **do**
(Select the left-most leaf node with the smallest projected
cost of all leaf nodes, and attach as children to the
selected node those nodes that can be reached by a
single production from the selected node.
Record the projected cost of each of these new nodes next
to the node in the search tree.)
Traverse the search tree from the goal node up to the root,
pushing the production associated with each arc traversed
onto a stack.
Solve the original problem by executing the productions as they
are popped off the stack.

most node with the smallest projected cost"). After this, the search tree will have taken the form displayed in Figure 10-11.

Note that the projected cost of the leaf node in the left branch is now five, indicating that this is perhaps not a good choice to pursue after all. The algorithm picks up on this and in the next pass through the loop instructs us to expand the tree from the right-most branch (which is the "left-most leaf node with the smallest projected cost"). Having been expanded in this fashion, the search tree will appear as in Figure 10-12.

At this point the algorithm seems to be on the right track. Because the projected cost of this last node is only three, the while loop will instruct us to continue

Figure 10-10 The beginning of our heuristic search

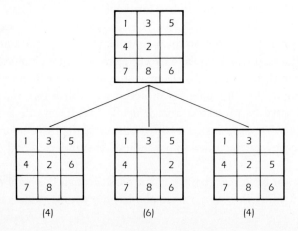

(4)   (6)   (4)

Figure 10-11

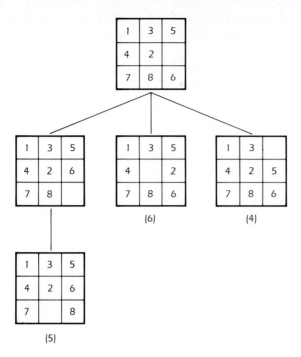

Figure 10-12

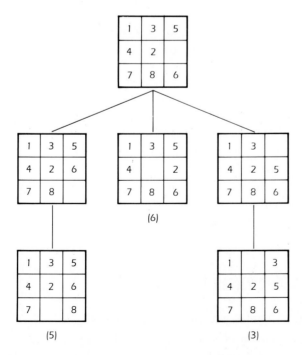

pursuing this path and the search will finally arrive at the goal with the search tree appearing as in Figure 10-13. Comparing this with the tree in Figure 10-6 shows that even with the temporary wrong turn taken early on by the new algorithm, the use of heuristic information has greatly decreased the size of the search tree and produced a much more efficient process.

After reaching the goal state, the while loop will terminate, and we will move on to traverse the tree from the goal node up to the root, pushing the productions encountered onto a stack as we go. Thus, the stack will appear as depicted earlier in Figure 10-7.

Finally, we are instructed to execute these productions as they are popped from the stack. At this point we would observe the puzzle solving machine raise its arm and begin to move the tiles.

Questions/Exercises

1. What analogy can be drawn between our heuristic system for solving the 8–puzzle and a mountain climber who attempts to reach the peak by considering only the local terrain and always proceeding in the direction of steepest ascent?

2. Using the heuristic information as presented in this section, apply the control-system algorithm of Figure 10-9 to the problem of solving the 8–puzzle configured as shown below:

1	2	3
4		8
7	6	5

3. Refine our method of computing the projected cost for a state so that the search algorithm of Figure 10-9 will not take the wrong branch as it did in the example in this section. Can you find an example where your system would still cause the search to go astray?

4. What would be the shape of the search tree produced by the algorithm in Figure 10-9 if the projected cost of all states were the same?

10–6 Applications of Artificial Intelligence

Having considered some of the techniques used in artificial intelligence, we turn now to the areas in which such techniques have found or are finding applications.

Figure 10-13 The search tree formed by our heuristic system

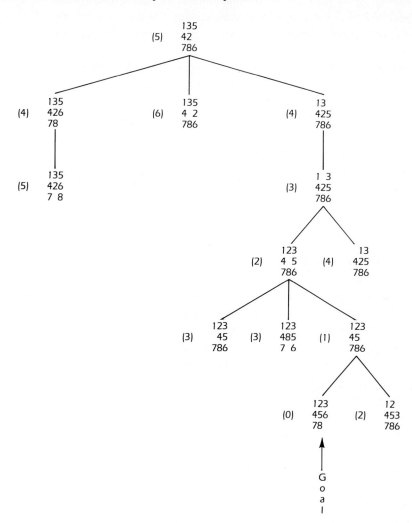

Language Processing

We begin with the task of translating statements from one language to another. Here, we find both traditional and artificial intelligence systems being used depending on the languages involved. The distinction centers around whether or not the semantics of a statement must be considered to produce the translation. For instance, traditional programming languages are designed so that they can be translated through the rather straightforward process of essentially finding the original statement (or statement part) in a table in which it is stored along with its translated equivalent.

Thus, the machine is never called upon to either understand or appear to understand the statements being translated, but rather it must merely recognize their syntax. We therefore classify such translation applications as being in the range of traditional computer applications.

In contrast is the problem of translating natural languages such as English where semantics plays an important role. For instance, to translate the word *fired* in the two sentences "John fired the employee" and "John fired the gun," one must understand the meaning of the sentence rather than convert individual words into the new language by means of a word-by-word conversion table. Thus, a considerable amount of intelligence (either simulated or real) is required to produce an accurate translation. In fact, understanding natural languages is one of the major pursuits of research in artificial intelligence today.

Robotics

Another application is found in the area of robotics or, from a less flamboyant perspective, machinery control. In particular, consider the use of computer-controlled systems in factory assembly lines (Figure 10-14). In this setting a machine is often asked to repeat a task over and over in an atmosphere where each execution of the task is exactly the same (or at least any variations can be handled in a straightforward manner). The important point is that the machine performs its task in a controlled environment. That is, if the task is to pick up assemblies and place them in boxes, the assemblies arrive on a conveyer belt at regular intervals and full boxes are consistently replaced by empty ones in the same location. Thus, the machine does not really pick up an assembly but merely closes its gripper at a particular time at a particular location and moves its arm to another location where, rather than placing the assembly in a box, it merely opens its gripper. Most would agree, then, that intelligence is not embedded in such an application.

A major difference arises if the machine must perform its task in an uncontrolled environment. Prominent examples occur in uninhabitable and unknown environments as found in such exotic pursuits as space exploration, or even in our factory assembly lines. Indeed, slight modifications of the task of picking up assemblies previously cited can result in the machine's being required to exhibit significant intelligent characteristics. For example, suppose the assemblies were delivered in a box containing an assortment of other parts rather than being isolated on a conveyer belt. The machine's task would include recognizing the correct assemblies, moving other parts out of the way, and picking up the correct objects. Assuming that the objects were placed in the box in an arbitrary manner, the retrieval of each assembly would require a unique sequence of steps that must be developed within the machine itself. Moreover, the machine would have to monitor and comprehend the situation constantly since parts in the box might shift, which would cause the required activities to change.

Figure 10-14 Assembly line robots welding car frames (Courtesy of Chrysler Motors Corporation)

Such concerns fall within the scope of artificial intelligence and comprise much of the subject of robotics. Since successes in this area can readily result in financial gain, it is not surprising that this subject has attracted major attention from the industrial sector of our society and that corresponding progress has been made in recent years.

Database Systems

Next we consider data storage and retrieval systems. These systems represent a major application of natural language-processing systems. The goal is to be able to request information from these systems by means of a natural language rather than requiring the human using the system to conform to a special and somewhat technical query language. However, artificial intelligence techniques are also used in the process of actually answering the question posed by the user.

Along these lines, traditional systems can merely retrieve the facts that were explicitly requested and previously stored, whereas the goal within artificial intelligence is to provide for the retrieval of both information that is related although not directly requested and information not explicitly stored. A need for the former capabilities is found in legal searches. A lawyer might need to retrieve information about all previous cases relating to the present litigation; however, whether or not a case relates to the current one is a vague concept requiring judgment. A common approach to this problem taken by today's computer systems is to request the searcher to identify key words and phrases that should appear in any relevant case. The system then searches through all the case histories and retrieves those cases containing these words and phrases. Such a system is really merely a sieve that reduces the number of cases that must be reviewed by the lawyer and may even overlook the most important case because it deals with "cars" rather than with "automobiles." A truly intelligent system, however, would produce a more reliable selection.

With regard to the ability to reply with information not explicitly stored, consider a database consisting of information about the presidents of the United States of America. When asked if there has ever been a president who was 10 feet tall, a traditional system would not be able to reply with the answer unless the height of each president was actually stored in the database. On the other hand, an intelligent system could reply correctly without knowing each president's height. The line of reasoning might go like this. If there had been a president who was 10 feet tall, that would have been significant and would be stored in the database. Therefore, since no president is recorded as being 10 feet tall, there have been no such presidents.

The conclusion that there have not been presidents who were 10 feet tall involves an important concept in database design—the distinction between closed-world databases and open-world databases. A closed-world database is one that is assumed to contain all true facts about the topic involved, whereas an open-world database does not encompass this assumption. Thus, the ability to reject the hypothesis of a 10-foot president in the previous example was based on the closed-world assumption that if the fact is not recorded then it must be false.

Still another goal of artificial intelligence research within the database environment deals with the problem of figuring out what the user of the system really wants to know or should be told instead of literally answering the question posed. For example, suppose we had a database consisting of the courses taught by the professors at a university along with the grades they awarded the students. Consider the following sequence of events: We ask the database for the number of A grades awarded by Professor Johnson last semester. The database replies, "none." We conclude that Professor Johnson was a rather demanding instructor and ask for the number of F grades awarded by Professor Johnson last semester. Again, the database replies, "none." We decide that Professor Johnson considers all students to be average except in extreme cases. Thus, we ask for the number of C grades awarded by Professor Johnson last semester. The database again replies, "none." At this point we begin to get suspicious and ask whether Professor Johnson taught a course last semester. The database replies, "no." If only it had said so in the first place!

Expert Systems

An important and increasingly popular extension of the intelligent database concept is the development of *expert systems*—software packages designed to assist humans in situations in which an expert in a specific area is required. These systems are designed to simulate the cause-and-effect reasoning that an expert would do if confronted with the same situation. Thus, just as a medical expert might know that a biopsy should be performed if an abnormality is noticed and an X ray shows the presence of mass in that location, a medical expert system should propose the same procedure.

It follows that a major task in constructing an expert system is to obtain the required knowledge from an expert. In fact, how this can be done has become a major area of research in the area of psychology. The problem is actually twofold. One task is to procure and maintain the expert's cooperation—an undertaking that may not be easy since the questioning involved is likely to be long and frustrating, and at the same time the idea of relinquishing knowledge to a system that might ultimately take the expert's place is not comforting to the expert. The other complicating factor is that most experts have never considered what reasoning process they use in reaching their conclusions. When asked, "How did you know to do that?" they often reply, "I don't know."

Once these acquisition problems are overcome, the knowledge gained from the expert must be organized into a format compatible with a software system. This organization is normally done by expressing the knowledge as a collection of rules in the form of if-then statements. For instance, the rule that an abnormality, confirmed by X rays, should lead to the performance of a biopsy might be expressed as:

```
if abnormality noticed and
    X ray shows presence of mass
then perform biopsy
```

Notice the similarity between such rules and the productions of a production system. The "if" portion of the rule essentially states the preconditions for performing or concluding the statement found in the "then" portion. Indeed, an expert system is usually implemented as a production system, with the rules obtained from the human expert being the productions and the underlying reasoning based on these rules being simulated by the control system. In this context the collection of productions is often called the system's knowledge base, and the control system is sometimes referred to as an inference engine.

(Those who read the optional section on declarative programming in Chapter 5 will recognize the similarity between the structure of an expert system and that of a Prolog program. In fact, a knowledge base is essentially a collection of Prolog facts and rules, and the inference engine corresponds to Prolog's problem-solving algorithm. This similarity is a major reason for the popularity of Prolog in the field of artificial intelligence. Indeed, Prolog is an excellent language in which to develop an expert system.)

Do not be misled, however, into thinking that an expert system is merely a large version of the puzzle-solving system discussed earlier. One distinction is that the underlying production system within an expert system is not necessarily charged with reaching a predetermined goal but is more likely to be charged with deriving well-founded advice. This means that the heuristics used are not measurements of closeness to a goal, since no precise goal is actually present. Rather, heuristics used in expert systems tend to be the rules of thumb used by the human expert.

Our claim that no precise goal may exist in the setting of an expert system may bother you, so let us consider this claim a bit further. Suppose either an expert or an expert system is charged with the problem of diagnosing diseases. Ideally, one would like both systems to conclude with a definitive statement of the form "The disease is X" where in place of X the statement gives the name of the disease present. Unfortunately, such precision may not be possible. Instead, the best answer might be, "The disease is most likely X." or perhaps, "The disease is either X or Y. Please perform the following test to determine which is more likely." Because of this ambiguity, the control system within an expert system may choose to follow several paths through the system's state space and report on the results of each. Indeed, if the production applied at some state is

> if rheumatoid factor present and
>   patient has pain in joints
> then 80% chance of rheumatoid arthritis

then any further reasoning based on the fact that the disease is rheumatoid arthritis has the potential of being invalid.

As in other research areas, early applications of expert systems were limited to only a few areas. Today, however, the number of areas in which expert systems are finding applications is rapidly increasing. One catalyst for this expansion is the realization that an expert system can be separated into its reasoning component and its knowledge component. That is, computer scientists have found that by removing the knowledge base from an existing expert system, one is left with a system of reasoning routines that is likely to be applicable in other settings as well. Thus, new expert systems in other areas can be constructed merely by attaching a new knowledge base to this already existing reasoning system. Indeed, this is essentially the observation that the control system we developed for solving the 8–puzzle could be applied to other problems merely by replacing the 8–puzzle productions with the productions representing those other problems.

Questions/Exercises

1. Explain the ambiguities involved when translating the sentence "They are racing horses."

2. In what sense is a closed-world database more powerful than an open-world database? In what sense is the maintenance of a closed-world database more demanding?

3. In what sense does the knowledge base in an expert system differ from a traditional database?

Chapter 10 Review Problems

1. Sometimes the ability to answer a question depends as much on knowing what facts are known as on the facts themselves. For example, suppose databases A and B both contain a complete list of employees who belong to the company's health insurance program but only database A is aware that the list is complete. What could database A conclude about a member who was not on its list that database B could not?

2. In the text we briefly discussed the problems of understanding natural languages as opposed to formal programming languages. As an example of the complexities involved in the case of natural languages, identify two situations in which the question "Do you know what time it is?" has different meanings.

3. As demonstrated by problem 2, humans may use a question for a purpose other than asking. An example is "Do you know that your tire is flat?" which is used to inform rather than to ask. Give examples of questions used to reassure, to warn, and to criticize.

4. Compare the roles of the prepositional phrases in the following two sentences (that differ by only one word):

   The pigpen was built by the barn.
   The pigpen was built by the farmer.

5. If a researcher were using computer models for studying the memorization capabilities and processes of the human mind, would the programs developed for the machine necessarily memorize to the best of the machine's abilities? Explain.

6. Which of the following activities would you expect to be performance oriented and which would be simulation oriented:
   a. The design of a flight simulator.
   b. The design of an automatic pilot system.
   c. The design of a database dealing with library materials.
   d. The design of a model of a nation's economy for testing theories.
   e. The design of a program for monitoring a patient's vital signs.

7. Identify a small set of geometric properties that could be used to distinguish between the symbols O, G, C, and Q.

8. Describe the similarities between the technique of identifying characteristics by comparing them to templates and the error correcting codes discussed in Chapter 1.

9. Describe two interpretations of the following line drawing depending on whether the the "corner" marked A is convex or concave:

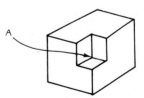

10. In the setting of a production system, what is the difference between a state graph and a search tree?

11. In the text we mentioned that a production system is often used as a technique for drawing con-

clusions from known facts. The states of the system are the facts known to be true at each stage of the reasoning process, and the productions are the rules of logic for manipulating the known facts. Identify some rules of logic that would allow the conclusion "John is tall" to be obtained from the facts that "John is a basketball player," "Basketball players are not short," and "John is either short or tall."

12. The following tree represents possible moves in a competitive game showing that player X currently has a choice between move A and move B. Following the move of player X, player Y will be allowed to select a move, and then player X will be allowed to select the last move of the game. The leaf nodes of the tree are labeled W, L, or T depending on whether that ending represents a win, loss, or tie for player X. Should player X select move A or move B? Why? How does selecting a "production" in a competitive atmosphere differ from a one-person game such as the 8–puzzle?

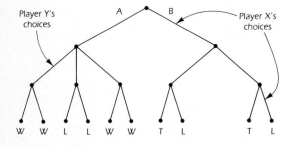

13. By considering the manipulation rules of algebra as productions, problems involving the simplification of algebraic expression can be solved in the setting of a production system. Identify a set of algebraic productions that would allow the equation $3/(2x + 1) = 2/(2x − 2)$ to be reduced to the form $x = 4$. What are some rules of thumb (that is, heuristic rules) used when performing such algebraic simplifications?

14. Draw the search tree that would be generated by a breadth-first search (Section 10-4, question 1) in an attempt to solve the 8–puzzle from the initial state shown below without using the assistance of any heuristic information:

	1	3
4	2	5
7	8	6

15. Draw the search tree that would be generated by the search algorithm of Figure 10-9 in an attempt to solve the 8–puzzle from the initial state in problem 14 if the number of tiles out of place is used as a heuristic.

16. Draw the search tree that would be generated by the search algorithm of Figure 10-9 in an attempt to solve the 8–puzzle from the initial state shown below assuming the heuristic used is the same as that developed in Section 10-5:

1	2	3
5	7	6
4		8

17. What is the distinction between the technique of deciding which way to go when applying the binary search to a list stored as a tree (Chapter 8) and the use of a heuristic when searching for a goal state in the context of a production system?

18. What heuristic do you use when searching for a route between two cities on a large road map?

19. List two properties that a heuristic should have if it is to be useful in a production system.

20. Suppose you have two buckets. One has a capacity of exactly 3 liters; the other has a capacity of 5 liters. You can pour water from one bucket to another, empty a bucket, or fill a bucket at any time. Your problem is to place exactly 4 liters of water in the 5-liter bucket. Formulate this problem as a production system.

21. Suppose your job is to supervise the loading of two trucks, each of which can carry at most 14 tons. The cargo is a variety of crates whose total weight is 28 tons but whose individual weights vary from crate to crate. The weight of each crate is marked on its side. What heuristic would you use for dividing the crates between the two trucks?

Problems for the Programmer

1. Write a program that matches input symbols to predefined templates and reports on its findings. Input the symbols in the form of a matrix of zeros and ones where zeros represent white pixels of the input image and ones represent black pixels. Design your program so that it does not require an exact match but rather allows for slight imperfections. Experiment with the problem of distinguishing between the symbols O, Q, and C.

2. Implement the puzzle-solving algorithm in Figure 10-9. Design your system to accept the initial puzzle state in the form of a three-by-three matrix and to display the solution as a series of such matrices. You may wish to experiment with different heuristics for determining the projected cost. (How should your program be designed to make such experimentation as easy as possible?)

3. Write a program that changes simple statements of the form "I am . . ." into questions of the form "Why are you . . . ?" Does your program correctly handle the statement "I am your friend"? (It should change "your" to "my" to produce "Why are you my friend?") What character-manipulating features are available in your programming language that simplify your programming task?

4. Write two programs, one performance oriented and the other simulation oriented, to play tic-tac-toe.

11 Theory of Computation

11–1 **A Bare Bones Programming Language**
Data Description Issues
Process Description Statements
The Scope of Bare Bones

11–2 **Turning Machines**
An Abstraction of a Real Machine
A Specific Example

11–3 **Computable Functions**
Functions and Their Computation
The Equivalence of Turing Machines and Bare Bones

11–4 **A Noncomputable Function**
Some Preliminaries
The Halting Problem

11–5 **Complexity and Its Measure**
Complexity of the Insertion Sort
Complexity of the Quick Sort
Orders of Complexity

11–6 **Problem Classification**
Polynomial Problems
Nonpolynomial Problems
NP Problems

In this chapter we discuss some theoretical ideas that ultimately center around the question of what algorithmic computers can and cannot do. We start by introducing a very simple programming language. Next we see that any problem that can be solved on a modern computer has a solution that can be expressed in that language. If a programming language is designed to encompass the features of this simple language, it is guaranteed to provide a means of expressing a solution to any problem that the machine is capable of solving. We then consider the question of whether or not more powerful machines can be constructed in the future and discover that there are problems that today's machines cannot solve and that apparently no future algorithmic machine will be able to solve. Finally, we find that even among the machine-solvable problems there appear to be those problems whose solutions are so complex that they are unsolvable from a practical point of view.

Many of the results in this chapter were originally obtained in the early twentieth century by mathematicians working in the area of mathematics known as logic and foundations. Thus, many of the points about the problem-solving ability of modern machines summarized here were known well before today's technology evolved. Moreover, this large area of knowledge and research that used to be classified as mathematics is now classified by many as computer science. Regardless of its classification, the subject presents a truly fascinating study of the power and limitations of mathematical reasoning. Paramount in the subject is the paper published by the German mathematician Kurt Gödel in 1931 that essentially shows that within any mathematical system encompassing the system of natural numbers (1, 2, 3, . . .) and the arithmetic operations of addition and multiplication, statements exist that can be neither proven nor disproven.

11–1 A Bare Bones Programming Language

Let us being by assuming that we have been asked to design a programming language for a new computer. The structure of the machine is similar to that described in Chapter 2. That is, the machine has a memory in which data can be stored in the form of zeros and ones, and attached to this memory is a CPU, which can retrieve data from memory, manipulate it, and place the results back in memory.

Although we do not know to what applications the machine will be applied in the future, we must design our language with enough flexibility so that its use does not later restrict the powers provided by the hardware itself. In other words, we do not want to discover at a future date that the hardware/software combination is not able to solve a problem that it otherwise could have solved had we provided other features in our programming language. On the other hand, we assume that considerations of expense dictate that we not provide an abundance of features that merely enhance convenience. Our task is to design a powerful yet concise programming language for the machine.

In this section we will describe a procedural programming language that fulfills the conditions just outlined. Because our ultimate purpose is to isolate the minimum requirements of a programming language, our language will have few of the conveniences found in other programming languages. It is therefore fitting that we refer to this language as Bare Bones.

Our description of Bare Bones will follow the format of the discussion of programming languages in Chapter 5. We first present the language features for data description, followed by the assignment statements, and then discuss the control statements in the language.

Data Description Issues

As we have seen, data in a machine is coded in terms of zeros and ones, and thus the meaning of the bit string is a matter of interpretation. After all, the machine does not associate meaning with the bit strings but merely performs bit manipulation operations as directed by a program. Thus, the variety of data types and structures available in most high-level programming languages can be viewed as a matter of convenience rather than of necessity. The purpose of these data types and structures is to assist a human trying to understand a program rather than to increase the ultimate capabilities of the language. Simplicity of a language itself can therefore be increased by avoiding the use of different data types and structures and instead considering each data item as merely a string of bits. Furthermore, the design of the language need not place a restriction on the length of such a string so that any such restriction will be a result of the machine's properties and not those of the language. Theoretically (that is, so far as the language is concerned) the strings manipulated by the language can be arbitrarily long.

Because our language adopts these simplifying concepts, there is no need for a syntactic structure by which data options are specified since there is only one data type and one data structure available. Thus, instead of using data description statements to present variable names and their properties, we can simply begin using the names as they are required in the procedural part of the program being written. An interpreter or translator can then set aside memory cells for data elements as each name is discovered in the process description rather than handling all such allocations prior to scanning the procedural part.

The only concern is that the interpreter or translator must be able to distinguish variable names from the other terms. This is done by carefully designing the syntax of Bare Bones so that the role of any term can be identified by its context. For this purpose, we adopt the policy of terminating each statement with a semicolon so that an interpreter or translator can easily separate statements and from there isolate the statement parts. We do, however, specify that a variable name consist only of letters from the traditional alphabet. Thus, the strings XYZ, Bill, and abcdefghi could be used as variable names, whereas G25, $o, or x.y could not.

Process Description Statements

Bare Bones contains only three assignment statements, each of which takes the form of modifying the contents of the variable identified in the statement. The first allows us to associate a string of zeros with a variable name. Its syntax is:

clear *name;*

where *name* can be any legal variable name.

The other assignment statements are essentially opposites of each other:

incr *name;*

and

decr name;

where again *name* represents any legal variable name. The first of these statements increments the value associated with the identified variable. Here the term *increment* refers to the interpretation of bit patterns as representing numeric values in base two notation. From the purely bit manipulative point of view, increment means to advance the binary odometer one position. Thus, if the pattern 101 were associated with Y before the statement:

incr Y;

were executed, the pattern 110 would be associated with Y afterward. That is, one would be added to the value assigned to Y.

In contrast, the statement "decr name;" is used to decrement the value associated with the identified variable or, in other words, to roll the binary odometer backward one position. An exception is when the identified variable is already associated with zero, in which case this statement leaves the value unaltered. Therefore, if the value associated with Y were 101 before the statement:

decr Y;

were executed, the pattern 100 would be associated with Y afterward. However, if the value of Y had been zero before executing the statement, the value would remain zero after execution.

Bare Bones contains only one control structure represented by a while/end statement pair. The statement sequence:

while name not 0 do;
.
.
.
end;

(where *name* represents any legal variable name) causes any statement or statement sequence positioned between the while and end statements to be repeated so long as the value of the variable *name* is not zero. To be more precise, when a while/end structure is encountered during program execution, the value of the identified variable is first compared to zero. If it is zero, the structure is skipped and execution continues with the statement following the end statement. If, however, the variable's value is not zero, the statement sequence within the while/end structure will be executed and control will be returned to the while statement, whereupon the comparison will be conducted again. Note that the burden of loop control is partially placed on the programmer who must explicitly request that the variable's value be altered within the loop body to avoid an infinite loop. For instance, the sequence:

```
          incr X;
          while X not 0 do;
              incr Z;
          end;
```

would result in an infinite process since the value associated with X will never be zero, whereas the sequence:

```
          clear Z;
          while X not 0 do;
              incr Z;
              decr X;
          end;
```

will ultimately terminate with the effect of transferring the value associated with X to the variable Z.

Observe that while and end statements must appear in pairs with the while statement appearing first. However, a while/end instruction pair may appear within the instructions being repeated by another while/end pair. In such a case, the pairing of while and end statements is accomplished by scanning the program in its written form from beginning to end while associating each end statement with the nearest preceding while statement not yet paired. Although not syntactically necessary, we often use indentation to enhance the readability of such structures. For example, the instruction sequence in Figure 11-1 would result in the product of the values associated with X and Y being associated with Z (although it has the side effect of destroying any nonzero value that may have been associated with X). (The while/end structure controlled by the variable W has the effect of restoring the original value of Y.)

Finally, we note that a Bare Bones program terminates when there are no further instructions.

The Scope of Bare Bones

Keep in mind that although we set the stage for this section with a proposal for a usable programming language, our goal here actually deals with what is possible, not what is practical. Bare Bones would probably prove to be more awkward than most machine languages if used in an applied setting. On the other hand, in Sections 11-2 and 11-3 we argue that this simple language does fulfill our goal of providing a no-frills language whose use places no additional restrictions on the power of the machine. That is, any problem that can be solved by the machine has a solution expressible in Bare Bones (although one could argue that such an expression would often prove to be unwieldy). Thus, languages such as this find their major applications within the theoretical concerns of computer science rather than within application programming. Moreover, they point out how much of high-level language design is aimed toward enhancing clarity rather than increasing processing power.

As a side issue, we note that through simple languages such as Bare Bones the relative power of various language features can be studied. For example, in Appendix

and

Figure 11-1 A Bare Bones program for computing X × Y

```
clear Z;
while X not 0 do;
   clear W;
   while Y not 0 do;
      incr Z;
      incr W;
      decr Y;
   end;
   while W not 0 do;
      incr Y;
      decr W;
   end;
   decr X;
end;
```

E we use Bare Bones as a tool to settle the question regarding the equivalence of loop and recursive structures raised in Chapter 4. There we find that our suspicion of equivalence was, in fact, justified.

For now we support our claims regarding the power of Bare Bones by demonstrating how its use allows the expression of some elementary operations. We first note that with a combination of the assignment statements any value can be associated with a given name. For example, the following sequence assigns the bit pattern 11 (the binary value three) to the name X by first clearing any previous association and then incrementing its value three times:

```
clear X;
incr X;
incr X;
incr X;
```

Another common activity in programs is to move data from one location to another as in the instruction MOVE TAX TO EXTRA. In terms of Bare Bones this means that we need to be able to assign to one name a bit pattern previously assigned to another name. This can be accomplished by first clearing the destination and then incrementing it an appropriate number of times. In fact, we have already observed that the sequence:

```
clear Z;
while X not 0 do;
   incr Z;
   decr X;
end;
```

transfers the value associated with X to Z. On the other hand, this sequence has the side effect of destroying the original value of X. To correct for this, we can introduce an auxiliary variable to which we first transfer the subject value from its initial location. We then use this auxiliary variable as the data source from which we restore the original variable while placing the subject value in the desired destination. In this manner, the movement of TAX to EXTRA could be accomplished by the sequence shown in Figure 11-2.

Figure 11-2 A Bare Bones implementation of the instruction "move TAX to EXTRA"

```
clear AUX;
clear EXTRA;
while TAX not 0 do;
    incr AUX;
    decr TAX;
end;
while AUX not 0 do;
    incr TAX;
    incr EXTRA;
    decr AUX;
end;
```

We will adopt the syntax:

move *name1* to *name2*;

(where *name1* and *name2* represent variable names) as a shorthand notation for a statement structure of the form in Figure 11-2. Thus, although Bare Bones itself does not have an explicit move instruction, we will often write programs as though it did, with the understanding that to convert such informal programs into real Bare Bones programs one would have to replace the move statements with their equivalent while/end structures using an auxiliary variable whose name does not clash with a name already used elsewhere in the program.

Questions/Exercises

1. Show that the statement "invert X;" (whose action is to convert the value of X to zero if its initial value is nonzero and to one if its initial value is zero) can be simulated by a Bare Bones program segment.
2. Show that even our simple Bare Bones language contains more statements than necessary by showing that the clear statement could be replaced with combinations of other statements in the language.
3. Show that the if-then-else structure can be simulated using Bare Bones. That is, write a program sequence in Bare Bones that simulates the action of the statement:

   if X not 0 then S1 else S2;

   where S1 and S2 represent arbitrary statement sequences.
4. Show that each of the Bare Bones statements can be expressed in terms of the machine language of Appendix B. (Thus, Bare Bones could be used as a programming language for such a machine.)
5. How can negative numbers be dealt with in Bare Bones?

11–2 Turing Machines

In Section 11-1 we hinted that with Bare Bones we could express an algorithm for solving any problem that any algorithmic machine is capable of solving. We discuss this claim in more detail in Section 11-3, but first we must develop a better understanding of the capabilities of algorithmic machines themselves.

An Abstraction of a Real Machine

We begin by concentrating on the major components of today's computing machinery: memory and the CPU. A machine's memory is nothing more than a row of cells, each of which can hold one of a finite number of different bit patterns. (If a machine's memory cells consisted of two bits each, each cell could contain one of the four patterns 00, 01, 10, 11.) We call the collection of these bit patterns the machine's alphabet. An important observation is that so long as a machine's alphabet has at least two different elements in it, we can devise a coding system by which any information can be represented in the machine's memory. Thus, a machine with only one bit per memory cell could store the same information as any other machine.

Next we note that the activity of a CPU is essentially to "look" at a cell in memory and change its content depending on the state of the machine at that time, where the machine's state is the collection of register values within the CPU. The number of states available to a given machine is limited since only a finite number of registers is present in any particular machine and thus only a finite number of ways exist to fill them with objects from the machine's alphabet.

Finally we observe that having interrogated one memory cell, the CPU can either halt or interrogate another cell whose location is again determined by the machine's state.

In summary, a computing machine can be viewed abstractly as consisting of a control unit, a list of memory cells each of which can contain a single object from a finite alphabet, and a finite collection of control states. A program for the machine is simply a definition of what action is to take place as the result of each possible state and memory cell value.

With these machine features in mind, let us consider the hypothetical computing machines described by Alan M. Turing in 1936 and now known as *Turing machines*. Keep in mind that we referred to these machines as being hypothetical. Such a machine can never actually be constructed since, as we will see, a Turing machine has an infinite amount of memory. The importance of these machines lies in the fact that they represent a generalization of real machines—a generalization that, because of its unlimited storage abilities, exceeds the capabilities of any of today's algorithmic machines. Moreover, indications are that no future machine will be able to exceed these capabilities either. Thus, Turing machines represent a theoretical limit to the capabilities of real machines.

Turing machines consist of a computing mechanism (that we envision as being mechanical, electrical, or even human) in combination with an infinitely long strip of tape divided into cells on which the computing mechanism can record symbols from a finite alphabet. The symbol to be recorded depends on the current content

Figure 11-3 An actual machine compared to a Turing machine

	Actual machine	Abstract Turing machine
Memory:	A finite number of cells organized in a row with each cell containing one of a finite number of possible bit patterns	An infinite number of cells organized sequentially on a tape with each cell containing one symbol from a finite alphabet
Control unit:	An electronic device	No particular technology—could be mechanical, electrical or human
States:	A finite collection of register value assignments	A finite collection of abstract states in which the machine might be found at any given time
Control unit/ Memory interface:	Where the control unit can retrieve and/or alter the contents of any memory cells as directed by its register values	Where the control unit can interrogate and possibly alter any memory cell depending on its current state and the contents of the interrogated cell

of the cell in question and the state of the machine at the time. Having written a symbol in the current cell, the computing mechanism can move its attention one cell to the right or the left on the tape or remain at the same location. Here again the action is determined by the condition of the machine together with the original content of the cell just examined. Each machine is defined to have a finite number of possible conditions called states, some of which may be halt states in the sense that once the machine reaches such a state no further action takes place.

The properties of Turing machines are remarkably similar to those of today's computers (Figure 11-3). The only significant difference is that a Turing machine has an infinite amount of memory, whereas today's machines are physically limited to a finite amount. This means that if any difference exists in the abilities of the two (which it does), the Turing machines should be more powerful. Again remember that we are interested in theoretical possibility, not in practicality. Although a machine with an infinite amount of memory may be more powerful than one with a finite amount, in reality it is impossible to build the more powerful version. On the other hand, in Section 11-3 we argue that our Bare Bones language, although very simple, is flexible enough to serve as a programming tool even for the more powerful infinite machine without restricting the machine's capabilities.

A Specific Example

To make the preceding discussion more concrete, we consider an example of a specific Turing machine. For this purpose we represent the machine's tape as a horizontal strip divided into cells in which we can record symbols from the machine's alphabet. We indicate the machine's current position on the tape by placing a pointer under the current cell. The alphabet for our example consists of the symbols 0, 1, and *. Thus, the tape of our machine might appear as follows:

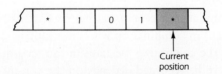

Current
position

Figure 11-4 A Turing machine for incrementing a value

Current state	Current cell content	Value to write	Direction to move	New state to enter
START	*	*	Left	ADD
ADD	0	1	Left	NO CARRY
ADD	1	0	Left	CARRY
ADD	*	*	Right	HALT
CARRY	0	1	Left	NO CARRY
CARRY	1	0	Left	CARRY
CARRY	*	1	Left	OVERFLOW
NO CARRY	0	0	Left	NO CARRY
NO CARRY	1	1	Left	NO CARRY
NO CARRY	*	*	Right	RETURN
OVERFLOW	(ignored)	*	Right	RETURN
RETURN	0	0	Right	RETURN
RETURN	1	1	Right	RETURN
RETURN	*	*	No move	HALT

By interpreting a string of symbols on the tape as representing binary numbers separated by asterisks, we recognize that this particular tape contains the value five. Our Turing machine will be designed to increment such a value on the tape by one. More precisely, it will assume that the starting position is at an asterisk marking the right end of a string of zeros and ones, and it will proceed by rolling the binary odometer one notch.

The states for our machine are START, ADD, CARRY, NO CARRY, OVER-FLOW, and HALT. The actions corresponding to each of these states and the content of the current cell are described in the table in Figure 11-4. We assume that the machine always begins in the START state.

Let us apply this machine to the tape pictured earlier that contains the value five. Observe that when in the START state with the current cell containing * (as is our case) we are instructed by the table to rewrite the *, move our position one cell to the left, and enter the ADD state. Having done this our situation can be described as follows:

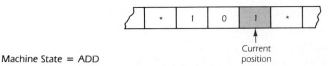

Machine State = ADD

To proceed we look at the table to see what to do when in the ADD state with the current cell containing 1. The table tells us to replace the 1 in the current cell with 0, move one cell to the left, and enter the CARRY state. Our situation would then be described by the following:

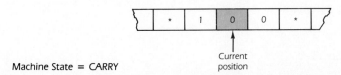

Machine State = CARRY

We again refer to the table to see what to do next and find that when in the CARRY state with the current cell containing 0 we should replace the 0 with 1, move one cell to the left, and enter the NO CARRY state. After doing this our situation will be as follows:

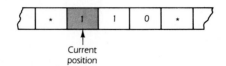

Machine State = NO CARRY

Current position

From this situation the table instructs us to proceed by replacing the 1 in the current cell with another 1, move one cell to the left, and remain in the NO CARRY state. Consequently, we will find our machine in the following condition:

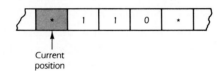

Machine State = NO CARRY

Current position

Now the table tells us to rewrite the asterisk in the current cell, move one position to the right, and enter the RETURN state. Continuing in this fashion, we will remain in the RETURN state as we move back to the right cell by cell until we finally arrive at the condition as follows:

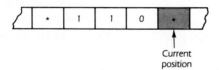

Machine State = RETURN

Current position

At this point we see that the table instructs us to rewrite the asterisk in the current cell and HALT. The machine would thus stop in the following configuration (the symbols on the tape now represent the value six as desired):

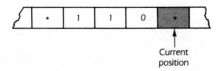

Machine State = HALT

Current position

In closing we note that this example has shown how a Turing machine might perform the action described by the statement:

incr X;

in the Bare Bones language of Section 11-1.

Questions/Exercises

1. Apply the Turing machine described in this section starting with the initial status described below:

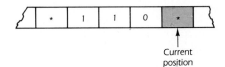

Machine State = START

2. Describe a Turing machine that would replace a string of zeros and ones with a single zero.
3. Describe a Turing machine that decrements the value on the tape if it is greater than zero or leaves the value unaltered if it is zero.
4. Identify an everyday situation in which calculating takes place. How is that situation analogous to a Turing machine?

11–3 Computable Functions

To summarize Sections 11-1 and 11-2, we have presented an elementary programming language, an abstract version of actual computers, and the theoretical Turing machines. The only pertinent difference between the last two is that Turing machines have an infinite amount of memory, which makes them a generalized version of real machines. Our goal is to compare the capabilities of the simple language with that of the machines. For this purpose, we need a measure of computing power that is common to all of the entities to be compared.

Functions and Their Computation

The measure we need is available in the concept of computable functions. To explain, let us first return to the example in Section 11-2 of a Turing machine that increments a value. We can consider this as a machine that accepts a value as an input and, based on that value, produces another value as an output. Such an association between input values and output values is called a *function.* Many functions are so common that they have been given names such as addition, which with each input pair associates an output value equal to the sum of the inputs; multiplication, which again accepts an input pair but outputs a value equal to the product of the inputs; and the successor function, which with each input value associates an output that is one greater than the input.

   Numerous techniques have been used to display or otherwise represent the associations of a given function. One is to present a table displaying the possible input values along with their corresponding output values. However, the table in

Figure 11-5 *The successor function*

Input	Output
0	1
1	10
10	11
11	100
100	101
101	110
110	111
111	1000
1000	1001
.	.
.	.
.	.

Figure 11-5 that attempts to describe the successor function points out a problem with such a technique. No limit exists to the number of possible inputs to the function being represented, thus no way is available for the table to be complete. Thus, a tabular form can display functions that have only a finite number of inputs.

Another way of describing a function that avoids the size limitations of tables is to describe (in an algorithmic style) how the output is obtained from the input. You have most likely seen this technique in the form of an algebraic formula. For example, to describe the function whose input values consist of temperatures measured in Centigrade and whose outputs consist of the Fahrenheit equivalences, we would write:

$$F = (9/5)C + 32$$

which describes how the conversion is done rather than presenting the results of the conversion in tabular form.

(We note that the addition function is traditionally handled with a combination of the tabular and algorithmic techniques. That is, students are taught to memorize the first part of the incomplete table in the form of addition facts and calculate the output in the case of more complex inputs, which was also our approach to the logical operations in Chapter 2.)

Our goal in this section ultimately deals with the problem of how we can figure out what the output of a given function is if we know the input value (or values). If there is a way of "calculating" this output value we say that the function is *computable*. We have placed calculating within quotation marks because it proves to have a rather nebulous meaning. Intuitively, to calculate means to go through a well-defined, step-by-step process such as that described by the temperature conversion formula or perhaps the process of looking up the result in a table.

The vastness in the number of functions that exists is enough to allow mathematical arguments that show that for any reasonable definition of "to calculate" there remain functions that are not computable. Thus, just as there are functions that cannot be displayed in tabular form, there are functions that cannot be represented by any algorithmic technique. However, to actually identify a noncomputable function requires a more precise definition of the concepts involved. We continue, then, by giving a definition for a form of computability that is widely accepted as encompassing the intuitive meaning of "to calculate" and that links the computing power of Turing machines with that of our simple Bare Bones language.

The Equivalence of Turing Machines and Bare Bones

We again return to the Turing machine example of Section 11-2. This machine can be used to find the output values for the successor function by placing the input value in its binary form on the tape, running the machine until it halts, and reading the correct output value from the tape. In other words, the Turing machine previously described actually calculates, or computes, the successor function outputs for us. We therefore say that the successor function is Turing machine computable. Following this lead, we consider a function to be *Turing machine computable* if a Turing machine can be designed that, given any input to the function, will calculate the function's corresponding output.

In the previous paragraph we ignored the fact that some Turing machines may never reach their halt state. Consider, for example, the machine with only one state, START, in which it always writes the symbol 0 in the current position on the tape, moves left one position, and reenters the START state. Such a machine, regardless of the input value, will never halt but will continue writing zeros and stepping to the left forever. Other Turing machines may halt for some input values but not for others. In such cases we say that the function computed by the machine is a *partial function*, meaning that it may have undefined outputs associated with some of its inputs. A major result in computer science is that the collection of all functions, including the partial ones, that are Turing machine computable has been identified and is known as the class of *partial recursive functions*.

Turning now to the Bare Bones programming language, we observe that any program written in Bare Bones can be considered as computing a function by considering the initial values of certain variables called input variables (including all those with nonzero initial values) as the function's input and the values of certain variables called output variables (which may or may not be the same as the variables used for input) when the program halts as the function's output. Under these conditions the program:

```
incr X;
```

can be considered as computing the successor function as clearly as the Turing machine example of Section 11-2. Moreover, some of the programs written in our language compute partial functions, as seen by the following example. (The program halts with X equal to zero if X started as zero. However, for any other starting value of X, the program becomes caught in an infinite loop.)

```
while X not 0 do;
end;
```

At this point we have identified two ways of "calculating" functions. One uses Turing machines and the other uses programs written in our Bare Bones programming language. The important point is that researchers have shown that the two are equivalent. That is, any function that can be computed by a Turing machine can be computed by a program in Bare Bones, and any function that can be computed by a program written in Bare Bones can be computed by some Turing machine. Thus, the partial recursive functions constitute an extremely important class of functions in computer science.

In closing we return to the problem posed at the beginning of Section 11-1 of developing a language capable of expressing the solution of any problem solvable by the given machine. Since the machine, having a finite memory, is merely a restricted version of a Turing machine, its capabilities are no greater than those of the more general Turing machines. Furthermore, we have found a simple language capable of expressing the solution of any problem solvable by a Turing machine, and that language theoretically fulfills the objective of providing a programming language for the machine without adding restrictions to the machine's capabilities. We say *theoretically* because such a language certainly does not possess the power of convenience offered by the less succinct high-level languages. On the other hand, each of the high-level languages discussed in Chapter 5 essentially contains the statements in Bare Bones as its core. It is through this collection of statements that the language is assured of usefulness.

Questions/Exercises

1. Describe a Turing machine that ultimately halts for some inputs but never halts for others.

2. Identify other functions whose output can be described as an algebraic expression involving its input.

3. Identify a function that cannot be described in terms of an algebraic formula. Is your function nonetheless computable?

4. Describe the function computed by the following Bare Bones program assuming the function's input is represented by X and its output by Z:

```
clear Z;
while X not 0 do;
    incr Z;
    incr Z;
    decr X;
end;
```

11−4 A Noncomputable Function

At this stage we have acquired two uses for the term *computable*. The first term refers to the intuitive meaning of "to calculate." The second term is in reference to the computing power of Turing machines or, equivalently, the Bare Bones programming language. A widely accepted conjecture known as the **Church–Turing thesis** is that the two terms are actually the same. That is, no step-by-step process can ever be defined that defines the calculation of a function that is not also Turing machine computable. To support this claim, many unsuccessful attempts have been made to define a computing machine more powerful than Turing's. In fact, many attempts have resulted in machines with less power. It is therefore common practice in computer science to drop the prefix "Turing machine" from the phrase "Turing machine computable" in recognition of the Church–Turing thesis. We follow this practice in this section. Thus, the noncomputable function presented here is in reality a function that is not Turing machine computable and is thus widely believed to be noncomputable in the general sense.

Some Preliminaries

Our presentation of a noncomputable function requires the understanding of two additional concepts. The first is Gödel numbering, which refers to a technique initially used by Kurt Gödel for assigning a unique positive integer to each object in a collection. The objects in Gödel's case were such things as formulas and proofs. In our case, they will be programs written in Bare Bones. Gödel's system was built around the properties of prime numbers and consisted of a more complex process than we need here. For our purpose the process summarized in Figure 11-6 suffices. We first consider any program written in Bare Bones as one single long string of characters (in which the instructions are separated by semicolons). We then code each character of this string into a bit pattern using the ASCII code. After this, any program would appear as a long string of zeros and ones that could be interpreted as representing a (rather large) number in binary notation. Observe that this process is also reversible; that is, given a number obtained with this process, we could perform the steps in reverse order and retrieve the original program. Thus, we see

Figure 11-6 Computing the Gödel number of a Bare Bones program

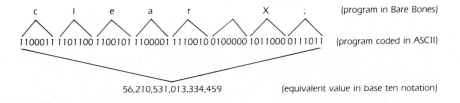

| c | l | e | a | r | X | ; | (program in Bare Bones) |
| 1100011 | 1101100 | 1100101 | 1100001 | 1110010 | 0100000 | 1011000 | 0111011 | (program coded in ASCII) |

56,210,531,013,334,459   (equivalent value in base ten notation)

that it is possible to associate any program written in Bare Bones with a unique positive integer. (In many applications it is important to note that this association is performed via a step-by-step process, thus making the association process itself computable.)

It is not important in our case whether the unique positive integers associated with the programs in Bare Bones are obtained by the process just described or by Gödel's original technique. The important point is that such an association is possible. Having established this possibility, we continue by assuming such an association has been carried out. Moreover, we call the number associated with a given program that program's *Gödel number*.

The second concept is that of a self-terminating program. Observe that any program written in Bare Bones must contain at least one variable name, and since each such variable consists of a string of letters, the names in a given program can be placed in alphabetical order. In terms of this order, we can speak of the first variable of a program. We say that a program is *self-terminating* if the program halts after being started with its first variable initialized at the program's own Gödel number and its other variables being set to zero. Thus, any program written in Bare Bones either is self-terminating or is not.

We should not go farther without emphasizing the role of self-reference built into the definition of a self-terminating Bare Bones program. Essentially, a program is self-terminating if and only if it ultimately halts if started with its own Gödel number as its input. Thus, the concept of a self-terminating program involves self-reference—the idea of an object referring to itself. This ploy has repeatedly led to amazing results in mathematics from such informal curiosities as the statement "This statement is false" to the more serious paradox represented by the question "Does the set of all sets contain itself?" What we have done, then, in defining the concept of a self-terminating program is to set the stage for a line of reasoning similar to "If it does, then it doesn't; but, if it doesn't, then it does," as we shall shortly see.

The Halting Problem

We are now in position to define a function that is not computable. It associates with each Gödel number of a program in Bare Bones (the function's input) a one or a zero (the function's output) depending on whether or not the program in question is self-terminating. More precisely we will define the function so that Gödel numbers of self-terminating programs produce the output value one and Gödel numbers of non-self-terminating programs product the output value zero.

Observe that the problem of computing this function is actually the problem of calculating whether or not programs ultimately halt after being started from a particular initial state; it is thus commonly referred to as the *halting problem*.

Our task now is to show that the preceding function is not computable. We will show that the assumption that it is computable leads to an impossible situation. Consequently, we will be forced to conclude that the function is not computable.

With this outline and Figure 11-7, we proceed with the assumption that the function is computable. This means that there must be a program in Bare Bones that computes the function. In other words, there is a program that halts with its output either equal to one if its input variable was the Gödel number of a self-terminating program or equal to a zero if not. We can assume that the variables in this program are named so that the input variable is the first in alphabetical order; otherwise we could simply rename them to have this property. Likewise, we may assume that the program's output variable is named X.

We could then modify the program by attaching the statements:

    while X not 0 do;
    end;

at its end. This new program must be either self-terminating or not. However, we are about to see that it can be neither! In particular, if this new program were self-terminating and we ran it with its input being equal to its own Gödel number, then when its execution reached the while statement that we added, the variable X would contain a 1. (To this point the new program is identical to the original program that produced a 1 if its input was the Gödel number of a self-terminating program.) At this point the program's execution would be caught forever in the while/end structure since we made no provisions for X to be decremented within the loop. But, this contradicts our assumption that the new program is self-terminating. Therefore, we must conclude that the new program is not self-terminating.

If, however, this new program were not self-terminating and we executed it with its input being its own Gödel number, it would reach the added while statement with X being assigned the value zero. In this case, the loop in the while/end structure would be avoided and the program would halt. But this is the property of a self-terminating program, so we are forced to conclude that the new program is self-terminating just as we were forced to conclude earlier that it is not self-terminating.

In summary, we see that we have the impossible situation of a program that on the one hand must be either self-terminating or not and on the other hand can be neither. Consequently, the assumption that led to this dilemma must be false. In other words, the function in question is not computable.

With this conclusion we have arrived at perhaps the most fascinating result within computer science (and mathematics as well). That is, there is a limit to what can be done through a step-by-step process (or, in mathematics, there is a limit to the power of logical deduction). Since the step-by-step process is fundamental to the concept of programming via algorithms, this limitation is inherited by computing machinery. In fact, this limitation represents an upper bound on the very essence of the computing process.

Figure 11-7 Proving the unsolvability of the halting problem

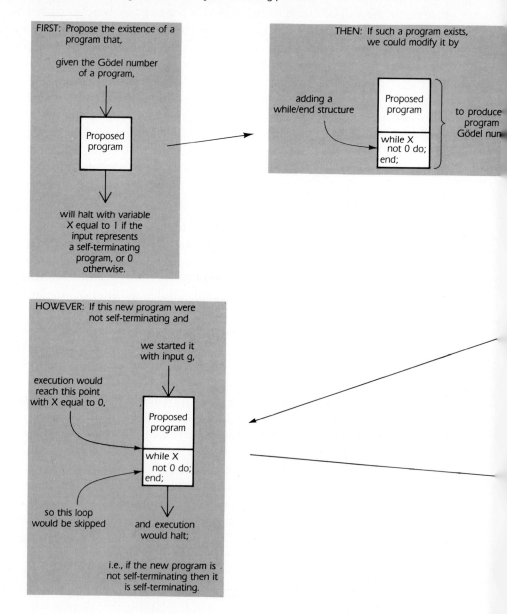

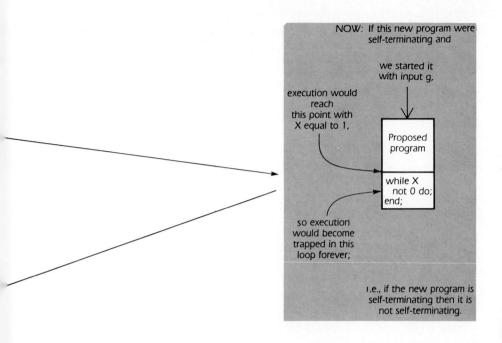

NOW: If this new program were self-terminating and

we started it with input g,

execution would reach this point with X equal to 1,

Proposed program

while X not 0 do; end;

so execution would become trapped in this loop forever;

i.e., if the new program is self-terminating then it is not self-terminating.

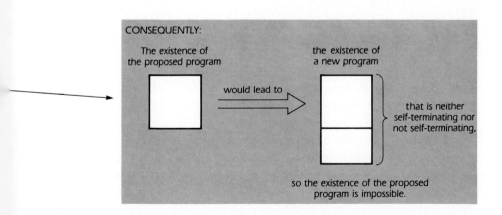

CONSEQUENTLY:

The existence of the proposed program

would lead to

the existence of a new program

that is neither self-terminating nor not self-terminating,

so the existence of the proposed program is impossible.

Earlier we agreed to substitute the single word *computable* for the phrase "Turing machine computable." Similarly, it is customary to drop the term "algorithmically" from the phrase "algorithmically solvable." A problem having an algorithmic solution is called a **solvable** problem, whereas a problem without an algorithmic solution, such as the halting problem, is called an unsolvable problem.

Finally, we should relate what we have just discussed to the ideas in Chapter 10. The popular press (and many scientists as well) would have us believe that the powers of computing machines include those required for intelligence itself. We have now seen that there are limits to the abilities of even infinite memory machines since they can solve only problems with algorithmic solutions. The question, then, is whether or not natural intelligence embodies more than mere algorithmic processes. Needless to say, this is a highly debatable and often emotional issue.

Questions/Exercises

1. Compute the following sentence:

   Turing machines were designed in an attempt to . . . .

2. What value would our Gödel numbering technique associate with the following simple Bare Bones program:

   decr X;

3. Is the program "incr X; decr Y;" self-terminating?

4. What is wrong with the following scenario:

   In a certain community everyone owns his or her own house. The house painter of the community claims to paint all those and only those houses that are not painted by their owners.

   (Hint: Who paints the house painter's house?)

11–5 Complexity and Its Measure

In Section 11-4 we investigated problems in terms of their solvability. In this section and in Section 11-6 we are interested in the more down-to-earth issue of whether or not a solvable problem has a practical solution.

The tool used for our investigation is a measure of the **complexity** of a problem. Here again we are using a term whose meaning should be clarified since complexity means different things to different people. One interpretation deals with the amount of branching and decision making involved in a problem's solution. Intuition tells us that following a twisted and entwined list of directions is more complicated than following instructions in the sequential order in which they are listed. However, such an interpretation of complexity ignores the fact that a machine does not really make any decisions when selecting the next instruction for execution but merely executes each instruction as it is indicated by the program counter. Consequently, a machine can execute one set of instructions as easily as another. Our intuitive interpretation, therefore, fails to grasp the meaning of complexity from the machine's point of view.

An interpretation of complexity that more accurately reflects the load placed on the computing machine is based on the number of steps that must be performed when executing the solution. Note that this is not the same as the number of instructions appearing in the written program. For example, a loop whose body consists of a single print statement but whose control requests the body's execution 100 times would appear to contain 100 print statements when executed. Thus, such a routine would be considered more complex than a list of 50 similar print statements even though the latter appears longer in written form. The point to remember is that our meaning of complexity is ultimately concerned with the time it takes a machine to execute an algorithm and not with the size of the algorithm in its written form. In a sense, then, our measure of complexity could be considered a measure of efficiency.

Keep in mind that what we are measuring with this concept is actually a property of a solution and not the problem directly. Thus, different solutions to the same problem might well be associated with different degrees of complexity. To assign a level of complexity to a problem, we select the complexity of the simplest solution to the problem in question. Unfortunately, finding the simplest solution to a problem and knowing that it is the simplest is often a difficult problem in itself. In fact, mathematicians have shown that some problems do not have a simplest solution. That is, regardless of what algorithm we use to solve some problems, there is always a more efficient method waiting to be discovered. It is not surprising, then, that the complexity of many problems is still unknown, as we discover in Section 11-6.

In reality when calculating the complexity of a solution, we do not try to count every step in the algorithm's execution. Rather, we concentrate on the significant or time-consuming steps. In defense of this looseness, note that the major use of complexity measure will be in making comparisons in which only a relative measure is actually required. This might be in the form of comparing different solutions to the same problem (as we are about to do) or comparing different problems (as in Section 11-6).

Observe that we have already used these techniques to compare the sequential and binary search algorithms in Section 4-6. There we found that when faced with a sorted list of 30,000 entries, the sequential search would interrogate an average of 15,000 entries whereas the binary search would consider at most 15.

Let us now consider the complexities of the insertion and quick sort algorithms. In each case it suffices to count the number of times two names are compared since this activity dominates both algorithms. Of course, the number of such comparisons depends on the number of names in the list. Thus, it is convenient to express the number of comparisons required in terms of the length of the list being searched. For this purpose we use the letter n in the following discussion to represent the number of names in the list.

Complexity of the Insertion Sort

We begin with the insertion sort (summarized in Figure 4-11). Recall that the process involved here is to select a list entry, called the pivot, compare this entry to those preceding it until its proper place is found, and then insert the pivot in this place. The first pivot chosen is the second list entry, the second is the third entry, the third is the fourth entry, etc. In the best possible case, each pivot will already be in its proper place and thus will need to be compared to only a single name before this is discovered. Thus, in the best case, sorting a list with n entries would require $n - 1$ comparisons. (The second entry would be compared to one name, the third entry to one name, etc.)

In contrast, the worst scenario would be that each pivot must be compared to all the preceding entries before its proper location could be found. For example, this would occur if the original list was in reverse order. In this case the first pivot (the second list entry) would be compared to one name, the second pivot (the third list entry) would be compared to two names, etc. Thus, the total number of comparisons when sorting a list of n entries would be $1 + 2 + 3 + \ldots + n - 1$, which is equivalent to $n(n - 1)/2$ or $(1/2)(n^2 - n)$. In particular, if the list contained 10 entries, the sort process would require 45 comparisons.

Having analyzed the insertion sort in both the best and worst possible cases, we might also consider what we would expect the average performance to be. In short, one would expect each pivot to be compared to half of the entries preceding it. This results in half as many comparisons as were performed in the worst case, or

insertion sort to sort a variety of lists of length 10, we would expect the average number of comparisons per sort to be 22.5.

Complexity of the Quick Sort

Let us now analyze the quick sort algorithm (summarized in Figure 4-17). We first consider the task of sorting a list whose order is exactly opposite to the desired order. That is, what should be the last name is initially the first, what should be the next to the last is second, etc. In this case the quick sort algorithm will designate the first name as the pivot entry, compare it to each of the other names (performing $n - 1$ comparisons), and finally place it at the end of the list by exchanging it with the last name in the list. It will then proceed by sorting first the names in front of the pivot entry (a list of length $n - 1$) and then the names following the pivot entry (a list of length 0).

The list of length 0 will require no comparisons, but the list of length $n - 1$ will require $n - 2$ comparisons before further divisions take place. In particular, its first entry (which was the last entry in the original list) will be designated as the pivot entry, then compared to each of the other entries (of which there are $n - 2$), and left in its current location. Note that this will result in the creation of two new lists to be sorted (one of length $n - 2$ and the other of length 0) in a manner similar to the previous step where two lists (of length $n - 1$ and 0) were produced.

This process will continue with additional recursive activations of the algorithm being applied to shorter and shorter lists until a list of length one is obtained. Observe that each such activation operates on a list of length one less than the previous activation and compares the first name of its list to the other names in its list before calling the next activation. Consequently, the first activation of the algorithm in the chain will perform $n - 1$ comparisons, the next $n - 2$, the next $n - 3$, etc. Thus, the total number of comparisons required will be:

$$(n - 1) + (n - 2) + \ldots + 1 = (1/2)(n^2 - n)$$

The quick sort technique is designed to divide the original list into shorter lists, each of which should be easier to sort. Such a technique performs best when the lists produced from the division are both the same size and thus half the size of the original. After all, little is gained from dividing a list if the division results in "smaller" tasks almost as large as the original. However, this is exactly what happens in the previous example. The preceding discussion thus constitutes a worst-case analysis of the quick sort algorithm.

We now turn to a best-case analysis. For this we assume that the original list is arranged so that each list division will result in two lists as nearly equal in size as possible. Thus, the divide-and-conquer approach of the quick sort algorithm will have its optimal effect.

Under these conditions the algorithm will first attack the list of n names in such a way that the initial sorting problem will be reduced to two smaller problems of sorting lists, each of length approximately $n/2$. These two problems will in turn be reduced to a total of four problems of sorting lists of length approximately $n/4$. This division process can be analyzed in terms of the tree structure in Figure 11-8 where we use each node of the tree to represent a single problem in the recursive process and the branches below each node to represent the smaller problems resulting from the division. Hence, we can find the total number of comparisons that occur when sorting the initial list by adding together the number of comparisons that occur at each node.

Our first task will be to determine the number of comparisons performed at each level of the tree. However, to avoid complications we will settle for a rough approximation. We first observe that each node appearing across any level of the tree requests the sorting of a unique segment of the list. This sorting process is accomplished by dividing the node's segment into two shorter segments that are ultimately sorted by the nodes below. To perform this division requires no more comparisons than there are names in the segment. (The first name in the segment is compared to each of the other names.) Hence, each level of the tree requires no

Figure 11-8 The hierarchy of problems generated by the quick sort algorithm

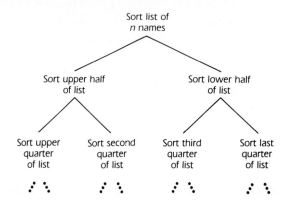

more comparisons than the total number of names in its list segments, and since the segments across a given level consist of disjoint portions of the original list, this total is no greater than the length of the original list. Consequently, each level of the tree requires no more than n comparisons. (Note that the bottom level is composed entirely of nodes representing the sorting of list segments of length one or zero and thus requires no comparisons.)

Next we need to determine the number of levels (or the depth) of the tree. For this, observe that the division process continues until lists of length no greater than one are obtained. Thus, the depth of the tree is equal to the number of times (starting with the number n) that we could repeatedly divide by two until the result is no larger than one. This is nothing more than the logarithm of n (base two), which we write as log n.

Figure 11-9 is a table of logarithms of values from 10 to 1000. Note that the entries in the table do not have integer values, whereas the depth of a tree is an integer. Thus, to get the actual depth of the tree obtained from sorting a list of n names, we round the value of log n up to the nearest integer. However, since the bottom level of the tree involves no comparisons, we can more accurately estimate the number of levels contributing to our comparison count by rounding the value of log n down to the nearest integer. We will denote this rounded value with the notation $\lfloor \log n \rfloor$. Thus, we estimate that if the list in question contained 10 names, the tree would contain $\lfloor \log \rfloor 10 = 3$ levels that involve comparisons.

Finally, we obtain $n \lfloor \log n \rfloor$ as our best-case estimate of the number of comparisons by multiplying the number of contributing levels ($\lfloor \log n \rfloor$) by the maximum number of comparisons in each level (n).

In summary given an arbitrary list of n names, we would expect quick sort to require between $n(\lfloor \log n \rfloor)$ (best-case) and $(1/2)(n^2 - n)$ (worst-case) comparisons

Figure 11-9 Logarithms (base two)

n	$\log n$	n	$\log n$
10	3.322	200	7.644
20	4.322	300	8.229
30	4.907	400	8.644
40	5.322	500	8.966
50	5.644	600	9.229
60	5.907	700	9.451
70	6.129	800	9.644
80	6.322	900	9.814
90	6.492	1000	9.966
100	6.644		

to sort it. In particular, when sorting a list of 10 names we would expect the quick sort to require between 30 and 45 comparisons.

(If you compare this projected performance to that of the insertion sort, you may wonder how the quick sort got its name. The answer is that the average performance of the quick sort algorithm tends to be closer to its best-case performance, which for large lists proves to be more efficient than the average performance of the insertion sort. For example, given a collection of arbitrary lists containing 100 entries each, the average number of comparisons required by the insertion sort would tend to be $(100)(99)/4 = 2475$, whereas the average performance of the quick sort would be closer to $100 \ (\lfloor \log 100 \rfloor) = 700$.)

Orders of Complexity

Although we may have made some approximations when computing the complexities of the insertion sort and quick sort algorithms, we were actually more precise than many situations require as well as being more precise than other situations may justify. For instance, we measured the average complexity of the insertion sort to be $n(n - 1)/4 = (1/4)(n^2 - n)$, but for large values of n the difference between $(1/4)(n^2 - n)$ and simply $(1/4)(n^2)$ becomes insignificant when compared to the size of the numbers involved. (If n were 100, the difference between the two expressions would be 25, whereas the two expressions themselves would be on the order of 2500.) Furthermore, for small values of n the time required to execute the statements that we did not count (we counted only the number of times names were compared) could easily be significant in comparison to the computed complexity. In short, our claim that the average complexity of the insertion sort is $(1/4)(n^2 - n)$ is probably no more accurate than another's claim that the complexity is $(1/4)(n^2)$.

Moreover, if we were to use our complexity measure to estimate the actual time required to execute an algorithm, we would find that differences between complexities such as $(1/4)n^2$ and simply n^2 have little significance. After all, distinctions determined by constant factors can be mitigated merely by executing the algorithm on different machines. On one machine an algorithm may appear to have a complexity of $(1/4)n^2$, while on another, slower machine the complexity might appear to be n^2. We see, then, that any constant coefficient involved in the computation of the complexity of an algorithm is more likely to be a property of the environment in which the algorithm is executed rather than the algorithm itself. However, given an algorithm whose complexity has been computed to be $(1/4)n^2$, we can conclude that its performance on any machine will be proportional to n^2.

Because of such uncertainties and variations, one rarely distinguishes between such expressions as $(1/4)(n^2 - n)$ and n^2 when determining the complexity of an algorithm. Instead, one tends to isolate the dominant term in the expression of the complexity while dropping any constant coefficients. Thus, although we computed the average complexity of the insertion sort to be $(1/4)(n^2 - n)$, we would actually claim no more than that the insertion sort should be expected to require a time period proportional to n^2 or, using other terminology, that the complexity of the insertion sort is on the order of n^2.

Computer scientists use O-notation (read "big oh notation") to represent such approximate measures. For example, the complexity of the insertion sort is considered to be $O(n^2)$ (read "on the order of n squared"). Thus, after all is said and done, two algorithms whose complexities are computed to be $(1/2)(n^2 - 5n + 2)$ and $(2/3)(n^2 + 2n - 3)$ would be considered to have essentially the same complexities, because both fall in the class of algorithms having complexity $O(n^2)$. In turn, both algorithms would be considered more efficient than an algorithm in the class $O(n^3)$.

Questions/Exercises

1. Suppose we found that a machine programmed with our insertion sort algorithm required an average of one second to sort a list of 100 names. How long would you estimate it would take to sort a list of 1000 names? How about 10,000?

2. If a machine required a minimum of one second to sort a list of 100 names using the quick sort algorithm, how long would you expect it to take to sort 1000 names?

3. How many comparisons would the quick sort algorithm require to sort a list of 10 names already in order?

4. Arrange the names Alice, Bill, Carol, David, Earl, Fred, and Gwen so as to require the least number of comparisons when sorted by the quick sort algorithm. How many comparisons would actually be required in this case?

11–6 Problem Classification

A *polynomial* (in x) is defined to be a mathematical expression of the form:

$$a_n x^n + a_{n-1} x^{n-1} + \ldots + a_0$$

where each subscripted a represents a constant numeric value, n represents a non-negative integer, and x is called the polynomial's variable. Thus, $3x^2 + 2x + 5$ is a polynomial (in x) and $w + 5$ is a polynomial (in w). Note that any polynomial describes a function by associating with each input the value obtained by replacing the polynomial's variable with the input value and performing the indicated algebraic calculations.

In contrast to polynomial expressions are the ***exponential*** expressions that have the form:

$$b^{ax}$$

where a and b represent constant numeric values and x again represents a variable. The actual letter used to represent the variable is arbitrary. Thus, examples of exponential expressions include 4^{2x} and 2^w. As with polynomials, each exponential expression describes a function obtained by substituting the input in place of the expression's variable and performing the indicated operations.

The significance of exponential expressions for our purpose is that if the constant b is greater than one and a is positive, the value of the expression will be larger than the value of any given polynomial if the input values are large enough. That is, if we pick any polynomial and proceed to compare its outputs to those of the exponential for similar inputs, as the inputs become larger we will find that the outputs of the exponential will eventually increase more rapidly than those of the polynomial and ultimately leave the polynomial outputs far behind.

Although an example of this phenomenon does not constitute a proof of its certainty, it is nonetheless instructive to take a look at the example given in the graph in Figure 11-10. Here we compare the outputs of the expressions x^2 and 2^x for input values in the range of 0 to 8. Note that although the exponential expression produces outputs smaller than those of the polynomial for some input values, its outputs overtake those of the polynomial as the inputs become larger.

Polynomial Problems

Observe that the complexities obtained in Section 11-5 either were polynomials themselves (such as $(1/4)n^2 - (1/4)n$) or were bounded by a polynomial (such as $n \lfloor \log n \rfloor$). (An expression is bounded by a polynomial if the expression's value for each possible input is always less than or equal to the polynomial's value for the same input. Thus, $n \lfloor \log n \rfloor$ is bounded by the polynomial n^2.) As a result, the insertion and quick sort algorithms belong to the class known as ***polynomial algorithms***, a class consisting of those algorithms whose complexity is bounded by a polynomial. Since our complexity is actually a measure of the time required to execute the algorithm, we often say that the algorithms in this class run in polynomial time.

Figure 11-10 The exponential 2^x compared to the polynomial x^2

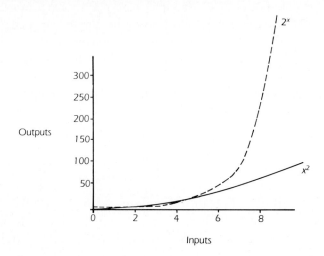

This relationship between complexity and an algorithm's run time is the key to the importance of the class of polynomial algorithms. An algorithm that is not in this class is characterized by extremely long run times as the size of its input increases. For instance, the graph in Figure 11-10 shows that an algorithm of complexity 2^n would become unbearably time-consuming when applied to large inputs. Consequently, such algorithms are seldom practical for routine use.

As mentioned earlier, problems are assigned degrees of complexity based on the complexity of their solutions. Thus, we find a class of problems (called **polynomial problems**) defined as being those problems with polynomial time solutions. Determining whether a theoretically solvable problem is or is not in this class is of major importance since it is closely related to the question of whether or not the problem has a practical algorithmic solution.

Nonpolynomial Problems

Unfortunately, solvable problems exist (called **nonpolynomial problems**) that fall outside the class of polynomial problems. For example, consider the problem of listing all possible committees of size one or more that could be formed from a group of n people. Since there are $2^n - 1$ such committees (we will allow a subcommittee to consist of the entire subcommittee, but we do not consider the empty committee to be a valid subcommittee—although it may be able to get more work done than any of the other subcommittees), any algorithm that solves this problem must have at least $2^n - 1$ steps and thus a complexity at least that large. In turn this problem does not have a polynomial time solution, and hence any solution becomes enormously time-consuming as the size of the group from which the committees are selected increases.

In contrast to our subcommittee problem, whose complexity is large merely because of the size of its output, problems exist whose complexities are large even though their ultimate output is merely a simple yes or no answer. An example involves the ability to answer questions about the truth of statements involving the addition of real numbers. For instance, we can easily recognize that the answer to the question "Is it true that there is a real number which when added to itself produces the value 5?" is yes, whereas the answer to "Is it true that there is a positive real number which when added to itself is 0?" is no. However, as such questions become more involved, our ability to answer them begins to fade. If we found ourselves faced with many such questions, we might be tempted to turn to a computer program for assistance. Unfortunately, the ability to answer these questions has been shown to require exponential time, thus even a computer will ultimately fail to produce timely answers as the questions become more involved.

NP Problems

An interesting phenomenon occurs if we make a slight change to our previous committee problem. Suppose we were told that it was possible to form a committee so that the total of the ages of its members would be a certain value and the problem was to find such a committee. One approach would be to begin listing all possible committees as before but to test the age total of each committee as it is listed. In this situation, the time required to solve the problem would depend on luck. If only one suitable committee existed and it was the last one tested, our process would again require the consideration of every possible committee and would therefore still require more than polynomial time. On the other hand, if a suitable committee were the first one tested, the process could terminate as soon as the committee was found. Thus, the time required to solve the problem depends on how early in the process a suitable committee is discovered.

Observe that solving our modified problem involves selecting which of many possible approaches to pursue. The situation is analogous to standing at the junction of many paths, one of which leads to a pot of gold (Figure 11-11). We can traverse any one path in only polynomial time, and if our choice turns out to be wrong, we can return to the junction and try again. However, there are more than a polynomial number of paths, and with enough incorrect choices, finding the gold could require more than a polynomial amount of time.

We call a problem that can be solved in polynomial time by a nondeterministic system a *nondeterministic polynomial problem* (or an *NP problem* for short). Of course, the class of NP problems contains the truly polynomial problems because if a problem can be solved by a (deterministic) algorithm in polynomial time, then it can certainly be solved in polynomial time by a nondeterministic system. Moreover,

Figure 11-11 The structure of an NP problem

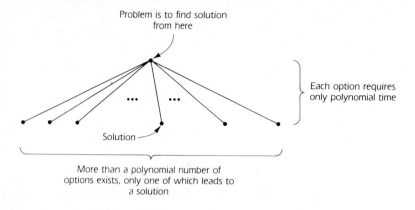

our subcommittee problem suggests that there are NP problems that are not true polynomial problems. That is, there appear to be problems that can be solved in polynomial time if we guess correctly but that would require nonpolynomial time otherwise—though no one has been able to prove this. In particular, no one has been able to show that there does not exist a strictly polynomial time algorithm for finding a subcommittee with the appropriate age total. Thus, the classification of the NP problems constitutes one of the mysteries in computer science today.

In summary, we have found that problems can be classified as either solvable (having an algorithmic solution) or unsolvable (not having an algorithmic solution), as depicted in Figure 11-12. Moreover, within the class of solvable problems are two subclasses. One is the collection of polynomial problems considered to have practical solutions. The second is the collection on nonpolynomial problems whose solutions are considered to be practical for only relatively small or carefully selected inputs. Finally, there are the mysterious NP problems that thus far have evaded precise

Figure 11-12 A graphic summation of problem classification

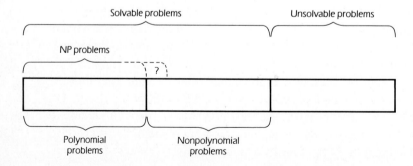

classification. They are contained in the class of solvable problems and contain the polynomial problems. Whether there are true polynomial solutions to all the NP problems remains an open question.

Questions/Exercises

1. For the same input value, will a polynomial expression always produce a value less than an exponential?
2. List all of the subcommittees that could be formed from a committee consisting of the two members Alice and Bill. List all the subcommittees that could be formed from the committee consisting of Alice, Bill, and Carol. What about the subcommittees from Alice, Bill, Carol, and David?
3. Given an example of a problem in each of the following classes:

    polynomial problems
    nonpolynomial problems

    Give an example of an NP problem that as yet has not been shown to be a polynomial problem.

Chapter 11 Review Problems

1. Show how a structure of the form:

    while X equals 0 do;

    .
    .
    .

    end;

    can be simulated with Bare Bones.

2. Write a Bare Bones program that places a 1 in the variable Z if the variable X is less than or equal to the variable Y and places a 0 in the variable Z if it is greater.

3. Write a Bare Bones program that places the Xth power of 2 in the variable Z.

4. In each of the following cases write a program sequence in Bare Bones that performs the indicated activity:
    a. Associate 0 with Z if the value of X is even; otherwise associate 1 with Z.
    b. Calculate the sum of the integers from 0 to X.

5. Write a Bare Bones routine that will divide the value of X by the value of Y. Disregard any remainder; that is, 1 divided by 2 should produce 0, and 5 divided by 3 should produce 1.

6. The example of a Turing machine that never halts given in the text used the fact that the tape was infinitely long. Design a Turing machine that never halts but uses no more than a single cell on its tape.

7. Design a Turing machine that will place zeros in all the cells to the left of the current cell until it reaches an asterisk.

8. Suppose a pattern of zeros and ones on the tape of a Turing machine is delimited by asterisks at either end. Design a Turing machine that will rotate this pattern one cell to the left assuming that the machine starts with the current cell being the asterisk at the right end of the pattern.

9. Design a Turing machine that will reverse the pattern of zeros and ones that it finds between the current cell (which contains an asterisk) and the first asterisk to the left.

10. Summarize the Church–Turing thesis.

11. What value would our Gödel numbering technique associate with the program: "incr A;"?

12. What Bare Bones program is represented by the number

    167,003,256,847,376,500,260,297,734,958,162,
    681,576,272,443

    when using our Gödel numbering system described in this chapter?

13. Is the following Bare Bones program self-terminating?

    ```
    while X not 0 do;
    end;
    ```

14. Analyze the validity of the following two statements:

    The next statement is true.
    The above statement is false.

15. Analyze the validity of the statement "The cook on a ship cooks for all those and only those who do not cook for themselves."

16. Summarize the significance of the halting problem in the field of theoretical computer science.

17. Is the problem of searching through a list for a particular entry a polynomial problem? Justify your answer.

18. Compute the complexity of the traditional grade school algorithms for addition and multiplication. That is, if asked to add two numbers each having n digits, how many individual additions must be performed, and if requested to multiply two n-digit numbers, how many individual multiplications are required?

19. Is a polynomial solution to a problem always better than an exponential solution? Explain.

20. Does the fact that a problem has a polynomial solution mean that it can always be solved in a practical amount of time? Explain.

21. Given the problem of dividing a group (of an even number of people) into two disjoint subgroups of equal size so that the difference between the total ages of each subgroup is as large as possible, Charlie Programmer proposes the solution of forming all possible subgroup pairs, computing the difference between the age totals of each pair, and selecting the pair with the largest difference. Mary Programmer, on the other hand, proposes that the original group first be sorted by age and then divided into two subgroups by forming one subgroup from the younger half of the sorted group and the other from the older half. What is the complexity of each of these solutions? Is the problem itself of polynomial, NP, or nonpolynomial complexity?

22. Sometimes a slight change in a problem can significantly alter the form of its solution. For example, find a simple solution to the following problem and determine its complexity class:

    Divide a group of people into two disjoint subgroups (of arbitrary size) such that the difference in the total ages of the members of the two subgroups is as large as possible.

    Now change the problem so that the desired difference is as small as possible. What is the complexity of your solution?

23. From the following list extract a collection of numbers whose sum is 3165:

    26, 39, 104, 195, 403, 504, 793, 995, 1156, 1673

    What is the complexity of your technique for solving this problem? Does this appear to be a polynomial problem, an NP problem, or a nonpolynomial problem?

Problems for the Programmer

1. Identify a small collection of instructions in a programming language you know that collectively provide all the features of Bare Bones. Show how each Bare Bones statement can be simulated with the instructions you picked.

2. Using only those instructions identified in programming problem 1 together with any I/O instructions you may need, write a program that will display a 0 at your terminal if a positive integer is typed and a 1 if zero is typed.

3. Write a program to list all the numbers that can be obtained by rearranging the various groupings of digits appearing in a given number. Why would you not want to execute this program for large input values?

4. Rewrite the program of programming problem 3 to print only those rearrangements whose digits total a particular value. What techniques can you apply to increase the efficiency of your solution?

5. Write a program to simulate a Turing machine.

6. Write a program for computing the Gödel numbers of Bare Bones programs using the numbering system adopted in the text.

7. Write an interpreter for our Bare Bones language.

Appendices

Appendix A: Popular Codes

Appendix B: A Typical Machine Language

Appendix C: Insertion Sort in Assembly Language

Appendix D: Syntax Diagrams for Pascal

Appendix E: The Equivalence of Loop and Recursive Structures

Appendix F: Answers to Questions/Exercises

A. Popular Codes

The following is a partial listing of some popular codes:

Symbol	ASCII	EBCDIC	BCD	Symbol	ASCII	EBCDIC	BCD
(space)	0100000	01000000	110000	N	1001110	11010101	100101
!	0100001	01011010		O	1001111	11010110	100110
"	0100010	01111111		P	1010000	11010111	100111
#	0100011	01111011		Q	1010001	11011000	101000
$	0100100	01011011	101011	R	1010010	11011001	101001
%	0100101	01101100		S	1010011	11100010	110010
&	0100110	01010000		T	1010100	11100011	110011
'	0100111	01111101	001100	U	1010101	11100100	110100
(	0101000	01001101	111100	V	1010110	11100101	110101
)	0101001	01011101	011100	W	1010111	11100110	110110
*	0101010	01011100	101100	X	1011000	11100111	110111
+	0101011	01001110	010000	Y	1011001	11101000	111000
,	0101100	01101011	111011	Z	1011010	11101001	111001
−	0101101	01100000	100000	[	1011011	01001010	
.	0101110	01001011	011011	\	1011100		
/	0101111	01100001	110001	]	1011101	01011010	
0	0110000	11110000	000000	^	1011110		
1	0110001	11110001	000001	_	1011111		
2	0110010	11110010	000010	a	1100001	10000001	
3	0110011	11110011	000011	b	1100010	10000010	
4	0110100	11110100	000100	c	1100011	10000011	
5	0110101	11110101	000101	d	1100100	10000100	
6	0110110	11110110	000110	e	1100101	10000101	
7	0110111	11110111	000111	f	1100110	10000110	
8	0111000	11111000	001000	g	1100111	10000111	
9	0111001	11111001	001001	h	1101000	10001000	
:	0111010	01111010		i	1101001	10001001	
;	0111011	01011110		j	1101010	10010001	
<	0111100	01001100		k	1101011	10010010	
=	0111101	01111110	001011	l	1101100	10010011	
>	0111110	01101110		m	1101101	10010100	
?	0111111	01101111		n	1101110	10010101	
@	1000000	01111100		o	1101111	10010110	
A	1000001	11000001	010001	p	1110000	10010111	
B	1000010	11000010	010010	q	1110001	10011000	
C	1000011	11000011	010011	r	1110010	10011001	
D	1000100	11000100	010100	s	1110011	10100010	
E	1000101	11000101	010101	t	1110100	10100011	
F	1000110	11000110	010110	u	1110101	10100100	
G	1000111	11000111	010111	v	1110110	10100101	
H	1001000	11001000	011000	w	1110111	10100110	
I	1001001	11001001	011001	x	1111000	10100111	
J	1001010	11010001	100001	y	1111001	10101000	
K	1001011	11010010	100010	z	1111010	10101001	
L	1001100	11010011	100011	{	1111011		
M	1001101	11010100	100100	}	1111101		

B. A Typical Machine Language

Machine Architecture

The machine has 16 general purpose registers named R0 through R15 (or R0 through RF in hexadecimal). Each register is one byte (8 bits) long. For identifying registers within instructions, each register is assigned the unique 4-bit pattern that represents its register number. Thus, R0 is identified by 0000 (hexadecimal 0), R1 is identified by 0001 (hexadecimal 1), and R15 is identified by 1111 (hexadecimal F).

Main memory consists of 256 cells. Each cell contains 8 bits (or one byte) of data. Since there are 256 cells in memory, each cell is assigned a unique address consisting of an integer in the range of 0 to 255. An address can therefore be represented by a pattern of 8 bits ranging from 00000000 to 11111111 (or a hexadecimal value in the range of 00 to FF).

Floating-point values are assumed to be stored in the format at the top of the next column.

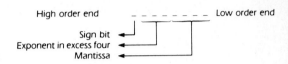

Machine Language

Each machine instruction is 2 bytes long. The first 4 bits consist of the op-code; the last 12 bits make up the operand field. The following table lists the instructions in hexadecimal notation together with a short description of each. The letters R, S, and T are used in place of hexadecimal digits in those fields representing a register identifier that will vary depending on the particular application of the instruction. The letters X and Y are used in lieu of hexadecimal digits in variable fields not representing a register.

Op-code	Operand	Description
1	RXY	LOAD the register R with the contents of the memory cell whose address is XY. *Example:* 14A3 would cause the contents of the memory cell located at address A3 to be placed in register R4.
2	RXY	LOAD the register R with the value XY. *Example:* 20A3 would cause the value A3 to be placed in register R0.
3	RXY	STORE the contents of the register R in the memory cell whose address is XY. *Example:* 35B1 would cause the contents of register R5 to be placed in the memory cell whose address is B1.
4	0RS	MOVE the contents of register R to register S. *Example:* 40A4 would cause the contents of register R10 to be copied into register R4.
5	RST	ADD the contents of registers S and T as though they were binary numbers and leave the result in register R. *Example:* 5726 would cause the binary values in registers R2 and R6 to be added and the sum placed in register R7.
6	RST	ADD the contents of registers S and T as though they represented values in floating-point notation and leave the floating-point result in register R. *Example:* 634E would cause the values in registers R4 and R14 to be added as floating-point values and the result to be placed in register R3.
7	RST	OR the contents of registers S and T and place the result in register R. *Example:* 7CB4 would cause the result of ORing the contents of registers R11 and R4 to be placed in register R12.
8	RST	AND the contents of registers S and T and place the result in register R. *Example:* 8045 would cause the result of ANDing the contents of registers R4 and R5 to be placed in register R0.
9	RST	EXCLUSIVE OR the contents of registers S and T and place the result in register R. *Example:* 95F3 would cause the result of EXCLUSIVE ORing the contents of registers R15 and R3 to be placed in register R5.
A	R0X	ROTATE the contents of register R one bit to the right X times. Each time place the bit that started at the low order end at the high order end. *Example:* A403 would cause the contents of register R4 to be ROTATED 3 bits to the right in a circular fashion.

B	RXY	JUMP to the instruction located in the memory cell at address XY if the contents of register R is equal to the contents of register number 0. Otherwise, continue with the normal sequence of execution.
		Example: B43C would first compare the contents of register R4 with the contents of register R0. If the two were equal, the execution sequence would be altered so that the next instruction executed would be the one located at memory address 3C. Otherwise, program execution would continue in its normal sequence.
C	000	HALT execution.
		Example: C000 would cause program execution to stop.

C. Insertion Sort in Assembly Language

```
            .TITLE   INSERT -- SORTS A LIST USING INSERTION SORT ALGORITHM
            .IDENT *VAX-11/8600*
;
; --------------
;   DATA SECTION
; --------------
;         CHANGE LSIZE BELOW TO SORT LISTS OF DIFFERENT SIZES.
;
            .PSECT   DATA,NOEXE,WRT
TERMFB:  $FAB      FNM=SYS$INPUT,-    ; FILE ACCESS   BLOCK
                   RAT=CR,-           ;    FOR TERMINAL.
                   FAC=<GET,PUT>
TERMRB:  $RAB      FAB=TERMFB,-       ; RECORD ACCESS BLOCK.
                   UBF=CRTBUF,-       ; USER BUFFER FOR $GET.
                   USZ=BFSIZE         ; BUFFER SIZE.
;
INSIZE:  .BLKW     1
;
CRTBUF:  .BLKB     80                 ; TERMINAL LINE BUFFER.
BFSIZE   =         .-CRTBUF
;
LSIZE    = 10                         ; LSIZE IS THE NUMBER OF NAMES IN LIST
;
NAME:    .BLKQ     LSIZE              ; SPACE FOR ARRAY OF NAMES.
TEMP:    .BLKQ     1                  ; FOR INTERCHANGING NAMES.
;
;
; -------------
; LOGIC SECTION
; -------------
;
            .PSECT   LOGIC,EXE,NOWRT
;
            .ENTRY   START,0
            $OPEN    FAB=TERMFB                ;    PREPARE
            BLBS     R0,CONT                   ;    FOR
            BRW      ERROR                     ;      I/O
CONT:    $CONNECT  RAB=TERMRB                  ;    OPERATIONS.
            BLBS     R0,CONT1
            BRW      ERROR
;
;         READ IN THE NAMES
;
CONT1:   MOVL      #0,R6                       ;R6 = INDEX TO NAMES ARRAY.
```

443

```
RD_NM:   $GET    RAB=TERMB                        ; GET NAME FROM TERMINAL.
         BLBS    R0,CONT2
         BRW     ERROR
CONT2:   MOVW    TERMRB+RAB$W_RSZ,INSIZE   ; SAVE LENGTH.
         MOVC5   INSIZE,CRTBUF,#^A/ /,-
                 #8,CRTBUF                 ; FILL OR TRUNCATE.
         MOVQ    CRTBUF,NAME[R6]
         AOBLSS  #LSIZE,R6,RD_NM           ; REPEAT LSIZE TIMES
;
; SORT THE LIST
;
; REGISTER USAGE:   R6 = INDEX OF PIVOT ENTRY
;                   R5 = INDEX OF HOLE
;                   R4 = INDEX OF NAME TO BE COMPARED WITH PIVOT
;                             (ADVANCES THROUGH SORTED PART)
;
;                   R7, R8    HOLD ADDRESSES OF NAMES FOR COMPARISON
;
         MOVL    #1,R6                     ; R6 POINTS TO SECOND NAME IN LIST
REPEAT:  MOVQ    NAME[R6],TEMP
         MOVL    R6,R5
         MOVL    R6,R4
WHILE:   SOBGEQ  R4,GO_ON                  ; MOVE R4 UP ONE NAME
         BRB     ENDWH                     ; GO TO ENDWH IF PAST TOP OF LIST
GO_ON:   MOVAQ   NAME[R4],R7
         MOVAQ   TEMP,R8
         CMPC3   #8,(R7),(R8)              ; COMPARE NAME[R4] AND PIVOT NAME
         BLEQ    ENDWH                     ; GO TO ENDWH IF NAME[R4] <= PIVOT NAME
         MOVQ    NAME[R4],NAME[R5]         ; MOVE NAME DOWN
         MOVL    R4,R5                     ; MARK NEW POSITION OF HOLE
         BRB     WHILE                     ; BACK UP TO WHILE
ENDWH:   MOVQ    TEMP,NAME[R5]             ; MOVE PIVOT ENTRY INTO HOLE
         AOBLSS  #LSIZE,R6,REPEAT          ; MOVE DOWN A NAME AND
                                           ;   GO BACK TO REPEAT
;
; WRITE NAMES
;
         MOVL    #0,R6                     ; R6 = INDEX TO ARRAY OF NAMES
WRT_N:   MOVAQ   NAME[R6],-
                 TERMRB+RAB$L_RBF          ; SET POSITION
         MOVW    #8,TERMRB+RAB$W_RSZ       ; SET LENGTH
         $PUT    RAB=TERMRB                ; WRITE NAME
         BLBS    R0,CONT3
         BRW     ERROR
CONT3:   AOBLSS  #LSIZE,R6,WRT_N           ; REPEAT LSIZE TIMES
;
         $CLOSE FAB=TERMFB
ERROR:   RET
;
         .END    START
```

D. Syntax Diagrams for Pascal

The following is a set of syntax diagrams for Pascal. The diagrams are arranged in a general to specific order. The first diagram describes the overall structure of a program as consisting of a program header followed by a declaration part that is in turn followed by a process part. The remaining diagrams further describe these components in a stepwise-refinement manner.

Components contained in rectangles are nonterminal in the sense that they are described in more detail by another diagram; symbols within ovals or circles are terminal in that no further definition is required for them. They are the symbols that actually appear in a program itself. The exceptions to this convention are the components called character, letter, and digit defined as follows:

Character—essentially any one of the symbols in the ASCII character set except the apostrophe
Letter—one of the alphabetic characters
Digit—one of the symbols 0, 1, 2, 3, 4, 5, 6, 7, 8, 9

These syntax diagrams do not describe the complete grammar of Pascal because syntax diagrams are unable to describe context-sensitive features of a grammar. For example, the diagrams shown here do not specify that different variables cannot have the same name or that the + operation is not defined for Boolean operands. On the other hand, most of a language's grammatical structure can be efficiently and clearly described with such diagrams; thus, even with their shortcomings, they have become a popular tool for language description.

Program

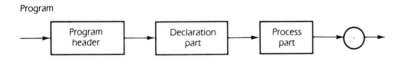

Program header

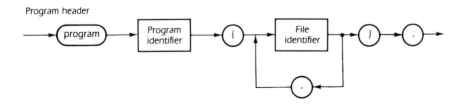

Process part

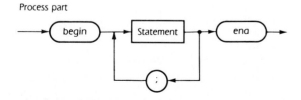

Declaration part

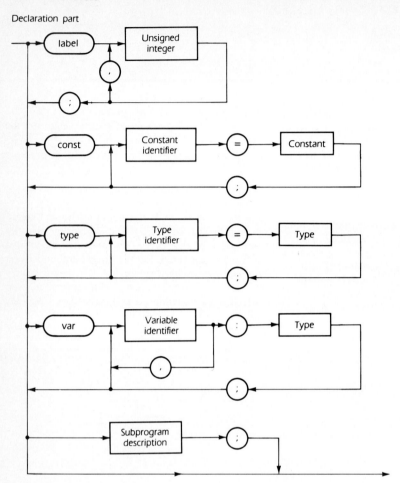

Subprogram description

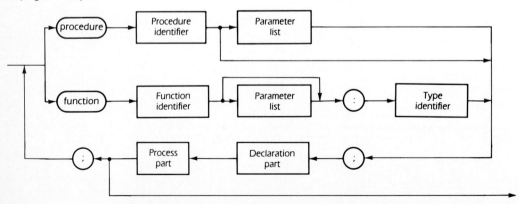

Statement

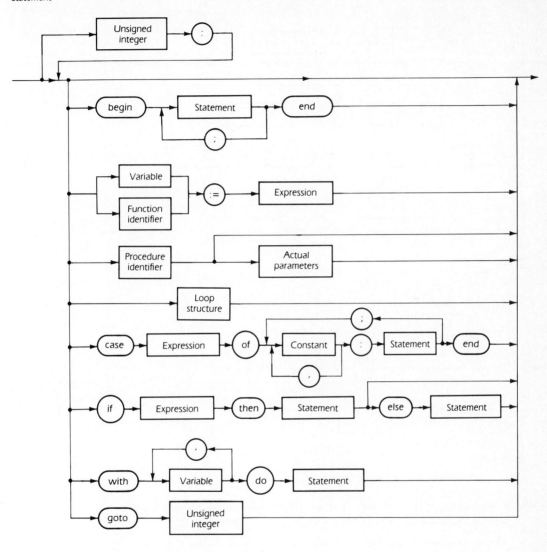

Loop structure

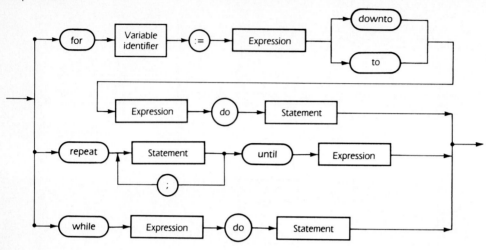

Field list

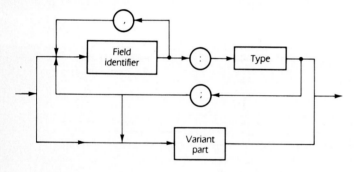

Variant part

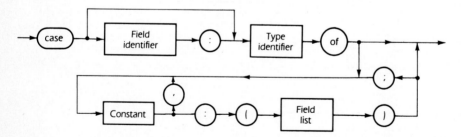

Parameter list

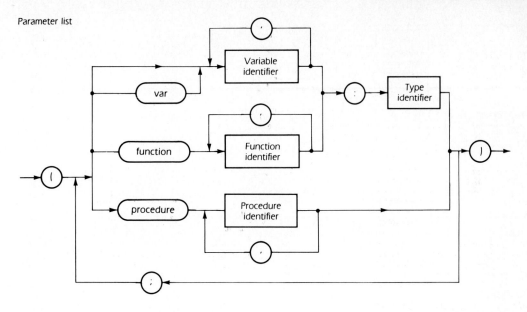

Actual parameters

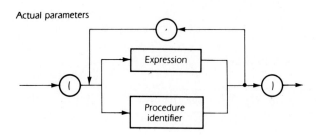

Type

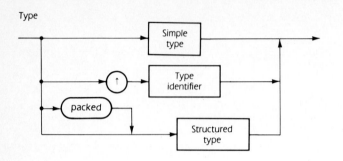

Simple type

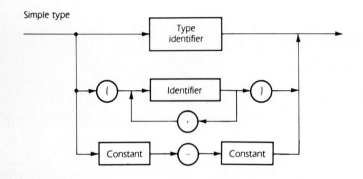

Structured type

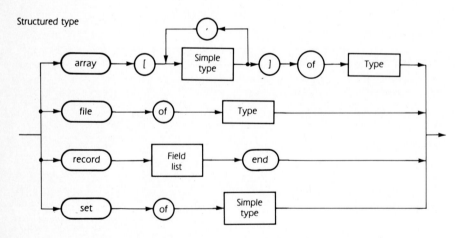

Variable

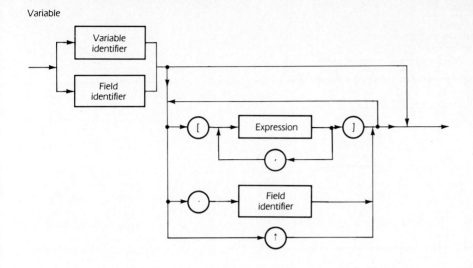

Constant

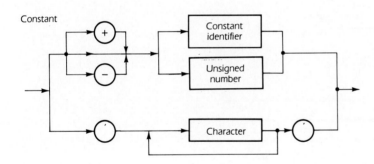

Expression

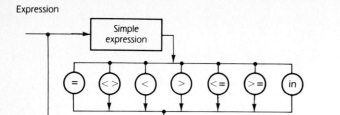

Simple expression

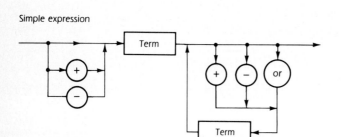

Term

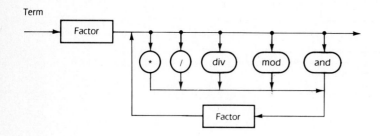

Factor

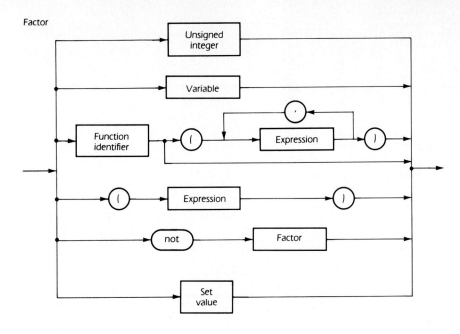

Set value

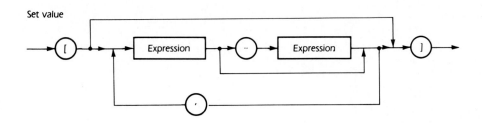

Unsigned constant

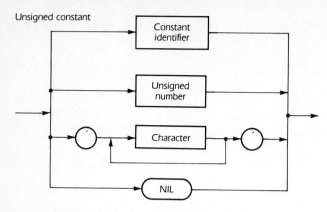

Unsigned number

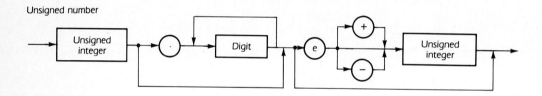

Unsigned integer

Identifier, field identifier, function identifier, constant identifier,
procedure identifier, type identifier, variable identifier

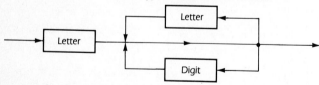

E. The Equivalence of Loop and Recursive Structures

In this appendix we use our Bare Bones language of Chapter 11 as a tool to answer the question posed in Chapter 4 regarding the relative power of loop and recursive structures. Recall that Bare Bones contains only three assignment statements (clear, incr, and decr) and one control structure (constructed from a while and end statement pair). Moreover, this simple language has the same computing power as a Turing machine, and thus, if we accept the Church–Turing thesis, we may conclude that any problem with an algorithmic solution has a solution expressible in Bare Bones.

The first step in the comparison of loop and recursive structures is to replace the loop structure of Bare Bones with a recursive structure. We do this by removing the while and end statements from the language and in their place providing the ability to divide a Bare Bones program into units along with the ability to call one of these units from another location in the program. More precisely, we propose that each program in the modified language can consist of a number of syntactically disjoint program units. We suppose that each program must contain exactly one unit called MAIN having the syntactic structure of:

MAIN: begin;
       .
       .
       .
    end;

(where the dots represent other Bare Bones statements) and perhaps other units (semantically subordinate to MAIN) that have the structure:

unit: begin;
      .
      .
      .
    return;

(where unit represents the unit's name that has the same syntax as variable names). The semantics of this unit system is that the program always begins execution at the beginning of the unit MAIN and halts when that unit's end statement is reached. Other program units can be called as subprograms by means of the conditional statement:

if name not 0 perform unit;

(where name represents any variable name and unit represents any of the program unit names other than MAIN). Moreover, we allow the units other than MAIN to call themselves recursively.

With these added features we can simulate the old while/end structure. For example, a Bare Bones program of the form:

while X not 0 do;
    S;
end;

(where S represents any sequence of Bare Bones statements) can be replaced by the unit structure:

MAIN: begin;
       if X not 0 perform unitA;
    end;

unitA: begin;
      S;
      if X not 0 perform unitA;
      return;

Consequently, we may conclude that the modified language has all the capabilities of the original Bare Bones.

It can also be shown that any problem that can be solved using the modified language can be solved using Bare Bones. One method of doing this is to show how any algorithm expressed in the modified language could be written in the original Bare Bones. However, this involves an explicit description of how recursive structures can be simulated with the while/end structure of Bare Bones, which in turn requires that we describe how the environments of the various unit activations can be saved in a stack storage structure using Bare Bones.

For our purpose, it is simpler to rely on the Church–Turing thesis as presented in Chapter 11. In particular, the Church–Turing thesis, combined with the fact that Bare Bones has the same power as Turing machines, dictates that no language can be more powerful than our original Bare Bones. We can thus conclude immediately that any problem solvable in our modified language can also be solved using Bare Bones.

Thus, we see that the power of the modified language is the same as that of the original Bare Bones. Moreover, the only distinction between the two languages is that one provides a loop control structure while the other provides recursion. We must therefore conclude that the two control structures are, in fact, equivalent in terms of computing power.

Part One

Chapter 1

Section 1–1

1. In the first case, memory cell number 6 would end up containing the value 5. In the second case, it would end up with the value 8.

2. Step 1 erases the original value in cell number 3 when the new value is written there. Consequently, step 2 does not place the original value from cell number 3 in cell number 2. The result is that both cells end up with the value that was originally in cell number 2. A correct procedure would be the following:

   Step 1. Move the contents of cell number 2 to cell number 1.
   Step 2. Move the contents of cell number 3 to cell number 2.
   Step 3. Move the contents of cell number 1 to cell number 3.

3. 32768 bits

4. △ □ ○ ◇ ◇ ○ △

5. a. 6AF2   b. E85517   c. 48

6. a. 010111111101100010111
   b. 0110000100001010
   c. 1010101111001101
   d. 0000000100000000

7. FFF

Section 1–2

1. A blocking factor of 16 would result in each data block being one inch long and would therefore produce a 50% waste due to interrecord gaps. A blocking factor of 32 would produce data blocks of twice the length of the interrecord gaps and thus a waste of only 33%.

2. In this application a constant expansion and shrinking will be taking place within the data. If the information were stored on tape, this would result in an endless rewriting process to accommodate the upheaval taking place within the data. (One envisions the last block of the data yo-yoing back and forth as reservations earlier on the tape are made, dropped, or become outdated.) When using disk storage, however, each change affects only the portion of the data stored on the track involved. Consequently, much less rewriting of data is required when updates are made.

3. If the tape is on-line, the program needs merely to start the tape. If, however, the tape is off-line, the normal procedure is for the program to request a human to mount the tape. This request is usually made by typing an appropriate message on a device called the message center being monitored by humans. After a human has mounted the tape, the program is told to continue again by means of the message center.

4. The point to remember here is that the slowness of mechanical motion compared with the speed of the internal functioning of the computer dictates that we minimize the number of times we must move the read/write heads. If we fill a complete surface before starting the next, we must move the read/write head each time we finish with a track. The number of moves would therefore be approximately the same as the total number of tracks on the two surfaces. If, however, we alternate between surfaces by electronically switching between the read/write heads on the two surfaces, we must mechanically move the read/write heads only after each pair of tracks has been filled. This technique requires half the number of mechanical motions as the previous technique and is therefore preferred.

Section 1–3

1. Computer Science

2. The two patterns are the same except that the second bit from the high order end is always 0 for upper case and 1 for lower case.

3. a. 1001001   0100000   1101100   1101001
      1101011   1100101   0100000   1101101
      1101001   1101100   1101011   0101110

b. 1010111 1101000 1100101 1110010
1100101 0100000 1100001 1110010
1100101 0100000 1111001 1101111
1110101 0111111

c. 0100010 1001000 1101111 1110111
0111111 0100010 0100000 1000011
1101000 1100101 1110010 1111001
1101100 0100000 1100001 1110011
1101011 1100101 1100100 0101110

d. 0110010 0101011 0110011 0111101
0110101 0101110

4.

5. a. 5   b. 9   c. 11   d. 6   e. 16   f. 18

6. a. 110   b. 1101   c. 1011   d. 10010
   e. 11011   f. 100

7. In 21 bits, we could store 3 symbols using ASCII. Thus, we could store values as large as 999. However, if we used the bits as binary digits we could store values up to 4,226,303.

Section 1–4

1. b, c, and e

2. Yes. If an even number of errors occurs in one byte, the parity technique will not detect them.

3. In this case, errors would have occurred in bytes a and d of question 1. The answer to question 2 would remain the same.

4. a. 01001001 00100000 11101100
11101001 01101011 11100101
00100000 01101101 11101001
11101100 01101011 10101110

b. 01010111 01101000 11100101
11110010 11100101 10100000
01100001 11110010 11100101
00100000 01111001 11101111
01110101 10111111

c. 10100010 11001000 11101111
11110111 10111111 10100010
00100000 01000011 01101000
11100101 11110010 01111001
11101100 00100000 01100001
01110011 01101011 11100101
01100100 10101110

d. 00110010 10101011 10110011
00111101 10110101 10101110

5. a. BED   b. CAB   c. HEAD

6. One solution would be the following:

A	0	0	0	0	0
B	1	1	1	0	0
C	0	1	1	1	1
D	1	0	0	1	1

Section 1–5

1. a. 42   b. 33   c. 23   d. 6   e. 31

2. a. 100000   b. 1000000   c. 1100000
   d. 1111   e. 11011

3. a. $3\frac{1}{4}$ b. $5\frac{7}{8}$ c. $2\frac{1}{2}$ d. $6\frac{3}{8}$ e. $\frac{5}{8}$

4. a. 100.1   b. 10.11   c. 1.001
   d. 0.0101   e. 101.101

5. a. 100111   b. 1011.110   c. 100000
   d. 1000.00

Section 1–6

1. a. 7   b. −1   c. 0   d. 5   e. −6   f. −7

2. a. 00000101   b. 10000101   c. 00010001
   d. 10010100   e. 00001001   f. 1001101

3. They both represent 0. This is one of the nuisances associated with sign-magnitude notation.

4. a. 6 since 1110 → 14 − 8
   b. −1 since 0111 → 7 − 8
   c. 0 since 1000 → 8 − 8
   d. −6 since 0010 → 2 − 8
   e. −8 since 0000 → 0 − 8
   f. 1 since 1001 → 9 − 8

5. a. 1101 since 5 + 8 = 13 → 1101
   b. 0011 since −5 + 8 = 3 → 0011
   c. 1011 since 3 + 8 = 11 → 1011
   d. 1000 since 0 + 8 = 8 → 1000
   e. 1111 since 7 + 8 = 15 → 1111
   f. 0000 since −8 + 8 = 0 → 0000

6. No. The largest value that can be stored in excess 8 notation is 7, represented by 1111. To represent a larger value at least excess 16 (which uses patterns of 5 bits) must be used. Similarly, 6 cannot be represented in excess 4 notation. (The largest value that can be represented in excess 4 notation is 3.)

7. a. 3   b. 15   c. −4   d. −6   e. 0   f. −16

8. a. 00000110   b. 11111010   c. 111011?
   d. 00001101   e. 11111111   f. 000000?

9. a. 11111111   b. 10101011   c. 000001?
   d. 00000010   e. 00000000   f. 100000(

10. a. With 4 bits the largest value would be 7 and the smallest would be −8.

b. With 6 bits the largest value would be 31 and the smallest would be -32.

c. With 8 bits the largest value would be 127 and the smallest would be -128.

11. a.
$$\begin{array}{rr} 0101 & 5 \\ +0010 \rightarrow & +2 \\ \hline 0111 & 7 \end{array}$$

b.
$$\begin{array}{rr} 0011 & 3 \\ +0001 \rightarrow & +1 \\ \hline 0100 & 4 \end{array}$$

c.
$$\begin{array}{rr} 0101 & 5 \\ +1010 \rightarrow & +(-6) \\ \hline 1111 & -1 \end{array}$$

d.
$$\begin{array}{rr} 1110 & (-2) \\ +0011 \rightarrow & +\quad 3 \\ \hline 0001 & 1 \end{array}$$

e.
$$\begin{array}{rr} 1010 & (-6) \\ +1110 \rightarrow & +(-2) \\ \hline 1000 & (-8) \end{array}$$

12. a.
$$\begin{array}{rr} 0100 & 4 \\ +0011 \rightarrow & +3 \\ \hline 0111 \rightarrow & 7 \end{array}$$

b.
$$\begin{array}{rr} 0101 & 5 \\ +0110 \rightarrow & +6 \\ \hline 1011 \rightarrow & -5 \end{array}$$
(incorrect due to overflow)

c.
$$\begin{array}{rr} 1010 & (-6) \\ +1010 \rightarrow & +(-6) \\ \hline 0100 \rightarrow & 4 \end{array}$$
(incorrect due to overflow)

d.
$$\begin{array}{rr} 1010 & (-6) \\ +0111 \rightarrow & +\quad 7 \\ \hline 0001 \rightarrow & 1 \end{array}$$

e.
$$\begin{array}{rr} 0111 & 7 \\ +0001 \rightarrow & +1 \\ \hline 1000 \rightarrow & -8 \end{array}$$
(incorrect due to overflow)

13. a.
$$\begin{array}{rr} 6 & 0110 \\ +1 \rightarrow & +0001 \\ \hline & 0111 \rightarrow \qquad 7 \end{array}$$

b.
$$\begin{array}{rrr} 3 & 0011 & 0011 \\ -2 \rightarrow & -0010 \rightarrow & +1110 \\ \hline & & 0001 \rightarrow \quad 1 \end{array}$$

c
$$\begin{array}{rrr} 4 & 0100 & 0100 \\ -6 \rightarrow & 0110 \rightarrow & +1010 \\ \hline & & 1110 \rightarrow \quad -2 \end{array}$$

d.
$$\begin{array}{rr} 2 & 0010 \\ +4 \rightarrow & +0100 \\ \hline & 0110 \rightarrow \quad 6 \end{array}$$

e.
$$\begin{array}{rrr} 1 & 0001 & 0001 \\ -5 \rightarrow & -0101 & +1011 \\ \hline & \rightarrow & 1110 \rightarrow \quad -4 \end{array}$$

14. No. Overflow occurs when an attempt is made to store a number that is too large for the system being used. When adding a positive value to a negative value the result must be between the values being added. Thus, if the original values are small enough to be stored, the result will be also.

Section 1–7

1. a. $\frac{5}{8}$ b. $3\frac{1}{4}$ c. $\frac{9}{32}$ d. $-1\frac{1}{2}$ e. $-\frac{11}{64}$

2. a. 01101011 b. 01111010 (round-off error)
   c. 01001100 d. 11101110
   c. 11111000 (round-off error)

3. 01001001 (9/16) is larger than 00111101 (13/32). The following is a simple way of determining which of two patterns represents the larger value:

   Case 1. If the sign bits are different, the larger is the one with 0 sign bit.
   Case 2. If the sign bits are both 0, scan the remaining portions of the patterns from left to right until a bit position is found where the two patterns differ. The pattern containing the 1 in this position represents the larger value.
   Case 3. If the sign bits are both 1, scan the remaining portions of the patterns from left to right until a bit position is found where the two patterns differ. The pattern containing the 0 in this position represents the larger value.

   The simplicity of this comparison process is one of the reasons for representing the exponent in floating-point systems with an excess notation rather than with two's complement.

4. The largest value would be 7½, which is represented by the pattern 01111111. As for the smallest positive value, you could argue that there are two "correct" answers. First, if you stick to the coding process described in the text, which requires the most significant bit of the mantissa to be 1 (called normalized form), the answer would be 1/32, which is represented by the pattern 00001000. However, most machines do not impose this restriction for values close to 0. For such a machine, the correct answer would be 1/256 represented by 00000001.

Chapter 2

Section 2–1

1. a. The store's stock of shoes.
   b. The floor space around the customer. (This is where the shoes being considered are usually piled.)
   c. The size and style of a shoe. (This is how the customer identifies a shoe when it is requested.)
   d. A pair of shoes.
   e. One major difference is that retrieving a shoe from stock leaves a hole, whereas retrieving the contents of a memory cell results in a copy of the contents being made so that the cell is left still holding the original value. Another is that the customer does not (or should not) perform alterations on the shoes and then request that the shoes be returned to stock, whereas such an alteration is one of the prime functions of the CPU.

2. On small machines this is often a two-step process consisting of first reading the contents from the first cell into a register and then writing it into the destination cell. On most large machines, this activity appears as one event.

3. The value to be written, the address of the cell in which to write, and the command to write.

4. The term *move* often carries the connotation of removing from one location and placing in another, thus leaving a hole behind. In most cases within a machine this removal does not take place. Rather, the object being moved is most often copied (or cloned) into the new location.

5. The terms *write* and *store* (or *read* and *load*) have very similar meanings. The distinction is similar to the distinction between *drive* and *ride* in the sense that we drive a car but ride a bike. As a rule of thumb, the terms *store* and *load* are most often used when we are speaking in terms of registers. For example, we might write something into memory from a location other than a register, and we might store the contents of a register in a location other than a memory cell.

6. A common technique, called relative addressing, is to state how far rather than where to jump. For example, an instruction might be to jump forward three instructions or jump backward two instructions. You should note, however, that such statements must be altered if additional instructions

are later inserted between the origin and the destination of the jump.

7. This could be argued either way. The instruction is stated in the form of a conditional jump. However, because the condition that 0 be equal to 0 is always satisfied, the jump will always be made as if there were no condition stated at all. You will often find machines with such instructions in their repertoires because it provides an efficient design. For example, if a machine is designed to execute an instruction with a structure such as "If . . . jump to . . ." this instruction form can be used to express both condition and unconditional jumps.

Section 2–2

1. a. STORE the contents of register 6 in memory cell number 8A.
   b. JUMP to location DE if the contents of R10 equals that of R0.
   c. AND the contents of registers 3 and 12, leaving the result in register 0.
   d. MOVE the contents of register 15 to register 4.

2. The instruction 15AB requires that the CPU query the memory circuitry for the contents of the memory cell at address AB. This value, when obtained from memory, is then placed in register 5. The instruction 25AB does not require such a request of memory. Rather, the value AB is placed in register 5.

3. a. 2356   b. A503   c. B7F3   d. 80A5

Section 2–3

1. hexadecimal 34

2. a. 0F   b. C3

3. a. 00   b. 01   c. four times

4. It will halt. This is an example of what is often called self-modifying code. That is, the program modifies itself. Note that the first two instructions place hexadecimal C0 at memory location F8, and the next two instructions place 00 at location F9. Thus, by the time the machine reaches the instruction at F8, the halt instruction (C000) will have been placed there.

Section 2–4

1. One set of registers is used for fetching, decoding, and executing microinstructions, while the other

set is used for fetching, decoding, and executing the machine language instructions as directed by the microprogram.

2. The pipe would contain the instructions B1B0 (being executed), 5002 (being decoded), and B0AA (being fetched). If the value in register 0 is equal to the value in register 1, the jump to location B0 will be executed and the effort expended on the last two of these instructions will be wasted.

3. If no precautions are taken, the information at memory locations F8 and F9 will be fetched as an instruction before the previous part of the program has had a chance to modify these cells.

4. a. The CPU that is trying to add 1 to the cell might first read the value in the cell. Following this the other CPU could read the cell's value. (Note that at this point both CPUs have retrieved the same value.) If the first CPU now finishes its addition and writes its result back in the cell before the second finishes its subtraction and writes its result, the final value in the cell will reflect only the activity of the second CPU.

   b. The CPUs might read the data from the cell as before, but this time the second CPU might write its result before the first. Thus, only the activity of the first CPU will be reflected in the cell's final value.

5. The instructions b, c, and e would be executed first in any order followed first by a and then by d.

6. Instruction d would be attempted first. This would cause instructions a and b to be executed, and then d would be completed. Note that c and e would not be executed since their results are never required.

Section 2–5

1. a. 00001011 b. 10000000 c. 00101101
   d. 11101011 e. 11101111 f. 11111111
   g. 11100000 h. 01101111 i. 11010010

2. 0011100 with the AND operation

3. 0011100 with the EXCLUSIVE OR operation

4. a. The final result would be 0 if the string contained an odd number of 1s. Otherwise it would be 1.

   b. The result is the value of the parity bit for even parity.

5. The logical EXCLUSIVE OR operation mirrors addition except for the case where both operands are 1, in which case the EXCLUSIVE OR produces a 0, whereas the sum is 10. (Thus, the EXCLUSIVE OR operation could be considered as an addition operation with no carry.)

6. Use AND with the mask 1011111 to change lower case to upper case. Use OR with 0100000 to change upper case to lower case.

7. a. 01001101 b. 11100001 c. 11101111

8. a. 57 b. B8 c. 6F d. 6A

9. 5

10. 00110110 in two's complement. 01011110 in floating-point. The point here is that the procedure used to add the values is different depending on the interpretation given the bit patterns.

11. The upper-case A, represented by 1000001, would precede the lower-case a, represented by 1100001.

12. One solution is:

    12A7 (LOAD register 2 with the contents of memory cell A7.)
    2380 (LOAD register 3 with the value 80 (= 10000000).)
    7023 (OR registers 2 and 3 leaving the result in register 0.)
    30A7 (STORE contents of register 0 in memory cell A7.)
    C000 (HALT.)

13. One solution is:

    15E0 (LOAD register 5 with the contents of memory cell E0.)
    A502 (ROTATE 2 bits to the right the contents of register 5.)
    260F (LOAD register 6 with the value 0F (= 00001111).)
    8056 (AND registers 5 and 6 leaving the result in register 0.)
    30E1 (STORE the contents of register 0 in memory cell E1.)
    C000 (HALT.)

Section 2–6

1. Since each state communicated represents 3 bits the measure of bps would be three times the baud rate.

2. Examples of simplex communication include traditional radio and television broadcasting. The station talks to the audience, but the audience cannot talk back via the same communication channel.

   Half-duplex communication is found in citizens band and other shortwave radio systems. In these cases, one person talks while the other listens and then the roles are reversed. The coordination of this exchange of roles is the purpose of such terminology as "over" or "over and out."

Full-duplex communication is found in telephone systems. Both parties can talk at the same time and still receive each other's voice.

3. a. 35FA (STORE the contents of register 5 in memory cell number FA.)
   b. 200,000 times.
   c. Not with today's technology. (If the lines being printed were 100 characters long, this speed would correspond to 2000 lines per second or 120,000 lines per minute.) This is why handshaking is necessary between the CPU and peripheral devices. Another approach to solving this problem is to provide the printer with memory cells (collectively called a buffer) of its own in which it can store those characters that have been received but not yet printed. With this addition, the printer is able to absorb short bursts of data so long as the average arrival rate does not exceed its physical capabilities.

4. "Don't send more characters. I'm still busy with the previous ones."
   "I'm ready for more characters."
   "I'm out of paper."

5. Even though a terminal is being used as an input device, information is normally transferred in both directions. One reason for this is validation. For instance, it is common for data received from a terminal to be echoed back to the terminal where it can be compared to its original form. If the echoed information is found to be the same as the original, one can assume that the machine at the other end of the line received it correctly. In such a case, the line often contains both transmitted and echoed data traveling in opposite directions at the same time and therefore must be full duplex.

Part Two

Chapter 3

Section 3–1

1. Hardware is to software as:
   a. records are to music
   b. television sets are to television programs
   c. books are to stories

2. In the case of microcomputers, access to the machine is normally controlled by controlling access to the room in which the machine is kept and is therefore of minor importance in their operating systems. Moreover, since microcomputers tend to be turned on and off between use, it is awkward to implement and enforce an accurate accounting system in software. Thus, this feature is not so significant on small systems as it is on large ones. On the other hand, controlling data and its access, providing for efficient device access, and the management of resources remain important tasks on small machines as well as on large ones.

3. With a statement equivalent to ILLEGAL COMMAND. Remember that an operating system determines the meaning of a command by comparing the string of characters typed to predefined strings and thus does not understand arbitrary sentences.

Section 3–2

1. How many times have you waited in line for access to one of a bank's drive-in tellers and wondered why the lines moved so slowly? How many tellers do you think were actually inside serving the windows? How many virtual tellers were being simulated? As another example, how about an image in a mirror?

2. So long as the system is operating correctly and the user does not attempt to circumvent the system, the distinction between virtual and real characteristics should have no significance. However, in the case of the mail-order business, by knowing that the business is not really a big operation a customer is able to guard against disappointment by placing Christmas orders earlier than would otherwise be done. Similarly, understanding the distinction between virtual and real characteristics can increase a user's success with the system. For example, knowing that the separation between one user's data and another's is actually an illusion created by the operating system might have a significant influence on whether or not truly sensitive data is stored in the system.

3.

Virtual Characteristics	Real Characteristics
Many employees	Few employees
Large inventory	Small inventory
Prestigious buildings	Garage
Potential for inefficient communication within business	Very efficient communication

Section 3–3

1. Planes waiting to leave a busy airport form a queue on the taxiway. This FIFO organization is rarely violated because of the physical inconvenience of getting one aircraft in front of those that have been waiting longer.

   Banks used to let separate queues form at each teller's window. However, this did not provide strict FIFO service to their customers. Many customers became irritated as they watched later arrivals advance to the head of a faster-moving queue. Today most banks have improved this situation by organizing a single queue in which all their customers wait for an available teller in the order in which they arrived at the bank.

2. Application a for sure. (It would become quite confusing if the letters did not appear on the screen in a timely fashion as they are typed.)

   Not application b.

   Application c is an example of requirements changing as capabilities change. Several years ago customers' accounts were reconciled at the end of the day in a batch processing environment. The only time coordination with the real world was for the job to be done by the next morning. Today with automatic bank tellers, each balance can be updated by a machine as deposits and withdrawals are made; this real-time processing is becoming the expected procedure.

3. a and b. In these applications all input data can be collected before the program package is submitted to the operating system for execution. On the other hand, the playing of a video game requires interaction with the user during execution and therefore is unsuitable for batch processing.

4. A major problem could arise if one of the machines in the network malfunctioned. This would mean that communication between any pair of the operating machines would be restricted to a one-way system.

5. The major problem is exemplified by the following situation. Suppose duplicate copies of a reservation system database are maintained at different locations within a network and only one ticket remains available for a particular activity. How would one ensure that this last ticket is not sold to different people at the same time? Note that this problem is not resolved simply by notifying the other copies of the database every time a transaction is made in one of them. The recognition of an available ticket and the transaction of a sale constitute a critical region.

Section 3–4

1. command processor: communicates with user
   scheduler: prepares jobs for execution
   file manager: maintains record of stored information
   resource allocator: coordinates the assignment of resources
   dispatcher: oversees execution of the scheduled activities
   utility software: removes programming burden from user

2. How about something like this?

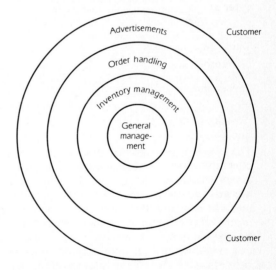

3. In most machines each letter occupies one byte of memory. Thus, this cell size is conducive to character manipulation.

4. While performing its functions, the operating system continually refers to these files with no particular pattern. This would result in repeated rewinding of the tape if the files were stored there.

However, various files or parts of a file can be easily retrieved from a disk pack.

5. In the final analysis there isn't any difference. In fact, many operating systems are built on this observation. In such systems each user-written program automatically becomes a utility program.

Section 3–5

1. If the programs required no external resources, it would take longer to run them in a time-sharing system because of the overhead of swapping back and forth between the two. However, most programs involve I/O operations and often have to wait for slow peripheral devices. In such cases, a time-sharing system is able to run another program during this waiting period. Consequently, the total time required to run two programs in a time-sharing system may actually be less than the sum of the individual time requirements.

2. Give the high-priority jobs longer time slices than the others or give time slices only to the jobs of highest priority.

3. First: Stop executing the current program.
   Second: Save the state of the current program.
   Third: Begin executing the interrupt routine.

4. First: Decide which program should be next.
   Second: Reload that program's state.
   Third: Reset the timer.
   Fourth: Start the program.

5. Approximately 20. We say approximately because the swapping overhead tends to decrease this value, whereas the fact that some programs will not use their entire slice tends to increase it.

Section 3–6

1. This system guarantees that the resource is not used by more than one program at a time; however, it dictates that the resource be allocated in a strictly alternating fashion. Once a program has used and relinquished the resource, it must wait for the other program to use the resource before the original program can access it again. This is true even if the first program needs the resource right away and the other program won't need it for some time.

2. If two cars enter opposite ends of the tunnel at the same time, they will not be aware of the other's presence. The process of entering and turning on the lights is another example of a critical region, or in this case we might call it a critical process. In this terminology we could summarize the flaw by saying that cars at opposite ends of the tunnel could execute the critical process at the same time.

3. a. This guarantees that the nonshareable resource is not required and allocated on a partial basis; that is, a car is given the whole bridge or nothing at all.
   b. This means that the nonshareable resource can be forcibly retrieved.
   c. This makes the nonshareable resource shareable, which removes the competition.

4. A sequence of arrows that form a closed loop in the directed graph. It is on this observation that techniques have been developed, allowing some operating systems to recognize the existence of deadlock and consequently to take appropriate corrective action.

Section 3–7

1. One is left with a less flexible system.

2. Just as the bootstrap routine is a small program used to start a larger one, a car's starter is a small motor used to start a larger one.

3. When turned on, the machine always starts fetching instructions from a predetermined area of main memory. This area of memory is constructed with nonvolatile cells in which is stored the bootstrap program. This program directs the loading of the general purpose operating system from bulk storage and then transfers control to this system.

   In a turnkey system the bootstrap program either may be the final application program itself (and thus no additional program must be loaded) or will load and start a particular application program rather than a general purpose operating system.

Chapter 4

Section 4–1

1. You will find that most algorithms used in everyday life fail to be algorithms from a rigorous point of view. This is sometimes true even when the term *algorithm* is used in identifying the process. For example, consider the long-division algorithm. To truly be an algorithm, this process must

be combined with a stopping criterion. Otherwise, the repetitive process may continue forever as when dividing 1 by 3.

2. The problem here is ambiguity. Natural languages developed as communication tools between intelligent beings and therefore lack the precision often required when expressing an algorithm. This is one of the main reasons that the high-level languages discussed in Chapter 5 use a well-defined subset of the English language rather than the complete florid system.

3. If you're thinking in terms of the ambiguity of which table or which pocket, you're missing the point here. The problem of termination is much more important. After all, once started, the process will continue to request the removal of coins forever. You may argue that in reality the process must stop because of the lack of coins. This, however, is a property of the algorithm's environment and not of the algorithm itself. The lack of coins does not actually terminate the algorithm's execution; it introduces ambiguity. In light of this argument, one way of modifying the sequence to form an algorithm would be the following:

Step 1. If there are no coins in your pocket, stop; otherwise, remove one of them and put it on the table.
Step 2. Return to step 1.

Section 4–2

1. One example is found in the composition of matter. At one level, the primitives are considered molecules, yet these particles are actually composites made up of atoms, which in turn are composed of electrons, protons, and neutrons. Today, we know that even these "primitives" are composites.

2. Once a program module is correctly constructed, it can be used as a building block for larger program structures without reconsidering the module's internal composition.

3. assign X the value of the
    larger input
assign Y the value of the
    smaller input
while (Y not zero) do
    (assign Remainder the value of the
    remainder after dividing X by Y,
    assign X the value of Y,
    assign Y the value of Remainder)
assign GCD the value of X

4. All other colors of light can be produced by combining red, blue, and green. Thus, a television picture tube is designed to produce these three basic colors.

Section 4–3

1. a. Use 667 3s.
  b. Use as many 3s as possible and then no more than two 2s.

2. a. Yes. Hint: place the first tile in the center so that it avoids the quadrant containing the hole while covering one square from each of the other quadrants. Then, each quadrant represents a smaller version of the original problem.
  b. The board with a single hole contains $2^{2n} - 1$ squares and each tile covers exactly three squares.
  c. Parts a and b of this question provide an excellent example of how knowing a solution to one problem helps solve another. See Polya's fourth phase.

3. It says, "This is the correct answer."

Section 4–4

1. Change the test in the while statement to read "target value not equal to current entry and there remain entries to be considered."

2. assign Z the value 0
assign X the value 1
repeat (assign Z the value Z + X,
    assign X the value X + 1)
until (X = 6)

3.
Cheryl	Alice	Alice
George	Cheryl	Bob
Alice	George	Cheryl
Bob	Bob	George

4. It is a waste of time to insist on placing the pivot above an identical entry in the list. For instance, make the proposed change and then try the new program on a list in which all entries are the same.

Section 4–5

1. The first sublist would consist of the names following Henry—that is, Irene, Joe, Darryl, Larry, Mary, Nancy, and Oliver. Next would be the names from this list preceding Larry—that is, Irene, Joe, and Darryl. At this point, the search process would find the target Joe at the center of the sublist in question.

2. 8

3.
Bob	Alice
Alice	Bob
Carol	Carol
Larry	Larry
John	John

4. This is an example of how unintelligent an algorithm can be. Rather than recognize that no work is needed, the algorithm will ultimately pick each name as the pivot entry and end up replacing it with itself.

   If the input list is in reverse order, the effect of the algorithm will be to exchange the first name with the last, then exchange the new first name with itself, and then turn its attention to the portion of the list between the first and last entries.

5. The effect will be that the first occurrence of the name will be interchanged with the last, then the first with the next-to-the-last, etc., until the first occurrence is exchanged with the second.

Section 4–6

1. No. The answer is not correct although it may sound right. The truth is that two of the three cards are the same on both sides. Thus, the probability of picking such a card is two-thirds.

2. No. If the dividend is less than the divisor, such as in 3/7, the answer given will be 1, although it should be 0.

3. No. If the value of X is zero and the value of Y is nonzero, the answer given will not be correct.

4. Each time the test for termination is conducted, the statement "Sum = 1 + 2 + ... + I and I less than or equal to N" is true. Combining this with the termination condition "I greater than or equal to N" produces the desired conclusion "Sum = 1 + 2 + ... + N." Since I is initialized at zero and incremented by one each time through the loop, its value must ultimately reach that of N.

Chapter 5

Section 5–1

1. A program in a third-generation language is machine independent in the sense that its steps are not stated in terms of the machine's attributes such as registers and memory cell addresses. On the other hand, it is machine dependent in the sense that arithmetic overflow and round-off errors will still occur.

2. The major distinction is that an assembler translates each instruction in the source program into a single machine instruction, whereas a compiler often produces many machine-language instructions to obtain the equivalent of a single source program instruction.

3. The declarative paradigm is based on developing a description of the problem to be solved. The object-oriented paradigm places emphasis on describing the components in the problem's environment.

4. The later-generation languages allow the program to be expressed more in terms of the problem's environment and less in terms of computer gibberish than do the earlier-generation languages.

Section 5–2

1. First, through the process known as lexical analysis, individual symbols in the program are grouped into strings representing objects such as numbers or words. Then, the parsing process is used to recognize instructions and clauses within instructions. Finally, as the various clauses in the program are recognized, the code generation step produces the equivalent instructions in the target language.

2. a. A translator produces a copy of the source program in a different language but does not execute the program. An interpreter executes the program from its source form without producing a formal, translated version.

   b. To change a program that is being translated, one must first change the source version of the program, then translate, link, and load the altered version before finally executing the program. In contrast, if an interpreter is used, one needs only to change the source program and then ask the interpreter to execute the new version.

3. The object version of a program usually contains many references to other program segments. These loose ends must be resolved by the linker before the program is ready to load into memory and be executed.

4. A relocatable module is a program segment in machine language that avoids references to explicit memory locations. Thus, the program will execute correctly regardless of where it is placed in

memory. This means that the loader need not be concerned with modifying the module to reflect its location in memory.

Section 5–3

1. Does the expression "X and Y or Z" mean that either both X and Y are true or Z is true, or does it mean that X is true as well as either Y or Z? This ambiguity can be resolved with parentheses by writing "(X and Y) or Z" in the first case and "X and (Y or Z)" in the second.

2. If the expression is evaluated from left to right, the result would be 7. If it is evaluated from right to left, the result would be 14. If it is evaluated according to the normal rules of arithmetic, the result would be 11.

3. A simple version would be this:

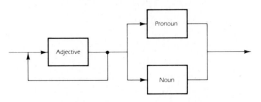

However, to allow for compound subjects the following would be in order:

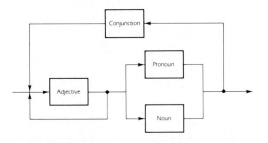

4. The definitions of terms in a natural language are not precise enough to avoid ambiguity. This is why many legal cases are argued in court on the basis of the meaning of a law, with opponents presenting different interpretations. In the case of programming languages this potential problem of ambiguity is removed by restricting the language used to a few well-defined statement forms.

5. Did John chase the parade or did he wait for the parade to pass before going for his afternoon jog?

Section 5–4

1. Probably something of the form XYZ(3,5). Note that the row is identified before the column.

2. a. The fractional part must be dropped leaving the value 26.
   b. Both the integer and the fractional part would be stored; however, the fractional part will probably be inaccurate since one-tenth cannot be represented exactly in binary notation.
   c. The four characters (2, 6, ., and 1) that represent the value will be stored in coded form.

3. a. A matrix with five rows (one for each employee) and seven columns (one for each day of the week).
   b. Perhaps a three-dimensional array with the dimensions represented by employees, days of the week, and weeks of the year.
   c. A vector of six entries (one for each game).
   d. A heterogeneous vector since the entries are of different types: name (of type character), quantity (of type integer), etc.

4. A constant in a program is a name that refers to a value that cannot change as the program executes. A variable is a name of a memory cell whose contents (and thus the value associated with the name) can vary during program execution.

5. In addition to moving the data, the data must be recoded to agree with the type associated with the new location.

6. a. 4   b. 1   c. 0   d. 1

7. Ada: at the first begin.
   BASIC: at line number 200.
   COBOL: at the statement PROCEDURE DIVISION.
   FORTRAN: at the second comment line.
   Pascal: at the second begin.

8. The ignored statements are:
   those beginning with -- in Ada
   those beginning with REM in BASIC
   those beginning with an asterisk in COBOL
   those beginning with C in FORTRAN
   those surrounded by brackets {} in Pascal

   These statements are provided to assist a human, not the machine.

Section 5–5

1.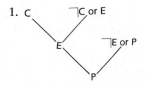

2. R, T, and V. For instance, we can show that R is a consequence by adding its negation to the col-

lection and showing that resolution can lead to the empty statement, as shown below:

```
      ¬R        ¬V or R
        \        /
S or V    \     ¬V      ¬S or V
      \      \  /      /
        \     ¬S      /
          \    /
           empty
```

3. No. The collection is inconsistent since resolution can lead to the empty statement, as shown below:

```
      ¬R or Q      ¬Q      P or Q or R
          \         /  \      /
R or ¬P    \     ¬R     P or R
      \      \   /      /
        \     ¬P      P
          \    /
           empty
```

A word of caution is in order here. The resolution process can be implemented in such a way that a collection of inconsistent statements will ultimately produce the empty clause, as was the case in this exercise. However, there are cases in which a collection of statements may be consistent, but there are infinitely many potential resolution patterns to consider. In such cases, a test for consistency based on resolving two clauses at a time can never check all possibilities and hence can never produce an answer. In short, a test for consistency based on resolution can answer no in the case of inconsistent statements but may not be able to answer yes in some cases of consistent statements. In fact, mathematicians have shown that there is no general-purpose definitive process for verifying consistency.

4. a. smaller(sue, carol)
      smaller(sue, john)
   b. smaller(sue, carol)
      smaller(bill, carol)
   c. smaller(carol, john)
      smaller(bill, sue)
      smaller(sue, carol)
      smaller(bill, sue)
      smaller(sue, john)

Chapter 6

Section 6–1

1. One could argue here as to whether the correct answer is the development phase or the modification phase. The ability to express one's ideas in terms of the application rather than the machine's features is certainly helpful in both cases.

2. This question is a trap. The answer is all of them.

3. All of the steps appear in this process, but in small systems they are sometimes difficult to distinguish. For example, in the case of a single small program a significant part of the design might be done in the context of a top-down programming process, thus closely associated with the program's implementation.

4. The implementation (during which time the programs are actually written) and the documentation of the system.

Section 6–2

1. The design of the system consists of analyzing the pieces from which the system will be constructed, whereas the process of programming is concerned with the sequential ordering of events.

2. No. In this sense the examples in this section are somewhat misleading. (On the other hand, we did point out that our second design is not strictly hierarchical.)

3. This question leads us to Section 6–3. For now note that less data is interchanged between the modules in the second design than in the first.

4. For CONTROL ACCESS we need stubs for GET PRIVILEGE, CONTROL MODIFICATION ACTIVITIES, and CONTROL DISPLAY ACTIVITIES. For CONTROL MODIFICATION ACTIVITIES we need stubs for CONTROL ACCESS, INSERT, DELETE, and DISPLAY.

Section 6–3

1. Because the purpose of a novel is to present a variety of interwoven plots, the reader finds a tremendous amount of coupling between the book's chapters. On the other hand, because an encyclopedia is designed to allow one to read about a particular topic independent of the others, there is little coupling between entries of an encyclopedia. (We say little coupling rather than no cou-

pling because there is a degree of implicit coupling between various entries. For example, a section on American history would be implicitly coupled to the topic of English history.)

2. The existence of coupling between courses is reflected by the listing of some courses as prerequisites for others. For example, many courses in the natural sciences are coupled to traditional courses in mathematics such as algebra or calculus.

3. From the users' point of view there should be none. However, we have seen that one of the major roles of an operating system is to coordinate the various user activities within the machine. From this point of view, a significant amount of sharing (and therefore coupling) exists between the users of the system at any given time.

4. Taking aspirin to relieve a headache gives some people an upset stomach. Here the term *side effect* refers to a result other than the intended one. The term has the same connotations in the programming context.

5. Explicit coupling includes the identification of the trump suit, which hand is dummy, who will lead, etc. Insights gained from the bidding process such as who holds which cards could be considered as implicit coupling.

Section 6–4

1. The related plots within a novel are often developed simultaneously in a single chapter. The result is a rather loose degree of cohesion based perhaps on the fact that the events presented are to have happened at the same time. In contrast, the organization of an encyclopedia promotes a high degree of cohesion within each entry.

2. This is a tough one. From one point of view, we could start by placing everything in a single module. This would result in little cohesion and no coupling at all. If we then began to divide this single module into smaller ones, the result would be an increase in coupling. We might therefore conclude that increasing cohesion tends to increase coupling.

   On the other hand, suppose the problem at hand naturally divides into three very cohesive modules, which we will call A, B, and C. If our original design did not observe this natural division (for example half of task A might be placed with half of task B, etc.), we would expect the cohesion to be low and the coupling high. In this case, redesigning the system by isolating tasks A, B, and C into separate modules would most likely decrease intermodule coupling as intramodule cohesion increases.

3. a. The common goal or interest of the club members. As various club activities are undertaken, committees and subcommittees are often formed to organize them. This can be viewed as a natural tendency to maximize cohesion. The cohesion of the club as a whole is weak compared with the specific tasks of the committees. Also, the duties of the officers of a club are modularized according to function. For example, the president presides over meetings, the secretary maintains records, and the treasurer manages the finances.

   b. The marketing of merchandise. Here again we find a natural tendency to seek greater cohesion within the organization. In this case it results in the formation of departments based on the type of merchandise being sold. In addition, we find the management divided according to function in a similar manner to the officers in a club.

   c. The registration of students. This activity is normally broken into its functional components to obtain a greater degree of cohesion. For example, one component might deal with confirming admission, another with selecting courses, still another with paying fees.

   d. The conveying of information. Again observe the natural desire to increase cohesion by subdivision. Newspapers are divided into sections according to subject matter.

Section 6–5

1.

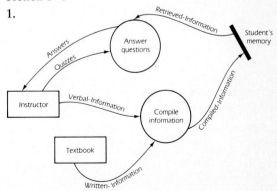

2. No. The data flow diagram does not deal with the order in which activities take place. Based on our diagram the system could be implemented so that

passwords are given by the user before, after, or during a request for information.

3.

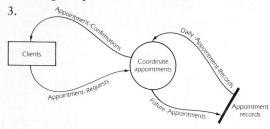

Section 6–6

1. In accompanying manuals, within the source program in the form of comments and well-written code, through interactive messages that the program itself writes at a terminal, through data dictionaries, and in the form of design documents such as structure charts and data flow diagrams.

2. In both the development and modification phases. The point is that modifications must be documented as thoroughly as the original program. (It's also true that software is documented while in its use phase. For example, a user of the system might discover problems, which are then reported in the system user's manual. Moreover, books written on the use and design of popular software systems are common. These are often written by people other than the original designers and after the software has been in use for some time and has gained popularity.)

3. Different people will have different opinions on this one. Some will argue that the program is the point of the whole project and thus is naturally the more important. Others will argue that a program is worth nothing if it is not documented since if you can't understand a program, you can't use it or modify it. Moreover, with good documentation the task of creating the program can be "easily" recreated.

Part Three

Chapter 7

Section 7–1

1. 5 3 7 4 2 8 1 9 6

2. If R is the number of rows in the matrix the formula would be R(J − 1) + (I − 1).

3. From the beginning address of 25 we must skip over 11(3 − 1) + (6 − 1) = 27 entries in the matrix, each of which occupies two memory cells. Thus, we must skip over 54 memory cells. The final address can therefore be found by adding 54 to the address of the first entry resulting in the address of 79.

Section 7–2

1. As an example, to find the fifth entry in a dense list multiply the number of cells in each entry by 4 and add the result to the address of the first entry. The situation is quite different in the case of the linked list since the address of the fifth entry is in no way related to the address of the first. Thus, to find the fifth entry, one must actually traverse each preceding entry.

2. The head pointer will contain the NIL value.

3. assign Last the value of the last name to be printed
   assign Finished the value false
   assign Current Pointer the value in the head pointer
   while (Current Pointer not NIL and Finished = false) do
       (print the entry pointed to by Current Pointer,
       if (the name just printed = Last) then
           (assign Finished the value true)
       assign Current Pointer the value in the pointer cell
           in the entry pointed to by Current Pointer)

4. assign Current the value in the head pointer
   assign Previous the value NIL
   assign Found the value false
   while (Current not NIL and Found is false) do
       (if (the entry pointed to by Current is the target entry)

then (assign Found the value true)
else (assign Previous the value of Current, and
    assign Current the value in the pointer
    cell of the entry pointed to by Current))
if (Found is true) then
  (if (Previous = NIL)
    then (assign head pointer the value in the
        pointer cell of the entry pointed to
        by Current)
    else (assign the pointer cell in the entry pointed
        to by Previous the value in the
        pointer cell in the entry pointed to
        by Current))

Section 7–3

1. One traditional example is the stack of trays in a cafeteria. Many of these are spring loaded to keep the top tray at a convenient level. In this case the term *push* is truly representative of the process of adding more entries to the stack.

2.

Activity	Stack Immediately Following Activity
Main program calls subprogram A.	Position in main program
	Position in subprogram A
Subprogram A calls subprogram B.	Position in main program
Subprogram B completes.	Position in main program
	Position in subprogram A
Subprogram A calls subprogram C.	Position in main program
Subprogram C completes.	Position in main program
Subprogram A completes.	Stack empty

3. The stack pointer would point to the cell immediately below the base of the stack.

4. if (the stack pointer points below the stack base)
  then (exit with error message)
  extract the stack entry pointed to by the stack pointer
  adjust the stack pointer to point to the next lower stack entry

5. Represent the stack as a one-dimensional array and the stack pointer as a variable of integer type. Then use this stack pointer to maintain a record of the position of the stack's top within the array rather than of the exact memory address.

Section 7–4

1.

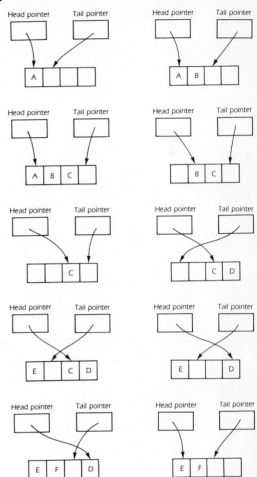

2. Both empty and full conditions are indicated by the equal head and tail pointers. Thus, additional information is required to distinguish between the two conditions.

3. if (Full is true) then (exit with error message)
  store the new entry in the location pointed to by the tail pointer
  advance the tail pointer
  if (the tail pointer points beyond the reserved block)
    then (alter the tail pointer to point to the first cell of the reserved block)
  if (head pointer = tail pointer)
    then (assign Full the value true)

Section 7–5

1. Root node is 11; leaf nodes are 1, 2, 6, 3, and 4.
2. The root pointer would be NIL.
3.

4.

6.

5. When searching for J:

When searching for P:

Section 7–6

1. Deposits and withdrawals to and from a checking account can be executed only through specific procedures that are supported by laws.

2. An abstract data type is a concept; an instance of that data type is an actual object of that type. For example, dog is a type of animal, whereas Lassie and Rex are instances of that type.

3. A traditional program module is normally designed to carry out a specific procedure and thus consists of a single routine. An instance of an abstract data type is designed to simulate the underlying type and thus may be capable of executing several procedures. For instance, an instance of a stack would be capable of pushing new entries on the stack as well as popping old entries from the stack.

4. A queue of integers might be implemented using either a dense or linked list as the underlying structure. Or, you may have answered as a circular queue restricted to a specific block of memory cells or a roaming block of cells, although this

latter implementation would prove dangerous to the other data structures residing in memory.

Section 7–7

1. One might be an escalator that should be able to receive shoppers at one level and deposit them at another. Another might be an entrance that should be able to introduce new shoppers into the system while removing others from the system.

2. Each object package contains those routines used to simulate the abstract object being represented.

3. A single object often consists of separate routines for performing the various operations on the object. For example, a stack object would have routines for pushing and popping entries. Each of these routines could be implemented as a submodule of the object.

4. No. An object may represent a very complicated structure that might require a variety of data structures to simulate it. (On the other hand, if an object is too complex, it is often redesigned as several objects working together.) Moreover, an object may have no underlying data structure. An example could be the object representing the front door in a system for simulating the traffic pattern in a bank lobby. Such an object would merely need to introduce new customers into the lobby and remove others but would not need an underlying storage system to hold these customers.

Chapter 8

Section 8–1

1. You should be led through these beginning stages:

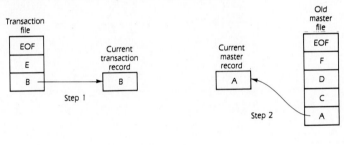

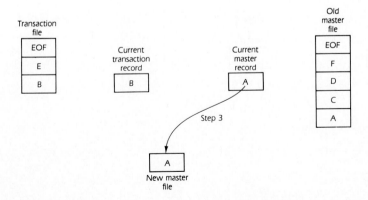

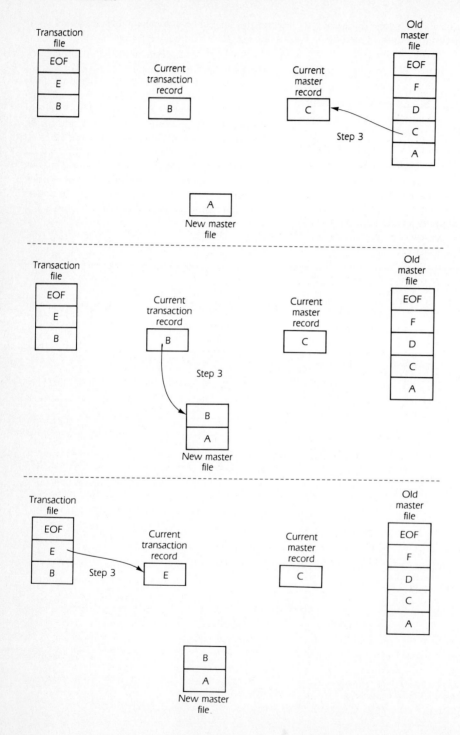

2. The idea is to first divide the file to be stored into many separate files containing one record each. Next group the one-record files into pairs and within each pair designate one file as the transaction file and the other as the old master. Since each file is sorted (it has only one record), we can now apply the merge algorithm to each pair. This will result with half as many files, each with two records. Furthermore, each of these two-record files will be sorted. We can group them into pairs, call one member of each pair the transaction file and the other the old master file, and again apply the merge algorithm to the pairs. Again we will find ourselves with fewer but larger files, each of which is sorted. Continuing in this fashion we will ultimately be left with only one file that consists of all the original records but in sorted order. (If an odd number of files occurs at any stage of this process, we need merely set the odd one aside and pair it with one of the larger files in the next stage.)

3. First sequentially read the tape until the position is reached where the new record belongs. Note that because a record is there now, we must read that record into main memory for safekeeping before writing the new one in its place. Having read this record, we are now beyond the "hole" on the tape, so we must rewind the tape and sequentially read back to the position of the hole. We can now write the new record into the hole. At this point we must place the record being held in memory back on the tape. It belongs at the current position (immediately after the record just inserted), but a record is already there. Therefore we must read this record into main memory before writing in its place. Having read this record, we are beyond the required hole and must rewind the tape and sequentially. . . . (Note that if the records were not the same size we would not know that retrieving one record would provide a hole big enough to hold its replacement.)

Section 8–2

1. Suppose the entries in the index were the smallest key field values from each segment and we were looking for the record with key field value 7. If the first entry in the index were 5, we would not know whether or not the target record is in the segment represented by this entry. Thus, we must go on to the next entry. If this next entry were 11, we would conclude that the previous entry was

the one we needed since our target key field, 7, is less than 11. Consequently, we would have to backtrack to the previous index entry to continue the search.

In contrast, suppose the entries in the index were the largest key field value from each segment. When looking for the entry 7, we might first find the entry 10. Since 10 is larger than the target key field value, we could conclude immediately that this is the segment of interest without going further in the index.

2. The purpose is to provide both direct and sequential access to the file. As pointed out in the section, sequential access is possible in an indexed file if the index is constructed so that it can be traversed sequentially as we did in the tree structure in Chapter 7. On the other hand, if the file is designed as an indexed sequential file, sequential processing might well be carried out more efficiently.

3. A list in some cases is easier to update. On the other hand, searching for an entry could take significantly more time than in the case of a tree.

4. It depends on how generally you interpret "the technique presented in this section." The point is that the partial-index system we presented relies on each physical segment being a contiguous part of the overall sorted file. Since the file cannot be physically divided according to two different orders, the technique could not literally be applied to different key fields in the same file. On the other hand, approximations to the technique can be implemented using a pointer system to represent the second order. Since an index based on this additional system will be less efficient than the one based on the physical storage order, we normally use it for the key field that will be used less frequently.

Section 8–3

1. This is a good example of the kinds of things that must be considered when selecting a hash algorithm. In this case the first three digits of the Social Security numbers would be a poor choice since these digits represent the area of the country in which the number was assigned. Consequently, citizens in one area of the country tend to have the same starting digits in their Social Security numbers, and this would result in more clustering than normal in the hashed file.

2. A poorly chosen hash algorithm will result in more clustering than normal and thus in more overflow. Since the overflow from each section of bulk storage is organized as a linked list, searching through the overflow records is essentially searching a sequential file.

3. The section assignments are as follows:
   a. 0   c. 3   e. 3   g. 3   i. 3
   b. 0   d. 0   f. 3   h. 3   j. 0

   Thus, all the records hash into sections 0 and 3 leaving sections 1, 2, 4, and 5 empty. The problem here is that the number of sections being used (6) and the key field values have the common factor of 3. (You might try rehashing these key field values using 7 sections and see what improvement you find.)

4. The point here is that we are essentially applying a hash algorithm to place the people in the group into one of 365 categories. The hash algorithm, of course, is the calculation of one's birthday. The amazing thing is that only 23 people are required before the probability is in favor of at least two of the birthdays being the same. In terms of a hashed file, this indicates that when hashing records into 365 available sections of bulk storage, clustering is likely to be present after only 23 records have been entered.

5. The sections of bulk storage identified by the hashing process are normally chosen to be tracks on the disk, with the overflow area as another one or more tracks.

Section 8–4

1. The operating system will first search the index to find which segment should be interrogated. Having established the desired segment number, the operating system might then check to see if that segment is already in main memory (it may be the same segment that was previously accessed). If it is already in main memory the operating system will search it and relay the correct record to the program. Otherwise, the segment must be retrieved from bulk storage and then searched.

2. The operating system in a time-sharing environment will do its best to use all time efficiently. If the required storage segment is not already in main memory, the operating system will ask the controller of the disk drive to retrieve the correct segment; but rather than wait for the data to arrive, the operating system will terminate the original program's time slice and start another program. After the controller has placed the requested segment in main memory, the operating system will return to the original program, give it the record it needed, and allow it to continue execution in the normal sequence of time slices.

3. No. For some reason this is a common mistake made by beginning programmers. Keep in mind that an index for a file must be maintained as the file is initially constructed and later modified. The operating system cannot perform the magic of creating an index for a previously non-indexed file.

Chapter 9

Section 9–1

1. The purchasing department would be interested in inventory records to place orders for more raw goods, whereas the accounting department would need the information to balance the books.

2. Employee, student, alumni, finance, registration, equipment/supplies, etc.

Section 9–2

1. No. The use of file systems invariably dictates that the application program be expressed in terms of the actual organization of records in the file. Thus, a change in the record structure would require changes in all programs accessing that file.

2.

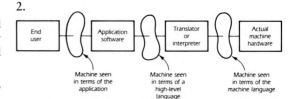

3. The application software translates the user's requests from the terminology of the application into terminology compatible with the database management system. The database management system in turn converts the requests into a form understood by the routines that actually manip-

ulate the data in bulk storage. These last routines perform the retrieval of data.

4. Yes. However, it is expensive and produces a less flexible piece of equipment than the traditional architecture. Nonetheless several manufacturers are moving in this direction.

Section 9–3

1. a. G. Jerry Smith
   b. Cheryl H. Clark
   c. S26Z

2. One solution would be:

   SELECT FROM JOB WHERE DEPT EQUALS "PERSONNEL" GIVING TEMP.
   PROJECT JOB–TITLE FROM TEMP GIVING LIST.

   In some systems this would result in a list with a job title repeated depending on how many times it occurred in the personnel department. That is, our list may contain numerous occurrences of the title secretary. It is more common, however, to design the PROJECT operation so that it removes duplicate tuples from the resulting relation.

3. One solution would be:

   MULTIPLY JOB BY ASSIGNMENT GIVING TEMP1.
   SELECT FROM TEMP1 WHERE JOB.JOB–ID EQUALS ASSIGNMENT.JOB–ID AND ASSIGNMENT.TERM–DATE EQUALS "*" GIVING TEMP2.
   MULTIPLY EMPLOYEE BY TEMP2 GIVING TEMP3.
   SELECT FROM TEMP3 WHERE EMPLOYEE.EMPL–ID EQUALS TEMP2.EMPL–ID GIVING TEMP4.
   PROJECT EMPLOYEE.NAME, TEMP2.DEPT FROM TEMP4 GIVING RESULT.

4. The model itself does not provide data independence. This is a property of the data management system. Data independence is achieved by providing the data management system the ability to present a consistent relational organization to the application software even though the actual organization may change.

5. Through common attributes. For instance, the EMPLOYEE relation in this section is tied to the ASSIGNMENT relation via the attribute EMPL–ID, and the ASSIGNMENT relation is tied to the JOB relation by the attribute JOB–ID. Attributes used to connect relations like this are sometimes called connection attributes.

Section 9–4

1. The concept is almost identical except that the end of file is indicated in the set environment by returning to the owner rather than by finding a special mark. Another difference is that retrieval of a record from a sequential file is combined with the advancement of one's position in the file, whereas the network model normally separates these activities. Although we didn't mention it in the text, the FIND–NEXT and FIND–OWNER commands shift one's position in the database but do not actually retrieve data. An additional operation called GET is normally used for actual retrieval.

2. First open the database and then do the following:

   FIND–NEXT JOB–SET
   FIND–NEXT JOB–SET
   FIND–NEXT FILLED–BY
   FIND–OWNER WORK–HISTORY
   Retrieve the current EMPLOYEE group and print that employee's name.
   FIND–NEXT FILLED–BY
   FIND–OWNER WORK–HISTORY
   Retrieve the current EMPLOYEE group and print that employee's name.
   Stop

3. No. When the database is first opened, no position in a WORK–HISTORY set is yet established; thus an instruction to find the next entry in such a set is meaningless.

4. No. You wouldn't know this from the discussion in the text, however. Indexes are often maintained on certain groups to allow timely response to frequently asked questions just as in indexed files. An example might be in an airline reservation system where information about flights and their passenger lists are frequently interrogated. Here indexes allow the application software to reach information without "walking" to it step by step.

5. Most likely not. In fact you would probably be considered strange for asking. The point here is to emphasize again that the database models being discussed are of concern to the application software and not to the end user.

Section 9–5

1. In the same manner as the operating system informs an application program of the EOF when processing a sequential file. That is, it may set a flag that can be checked by the program or it can auto-

matically transfer control to another part of the application program.

2. GET–FIRST JOB WHERE JOB–ID EQUALS "T25"
While still under this parent continue to
GET–NEXT EMPL–ASSIGNMENT UNDER PARENT and print that employee's name.
Stop.

3. This depends on your point of view. If you're interested in the parts made by each manufacturer, you would probably want trees of the form:

but if you're looking for those manufacturers producing a certain part, the form:

would be in order.

4. They're very much the same; however, a group occurrence can be a member of more than one set (but of different types) in the network system, whereas a child can have only one parent in the hierarchical model.

Part Four

Chapter 10

Section 10–1

1. Our purpose here is not to give a decisive answer to this issue but to use it to show how delicate the argument over the existence of intelligence really is.

2. Although most of us would probably say no, we would probably claim that if a human dispensed the same products in a similar atmosphere, awareness would be present even though we might not be able to explain the distinction.

Section 10–2

1. In the case of sending pictures to the earth, the system needs only to relay the picture, whereas to use the picture for maneuvering, the robot must be able to "understand" the meaning of the picture.

2. The possible interpretations for one section of the drawing do not match any of those of another section. To embed this insight into a program, one might isolate the interpretations allowable for various line junctions and then write a program that tries to find a set of compatible interpretations (one for each junction). In fact, if you stop and think about it, this is probably what your own senses did in trying to evaluate the drawing. Did you detect your eyes scanning back and forth between the two ends of the drawing as your senses tried to piece possible interpretations together?

(If this subject interests you, you'll want to read about the work of people such as D. A. Huffman, M. B. Clowes, and D. Waltz.)

3. There are only two. One is the concave scene observed when viewing the corner of a box from the inside; the other is the convex scene obtained when viewing the corner of a box from the outside. (This is the kind of analysis we were talking about in the previous answer when we referred to isolating the possible interpretations.)

4. We must be looking at the edge of a box from the inside. If we were on the outside, the image would have to be something like that below:

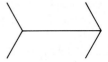

Section 10–3

1. Production systems provide a uniform approach to a variety of problems. That is, although apparently different in their original form, all problems reformulated into terms of production systems become the problem of finding a path through a state graph.

2.

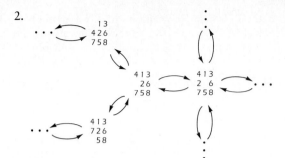

3. The states might include that of starting the maze, finishing the maze, deciding which way to go from the current position, or being stuck at a dead end. These individual states are so closely associated with particular positions in the maze that we can identify them by the positions labeled below. Thus, we could speak of being in state S (the starting state), state B (deciding which way to go from that position), or state G (having reached the goal).

The productions consist of the movements from one location to another. Thus, the state graph would have the following form:

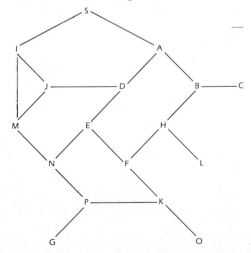

Section 10–4

1. If we agree to stop the search after a depth of five expansions, the search tree at one point might appear as shown below. The nodes are labeled in the order in which they were expanded. If the search were to continue, the next node to be expanded would be the middle child of the root.

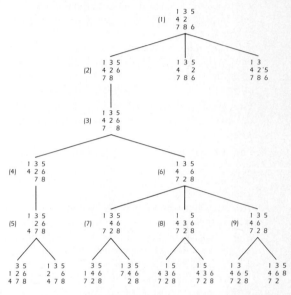

2. The process of following a depth-first search is essentially that of staying with a single attempted solution rather than freely jumping between different ones. This dedication to a particular solution is inherent in a system that actually executes the productions in the outside world as they are suspected of being a part of the solution. That is, if our puzzle solving machine actually began moving tiles as the search tree was developed, any final solution would have to begin with those particular moves and thus would consist of a path along that particular branch in the search tree.

3. No. When using a depth-first search the most recently discovered occurrence of a duplicated state could easily be higher in the tree than the previous occurrence.

4. Remember that the control system must execute the productions as they are popped off the stack. At execution time, the instruction MOVE THE TILE IN THE UPPER RIGHT HAND CORNER DOWN would be easier to execute than the instruction MOVE THE 5 TILE DOWN. The lat-

ter form requires the system to return to the puzzle image to find where the 5 tile is located at that time.

Section 10–5

1. Our heuristic system for solving the 8–puzzle is based on an analysis of the immediate situation just as that of the mountain climber. This short-sightedness is what allowed our algorithm to proceed initially along the wrong path in the example of this section just as a mountain climber can be led into trouble by always plotting a course based only on the local terrain. (This analogy often causes heuristic systems based on local or immediate information to be called hill-climbing systems.)

2. The system will rotate the 5, 6, and 8 tiles either clockwise or counterclockwise until the goal state is reached.

3. The problem here is that our heuristic scheme ignores the value of keeping the hole adjacent to the tiles that are out of place. If the hole is surrounded by tiles in their correct position, some of these tiles must be moved before those tiles still seeking their correct place can be moved. Thus, it is incorrect to consider all those tiles surrounding the hole as actually being correct. To fix this flaw, we might first observe that a tile in its correct position but blocking the hole from incorrectly positioned tiles must be moved away from its correct position and later moved back. Thus, each correctly positioned tile on a path between the hole and the nearest incorrectly positioned tile will account for at least two moves in the remaining solution. We could therefore modify our projected cost calculation to be as follows:

First, calculate the projected cost as before. However, if the hole is totally isolated from the incorrectly positioned tiles, find a shortest path between the hole and an incorrectly positioned tile, multiply the number of tiles on this path by two, and add the resulting value to the previous projected cost.

With this system the leaf nodes in Figure 10-10 would have projected costs of 6, 6, and 4 (from left to right), and thus the correct branch would be pursued initially.

Our new system is not foolproof. For example, consider the following configuration. The solution is to slide the 5 tile down, rotate the top two rows clockwise until those tiles are correct, then move the 5 tile back up, and finally move

the 8 tile to its correct position. However, our new heuristic system wants us to start by moving the 8 tile since the state obtained by this initial move has a projected cost of only 6 compared with the other options that have costs of 8.

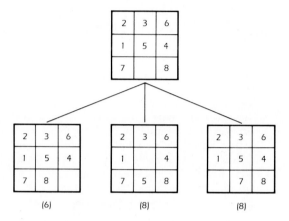

(6)   (8)   (8)

4. The search tree would be little more than a linked list representing the result of depth-first search without a depth limit since the "left-most leaf node with the smallest projected cost" would always be the left-most leaf node. Thus, the search tree would consist of only the left-most possible path.

Section 10–6

1. Is the sentence describing what kind of horses they are, or is it telling what some people are doing?

2. A closed-world database can draw conclusions that an open-world database cannot. However, the maintenance of a closed-world database is more demanding since any statement that cannot be derived from the facts in the database will be considered false. This leads to some rather surprising repercussions. A standard example is that of a database containing only a single statement of the form "P or Q." Since the database cannot derive P alone from its facts, it must conclude that P is false. Likewise, it must conclude that the statement Q is false. But, these two conclusions together contradict the statement in the database.

3. A traditional database contains facts such as an employee's name, address, and employee number. In contrast, a knowledge base often contains rules such as "if raining, check rain gauge."

Chapter 11

Section 11–1

1. clear AUX;
   incr AUX;
   while X not 0 do;
       clear AUX;
       clear X;
   end;
   while AUX not 0 do;
       incr X;
       clear AUX;
   end;

2. while X not 0 do;
       decr X;
   end;

3. move X to AUX;
   while AUX not 0 do;
       S1
       clear AUX;
   end;
   move X to AUX;
   invert AUX;
   wile AUX not 0 do;
       S2
       clear AUX;
   end;

4. If we assume that X refers to the memory cell at address 40 and that each program segment starts at location 00 we have the following conversion table:

	Address	Contents
clear X;	00	20
	01	00
	02	30
	03	40

	Address	Contents
incr X;	00	11
	01	40
	02	20
	03	01
	04	50
	05	01
	06	30
	07	40

	Address	Contents
decr X;	00	20
	01	00
	02	11
	03	40
	04	22

	Address	Contents
while X not 0 do;	05	01
	06	40
	07	03
	08	50
	09	02
	0A	B1
	0B	06
	0C	33
	0D	40
	00	20
	01	00
	02	11
	03	40
	04	B1
end;	05	WZ
	WX	B0
	WY	00

5. Just as in a real machine, negative numbers could be dealt with via a coding system. For example, the right-most bit in each string could be used as a sign but with the remaining bits used to represent the magnitude of the value.

Section 11–2

1. The result will be the following diagram:

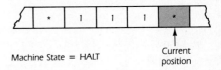

Machine State = HALT   Current position

2.

Current State	Cell Content	Value to Write	Direction to Move	New State to Enter
START	*	*	left	STATE 1
STATE 1	0	0	left	STATE 2
STATE 1	1	0	left	STATE 2
STATE 1	*	0	left	STATE 2
STATE 2	0	*	right	STATE 3
STATE 2	1	*	right	STATE 3
STATE 2	*	*	right	STATE 3
STATE 3	0	0	right	HALT
STATE 3	1	0	right	HALT

3.

Current State	Current Cell Content	Value to Write	Direction to Move	New State to Enter
START	*	*	left	SUBTRACT
SUBTRACT	0	1	left	BORROW
SUBTRACT	1	0	left	NO BORROW

(continued)

3. (cont.)

BORROW	0	1	left	BORROW
BORROW	1	0	left	NO BORROW
BORROW	*	*	right	ZERO
NO BORROW	0	0	left	NO BORROW
NO BORROW	1	1	left	NO BORROW
NO BORROW	*	*	right	RETURN
ZERO	0	0	right	ZERO
ZERO	1	0	right	ZERO
ZERO	*	*	no move	HALT
RETURN	0	0	right	RETURN
RETURN	1	1	right	RETURN
RETURN	*	*	no move	HALT

4. The point here is that the concept of a Turing machine is supposed to capture the meaning of "to compute." That is, anytime a situation occurs in which computing is taking place the components and activities of a Turing machine should be present. For example, a person figuring income tax is doing a certain degree of computing. The computing machine is the person and the tape is represented by the paper on which values are recorded.

Section 11–3

1. The machine described by the following table will halt if started with an even input but will never halt if started with an odd input:

Current State	Current Cell Content	Value to Write	Direction to Move	New State to Enter
START	*	*	left	STATE 1
STATE 1	0	0	right	HALT
STATE 1	1	1	no move	STATE 1
STATE 1	*	*	no move	STATE 1

2. The computation of a loan payment, the area of a circle, or a car's mileage.

3. Mathematicians call such functions transcendental functions. Examples include the logarithmic and trigonometric functions. These particular examples can still be computed but not by algebraic means. For example, the trigonometric functions can be calculated by actually drawing the triangle involved, measuring its sides, and only then turning to the algebraic operation of dividing.

4. The function is multiplication by 2.

Section 11–4

1. ... capture the meaning of "to compute" or equivalently "to calculate."

2.

$$decr\ X. \qquad \text{(program)}$$
$$\downarrow$$
1100100110010111000111110010010000010110000111011 (ASCII code)
$$\downarrow$$
443,301,799,406,651 (Gödel number in base ten)

3. Yes. In fact, this program will halt for any input value. Thus, it must halt if its input is its own Gödel number.

4. The point here is that the logic is the same as in our argument that the halting problem does not have an algorithmic solution. If the house painter paints his or her own house, he or she doesn't and vice versa.

Section 11–5

1. If the machine sorts 100 names in an average of one second, it can perform $(1/4)(10,000 - 100)$ comparisons in one second. This means that each comparison takes approximately 0.0004 second. Consequently, sorting 1000 names (which requires an average of $(1/4)(1,000,000 - 1000)$ comparisons) would require roughly 100 seconds or $1\frac{2}{3}$ minutes.

2. To sort a list of 100 names using the quick sort algorithm requires at least $100 \lfloor \log 100 \rfloor = 600$ comparisons. Since it takes the machine one second to do this, it requires about 0.0016 second for each comparison. Because to sort a list of 1000 names requires at least $100 \lfloor \log 1000 \rfloor = 9000$ comparisons, at least 15 seconds would be required.

3. Surprising as it may seem, this is a worst-case example for the quick sort algorithm. Thus, to sort 10 names will require $1/2(100 - 10)$ or 45 comparisons.

4. The list David, Carol, Alice, Bill, Gwen, Earl, Fred would require only 10 comparisons.

Section 11–6

1. No. Depending on which polynomial and exponential are compared, either may be small in comparison to the other for small inputs. In fact, it is true that exponential algorithms are sometimes preferred as opposed to polynomial ones when the application involves only small inputs.

2. From Alice and Bill we could form these three subcommittees:
   1. Alice
   2. Bill
   3. Alice, Bill

From Alice, Bill, and Carol we could form these subcommittees:
1. Alice
2. Bill
3. Carol
4. Alice, Bill
5. Alice, Carol
6. Bill, Carol
7. Alice, Bill, Carol

From Alice, Bill, Carol, and David we could obtain 15 different subcommittees. The point here is that the number of subcommittees is growing exponentially and from this point on the job of listing all the possibilities becomes a laborious task.

3. Within the class of polynomial problems is the sorting problem, which can be solved by polynomial algorithms such as the insertion sort or the quick sort.

Within the class of nonpolynomial problems is the task of listing all the subcommittees that could be formed from a given parent committee.

Any polynomial problem is an NP problem, but the problem of finding a subcommittee whose age total is a given value is an example of an NP problem that has not been shown to be a polynomial problem.

Additional Reading

Introduction

1. Goldstine, H. H. *The Computer from Pascal to von Neumann.* Princeton, N.J.: Princeton Univ. Press, 1972.
2. Heminway, M., ed. *Datapro 70 the EDP Buyer's Bible.* Datapro Research Corp., updated monthly.
3. Kotelly, G., ed. *Mini-Micro Systems.* Denver, Colo.: Cahners Publishing Co., published monthly.
4. Randell, B. *The Origins of Digital Computers.* New York: Springer-Verlag, 1973.
5. Shurkin, J. *Engines of the Mind.* New York: W. W. Norton and Company, 1984.

Chapter 1: Data Storage

1. Cavanagh, J. J. F. *Digital Computer Arithmetic: Design and Implementation.* New York: McGraw-Hill, 1984.
2. Gear C. W. *Computer Organization and Programming.* New York: McGraw-Hill, 1974.
3. Knuth, D. E. *The Art of Computer Programming.* Vol. 2. Menlo Park, Calif.: Addison-Wesley, 1969.
4. Levy, H. M., and Eckhouse, R. H., Jr. *Computer Programming and Architecture.* Bedford, Mass.: Digital Equipment Corp., 1980.
5. Tanenbaum, A. S. *Structured Computer Organization.* Englewood Cliffs, N.J.: Prentice-Hall, 1984.
6. Waser, S., and Flynn, Michael J. *Introduction to Arithmetic for Digital Systems Designers.* New York: Holt, Rinehart and Winston, 1982.

Chapter 2: Data Manipulation

1. Brink, J., and Spillman, R. T. *Computer Architecture and VAX Assembly Language Programming.* Menlo Park, Calif.: Benjamin/Cummings, 1986.
2. Hillis, W. D. *The Connection Machine.* Cambridge, Mass.: MIT Press, 1985.
3. Hwang, K., and Briggs, F. A. *Computer Architecture and Parallel Processing.* New York: McGraw-Hill, 1984.
4. Knuth, D. E. *The Art of Computer Programming.* Vol. 1. Menlo Park, Calif.: Addison-Wesley, 1973.
5. Levy, H. M., and Eckhouse, R. H., Jr. *Computer Programming and Architecture.* Bedford, Mass.: Digital Equipment Corp., 1980.
6. Mano, M. M. *Computer Systems Architecture.* Englewood Cliffs, N.J.: Prentice-Hall, 1976.
7. Stone, H. S. *High-Performance Computer Architecture.* Menlo Park, Calif.: Addison-Wesley, 1987.

Chapter 3: Operating Systems

1. Comer, D. *Operating System Design: The XINU Approach.* Englewood Cliffs, N.J.: Prentice-Hall, 1984.
2. Deitel, H. M. *An Introduction to Operating Systems.* Menlo Park, Calif.: Addison-Wesley, 1983.
3. Holt, R. C.; Graham, G. S.; Lazowsha, E. D.; and Scott, M. A. *Structured Concurrent Programming with Operating System Applications.* Menlo Park, Calif.: Addison-Wesley, 1978.
4. Lister, A. M. *Fundamentals of Operating Systems.* New York: Macmillan, 1979.
5. Peterson, J. L., and Siberschatz, A. *Operating System Concepts.* Menlo Park, Calif.: Addison-Wesley, 1983.
6. Tanenbaum, A. S. *Computer Networks.* Englewood Cliffs, N.J.: Prentice-Hall, 1981.
7. Theaker, C. J., and Brookes, G. R. *A Practical Course on Operating Systems.* New York: Springer-Verlag, 1983.

Chapter 4: Algorithms

1. Aho, A. V.; Hopcroft, J. E.; and Ullman, J. D. *Data Structures and Algorithms.* Menlo Park, Calif.: Addison-Wesley, 1983.
2. Deo, N.; Nievergelt, J.; and Reingold, E. M. *Combinatorial Algorithms.* Englewood Cliffs, N.J.: Prentice-Hall, 1977.
3. Dijkstra, E. W. *A Discipline of Programming.* Englewood Cliffs, N.J.: Prentice-Hall, 1976.
4. Gries, D. *The Science of Programming.* New York: Springer-Verlag, 1981.
5. Harbin, R. *Origami—The Art of Paper Folding.* London: Hodder Paperbacks, 1973.
6. Hu, T. C. *Combinatorial Algorithms.* Menlo Park, Calif.: Addison-Wesley, 1982.

7. Knuth, D. E. *The Art of Computer Programming.* Vol. 2 & 3. Menlo Park, Calif.: Addison-Wesley, 1969, 1973.
8. Polya, G. *How to Solve It.* Princeton, N.J.: Princeton Univ. Press, 1973.
9. Wirth, N. *Algorithms + Data Structures = Programs.* Englewood Cliffs, N.J.: Prentice-Hall, 1976.

Chapter 5: Programming Languages

1. Aho, A. V.; Sethi, R.; and Ullman, J. D. *Compilers: Principles, Techniques, and Tools.* Menlo Park, Calif.: Addison-Wesley, 1986.
2. Clocksin, W. F., and Mellish, C. S. *Programming in Prolog.* New York: Springer-Verlag, 1984.
3. Cox, B. J. *Object-Oriented Programming: An Evolutionary Approach.* Menlo Park, Calif.: Addison-Wesley, 1986.
4. Ghezzi, C., and Jazayeri, M. *Programming Language Concepts.* New York: John Wiley and Sons, 1982.
5. Hogger, C. J. *Introduction to Logic Programming.* New York: Academic Press, 1984.
6. MacLennan, B. J. *Principles of Programming Languages: Design, Evaluation, and Implementation.* New York: Holt, Rinehart and Winston, 1983.
7. Pratt, T. W. *Programming Languages.* Englewood Cliffs, N.J.: Prentice-Hall, 1984.
8. Rogers, J. B. *A Prolog Primer.* Menlo Park, Calif.: Addison-Wesley, 1986.
9. Tucker, A. B. *Programming Languages.* New York: McGraw-Hill, 1986.

Chapter 6: Software Engineering

1. Fox, J. M. *Software and Its Development.* Englewood Cliffs, N.J.: Prentice-Hall, 1982.
2. Leong-Hong, B. W., and Plagman, B. K. *Data Dictionary/Directory Systems.* New York: John Wiley and Sons, 1982.
3. Pressman, R. S. *Software Engineering: A Practitioner's Approach.* New York: McGraw-Hill, 1987.
4. Sommerville, I. *Software Engineering.* Menlo Park, Calif.: Addison-Wesley, 1982.
5. Yourdon, E. *Techniques of Program Structure and Design.* Englewood Cliffs, N.J.: Prentice-Hall, 1975.
6. Yourdon, E. *Structured Walkthroughs.* Englewood Cliffs, N.J.: Prentice-Hall, 1979.
7. Yourdon, E., and Constantine, L. L. *Structured Design.* Englewood Cliffs, N.J.: Prentice-Hall, 1979.

Chapter 7: Data Structures

1. Baron, R. J., and Shapiro, L. G. *Data Structures and Their Implementation.* New York: Van Nostrand Reinhold, 1980.
2. Helman, P., and Veroff, R. *Intermediate Problem Solving and Data Structures.* Menlo Park, Calif.: Benjamin/Cummings, 1986.
3. Horowitz, E., and Sahni, S. *Fundamentals of Data Structures.* Rockville, Md.: Computer Science Press, 1976.
4. Knuth, D. E. *The Art of Computer Programming.* Vol. 1. Menlo Park, Calif.: Addison-Wesley, 1973.
5. Kruse, R. L. *Data Structures and Program Design.* Englewood Cliffs, N.J.: Prentice-Hall, 1984.
6. Tenenbaum, A. M., and Augenstein, M. J. *Data Structures Using Pascal.* Englewood Cliffs, N.J.: Prentice-Hall, 1981.
7 Tremblay, J., and Sorenson, P. G. *An Introduction to Data Structures with Applications.* New York: McGraw-Hill, 1984.
8. Ullman, J. D. *Structures and Algorithms.* Menlo Park, Calif.: Addison-Wesley, 1983.

Chapter 8: File Structures

1. Bradley, J. *File and Data Base Techniques.* New York: Holt, Rinehart and Winston, 1982.
2. Hanson, O. *Design of Computer Data Files.* Rockville, Md.: Computer Science Press, 1982.
3. Horowitz, E., and Sahni, S. *Fundamentals of Data Structures.* Rockville, Md.: Computer Science Press, 1976.
4. Tremblay, J., and Sorenson, P. G. *An Introduction to Data Structures with Applications.* New York: McGraw-Hill, 1984.
5. Zoellick, B., and Folk, M. J. *File Structures: A Conceptual Toolkit.* Menlo Park, Calif: Addison-Wesley, 1987.

Chapter 9: Database Structures

1. Date, C. J. *An Introduction to Database Systems.* Menlo Park, Calif.: Addison-Wesley, 1981.
2. Loomis, M. E. S. *The Database Book.* New York: Macmillan, 1987.
3. Ullman, J. D. *Principles of Database Systems.* Rockville, Md.: Computer Science Press, 1980.

Chapter 10: Artificial Intelligence

1. Charniak, E., and McDermott, D. *Introduction to Artificial Intelligence.* Menlo Park, Calif.: Addison-Wesley, 1985.

2. Cohen, P. R., and Feigenbaum, E. A., ed. *The Handbook of Artificial Intelligence.* Los Altos, Calif.: William Kaufman, 1982.

3. McCorduck, P. *Machines Who Think.* New York: W. H. Freeman and Co., 1979.

4. Nilsson, N. J. *Principles of Artificial Intelligence.* Los Altos, Calif.: Tioga, 1980.

5. Rich, E. *Artificial Intelligence.* New York: McGraw-Hill, 1983.

6. Weizenbaum, J. *Computer Power and Human Reason.* New York: W. H. Freeman and Co., 1979.

7. Winston, P. H. *Artificial Intelligence.* Menlo Park, Calif.: Addison-Wesley, 1984.

Chapter 11: Theory of Computation

1. Ballard, D. H., and Brown, C. M. *Computer Vision.* Englewood Cliffs, N.J.: Prentice-Hall, 1982.

2. Brainerd, W. S., and Landweber, L. H. *Theory of Computation.* New York: John Wiley and Sons, 1974.

3. Hofstadter, D. R. *Gödel, Escher, Bach: An Eternal Golden Braid.* St. Paul: Vintage Book Co., 1980.

4. Kfoury, A. J.; Moll, R. N.; and Arbib, M. A. *A Programming Approach to Computability.* New York: Springer-Verlag, 1982.

5. Lewis, H. R., and Papadimitriou, C. H. *Elements of the Theory of Computation.* Englewood Cliffs, N.J.: Prentice-Hall, 1981.

6. Manna, Z. *Mathematical Theory of Computation.* New York: McGraw-Hill, 1974.

7. McNaughton, R. *Elementary Computability, Formal Languages, and Automata.* Englewood Cliffs, N.J.: Prentice-Hall, 1982.

8. Pearl, J. *Heuristics: Intelligent Search Strategies for Computer Problem Solving.* Menlo Park, Calif.: Addison-Wesley, 1984.

9. Sowa, J. F. *Conceptual Structures: Information Processing in Mind and Machine.* Menlo Park, Calif.: Addison-Wesley, 1984.

Index

Abstract data type 304–7
Accumulator register 62
Actual parameter 217
Ada 220–21
Address 27
Aiken, Howard 8
Algebraic coding theory 42
Algorithm 4–6, 129–83
Algorithmic machine 6
American National Standards Institute 36, 221
American Standard Code for Information Interchange (ASCII) 36
Application software 313, 340
Arc
   in a graph 383
   in a tree 296
Area (in network database) 351
Argument 215. *See also* Parameter
Arithmetic/logic unit 62
Arithmetic shift 83
Array 205–7, 277–79
   heterogeneous 206
   homogeneous 206
Artificial intelligence 374–405
   performance oriented approach 376
   simulation oriented approach 376
Assembler 186
Assembly language 186
Assertions
   in algorithm development 164–68, 178
   in proof of correctness 176–78
Assignment statements 208–9
Attribute (in a relation) 343

Babbage, Charles 7

Bare Bones language 407–12
Base two. *See* Binary system
BASIC 221
Batch processing 106–7
Baud rate 89
Bell Laboratories 8, 103
Binary coded decimal (BCD) 36
Binary search 156–61
   complexity of 173
Binary system 36–38, 43–46
Bit 25
Blocking factor 34
Body (of a repetitive structure) 149
Boole, George 204
Boolean data type 204
Bootstrap 124–25
Bootstrapping 125
Bottom-up methodology 145
Bps (bits per second) 89
Branch (of a tree) 296
Breadth-first search 391
Buffer 89
Buffering 89
Bulk storage 30–35
Bus 62
Byron, Augusta Ada 221
Byte 26

Capacitor (memory device) 25–26
Case control structure 210–11
Cathode ray tube (CRT) 12
Cell (memory) 26
Central processing unit (CPU) 11, 62–66
Channel 88
Character data type 203
Character recognition 379–80

Character strings 205
  operations on 209, 218
Children (in a tree) 296
Chip 25
Church-Turing thesis 421
  application of 455–56
Circular queue 293
Clause form 230
Closed-world database 400
CLOSE statement 333
COBOL 221–23
Cohesion (intramodule) 256–58
Column major order 278
Command processor 111
Comment statement 220, 255, 264
Commutative production system 347
Compiler 188
Complement (of a bit pattern) 49
Complexity
  of an algorithm 427
  of a problem 426–27
  orders of 431–32
Computable function 419
Concatenation 209
Conceptual vs. real
  in databases 339–42
  in data structures 285–86, 289, 293,
    299–307
  in operating systems 104–5
Concurrent processing 77
Constant 207–8
Control coupling 251
Control-driven machine 78
Controller 12–13, 88–89
Control of repetitive structures
  iteration 149–52
  recursion 161–64
Control structures 209–19
Control unit 62
Core 123
Core wars 91–92

Coupling (intermodule) 251–56
CP/M 103
Critical region 120

Database 336–67, 399–400
Database administrator (DBA) 339
Database management system (DBMS) 340
Data control block (DCB) 332
Data coupling 252–53
Data dictionary 264–65
Data-driven machine 78
Data flow diagram 260–62
Data independence 340
Data structure 205–7, 276–313
Data type 203–4
Deadlock 120–21
Declaration part (of a program) 203
Demand-driven machine 79
Depth (of a tree) 296
Depth-first search 391
Dewey, J. 141
Digital Research 103
Direct access file 326
Direct memory access (DMA) 88
Diskette 11
Disk pack 11
Disk storage 32–33
Dispatcher 112
DOCTOR (ELIZA) program 377
Documentation 220, 245, 263–65
Double precision 52, 56
Duplex (half vs. full) 88

Editor 114
Efficiency (of an algorithm) 172–74
8-puzzle 378
Encapsulation 306
End-of-file (EOF) mark 317
ENIAC 10
Error correcting code 41–43
Euclidean algorithm 140

Even parity 40
Excess notation 47–49
Expert systems 401–2
Exponent field 54
Exponential expression 433

Factorial (of a nonnegative integer) 181
Feature evaluation 380
Feature extraction 380
Fibonacci sequence 180
Field (in hierarchical database) 361
File 112, 272, 314
    organization of 314–35
File manager 112
FIND-NEXT (network operation) 253
FIND-OWNER (network operation) 254
First-in-first-out (FIFO) 106
Fixed-format language 200
Floating-point notation 38, 54–57
    normalized form 459
Floppy disk 11
Formal parameter 217
FORTRAN 225
Free-format language 201
Function
    abstract 417
    computation of 417–19
    program unit 217
Functional cohesion 257

Generations (of programming languages)
    185–90
GET-FIRST (hierarchical operation) 362
GET-NEXT (hierarchical operation) 363
Global program elements 254
Gödel, Kurt 407, 421
Gödel number 422
GOTO statement 210
Graph (directed) 123, 383
Group (in network database) 351
Group occurrence 351

Halting problem 422
Hamming, R. W. 41
Hamming distance 41
Handshaking 87
Hard-copy device 12
Hardware 10, 100
Hash algorithm 326
Hashed file 326–31
Head (of queue) 291
Head pointer 283, 291
Heuristic 391–95
Hexadecimal notation 29
Hierarchical database model 341, 360–64
High order (bit) 28
Host language 341

If control structure 136–37
Image analysis 378–81
INDEX (program function) 218
Indexed file 320–26
Indexed sequential file 326
Inference engine 401
Input/output (I/O) device 11–12
Input/output (I/O) program statements 219
Insertion sort 152–56
    complexity of 428
Instruction pointer 280
Instruction register 70
Integer data type 203
Integrated software 189
Interactive processing 107–8
Interpretation 195–97
Interpreter 195
Inter-record gap 31
Interrupt 115
Interrupt routine 116
Inverted file 323
Irrevocable control strategy 386
Iterative structure 149. *See also* Loop
    structure

Jacquard, Joseph 9
Jacquard loom 9
JCL (Job control language) 107
Job queue 106
Jump (conditional vs. unconditional) 69

K (kilo) 27
Kemeny, John 221
Key field 317
Key words 201
Knowledge base 401
Kurtz, Thomas 221

Label (of an instruction) 210
Language processing 397–98
Last-in-first-out (LIFO) 287
Leaf node 296
Least significant bit 28
Left child pointer 297
Leibniz, Gottfried Wilhelm 7
LEN (program function) 218
Lexical analysis 193–94
Library 115
LIFO. *See* Last-in-first-out
Linker 194
List 280–86
   dense 282–83
   linked 283–85
Loader 195
Load factor 324
Local program elements 254
Logical cohesion 256
Logical record 33–35
Logical shift 83
Loop invariant 177
Loop structures 147–56, 210–12, 455–56
   control of 149–52
Low order (bit) 28

Machine cycle 70
Machine independence 186–89

Machine language 66
Machine-level instructions
   AND 64, 80–81
   BRANCH 65
   EXCLUSIVE OR (XOR) 64, 82–83
   JUMP 65, 69
   LOAD 64
   OR 64, 81–82
   ROTATE 83
   SHIFT 83
   STORE 64
Mainframe computer 13–15, 17–18
Main memory 11, 26–28
Mantissa field 54
Mark I 8
Mask 81
Masking 81
Master file 319–20
Member (in network database) 350
Memory mapped I/O 86
Merge sort 320, 475
Microcomputer 13–16
Microprogram 76
Microsecond 34
Microsoft Corporation 103
Millisecond 33
Minicomputer 13–14, 16–17
Mnemonic 185
Modular design 137–40, 246–51
Modus tollens 230
Most significant bit 28
MS-DOS 103
MULTIPLY (relational operation) 347

Nanosecond 34
Natural language processing 398
Network 109
Network database model 341, 350–60
NIL pointer 283
Node
   in a graph 383
   in a tree 296

Nondeterministic polynomial (NP) problems 435
Nonloss decomposition 346
Nonpolynomial problems 434
Normal forms 346
NP problems 435
NULL pointer 283
Numerical analysis 56

Object program 193
Odd parity 40
Off-line 30
Onion-skin diagram 112–13, 342
On-line 30
Op-code 67
OPEN statement 332
Open-world database 400
Operand field 67
Operands 68–69, 185
Operating system 100–27
    file control 332–33
Overflow error 38, 52
Owner (in network database) 350

Parallel communication 89
Parallel processing 77
Parameter 214–17, 254
Parent node 296
Parity bit 40–41
    application of 42–43
Parsing 194
Partial function 419
Partial index 323
Partial recursive function 419
Pascal 225
Pascal, Blaise 7, 225
Peripheral devices 12
Physical record 33–35
Pipelining 76–77
Pixel 379
Poincaré, H. 144

Pointer 280–82
Pointer data type 280
Polya, G. 141, 245
Polynomial algorithm 433
Polynomial expression 432
Polynomial problems 434
Pop (stack operation) 287
Port 86
POS (program function) 218
Precedence rules 199
Primary key 323
Primitives 132–34
Problem solving 141–46
Procedural part (of a program) 203
Production systems 382–85
    control system 383
    goal state 382
    production 382
    start state 382
Program counter 70
Programming languages 184–240
    generations of 186–90
Programming paradigms
    declarative 191, 228–37
    object-oriented 192, 307–9
    procedural 190
PROJECT (relational operation) 347
Projected cost 393
Prolog 234–37
Proof of correctness 176–78
Pseudocode 134–37
Push (stack operation) 287

Queue 106–7, 291–95
Quick sort 164–72
    complexity of 428–31

Radix point 45
Random access file 326
Random access memory (RAM) 123
Read only memory (ROM) 123
Real data type 203

Real-time processing 108
Recursion 163
Recursive structures 156–72, 455–56
    control of 161–64
Region growing 380
Region splitting 380
Register 62
Relation 343
Relational database model 341, 343–50
Relative addressing 460
Repeat control structure 151–52
Resolution 229
Resolvent 229
Resource (shareable/nonshareable) 118–19
Resource allocator 112, 119
Revocable control strategy 386
Right child pointer 297
Robotics 398–99
Root node 296
Root pointer 297
Round-off error 38, 55–57
Row major order 278

Scheduler 111
Search tree 387–89
Secondary key 323
Sectors (of a disk track) 32
Segment (in hierarchical database) 361
SELECT (relational operation) 347
Self-terminating program 422
Semantics 131–32, 198–99
Sentinel 317
Sequential file 315–20
Sequential search 147–48
    complexity of 173
Serial communication 89
Set (in network database) 250
Siblings (in a tree) 296
Side effect 254–56
Sign bit 47
Sign-magnitude notation 47

Simplex 88
Soft-copy device 12
Software, 10, 100
Software engineering 241–67
Software life cycle 242–45
Software verification 174–78
Solvable problem 426
Source program 193
Spooling 122
Stack 286–91
    applications of 287–88
Stack pointer 288
Starvation 127
State
    of production system 382
    of program 116
    of Turing machine 414
State graph 383
Stepwise refinement 145
Stibitz, George 8
Structure chart 248
Structured programming 210
Subprogram 213–14
Successor function 418, 419
Syntax 131–32, 199–202
Syntax diagram 201, 445–54
System requirements 244
System specifications 244
System/360 (IBM) 103

Tail (of queue) 291
Tail pointer 292
Tape storage 30–32
Terminal node 296
Throughput 77
Time-sharing 109, 116–18
Time slice 116
Top-down methodology 149, 259–60
Top of stack 287
Towers of Hanoi 181–82
Track 32

Transaction file 319–20
Transcendental functions 482
Translation 193–97
Translator 193
Tree 296–304
  binary 297
Tuple (in a relation) 343
Turing, Alan M. 377, 413
Turing machine 412–17
Turing machine computable 419
Turing test 377
Turnkey system 125
Twins (in a tree) 296
Two's complement notation 38, 49–52

UNIX 103
Utility software 113–15

Variable 207
Virtual 104–5, 276. *See also* Conceptual vs.
  real
von Helmholtz, H. 141, 143
von Neumann, John 66

Weizenbaum, Joseph 377
While control structure 137
Wirth, Niklaus 225
Word (unit of memory) 26
Word processor 114